COMMUNITIES IN DISPUTE

SBL

Society of Biblical Literature

Early Christianity and Its Literature

Gail R. O'Day, General Editor

Editorial Board:
Warren Carter
Beverly Roberts Gaventa
David Horrell
Judith M. Lieu
Margaret Y. MacDonald

Number 13

COMMUNITIES IN DISPUTE

CURRENT SCHOLARSHIP ON THE JOHANNINE EPISTLES

Edited by

R. Alan Culpepper and Paul N. Anderson

SBL Press
Atlanta

Copyright © 2014 by SBL Press

All rights reserved. No part of this work may be reproduced or transmitted in any form or by any means, electronic or mechanical, including photocopying and recording, or by means of any information storage or retrieval system, except as may be expressly permitted by the 1976 Copyright Act or in writing from the publisher. Requests for permission should be addressed in writing to the Rights and Permissions Office, SBL Press, 825 Houston Mill Road, Atlanta, GA 30329 USA.

Library of Congress Cataloging-in-Publication Data

Communities in dispute : current scholarship on the Johannine epistles / edited by R. Alan Culpepper and Paul N. Anderson.
    p. cm. — (Society of Biblical Literature Early Christianity and its literature ; number 13)
    Includes bibliographical references and index.
    ISBN 978-1-62837-015-7 (paper binding : alk. paper) — ISBN 978-1-62837-016-4 (electronic format) — ISBN 978-1-62837-017-1 (hardcover binding : alk. paper)
    1. Bible. Epistles of John—Criticism, interpretation, etc. I. Culpepper, R. Alan. II. Anderson, Paul N., 1956–.
    BS2805.52.C66 2014
    227'.9406—dc23   2014039766

Printed on acid-free, recycled paper conforming to
ANSI/NISO Z39.48-1992 (R1997) and ISO 9706:1994
standards for paper permanence.

Contents

Abbreviations vii

Introduction
   R. Alan Culpepper and Paul N. Anderson 1

Setting the Stage: The Context for the Conversation
   R. Alan Culpepper 3

Part 1: The Relationship between the Gospel and the Epistles

Raymond Brown's View of the Crisis of 1 John: In the Light of
   Some Peculiar Features of the Johannine Gospel
   Urban C. von Wahlde 19

The Community that Raymond Brown Left Behind: Reflections
   on the Johannine Dialectical Situation
   Paul N. Anderson 47

The Relationship between the Gospel of John and 1 John
   R. Alan Culpepper 95

Part 2: The Church in the Johannine Epistles

The Audience of the Johannine Epistles
   Judith M. Lieu 123

The Missional Role of ὁ Πρεσβύτερος
   Peter Rhea Jones 141

Part 3: The Theology and Ethics of the Epistles

The Cosmic Trial Motif in John's Letters
    Andreas J. Köstenberger 157

Spirit-Inspired Theology and Ecclesial Correction: Charting
    One Shift in the Development of Johannine Ecclesiology
    and Pneumatology
    Gary M. Burge 179

The Antichrist Theme in the Johannine Epistles and Its Role
    in Christian Tradition
    Craig R. Koester..187

On Ethics in 1 John
    Jan G. van der Watt 197

The Significance of 2:15–17 for Understanding the Ethics of
    1 John
    William R. G. Loader...223

Completed Love: 1 John 4:11–18 and the Mission of the New
    Testament Church
    David Rensberger..237

Response

Moving the Conversation Forward: Open Questions and
    New Directions
    Paul N. Anderson 275

Works Cited..289
Contributors...313
Ancient Sources Index..315
Name Index..329

Abbreviations

4 Regn.	Dio Chrysostom, *De regno iv* (*Or.* 4)
AB	Anchor Bible
Abr.	Philo, *De Abrahamo*
ABRL	Anchor Bible Reference Library
ACNT	Augsburg Commentaries on the New Testament
AcTSup	Acta Theologica Supplementum
Agr.	Philo, *De agricultura*
AJEC	Ancient Judaism and Early Christianity
Alex.	*Ad Alexandrinos* (*Or.* 32)
Amic.	Cicero, *De amicitia*
AMP	Amplified Bible
AnBib	Analecta Biblica
Andr.	Euripides, *Andromache*
ANF	*Ante-Nicene Fathers*
Ant.	Josephus, *Jewish Antiquities*
ANTC	Abingdon New Testament Commentaries
ASV	American Standard Version
BBE	Bible in Basic English
BDAG	Bauer, Walter, Frederick W. Danker, William F. Arndt, and F. Wilbur Gingrich. *Greek-English Lexicon of the New Testament and Other Early Christian Literature*. 3rd ed. Chicago: University of Chicago Press, 1999.
BDF	Blass, Friedrich, Albert Debrunner, and Robert W. Funk. *A Greek Grammar of the New Testament and Other Early Christian Literature*. Chicago: University of Chicago Press, 1961.
BECNT	Baker Exegetical Commentary on the New Testament
BETL	Bibliotheca ephemeridum theologicarum lovaniensium
BHT	Beiträge zur historischen Theologie
BibLeb	*Bibel und Leben*

BIS	*Biblical Interpretation Series*
BJRL	*Bulletin of the John Rylands University Library of Manchester*
BK	*Bibel und Kirche*
BL	*Bibel und Liturgie*
BR	*Biblical Research*
BTB	*Biblical Theology Bulletin*
BWA(N)T	*Beiträge zur Wissenschaft vom Alten (und Neuen) Testament*
BZ	*Biblische Zeitschrift*
BZNW	*Beihefte zur Zeitschrift für die neutestamentliche Wissenschaft*
CBQ	*Catholic Biblical Quarterly*
CCSL	*Christianorum: Series latina*
CEB	Contemporary English Bible
CEV	Contemporary English Version
Cher.	Philo, *De cherubim*
Contempl.	Philo, *De vita contemplativa*
Decal.	Philo, *De decalogo*
Deus	Philo, *Quod Deus sit immutabilis*
Diatr.	Epictetus, *Diatribai*
Did.	Didache
DivThom	*Divus Thomas*
ECC	Eerdmans Critical Commentary
EDNT	*Exegetical Dictionary of the New Testament.* Edited by Horst Balz and Gerhard Schneider. Grand Rapids: Eerdmans, 1990–1993.
EKKNT	Evangelisch-katholischer Kommentar zum Neuen Testament
Eph.	Ignatius, *To the Ephesians*
Epigr.	Martial, *Epigrammaton libri*
Ep. Tra.	Pliny the Younger, *Epistulae ad Trajanum*
ERV	English Revised Version
ESV	English Standard Version
Eth. eud.	Aristotle, *Ethica eudemia*
Eth. nic.	Aristotle, *Ethica nichomachea*
ExpTim	*Expository Times*
Flacc.	Philo, *In Flaccum*
FM	*Faith and Mission*

frg.	fragment
Fug.	Philo, *De fuga et inventione*
GNT	Good News Translation
Haer.	Irenaeus, *Adversus haereses*
HBT	*Horizons in Biblical Theology*
Herm. Mand.	Shepherd of Hermas, *Mandate*
Hist.	Thucydides, *History of the Peloponnesian War*
Hist. eccl.	*Historia ecclesiastica*
HNT	Handbuch zum Neuen Testament
HNTC	Harper's New Testament Commentaries
HTKNT	Herders theologischer Kommentar zum Neuen Testament
HUT	Hermeneutische Untersuchungen zur Theologie
Hyp. Arch.	Nag Hammadi Codices II 4, Hypostasis of the Archons
IBC	Interpretation: A Bible Commentary for Teaching and Preaching
ICC	International Critical Commentary
Int	*Interpretation*
JBL	*Journal of Biblical Literature*
JSJSup	Journal for the Study of Judaism Supplement Series
JSNT	*Journal for the Study of the New Testament*
JSNTSup	Journal for the Study of the New Testament: Supplement Series
JSPSup	Journal for the Study of the Pseudepigrapha: Supplement Series
JTS	*Journal of Theological Studies*
KEK	Kritisch-exegetischer Kommentar über das Neue Testament (Meyer-Kommentar)
KJV	King James Version
LB	The Living Bible
Leg.	Plato, *Leges*
Legat.	Philo, *Legatio ad Gaium*
LNTS	Library of New Testament Studies
Lys.	Plato, *Lysis*
Magn.	Ignatius, *To the Magnesians*
Mart. Pol.	*Martyrdom of Polycarp*
MNTC	Moffatt New Testament Commentary
Met.	Apuleius, *Metamorphosis*

Metaph.	Aristotle, *Metaphysica*
Mor.	Plutarch, *Moralia*
Mos.	Philo, *De vita Mosis*
NAB	New American Bible
NAC	New American Commentary
NASB	New American Standard Bible
NCB	New Century Bible
NCV	New Century Version
NEB	New English Bible
NET	New English Translation
NIB	*New Interpreter's Dictionary of the Bible*
NIBCNT	New International Biblical Commentary on the New Testament
NICNT	New International Commentary on the New Testament
NIGTC	New International Greek Testament Commentary
NIV	New International Version
NJB	New Jerusalem Bible
NJKV	New King James Version
NLT	New Living Translation
NovTSup	Novum Testamentum Supplements
NRSV	New Revised Standard Version
NTD	Das Neue Testament Deutsch
NTL	New Testament Library
NTS	*New Testament Studies*
Opif.	Philo, *De opificio mundi*
Orest.	Euripides, *Orestes*
ÖTK	Ökumenischer Taschenbuch-Kommentar
Phaedr.	Plato, *Phaedrus*
Phil	Polycarp, *To the Philippians*
Phld.	Ignatius, *To the Philadelphians*
Pol.	Aristotle, *Politica*
Post.	Philo, *De posteritate Caini*
Presb	*Presbyterion*
PRSt	*Perspectives in Religious Studies*
QG	Philo, *Quaestiones et solutiones in Genesin*
REB	Revised English Bible
Res.	Tertullian, *Resurrection of the Flesh*
Resp.	Plato, *Respublica*
RevExp	*Review and Expositor*

RBL	*Review of Biblical Literature*
RNT	Regensburger Neues Testament
RSV	Revised Standard Version
Sacr.	Philo, *De sacrificiis Abelis et Caini*
SBLDS	Society of Biblical Literature Dissertation Series
SBLECL	Society of Biblical Literature Early Christianity and Its Literature
SBLSymS	Society of Biblical Literature Symposium Series
SemeiaSt	Semeia Studies
SHBC	Smyth & Helwys Bible Commentary
SJOT	*Scandinavian Journal of the Old Testament*
Smyrn.	Ignatius, *To the Smyrnaeans*
SNTSMS	Society for New Testament Studies Monograph Series
SNTW	Studies of the New Testament and Its World
Somn.	Philo, *De somniis*
SP	Sacra Pagina
Spec.	Philo, *De specialibus legibus*
SR	*Studies in Religion*
TBT	*The Bible Today*
TEV	Today's English Version
THKNT	Theologischer Handkommentar zum Neuen Testament
TLZ	*Theologische Literaturzeitung*
TNIV	Today's New International Version
TNTC	Tyndale New Testament Commentaries
Tract. ep. Jo.	*In epistulam Johannis ad Parthos tractatus*
Trall.	Ignatius, *To the Trallians*
TRu	*Theologische Rundschau*
TTS	Theologische Texte und Studien
TUGAL	Texte und Untersuchungen zur Geschichte der altchristlichen Literatur
TZ	*Theologische Zeitschrift*
UBS	United Bible Societies
Unit. eccl.	Cyprian, *De catholicae ecclesiae unitate*
Vir. Illus.	Cornelius Nepos, *De Viris Illustribus*
Virt.	Philo, *De virtutibus*
Vit.	Diogenes Laertius, *Lives of Eminent Philosophers*
WBC	Word Biblical Commentary
WUNT	Wissenschaftliche Untersuchungen zum Neuen Testament

WW	*Word and World*
ZBK	Zürcher Bibelkommentar
ZNT	*Zeitschrift für Neues Testament*
ZTK	*Zeitschrift für Theologie und Kirche*

Introduction

R. Alan Culpepper and Paul N. Anderson

The Epistles of John involve only seven chapters of the New Testament, but they offer one of the most interesting windows into the life of the early church available, with extensive implications for understanding (and misunderstanding) a host of interpretive issues. First John does not identify its audience, and the author does not introduce himself. The author of 2 John and 3 John refers to himself as "the Elder" (ὁ πρεσβύτερος in Greek). Were all three texts written by the same author? If so, then why the differences in the author's self-identification? And the audiences of 2 and 3 John are specified as "the elect lady and her children" (2 John 1) and "the beloved Gaius" (3 John 1). Why the differences in declared audiences? Further, there is a considerable difference in length between the letters: the five chapters of 1 John are five times as long as 2 and 3 John combined. How are these facts to be understood and thus interpreted?

Another set of issues emerges also at the start: the relation of the Johannine Epistles to the Johannine Gospel and Apocalypse. While Revelation is the most distinctive among the five Johannine writings (and the only one to assert the name of its author, indirectly and directly: "John," Rev 1:1, 4, 9; 22:8), its style and form are considerably different from the other Johannine writings. That is why most scholars feel it is safer to leave it out of discussions related to the Gospel and Epistles of John, despite a number of Johannine similarities. The relation of the Gospel to the Epistles of John, however, cannot be ignored, and questions range from which was earlier and later, whether they represent a similar setting, whether their authorship was common, and whether purposes were similar or different. It could even be that a multiplicity of authorial and editorial hands were involved in the production of the Johannine corpus, and such a likelihood is bolstered by the inclusion of first-person plural language ("we," "us," and "our"—in the Gospel and the Epistles), raising doubts that a single individual was responsible for all of these writings or that they were written to the same situation.

As a result, understanding the content of the Johannine Epistles hinges directly upon solid inferences of the contexts in which they were written, the concerns of their authors and editors, the relations of these writings to other contemporary literature (especially the Johannine), and the literary features of each composition. As Raymond Brown has made us aware, while the Johannine "eagle," representing the elevated perspective of the Fourth Gospel, soars above the ground it surveys, the Johannine Epistles betray eaglets fighting over their place in the nest, with schisms, rejections, embraces, and invective language—all showing a far less tidy portraiture of early Christianity than more romanticized views have allowed.

If the Johannine leadership and its adversaries reflect communities in dispute, however, what about Johannine scholarship over the last several decades? Indeed, as this collection of incisive essays by leading Johannine scholars shows, some points of convergence are evident, but top scholars also take issue with each other as to how this material came together, what was going on within the Johannine situation, and what its content implies for both theological and ethical interpretations of the New Testament. Therefore, today's "Johannine School"—the international community of Johannine scholars today—also finds itself in dispute about important issues, not simply tangential ones, and this collection of essays throws some of those similarities and differences into sharp relief.

These papers were invited and delivered at the Symposium on the Johannine Epistles at the McAfee School of Theology at Mercer University in Atlanta, Georgia, November 17–19, 2010, and they are gathered into three sections within the present volume. Part 1 deals with "The Relationship between the Gospel and the Epistles"; Part 2 addresses "The Church in the Johannine Epistles"; Part 3 concludes, then, with "The Theology and Ethics of the Epistles." Alan Culpepper introduces the volume by setting the stage for the conversation, providing terse summaries of the papers' contributions, and Paul Anderson introduces each section by outlining some of the key issues in each part and concludes with an overview of the collection—moving the discussion forward regarding emerging aspects of consensus as well as continuing, open questions.

So, regarding state-of-the-art discussions of earlier communities in dispute and the texts by which they are illumined ... let the conversation begin!

Setting the Stage:
The Context for the Conversation

R. Alan Culpepper

The title for this volume conveys an obvious double entendre: *Communities in Dispute*. It signals both that the essays in this volume deal with the Johannine Epistles as artifacts of ancient communities in dispute, as some think, over the gospel tradition and that they represent the disputes in current scholarship over the interpretation of these short letters.

Short they may be, tucked away near the end of the New Testament between 2 Peter and Jude, but they provide unparalleled insights into the development of early Christianity. They are the only letters attached to any of the Gospels, canonical or apocryphal. They are the written by an "Elder." First John in particular contains a mix of pastoral and polemical, ethical and christological material. Second and Third John, of all the New Testament letters, follow the Hellenistic conventions of letter writing most closely. Taken together, these three letters offer a window into the disputes among individuals and communities related to the Johannine tradition, if not the Gospel itself. How were doctrinal and ethical debates brokered? What authority did the church or community leaders have? How are the Epistles related to the Gospel—chronologically and theologically?

The "disputes" over these issues reach back over a century in New Testament scholarship. The springboard for much of this debate has been the question of the authorship of the Epistles. Were they written by the Apostle John, the Fourth Evangelist, and the author of the Revelation of John, as tradition and orthodoxy hold, or were they written by another early Christian leader, John the Elder, or an otherwise unknown associate or disciple of the Beloved Disciple or the Fourth Evangelist?

C. H. Dodd broke from tradition in an article on the relationship between the Gospel and the Epistles in 1937 and in his commentary on the

Epistles in 1946 by assigning the letters to someone other than the Evangelist. Subsequent contributions to this debate have generally followed the lines of argument he set forth: linguistic evidence and theological similarities and differences (eschatology, the interpretation of Jesus's death, and the Holy Spirit).

These issues were taken up by Raymond Brown and set in a broader thesis regarding the relationship between the Gospel and the Epistles attributed to John. Brown's views are summarized in detail in several of the essays in this volume (Anderson, Burge, Culpepper, and von Wahlde), as his position has become a point of departure for most subsequent treatments of the Epistles, both those that take issue with Brown and those that seek to advance or refine his thesis that the Elder wrote after the Gospel was substantially completed, assumed its theological tradition, and debated with those who had broken away from the Elder's community over differences in how they interpreted the Gospel.

Conversely, Judith Lieu, her former students, and others outside the Brown school have argued that the Johannine Epistles must be read on their own terms, quite apart from their relationship to the Gospel, as pastoral letters more concerned with encouragement and ethics than with theological polemics. Where there are commonalities between the Gospel and the Epistles, they may be due to their common but independent dependence on community tradition. Where they differ, the Elder may be following the community tradition rather than departing from the Gospel. The Gospel's theology is dominated by its Christology; 1 John focuses on God and differs from the Gospel in maintaining a more traditional understanding of the atonement and the parousia.

The essays that follow play across the multiple combinations of interpretations of the language and style of the Epistles, the historical settings they reflect, their major themes, the nuances of their theology, and their relationship to or independence from the Gospel. They were invited by the editors and presented at the McAfee School of Theology Symposium on the Johannine Epistles (November 2010), building a progression from compositional to situational to interpretive sets of analysis. That progression is reflected in the three parts of the present volume, facilitating literary, historical, and theological considerations along the way.

Urban von Wahlde takes up the question of the literary and theological relationship between the Gospel and the Epistles in dialogue with Brown's view of the crisis reflected in 1 John. One finds "astounding differences" in the perspectives on 1 John in current scholarship. Von Wahlde claims that the interpretation of this letter "is more thoroughly controverted than almost any other document in the New Testament," a claim he documents with a survey of the ways in which the historical situation of the community is reconstructed in a sample of recent commentaries on the Epistles. Before addressing the historical setting of the Epistles and their relationship to the Gospel, von Wahlde acknowledges his indebtedness to Brown's thesis, articulated in his masterful commentary in 1982. Nevertheless, he contends that Brown's view of "the so-called dominant strain of Johannine theology does not do full justice to the Gospel."

Four features of the Gospel remain problematic for von Wahlde: (1) "the Johannine Jesus was 'a revealer without a revelation'" (quoting Bultmann 1951, 1955, 2:66); (2) "the death of Jesus is conceived of primarily as a departure to the Father and not as an atoning sacrifice"; (3) there is a puzzling "ethical vacuum" in John; "it offers no explicit moral instruction" (Meeks 1996, 318); and (4) John's focus on "knowing" and "not knowing" is peculiar. These four features of the Gospel can be explained as deriving from its "dominant theology": (1) Jesus came to give eternal life through the Spirit; (2) to receive the Spirit one must believe in Jesus; and (3) reception of the Spirit brings prerogatives that are well known in the Jewish Scriptures.

This dominant Johannine theology was "totally Jewish." It reflects six aspects of Jewish understanding of the Spirit: (1) the outpouring of the Spirit is eschatologically significant; (2) the coming of the Spirit promises new life for those who receive it; (3) recipients of the Spirit have no need for teaching; (4) those who have the Spirit have knowledge of God; (5) the Spirit brings cleansing from sin; and (6) those who have the Spirit have no need for ethical instruction, because they spontaneously live according to God's commandments.

First John's relationship to the dominant theology of the Gospel can be assessed on the basis of the way it addresses each of the peculiar features defined above. The author of 1 John could not accept the Gospel's theology without qualification: (1) the Spirit is the source of revelation, but it also confirms the validity of the words of Jesus; (2) 1 John holds a view of ethical perfectionism but insists on the root of all ethics: the command to love one another; (3) the author of 1 John claims to know Jesus but denies that his opponents, who also claim to know Jesus, have such knowledge; (4) for the author of 1 John the death of Jesus is much more than a departure to the Father—it is salvific, an atonement.

Von Wahlde also observes that "there are elements in [the Gospel] that clearly support the thought of 1 John and could have been used to refute his opponents." On the other hand, if the Paraclete passages were part of the Gospel when its dominant theology was developed, the Elder of 1 John would surely have used them. Brown paved the way for understanding the development of the Johannine tradition, but the actual scope of that development requires an even more nuanced interpretation of the course of the development of the Johannine tradition and the Elder's place in that history.

Paul Anderson develops a dialectical view of the Johannine setting in an essay playfully entitled, "The Community that Raymond Brown Left Behind" (see Brown 1984). In *The Community of the Beloved Disciple* (1979), Brown developed his view of the development of the Johannine community through four phases and the interaction of six groups. Brown's later work refines the initial presentation of his theory. In *The Epistles of John* (1982), Brown notes echoes of the Johannine writings in early Christian writers between 90 and 100 CE. *The Churches the Apostles Left Behind* (1984) characterizes two strengths of the community of the Beloved Disciple as (1) the priority of individual connectedness to Jesus and (2) the resulting egalitarian character of such an ethos. *An Introduction to the Gospel of John* (2003), completed by Frank Moloney following Brown's death in 1998, simplifies his theory of the composition of the Gospel, adds insights on the relationship between the Johannine and Synoptic traditions, and consolidates his earlier six groups into four. The principal elements of Brown's overall theory are a two-edition theory of the Gospel's composition, John's autonomy in relation to other traditions, and a history of the Johannine community. From this cogent summary, Anderson turns to the question of how Brown's theory has fared in the intervening years. Anderson identifies three critiques in particular: (1) Brown's two-level reading of the Johannine narrative threatens to focus on the later levels while displacing the earlier ones; (2) close relations between Jews and Christians during this time were warm and reciprocal (e.g., Katz, Kimelman, and Reinhartz); and (3) the Gospels, including John, were written for all Christians, not particular communities (Bauckham).

Developing his own overall theory of the Johannine tradition in dialogue with Brown's, Anderson contends for "the dialogical autonomy of the Johannine tradition," which includes (1) a two-edition model of composition, with the Epistles being written during this composition process; (2) an "interfluential" theory of gospel relations; and (3) seven crises over seven decades of Johannine history. Anderson posits a first edition of the Gospel by the Evangelist (80–85 CE), the writing of the Johannine Epistles by the Elder (85–95 CE), and the finalization of the Gospel (100 CE) by the Elder. Anderson reconstructs the development of the Johannine tradition through the following dialectical relationships: John's dialogical autonomy develops in ways parallel to other traditions; interfluential contacts occur between the pre-Markan and early Johannine traditions; augmentation and correction is made of written Mark; John has a formative impact upon Luke; John has a possible influence upon the Q tradition; Johannine preaching (and some writing) continues; Matthean and Johannine traditions engage in an interfluential set of dialogues; the Johannine Epistles are written by the Elder; the Johannine Gospel was supplemented and finalized by the Johannine Elder; the "spiritual" Gospel poses a bi-optic alternative to the "somatic" Gospels; and the second Markan ending bears Johannine echoes within it. These relationships can further be related to three periods in the history of the Johannine tradition: an early Palestinian period, developing an autonomous Johannine tradition (30–70 CE); the first Asia Minor phase, forging a Johannine community (70–85 CE); and a second Asia Minor phase, with dialogues between Christian communities (85–100 CE).

R. Alan Culpepper: my contribution to the symposium deals with the relationship between the Gospel and 1 John. As the previous papers have made clear, the setting of the Epistles and the development of the Johannine tradition are inextricably tied to the question of the relationship between the Gospel and 1 John. Historically the debate was over common or different authorship, but increasingly analysis has turned to the issues of sequence and whether 1 John is dependent or independent of the Gospel. Five positions are represented in current scholarship: (1) the Gospel was written before 1 John; (2) 1 John was written before the Gospel; (3) 1 John is independent of the Gospel; (4) the sequence cannot be determined; and (5) 1 John was written sometime during the period of the composition of the Gospel. The body of the paper is devoted to identifying the adherents and arguments for each of these five positions. Beyond analysis of the grammar and style, theology, and polemical elements of 1 John, discussions now consider the question of whether the Elder was the Beloved Disciple or the redactor of the Gospel. How should we interpret the structural parallels between the two writings? Did the Elder pattern 1 John after the completed Gospel, or was the redactor, who added John 21 to the Gospel, influenced by the structure of the Epistle? The theological development of the Johannine tradition, the delineation of stages in the composition of the Gospel, and the identity of the Elder's opponents are all relevant to the question of the relationship between these two writings, especially for those who see a close relationship or interdependence between them. There seems to be a trend toward concluding that 1 John was written during the process of the composition of the Gospel, rather than before or after it was written, but numerous issues are still debated and unresolved.

Judith Lieu forges her own path through the issues, focusing especially closely on 2 and 3 John. In contrast to the readings of the Epistles based on reconstructions of the history of the Johannine community and the relationship of the Epistles to the Gospel, Lieu offers an inductive description of the audience of the Johannine Epistles from the Epistles themselves, as letters, without reference to the Gospel. At the outset, the differences between 1 John and the two shorter letters must be recognized. Third John follows most closely the pattern of private letters. Gaius is treated as separate from "the brothers" or "the church." Various proposals have been offered regarding Gaius's role in relationship to church or community, perhaps as a leader, but these remain conjectural. Second John is more complex, a mix of self-conscious elements and features of a private letter, and his relationship with the audience is more distant. The "elect lady" may be either a real woman or a reference to a community: "The implied audience of the *substantive content* of the Letter is treated as a group of equally responsible adult members; the implied recipient of the Letter is a woman and her family, who are in epistolary contact with her sister and cousins" (emphasis original). Comparisons can be drawn with the Pastoral Epistles. First John, in contrast, provides no names or location; it appeals to no events identified by shared referential knowledge, and it lacks almost all the generic marks of a letter. Even if 1 John were originally an oral address (a sermon or homily), as a letter it functions in a different way in relation to its audience. There is no suggestion that the author and audience have had any prior association. The prologue suggests they have not. The author ("I") writes the Epistle, but his use of the corporate "we" addresses the audience. Unlike Ignatius, the author does not use epistolary conventions to reinforce his own authority. Further, the Epistles must be treated individually, because the process by which they were collected and the relationships among them remain unclear.

The majority of early Christian letters embody a narrative; they refer to past events or anticipate future events. Third John suggests a relatively specific narrative, whereas 2 John offers little history or anticipated future. First John adduces both past and future, but "plays less of a role in determining the future." The past is expressed in reference to the coming of the Son, the prologue, and the going out of the antichrists. The interpretation of the third element is pivotal: only the author has experienced it directly; the audience has merely heard about it. The audience of 1 John, in contrast to the audiences of most other New Testament letters, is not within "a continuous dynamic narrative, neither does it act as a catalyst within such a narrative."

Like many letters, the Johannine Epistles also have a rhetorical function: to shape the audience. The interplay between "we" and "you" reaches a crisis in 1 John 4:4–6. Where will "you" stand? The rhetorical strategy of the letter, to create fellowship, is achieved, but the nature of this fellowship is not specified. The antichrists represent for the audience the failure to remain true. The threat is more immediate in 2 John, as fraternization with the antichrists appears to be a real possibility, if 2 John is judged to be a real letter. Third John, as has been said, creates a sense of presence and a strong network of identification, and it issues an appeal to loyalty.

The relationships between the Epistles and the language they share with the Gospel also beg to be explained. As Lieu affirms, "the idea of 'community' cannot be avoided," but the Epistles offer little that can be used to describe the community beyond the designation ἐκκλησία, the Elder, and the reference to "the friends" in 3 John 15. These and other such references in the Epistles "do little to create a distinctively 'Johannine' community." The "Johannine Community" as it has often been evoked—with a history, personalities, opponents, and tradition—is therefore a construct, not necessarily wrong, but not a foundation within the texts themselves.

Peter Rhea Jones interprets the role of the πρεσβύτερος as "missional," based on an inductive reading of the Epistles. The exordium, the opening of 1 John, sets the direction for the corpus of letters as it appeals to those who are already believers to join in fellowship with the Elder and those of his community in their "privileged fellowship with the Father and the Son." The departure of those who "went out" from the community in 1 John 2:19 signals a rival mission, but while 1 John alerts recipients to the threat of this rival mission, the Epistle is itself missional. The role of the Elder in 2 John is also missional, "as shepherd of the flocks." The Elder writes, like a bishop, as one who assumes authority to give instruction to a church or circle of churches, but he establishes common ground, appeals to common Johannine tradition, and seeks to persuade the recipients of the Epistle. Even the refusal of hospitality, which he urges, is missionally motivated. An inductive reading of 3 John nuances the role of the Elder further. The problem posed by Diotrephes's challenge to the Elder is not just that he does not acknowledge the Elder's authority but that he opposes the Elder's mission. As in 2 John, the Elder employs warmth and persuasion in his appeal for Gaius's support and collaboration. As Lieu suggests, the doctrinal differences between the Elder and Diotrephes may be secondary to the issues of leadership and party as they concern missional policy. Jones builds a strong case, therefore, for understanding the Elder as "above all a missional leader who belonged to a church whose ecclesiology was missiological."

Andreas Köstenberger analyzes the theme of the cosmic trial in the Johannine Epistles, arguing that it provides an overarching framework for John's theology and for other Johannine motifs and transcends the differences in genre among the Gospel, Epistles, and Revelation. A set of six polarities define John's worldview. The cosmic conflict between God and Satan builds in intensity from the Gospel to the Epistles to the book of Revelation. On the assumption that the Gospel was written before 1 John, Köstenberger analyzes the cosmic trial motif in the Gospel first. In the Gospel the trial is centered on the question of the true identity of Jesus as the Messiah, the Son of God. First John particularizes the cosmic trial at the ecclesial level, and "John's Epistles contain virtually all the same ingredients of the cosmic trial motif as does the Gospel." In 1 John the cosmic trial motif is related to John's depiction of the world, witness, judgment, Satan, the antichrist, and truth. Köstenberger summarizes the Epistle's characterization of each of these in turn. The book of Revelation is "thoroughly saturated" with the notion of cosmic conflict, so it shares many terms and themes with 1 John. Following this survey of the literary development of the theme of cosmic conflict, Köstenberger analyzes the roots of the Johannine community hypothesis and offers four reasons why an alternative explanation is preferable. The Johannine community hypothesis as developed by J. Louis Martyn, Wayne Meeks, and Raymond Brown is deficient, Köstenberger argues, "on account of its failure to account for four features which intersect in the above-surveyed cosmic trial motif: its underlying worldview; its missionary thrust; its spiritual orientation; and its salvation-historical point of reference." A more adequate understanding of the Gospel and Epistles finds them written from a first-century CE Jewish monotheistic worldview, based on the cosmology and theology of the Old Testament. The missionary thrust of the Johannine literature militates against the sectarian view of John adopted by the Johannine community hypothesis. The regeneration language of 1 John is connected to the cosmic trial motif; and the conflict at the social, ecclesial level is secondary to the broader salvation-historical theme. At its root, therefore, the cosmic conflict deals with the life of Jesus, and "the Epistles testify to the implications of the life and work of Jesus Christ upon those who do and do not confess him as Christ." Finally, the consistency of the cosmic trial motif across the five Johannine writings adds further plausibility to the view that they are the work of one and the same author.

Gary M. Burge addresses the topic of "Spirit-Inspired Theology and Ecclesial Correction." Beginning with the observation that the false teachers about whom the Elder warns the community were prophets who claimed some spiritual authority and that "the world" is listening to them (1 John 4:5), Burge asks, "What ecclesial and theological environment would lend itself to this sort of pastoral crisis?" Agreeing with Brown's thesis, he responds "a community deeply invested with spirit-experience found itself in jeopardy because of the very intense spirituality it had so eagerly promoted." The Spirit is more prominent in John than any of the other Gospels. The promised Spirit would sustain the presence of Jesus by dwelling within the disciples, reminding them of what Jesus had taught and leading them into new truths. The Johannine community therefore "possess[ed] a heightened awareness of the indwelling Spirit," but prophet-teachers with novel teachings could also claim the Spirit's authority. In such a context, a pastoral leader cannot claim personal or ecclesiastical authority; "he must appeal to the discernment of spirits as a chief strategy." Each member of the community has received the same anointing of the Spirit as the false teachers. The spirits must be tested, however, and they must be judged according to tradition, especially as it speaks to ethics and right belief. Therefore, the Elder reminds the community what they had heard "from the beginning." The leadership of the Spirit must cohere with what Jesus had said. Conflicts between inspiration and tradition continue in every generation, and the Pentecostal community today is well versed in handling such questions.

Craig Koester takes up the related theme of the antichrist in the Johannine Epistles. The term "antichrist" first appears in these letters. The usual picture of the antichrist, as it developed in Christian history, is that he is an agent of Satan, a political ruler during the final years of the present age, leading up to a cosmic battle in which Christ, having returned, will destroy the antichrist. Surprisingly little of this picture is evident in 1 or 2 John. Koester thus pursues three questions: "First, how do the Johannine Epistles portray the antichrist? Second, how do the Epistles depict the eschatological battle? And third, how do the Epistles encourage or subvert the polemical use of antichrist language?" Irenaeus and Hippolytus combined the antichrist of the Epistles with the tyrannical rule of Revelation and 2 Thess 2. In the Johannine Epistles, however, there are no signs and wonders, no persecution of the saints, and the antichrist does not make himself an object of worship. The antichrist offers a substitute belief by denying the claim that Jesus was the Christ. The implication was that Jesus's humanity had no salvific significance. Accordingly, the antichrist is not incarnate in any human person either but resides among those who "do not confess that Jesus Christ has come in the flesh" (2 John 7). In this way, the one becomes many: all who deny the incarnation, or Jesus's humanity, are the antichrist.

The eschatological battle, therefore, is not a clash of armies but a battle of words, and the world accepts the deceits of the antichrist. The author, however, announces victory: "a victory that is manifest not in fire from heaven but in faith on earth." Wherever people confess that Jesus Christ has come in the flesh, there is a victory. The battle does not lie off in the future, but is being waged and won in the present.

In the context of the Johannine Epistles, this antichrist language warns readers that when they adopt the Christology of the opponents they do not merely embrace an alternative Christology; they join the agents of evil. Similarly, however, those who voice the confession of the community but deny it with their lives also exhibit traits of the antichrist. The antichrist cannot simply be consigned to the opponents. Instead, the antichrist works within the community of faith. As Augustine wrote, whoever "in his deeds denies Christ is an antichrist" (*Tract. ep. Jo.* 3.4, 8). The potential of self-deception, therefore, carries with it the importance of self-examination for those within the author's community also.

Jan van der Watt challenges the tendency to minimize the place of ethics within the Johannine writings, as do all three of the last three essays in the book's final section. Van der Watt's contribution, "On Ethics in 1 John," highlights three central aspects of 1 John's ethics: the ethical implications of fellowship, the family as a social basis for motivating ethics, and following the example of Jesus as the guiding principle for ethics.

First John begins with the assertion that "God is light." The metaphor is foundational for the Epistle's ethics. God is the norm by which right is measured. God is also "in the light" (1:7), which means that God is knowable, and this knowledge leads to ethical behavior. Those who know God have fellowship with God and with one another, but the Epistle gives no further explanation regarding what it means to "walk in the light." Later, in 2:7–10, love and hate are added as criteria for right behavior.

The believer's filial relationship to God motivates ethical behavior. Indeed, one who is "born of God" does not sin, cannot sin. By the same token, the righteous person shows that he or she has been born of God. In antiquity, one's identity and social position were defined by one's birth or family of origin. Children of God have life from God and live in the sphere defined by God: light, or right behavior. Life and behavior are further linked in the assertion that the difference between life and death is loving instead of hating. Because God's love resulted in life, we should also love (4:7–12). The social dynamics of the ancient family are therefore the matrix within which Johannine ethics must be understood.

Because one's deeds are determined and inspired by one's identity, ethics in 1 John is a product of one's relationship to Jesus. Jesus is the exemplary standard for the believer, hence the recurrence of the particles "as" and "just as" (ὡς, καθώς). The Elder admonishes the community to "walk in the light" *just as* God is light or *just as* Jesus did. These admonitions assume that the recipients knew how Jesus lived, or that they knew the Gospel, or at least the tradition contained in it. Those born of God abide or remain in this relationship and keep God's commandments so that God's love can reach its aim in them. Living as Jesus lived requires that his followers act righteously and be pure. The ultimate criterion of right behavior, however, is God's love manifested in Jesus. If love does not characterize one's behavior within familial relationships (physical or fictive), one cannot claim to love God. On the contrary, right behavior is based on reciprocity: "God loves the believers and in order to reciprocate, they should 'return' his love by loving the children of God in a like manner."

William Loader turns to the significance of 2:15–17 for understanding the ethics of 1 John. Beginning with the assumption that the text is about sexual desire, Loader finds that it is about more than that and may not be about sexual desire at all. If the three phrases in verse 16 are a minicatalogue of vices, however, then the second item, "the lust of the eyes," may be a sexual reference. On the other hand, with Brown, one may find that the three are neutral aspects of human nature and part of biological life, but the third element—pretentiousness or vainglory in material goods—is clearly negative. Here, as with the first two items, the author addresses inappropriate responses that are typical of the world. Loader surveys literary parallels and analogies to the phrases in this list, and then he turns to the social realities of the time, especially "the culture of depravity present in the banquets of the rich," which were marked by gluttony, drunkenness, and sexual excess. A survey of attacks on the excesses of such banquets suggests that the three items in the triad are related—they are "the depraved excesses of the rich." Loader acknowledges that this interpretation remains only a hypothesis, but it coheres well with the ethical vision of the rest of the Epistle. In a context in which many lived on the raw edge of poverty, the community ethic demanded the sharing of goods with those most in need (1 John 3:17). Understood in this context, the triad in 2:15–17 serves a fundamental concern of 1 John's ethics: it attacks "the neglect of the ethical obligation of support for the poor."

David Rensberger makes the case that the verb τελειόω should not be translated "perfected" in 1 John 4:11–18, as it usually is (KJV, NRSV). Instead, in this context it means "completed": "his love is completed in us." Rensberger contends that in Koine Greek τελειόω did not mean what "perfect" does in modern English. This translation can be traced back to the fourteenth century translation attributed to John Wycliffe, who worked from the Latin Vulgate, not the Greek text of the New Testament. William Tyndale offered the same translation, and this tradition has been followed with few variations up to the present. Translators have no doubt assumed that this was the best translation. Some private translations by individual translators first began to employ other terms to express the meaning of this verse; James Moffatt used "complete" in his 1913 translation of 1 John 4:12. For this verse, William Beck offered the insightful translation "and His love has accomplished in us what He wants." Despite the appeal of the phrase "perfect love," "perfect" does not carry the same meaning as τελειόω. As Rensberger observes, "the meaning of 'perfect' in English has slipped significantly from the meaning of *perfectus* in Latin, to the point that we may be confusing ourselves about what the ancient texts are actually saying."

The basic meaning of τελειόω, in contrast, is to "complete, bring to an end, finish, accomplish" (BDAG). In the Gospel of John, Jesus uses the verb when speaking of completing the work(s) the Father gave him to do (4:34; 5:36; 17:4). These sayings are close to those in 1 John 4, but the term cannot be translated by "perfect" in these verses. The same is true for Jesus's exclamation in 19:30. Rensberger's exegesis of 1 John 4 demonstrates that the sense of carrying a task through to completion or bringing it to its intended goal is the meaning here also, rather than making something perfect or flawless. But here, God's love is placed in human hands with the charge that they continue the revelation of God by loving one another. When they do, they bring God's love to its intended consummation. Rensberger sees further the implications of these statements for the mission of the church. Even at a late stage in the development of New Testament Christianity, the perceived goal is not institutional development but the generation of communities of love.

So, the stage is set. The backdrop is in place, the plot—the knotty interpretive issues, and the "disputes" both within the Epistles and between the lines of interpretation they have evoked—is endlessly engaging, and the characters—again both the personae and the named characters in the letters as well as the diverse group of scholars who contributed to this volume—continue to be in "dispute." If there is no unanimity or final resolution to the plot, then it invites the reader, and future scholars, into the conversation. The disputes are important both because the issues in dispute matter and because scholarship advances through this process of investigation and debate. In the process rich insights into these letters emerge.

Part 1
The Relationship between the Gospel and the Epistles

The relation between the Gospel and Epistles of John is fraught with perplexities. On one hand, much of the vocabulary and sentence construction between these two sets of writings are similar, while differences also abound. They certainly represent the same sector of the early Christian movement, but were they written around the same time, by the same person, to the same audience, or might there be a multiplicity of answers to each of these questions? Therefore, any attempt to ascertain the character of the Johannine situation, as well as the meaning of its writings' content, must first begin with seeking to understand the relationship between the Johannine Gospel and Epistles. In so doing, it is worth noting that the great Johannine commentaries over the last century or so have distinguished themselves as such precisely because they have engaged both the Gospel and Epistles of John. These include the commentaries by Rudolf Bultmann (1971, 1973), Rudolf Schnackenburg (1984, 1992), Raymond Brown (1966, 1970, 1982, 1988), and more recently Urban von Wahlde (2010a). Characteristic also of these great programmatic works is the ways they also address literary, historical, and theological features of these texts, and decisive contributions in the future will also need to follow their lead.

Nonetheless, it is fair to say that the most significant contribution over the last half century or more to the larger Johannine questions has been that of Raymond Brown. Not only did he produce three unrivalled commentaries on the Gospel and Epistles of John for the Anchor Bible Commentary series (1966, 1970, 1982), but he also wrote important monographs on the Johannine situation (1979a, 1984) and other related subjects. Therefore, engaging his set of paradigms is an inescapable place to begin when considering state-of-the-art research on the Johannine Epistles. Brown's paradigms are not the only ones worth considering, however, so the leading contributions of other scholars must also be drawn into the discussion, evaluating their approaches along the way.

Here the relation of the Johannine Gospel and Epistles will involve further questions: which was written first, the Gospel or the Epistles? More pointedly, is the "new commandment" of the Gospel earlier than the "old commandment" in the Epistles (implying that the Epistles are later than the Gospel), or is the Word-life-light combination of themes in 1 John 1:1–3 developed more fully (and thus later) in John 1:1–18? Or, might the Gospel have been produced in more than one edition, or the Epistles written over an extended period of time, so that some overlapping of composition timeframes might also be plausible? And, if the Gospel's author and final editor were two different people, might either of them have authored the Epistles? Further, were the Epistles written in the same order that they are found canonically, or might their composition have been in a different order? Whatever the case, 1 John is the most similar to the Gospel of John; therefore, that relationship must be examined most closely. And, as 2 John is closest in its content to 1 John, that relationship will also be an important one to consider. Then again, how does 3 John relate to the other Johannine texts, as it is the most distinctive? Some of these considerations will follow also in other sections of this collection.

Note that in the three essays below, each of the authors adopts a distinctive approach to the composition of and relationships between these four texts. Their approaches and outcomes also bear implications for understanding the context of the Johannine Epistles, as well as their theological and ethical content. Nonetheless, these essays make robust attempts not only to engage and evaluate earlier paradigms; they also seek to establish new ones worth building on for contemporary and future interpreters.

Raymond Brown's View of the Crisis of 1 John: In the Light of Some Peculiar Features of the Johannine Gospel

Urban C. von Wahlde

If there is one thing that can be said with some certainty about 1 John, it is that interpretation of the document is more thoroughly controverted than almost any other document in the New Testament. It is like a Rorschach test. Scholars see in it all sorts of variations! Since the appearance of Raymond Brown's masterful commentary, a number of other major commentaries have appeared with astounding differences in their view of what is going on in 1 John.[1]

Stephen Smalley (1984, xxiii–xxxii) holds that the author addresses two groups still within the community but who have various views in need of correction. The first is a group of Jewish Christians who continue to have difficulty accepting the messiahship of Jesus. A second group is composed of Hellenistic Christians influenced by dualistic thought, who continued to have difficulty with the humanity of Jesus and so are close to what was later termed docetism. Thus, both of these groups within the community need to have their christological views nuanced. The one group needs to emphasize the divinity of Jesus, and the other needs to focus on the humanity.

According to Smalley, both groups also need to have their views of ethics corrected. The first group, which has a Jewish Christian background, needs to move beyond their focus on the Jewish law.[2] The second

---

[1]. For a valuable review of scholarship on the Epistles since the commentary of Alan Brooke (1912), see Smith 2009.

[2]. In Smalley's view, this polemic against the old law is evident primarily in the discussion of the new and old commandment in 2:7–8.

group needs to focus on mutual love as a reaction to moral indifferentism.[3] Finally, a third group consists of more radical members of either or both of the first two groups. These more radical members had departed from the community and are now the secessionists referred to in 1 John 2:18–19. Like Brown, Smalley agrees that the views of the opponents are based on a reading of the Gospel, but he is the only scholar reviewed here who sees three groups of opponents.

Rudolf Schnackenburg (1992, 18) holds the view that the opponents are of gnostic leaning and from a predominantly gentile group.[4] They attempt an interpretation of the Johannine tradition with which the author disagrees. Schnackenburg focuses on seven statements that he feels are central to the position of the opponents. However, in addition to these statements, Schnackenburg also notes a number of "positive statements of Christological faith." He comments: "Even if these are not directed emphatically against the heretics, they do, taken as a whole, create a picture of the faith in its light and shade which ought to protect the church against these dangerous influences" (1992, 19). These statements include emphasis on what was "from the beginning," incarnation, atoning death, unique sonship, and divinity of Jesus.

Georg Strecker (1996, 69–76) has proposed that the opponents in 1 John are to be identified as docetists. Their beliefs are to be discerned from 1 John itself, but the entire letter is not concerned with the crisis. Rather, the crisis is mirrored only in 1 John 2:22–23; 4:1–6, and 5:6–8 (Strecker 1996, 70 n. 55). After a survey of early docetic views, Strecker concludes that the closest parallels to the opponents of 1 John are the groups opposed by Ignatius of Antioch.

Strecker finds similarities to Ignatius's opponents in the denial that Jesus is the Christ and Son of God and the denial that Jesus Christ came in the flesh. He also suggests that the opponents devalued the Eucharist. He argues this on the grounds that the Gospel puts much value on

---

3. Smalley refers to 1 John 3:10–11 as the major text dealing with this issue.

4. According to Schnackenburg, the views of the opponents can be gathered from the specific confessional statements about Jesus as the Christ, as the Son of God, as coming in the flesh, and as coming in water and blood. According to Schnackenburg, that the opponents are predominantly gentiles is indicated primarily by the lack of argument from Scripture offered in 1 John and by the author's preference for "Son of God" as a title for Jesus.

the Eucharist and so was probably attempting to counter opponents.⁵ He claims that nothing can be known about the anthropology or ethics of the opponents (1996, 74).⁶

Hans-Josef Klauck (1991a), basing himself on what he sees as the essential ambiguity of the data in the Epistles, rather than attempting to provide a definitive picture of the opponents, looks for the element in the Johannine tradition that has given rise to the problem. For Klauck, this element is the baptism of Jesus. This could be interpreted as the melding of Jesus and the Christ in a docetic way, but whether the Spirit departs from Jesus before his death or simply does not suffer is not answered by the Gospel. Klauck (1991a, 41, 295) sees the baptism of the believer as the point of the reception of the Spirit and argues that a number of the elements of the opponents' beliefs reflect a radicalizing of various elements of the Johannine tradition connected with the Spirit. For example, he understands the opponents to be transformed by their reception of the Spirit into a "pneumatic existence" that is no longer subject to the conditions of the material world. They have knowledge of God and fellowship with God; they have a purely present eschatology; the children of God

---

5. I do not find Strecker clear on this point. In 1 John itself, I find no reference by either the author or the opponents regarding the Eucharist. If its neglect has been a problem the author opposed, surely there would be some mention of it. To argue from the traditions in the Gospel is tenuous, given the fact that Strecker holds 1 John and the Gospel to be independent compositions of a fairly large Johannine "school." See Strecker 1996, 74. However, I would agree with Strecker that the Eucharist became a topic of concern in the final stage of the community's development, and it may be that this conflict (from a period later than that of 1 John) is what is echoed in Ignatius's letter. More will be said of this below.

6. Thus, Strecker would hold a view opposite to that of Beutler (see below). Also most scholars find a considerable emphasis on ethics throughout the Epistle. Perhaps the most significant problem with the approach taken by Strecker is that by limiting so severely statements dealing with the crisis, he does not seem to take adequate account of a large number of other statements with which the author of 1 John clearly disagrees and which he seeks to refute. Strecker also does not account for the fact that the views of the author and those of the opponents are so similar in many respects: "No sufficient evidence can be presented to show that the author of the Johannine Letters used the Fourth Gospel, as I will demonstrate below" (1996, xl). So also Schnelle: "the derivation of their [the opponents'] theology from the Gospel of John must be called pure speculation, especially since there is no passage in 1 John regarding the opponents that can be regarded as even a remote reference to the Gospel" (1992, 70 n. 169). In this respect, both Strecker and Schnelle are at odds with the majority of modern scholars.

have complete freedom from sin. They no longer have need of forgiveness. For them the gift of life and the atoning death of Jesus lose their soteriological meaning (1991a, 41, 295).[7]

Although Klauck associates the various claims of the opponents with a radicalized pneumatology, he does not ground this claim sufficiently but instead chooses to focus on the similarities with docetic trends elsewhere in early Christianity. Just recently, in her commentary on the Johannine Epistles, Judith Lieu (2008a) has proposed that 1 John is not concerned with refuting opponents at all but simply with exhortation of the community and that in many cases that which is discouraged is not necessarily the view of any group of opponents.[8] In some ways, it could be said that this represents the antithesis of the view of Brown (and of many other scholars).

Other Recent Views

Other recent commentators have forged positions that reflect varying modifications of the positions evident in the major commentaries; but, because of the limits of format, they have not been able to argue these theories so extensively. Because commentators will at times see a mixture of influences, it is often difficult to know to which group to assign a commentator.

Among those seeing an exaggerated pneumatology as the primary factor in the position of the opponents is Kenneth Grayston (1984), who was among the first of this group to make such a proposal.[9] Lieu (1986, 171–80), in her commentary on 2 and 3 John, also raises in an extended way the question of the role of the Spirit in the controversy. Lieu does so in the context of the repeated assertions of the author regarding the importance of the tradition vis-à-vis the role of the Spirit. In her view the

---

7. In this regard, Klauck's view is close to mine. He in fact spells out a number of prerogatives of the outpouring of the Spirit that would account for elements of the opponents' position, as I do.

8. For example, see Lieu (2008a, 60) regarding "sinlessness" and (2008a, 67) regarding "knowing" God.

9. Smith also proposes that at the time of 1 John the community was in the process of constructing "criteria by which genuine and false claims to Spirit inspiration had to be worked out" (1991, 106).

problem of the relation of Spirit to tradition is "met ... by understanding both tradition and Spirit Christocentrically."[10]

Among those seeing the opponents as docetic is D. Moody Smith Jr. (1991, 130–32). He believes that "1 John presupposes familiarity with the Christian message and tradition as it is known from the Gospel of John or something substantially like it" (28). In the view of R. Alan Culpepper (1998, 48–54), the opponents have many traits of docetists and may have later developed into Valentinian Gnosticism. The opponents held an even higher Christology than the author but one that removed Jesus from any connection with the flesh.

Johannes Beutler (2000, 20–24) sees the focus of disagreement as being rooted in anthropology rather than in Christology or ethics. The opponents are "Pneumatiker," persons filled with the Spirit, and are defined by their attitudes toward community with God, sinlessness, knowledge of God, abiding in him, being in the light, having an anointing, and so on. They claim that these characteristics are a result of the anointing they have from the Spirit, and these do away with the need for Jesus as "anointed," as "Son of God," and as a bringer of salvation. The author resists this by distinguishing a true possession of the Spirit from the false one asserted by the opponents. Thus, Beutler continues the direction of recent scholarship that focuses on the understanding and role of the Spirit as essential.

Taking his cue from Schnackenburg, John Painter (2002, 79–94) focuses his understanding on seven statements that are thought to reflect the view of the opponents.[11] He argues that the conflict evident in 1 John is based on divergent interpretations of the tradition and that it centers on issues of Christology and ethics. The conflict has been created, however, by the influx of considerable numbers of converts who are not of Jewish background and who attempt to interpret the tradition without respect to its Jewish background (Painter 2002, 80, 330; 1986, 50–51). Painter concludes that the position of the opponents is not a single logical whole, and so there are inevitably "loose ends" that cannot be fully understood within the context of the Epistle.

Brown himself (1982, 69) views 1 John as concerned with the interpretation of the Johannine tradition as it appeared in the Gospel of John. The

---

10. Lieu (1986, 177) articulates well the tensions between Spirit and "tradition" and between Spirit and Jesus.

11. Earlier versions of Painter's view had been worked out in his book on John (1980, 115–25) and his article on the "'Opponents' in 1 John" (1986).

"tract" (Brown's term for 1 John) was intended to put forward the correct interpretation of the Gospel by emphasizing elements that were less dominant, over against what the author thought was a misinterpretation, which focused on elements of the tradition that were dominant in the Gospel.[12] Brown went so far as to suggest that one could argue that the minor elements had been added by a redactor, but he feared the accusation that such arguing was only a circular method by which one excluded what did not agree with the dominant view.

I have titled my paper as I have because, as will be apparent, I owe much to the work of Brown but at the same time do diverge at significant points. Since I first read Brown's commentary for a review in the *Biblical Theology Bulletin* (1983), I have found it to be in very many respects an accurate view. However, I believe that it is possible to sharpen and refine elements of his view and in some cases propose changes that make his general view of 1 John and of its relation to the Gospel even more persuasive. Specifically, I would propose, along with Brown, that 1 John was written

---

12. Brown expresses his basic position as follows: "I shall try to show that *every idea of the secessionists (as reconstructed from the polemic of I and II John) can be plausibly explained as derivative from the Johannine tradition as preserved for us in* [*the Gospel of John*]" (Brown, 1982, 72, emphasis original).

Yet Brown is somewhat ambiguous in describing the two strains of thought regarding the various topics. In his summary of his theory, he comments: "The Johannine tradition enshrined in [the Gospel of John], as it came to both the author and to his adversaries, was relatively 'neutral' on some points that had now come into dispute. Either it did not contain direct answers for the divisive questions, or it contained texts that each side could draw upon for support" (1982, 69). This last alternative is not well expressed, but it is clear from other statements by Brown that the "texts that each side could draw upon" is meant to refer to two sets of texts, one of which would favor the author's view and the other of which would favor the secessionists' views.

That this is so is clear from other statements that Brown makes. For example, Brown observes that if one were to claim that "every passage which does not favor the secessionist position had been added by a redactor in order to refute the secessionists.... Then one is open to the charge of circular reasoning by establishing kinship between secessionist thought and a Gospel from which one has excluded all difficult passages" (73). On p. 98, Brown refers to the elements of the tradition that refute the views of the secessionists as "minor indications." Thus, we may restate Brown's view by saying that his opponents emphasized elements, many of which constituted what might be called more dominant positions in the Gospel, while the author of 1 John sought to argue for the importance of elements of the Johannine tradition that were present in the Gospel but were represented by "minor indications."

to correct a misinterpretation of the Gospel's tradition. Moreover, I would agree with Brown in saying that many of the views of the author of 1 John can be found in the Gospel, but that in the Gospel, they represent views that are only minimally present.

However, I also believe that his view of the so-called dominant strain of Johannine theology does not do full justice to the Gospel, and it is in that respect that I would disagree with Brown. My purpose here is to try to draw together some significant features of the Johannine Gospel and to show how 1 John sheds light on those features and puts them into context within the full Johannine corpus. I would propose that, if what I am about to say is correct, we may gain a significant new understanding of the Johannine tradition, both the Gospel and Epistles.

In order to help following along the way, I have prepared a chart of the four parts of my presentation.

Where We Are Going

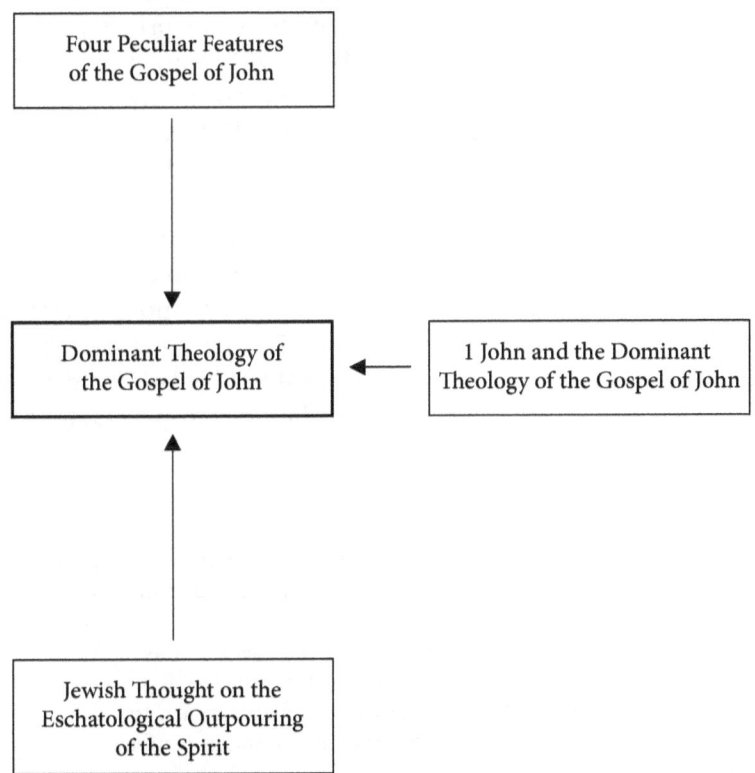

1. Four Peculiar Features of the Gospel of John

There are several prominent features of the Gospel that remain puzzling to scholars. These are features that might be called "macrofeatures," features that are evident in the Gospel as a whole and that are, at the same time, unique to the Gospel of John within the New Testament. All of these features were recognized by Brown, either in his commentary on the Gospel or on the Epistles. They are also very widely recognized by other scholars and always described as somehow "peculiar." I would like to call attention to them, because I believe that they form an important element in Johannine theology and, thus, that a better understanding of them may be gained when they are addressed from the perspective of 1 John. But first, we must note them as they appear in the Gospel.

The first of the features is articulated well by Bultmann's (1951, 1955, 2:66) famous statement that the Johannine Jesus was "a revealer without a revelation." Although we might well debate the absoluteness of Bultmann's statement, it certainly is true that there is a massive concentration on Christology, and this might well be said to be the primary content of Jesus's revelation. For example, Smith (1984, 178) comments: "Aside from his discourses and disputes about himself and his own role, Jesus utters no teaching whatever during his public ministry." Brown (1979b, 64; 1994, 197–98) himself recognized this, although he disagreed with the absoluteness of the statement.

The second feature is that, in the Gospel, the death of Jesus is conceived of primarily as a departure to the Father and not as an atoning sacrifice. This observation has been put forward also by, among others, Smith (1984, 178) and in a more detailed way by J. Terence Forestell in his book, *The Word of the Cross* (1974)[13] and by Godfrey Nicholson in his book *Death as Departure* (1983).[14] Brown describes the Gospel's view of Jesus's

---

13. For a succinct statement of Forestell's view, see Forestell (1974, 191): "The cross of Christ in Jn is evaluated precisely in terms of revelation in harmony with the theology of the entire gospel, rather than in terms of vicarious and expiatory sacrifice for sin."

14. For a succinct statement of Nicholson's view, see Nicholson (1983, 167): "As we have tried to demonstrate, the interpretation of the death of Jesus which [the evangelist] achieves is rather subtle: Jesus' death is really his return to the Father; Jesus came to return rather than to die; the focus of attention lies just beyond the cross in the moment of return—the "hour" of the glorification of Jesus."

death as his "ascension" and later comments: the Gospel of John "presents the death of Jesus as a glorification and ascension … but it contains minor indications that the sacrificial and vicarious character of Jesus' death was known and perhaps taken for granted" (1982, 33, 98). Of course, the belief that the death of Jesus was somehow an atonement for sin is commonly held throughout early Christianity.

The third feature is what has been called the "ethical vacuum" in the Gospel. Again several scholars have called attention to this; for example, in his article entitled "The Ethics of the Fourth Evangelist," for Smith's *Festschrift*, Wayne Meeks (1996, 318) comments: "What is wrong with the Fourth Gospel as a vehicle of moral formation? First, its form is wrong: It offers no explicit moral instruction." Smith's (1984, 178, cited above) own view of the matter can be discerned from his more general comment that in the Gospel Jesus "utters no teaching whatever during his public ministry." Brown, in his commentary on the Epistles (1982, 81), said: "No specific sins of behavior are mentioned in [the Gospel of John], only the great sin which is to refuse to believe in Jesus (8:24; 9:41)." Brown said elsewhere (1979, 66): "There is no body of ethical maxims in the Johannine tradition as it is known to us from the Gospel."

The fourth peculiar feature of the Gospel is the considerable focus on "knowing" and "not knowing" in the Gospel.[15] This is the feature that has, more than anything else, led people to ask about a relationship of the Gospel to Gnosticism. This led Bultmann to suppose that the discourses in the Gospel had been derived from gnostic sources and had been "baptized" to make them apply to Jesus. In more recent proposals, which have understood the relation of the Gospel to Gnosticism less directly, scholars have suggested that this feature accounts for the attractiveness of the Gospel to gnostics.[16]

Thus we have four distinctive, and indeed unique, features of the Johannine Gospel: (1) a marked absence of what would ordinarily be called "revelation" by Jesus; (2) the presence of an interpretation of the death of Jesus that is not soteriological; (3) the absence of any significant ethical teaching; and an (4) intense focus on "knowing" God.

---

15. Brown (1966, 514) says that the Greek verb γινώσκω appears fifty-six times and the Greek verb οἶδα appears eighty-five times in the Gospel.

16. For a survey of the changing attitudes toward the relation of the Johannine tradition with Gnosticism, see von Wahlde (2010b).

I would like to address these four "mega" problems in my presentation—a project that may not be as impossible as it sounds.

2. The Dominant Theological Plan of the Gospel

If we return for a moment to the chart showing the overview of "Where We Are Going," we will see that, next, I would like to look briefly at the "dominant theology of the Gospel." Specifically, I would like to propose that the "peculiar features" of the Gospel that I have just described can be explained as deriving from the dominant theology of the Gospel.

Of course, for the present occasion, I can only sketch an approach to this proposal, but I hope this sketch will not be a distortion or a falsification of the evidence. For those whose interest is piqued, another avenue is available. I have addressed these issues from a slightly different perspective but much more thoroughly in the context of my commentary published by Eerdmans in their Critical Commentary Series. But a look at these features, first, from the perspective of the Gospel itself, then from the perspective of Old Testament hopes for the outpouring of the Spirit, and then from the perspective of 1 John may be of help in furthering our understanding of 1 John and of its relation to the Gospel.

According to the Gospel of John, the essential purpose of Jesus's ministry was to give eternal life through the Spirit. Furthermore, this Spirit was regularly identified in the Gospel by the image of "living water." In John 3:3–8, Jesus explains this to Nicodemus: it is necessary to be born of the Spirit; "that which is born of the flesh is flesh and that which is born of the Spirit is Spirit" (3:6; all translations from the Gospel and Letters of John are my own). In 4:10–15 Jesus offers the Spirit to the Samaritan woman under the imagery of living water. In 7:37–39, Jesus explains that living water will flow from his side when he is glorified, and the author then explains that this refers to the Spirit, which those who believed in Jesus would receive when Jesus was glorified. After numerous other references to the fact that Jesus gives eternal life, we come to the moment of his death, when it is said that Jesus "gave up the Spirit (19:30), a statement that is inherently ambiguous but could well refer to the "release" of the Spirit. Finally, in 20:22, we hear that Jesus bestows the Spirit on his disciples on the evening of the resurrection. In this event, we have the culmination of Jesus's promise throughout the Gospel. There cannot be any doubt that this is the primary hoped-for benefit of belief in Jesus. It is to those who believe in Jesus that the Spirit will be given.

In the light of this promise by Jesus, the most important action of the individual who hopes to receive the Spirit is *to believe in Jesus*. It is only to those who believe in Jesus that the Spirit will be given. When we look at the Gospel either in overview or in detail, we see that the overriding emphasis of the Gospel is thus the encouragement of this belief. Finally, it is made clear again and again in the Jewish Scriptures that the outpouring of the eschatological Spirit will take place, but also that it will have certain effects upon those persons who receive this Spirit. However, in the Gospel, the relationship of these effects to the bestowal of the eschatological Spirit is *implicit* rather than *explicit*.

Consequently, it is important that we look at the background of this thought in those Scriptures. This will be the third part of my presentation. However, before we do that, it will be helpful to stop briefly and reflect on what might be called "the nature of the eschatological age" in the classical (nonapocalyptic) worldview of the Jewish Scriptures.

A Note on the Nature of the Eschatological Age

We are about to observe several Old Testament texts in which the prerogatives of the eschatological Spirit are articulated. It is important to notice that these prerogatives are articulated in a simple, absolute way. In all cases, the Old Testament authors are speaking about what are variously called "the end times," "the age of fulfillment," or "the eschatological age." The "eschatological age" as it was understood in Judaism, is, *by definition, an age of perfection*, an age in which all evil is removed and there is no hint of imperfection.

If the Jewish believers within the Johannine community believed that the end times had truly arrived with the giving of the eschatological Spirit, then these texts told them what to expect, and *there would be no reason to qualify the prerogatives that accompanied that outpouring of God's Spirit!*[17] It is for this reason that such traditional, "classical," canonical eschatology could be said to be truly "realized."[18]

---

17. Although the "realized" eschatology of the Gospel of John is often thought to be an advancement created by the Johannine author, in fact, realized eschatology is simply the eschatology envisioned by the worldview of "classical" (i.e., nonapocalyptic) Judaism.

18. The absence of dualism in the Old Testament has long been recognized. K. G. Kuhn comments: "This dualistic ideology [as found in the sectarian documents from

3. The Background of This Theology in the Jewish Scriptures

I mentioned above that the so-called dominant Johannine theology was a totally *Jewish* interpretation of the ministry of Jesus. There are six aspects of this Jewish understanding of the Spirit and its effects that are reflected in the dominant theology of the Gospel, so let us look at each of these features briefly and see some texts that support this view.

3.1. The Eschatological Outpouring of the Spirit

First, we see that the canonical Jewish Scriptures clearly promise an outpouring of the Spirit in the end times. The text that is probably the most familiar to Christians is the one from the book of Joel [3:1–2 LXX; 2:28–29 MT] quoted in Acts 2:17, on the Feast of Pentecost.

> *Then afterward I will pour out my spirit on all flesh*; your sons and your daughters shall prophesy, your old men shall dream dreams, and your young men shall see visions. Even on the male and female slaves, *in those days, I will pour out my spirit.* (NRSV)

This text shows clearly that the Christian community understood the bestowal of the Spirit to be promised in Scripture. But there are numerous other similar references: for example, Isa 32:14–15 and Isa 44:3. In addition, Ezekiel makes at least three references to such an outpouring: Ezek 11:17–19, 36:26–27, and 39:29.

3.2. New Life through the Spirit

Second, the person who receives God's Spirit receives a new form of life. As Ezek 36:26 says:

> A new heart I will give you and *a new spirit I will put within you*. (NRSV)

Qumran] is totally alien to Old Testament thought nor can it be explained as an outgrowth of the Old Testament" (1952, 303). Kuhn's observation is noted approvingly by Brown (1965, 142), who also comments: "In the Qumran literature we find a new outlook. All men are aligned in two opposing forces, the one of light and truth, the other of darkness and perversion, with each faction ruled by a spirit or prince." Of course, what applies to Qumran applies to apocalyptic dualism generally.

This notion is to be understood in the larger context of the Jewish Scriptures, in which natural life comes from an infusion of a natural spirit—and with the correlation that the giving of the Spirit of God will elevate the person to the level of the life of God, which is "eternal life." This is clear from Ezek 37:4–6:

> Then he said to me, "Prophesy to these bones, and say to them: O dry bones, hear the word of the Lord. Thus says the Lord God to these bones: I will cause breath to enter you, and you shall live. I will lay sinews on you, and will cause flesh to come upon you, and cover you with skin, and put breath in you, and you shall live; and you shall know that I am the Lord." (NRSV)

Ezekiel 37:14 makes it clear that this is not a natural spirit but God's Spirit:

> *I will put my spirit in you that you may live.*

3.3. No Need for Teaching

Third, when a person receives the promised Spirit of God, that person thenceforth will be taught by the Spirit. As is said in Jer 31:34 (38:34 LXX):

> *No longer shall they teach one another*, or say to each other, "Know the LORD," for they shall all know me, from the least of them to the greatest, says the LORD; for I will forgive their iniquity, and remember their sin no more. (NRSV)

Also Jer 24:7:

> I will give them a heart to know that I am the LORD; and they shall be my people and I will be their God, for they shall return to me with their whole heart. (NRSV)

3.4. Knowledge of God

As can be seen from the passages just quoted (Jer 31:34 MT; 38:34 LXX), when a person possesses the promised Spirit, one is also enabled to truly and thoroughly "know" God:[19]

---

19. So also Brown (1982, 280) in an extended discussion; Lieu (2008a, 68–69) and others.

> *No longer shall they ... say to each other, "Know the LORD," for they shall all know me,* from the least of them to the greatest, says the LORD. (NRSV)

3.5. Cleansing from Sin by the Spirit

When a person receives the promised Spirit, the person is cleansed of sin. Ezekiel 36:25–27 says:

> *I will sprinkle clean water upon you, and you shall be clean from all your uncleannesses,* and from all your idols I will cleanse you. A new heart I will give you, and a new spirit I will put within you; and I will remove from your body the heart of stone and give you a heart of flesh. (NRSV)

Cleansing of sin by the Spirit is *implicit* in this text and is *explicit* in similar statements in the Dead Sea Scrolls.[20] In 1QS 4:21, we read that:

> [God will] cleanse him *with the spirit of holiness* from every irreverent deed. He will sprinkle over him the spirit of truth like lustral water (in order to cleanse him) from all the abhorrences of deceit and from the defilement of the unclean spirit. (García Martínez and Tigchelaar 1997)

In 1QH 8:19–20 we read:

> I have appeased your face by the spirit which you have given me, to lavish your favor on your servant for [ever], *to purify me with your holy spirit,* to bring me near by your will according to the extent of your kindnesses. (García Martínez and Tigchelaar 1997)

3.6. No Need for Ethics

Finally, when a person possesses the promised Spirit, the person will spontaneously live as God wants. As Ezek 36:27 says:

> I will put my spirit within you, and make you follow my statutes and be careful to observe my ordinances. (NRSV)

---

20. Lieu (2008, 56) points to texts such as Ps 51:2, Pss. Sol. 9:6; 10:1, and 1QH XIV, 8 as expressing similar sentiments regarding remission of sin.

Similarly, Jer 31:33–34 says:

> But this is the covenant that I will make with the house of Israel after those days, says the LORD: I will put my law within them, and I will write it on their hearts; and I will be their God, and they shall be my people. No longer shall they teach one another, or say to each other, "Know the LORD," for they shall all know me, from the least of them to the greatest, says the LORD; for I will forgive their iniquity, and remember their sin no more. (NRSV)

According to this statement, and in agreement with the previous ones, the possession of the eschatological Spirit will mean that a person spontaneously responds to, and behaves in accordance with, the commandments of God.

Do these prerogatives of the reception of the Spirit as expressed in the Jewish Scriptures account for both the peculiar features of the Gospel and also its dominant theology? I would answer "yes" and would argue that the various features of the Gospel I listed earlier are most completely explained within this perspective. To review: (1) Having received the Spirit will give believers the life of God—the essential, hoped-for gift according to the Gospel. (2) Jesus is presented as a revealer without a revelation; because once believers have the Spirit, they will have no need of anyone's teaching ("revelation"). The Spirit will take over this function. (3) Having the Spirit will make the believer "know" the Lord. (4) Having the Spirit will make the believer spontaneously follow the ordinances of God. There will be no need for ethical instructions. (5) The Spirit will free them from sin. There will be no reason to speak of the death of Jesus as atoning for sin.

Thus, to this point, we have seen: (1) that there are a number of commonly recognized features of the Gospel of John that are unexpected and quite different from "normal" Christian theology; (2) that the dominant theological stratum of the Gospel presents Jesus as offering the eschatological Spirit; (3) that this hope for the outpouring of the Spirit represents a clear strand of Jewish eschatological hopes; and (4) that the prerogatives of this Spirit account for both the dominant theology of the Gospel and the peculiar features so distinctive of the Gospel.[21]

---

21. It is significant to note that, not only in the Old Testament but also in the Dead Sea Scrolls, these prerogatives are attributed to the Spirit (of truth). For example, 1QS IV, 21–22 (referred to above) states: "He (God) will sprinkle over him the Spirit of

4. A Confirmation of the Proposal:
These Same Features from the Perspective of 1 John

We now come to the final—and crucial—part of my proposal. What does the thought of 1 John have to say about these various features? In his commentary on the Johannine Epistles, Brown proposed that 1 John was reacting to the thought of the Gospel and that the Epistle was attempting to correct and to nuance aspects of the "dominant" theology in the Gospel. I would agree with this view; however, as we have seen above, I believe it is possible to define more precisely the theological contours of the dominant theology (and its background) to which the author of 1 John reacted.

While what we have seen so far may seem possible and perhaps convincing to some, to others it may seem too general to be certain. However, when we turn to 1 John, we observe something remarkable. As we will see, 1 John addresses—and modifies—each of these features in a way that makes it all but impossible to believe that the correspondence is accidental. In order to see this, we must return to these features one more time.

4.1. Did Jesus Come to Give Eternal Life?

First, it is clear that both the Gospel and 1 John agree that Jesus came to give eternal life. This is so clear that it does not require discussion. For example, in 1 John 2:25, we read:

> And *this is the promise that [Jesus] promised us: eternal life.*

In 1 John 5:11–12 we read:

> And *this is the witness: that God gave us eternal life* and this life is in his Son.

Truth like lustral water (in order to cleanse him) from all the abhorrences of deceit and (from) the defilement of the unclean spirit, in order to instruct the upright ones in the knowledge of the Most High, and to make them understand the wisdom of the sons of heaven to those of perfect behavior" (García Martínez and Tigchelaar 1997). Thus we see the reception of the Spirit takes away sin, gives knowledge, and prevents future sin. The one element "missing" from this description is the conviction that the Spirit will be the sole source of teaching, although this could undoubtedly be considered an aspect of instruction by the Spirit.

4.2. Did Jesus Come to Give a Revelation?

As we have seen, the focus of the Gospel is on Christology: was Jesus truly a divinely sent herald of the giving of the Spirit? In order for someone to believe Jesus's proclamation that he was the herald of the giving of the Spirit, it had to be proved that Jesus was who he said he was. If he was not truly the Son sent by the Father, then his words and promises would be meaningless. If Jesus genuinely promised and bestowed the eschatological Spirit, then, according to the Jewish Scriptures, believers would have no need for what might be called the historical teaching of Jesus, because the Spirit would teach them all they needed to know, as Ezekiel and Jeremiah say.

But what does 1 John have to say about this? The author presents what might be called a "yes … but" position. He agrees that, *yes*, the inspiration of the Spirit is essential, *but* at the same time he argues that the true believer must remain faithful to what might be described as the historical words of Jesus. The author strongly affirms the role of the Spirit and that the Spirit will teach the believer. In fact, he presents a view that is remarkably close to the view of the opponents and at the same time echoes the wording of Jer 31:34. In 1 John 2:27, the author says:

> And as for you—*the anointing that you received from [God] abides in you, and you do not have need that anyone teach you, but as [God's] anointing teaches you about all.*

Earlier, in 2:20–21, he had said:

> *You have an anointing from the Holy One and you know all. I did not write to you that you do not know the truth but that you know it.*

So the author of 1 John acknowledges the importance of inspiration by the Spirit.[22] The Spirit enables the believer to know all and makes it

---

22. It should also be pointed out that in the Jewish Scriptures, it was understood that the term "anointing" could be used either metaphorically or literally. In the coronation of the king, there was a literal anointing with oil, but this was intended as a metaphor for the giving ("anointing") by the Holy Spirit. There can be no other explanation of the words of the author of 1 John that speak of an "anointing from the Holy One."

unnecessary for them to have any other teacher. We know that the author of 1 John is referring to Jewish eschatological hopes, because his wording in these verses is such a clear reference to the text of Jer 38:34 (LXX). But, then, how does the author differ from his opponents? The author does affirm what the Jeremiah text has to say, but he then goes on to balance this view with another perspective. In doing so, the author of 1 John (1:1–3) insists that the believer must remain faithful to

> *that which was from the beginning*, which we have heard, which we have looked at with our eyes, which we have seen and our hands have touched, that which concerns the word of life—and the life was revealed, and we have seen and we bear witness ... whatever we have seen and we have heard, *we proclaim to you* also so that you also may be in fellowship with us.

That which is "from the beginning" is essential. The author is opposed to what is "new" and what derives from the time after the beginning. In 2:24, the author urges his readers:

> As for you—*let what you heard from the beginning abide in you.* If it abides in you, (*what you heard from the beginning*) you abide in the Son and in the Father."

In 3:11, at the beginning of what many consider to be the start of the second half of the tract, the author states:

> This is the proclamation *that you heard from the beginning*, that we should love one another.

In 2:7, the author explains that keeping the word of Jesus is a commandment that they have had from the beginning.

> Loved Ones, I am not writing to you about a new commandment but an old one that you have had from the beginning. The "old" commandment is the word that you heard.[23]

---

23. There has been some discussion about the meaning of this verse. Brown (1982, 265–67) proposed that "word" did not mean "message" but rather was the Greek equivalent of the Hebrew דבר which was a synonym for "commandment." But this could hardly be the case, since the sentence would then be meaningless: "the com-

The view that the author is opposing is perhaps stated most clearly in 2 John 9:

> Everyone *who is "progressive" and who does not remain in the teaching of the Christ*, does not possess God; the one who remains in the teaching has both the Father and the Son.

So we can see that for the opponents, the earthly ministry and the words of Jesus during that period did not have any special value, but for the author of 1 John they did. In fact, the author of 1 John explains that if the believers listen to the Spirit they will find out that the Spirit will teach them *to abide in the teaching of Jesus*:

> And as for you—the anointing that you received from [God] abides in you, and you do not have need that anyone teach you, but as [God's] anointing teaches you about all and it is true and not false, and just as it taught you, you abide in [Jesus]. (2:27)[24]

For the author of 1 John, the inspiration by the Spirit was not the only source of revelation. Rather, it was understood to function *in relation to the words of Jesus* and to confirm the permanent validity of his words. So we see that the peculiar feature of the Johannine Jesus—seemingly without a revelation—can be explained as deriving from Jewish eschatology but at the same time is corrected and nuanced by the author of 1 John.

4.3. What about the Lack of Ethics in the Gospel?

Third, we must ask about the ethical vacuum in the Gospel. We saw that in the Gospel, two features of the Spirit-centered eschatology combine to explain this. On one hand, one could argue that there is no need for written "rules" and "commandments," since the Spirit would teach them what constitutes life properly lived. On the other hand, an even more likely factor becomes apparent. According to the Jewish Scriptures, the reception of the Spirit so transformed the person that the person will never

---

mandment is the commandment." For a detailed justification of the meaning proposed here, see von Wahlde 1990, 16–18, 57–59; 2010b, 2:617, 623, 633–35, 3:62, 67–69.

24. Surprisingly, Lieu (2008, 111–13) hardly pauses to consider the possibility of a reference to Jer 31:34 here. Brown (1982, 375) considers a reference to Jer 31:34 much more seriously.

sin again and so will not need ethics. This is what is referred to as "ethical perfectionism."[25]

What does 1 John have to say about this? From the pages of 1 John, it becomes clear that the author is concerned to address this view also. Again he has what could well be called a "yes" (that's true) "but" (nevertheless) position. Yes, the author holds to a view of perfectionism, and several texts make this explicit. In 1 John 3:6, the author says:

> *Everyone abiding in [Jesus] does not sin.* Everyone sinning has neither seen him [Jesus] nor known him [Jesus].

Two verses later, the author is even clearer:

> *Everyone begotten of God does not commit sin* because [God's] seed abides in [the believer], and [*the believer*] *is not able to sin* because he has been begotten of God.

If these were the only statements regarding sinfulness in 1 John, it would appear that the author had no disagreement with his opponents on the matter. But toward the end of his tract (5:16–18a), the author returns to the issue of sin and makes it clear once again that it is not in the character of a believer to sin, but that it is nevertheless possible. In other words, we see another example of the author's "yes … but" approach:

> *If anyone sees his brother sinning a sin not unto death*, he [the believer] will ask, and he [God] will give life to him [the sinner], to those [sinners] not sinning unto death.

Perhaps the clearest statement on the matter appears in 3:1–3, where the author had said:

> Behold how great a love the Father has given us that we may be called *children of God; and we are.* Because of this the world does not know

---

25. Lieu (2008, 57) sees this as a consequence of the dualist worldview. However, while it is true that sinlessness could be seen by the author of 1 John as characteristic of one who walks in the light, it is even more to the point that sinlessness was understood in nondualistic Judaism to be the result of the presence of the eschatological Spirit. Lieu (2008, 57, 60–62) seems to think the author of 1 John categorically denies the possibility of sinlessness.

us—because it did not know [the Father]. Beloved, now we are children of God, and it has not yet been revealed *what we will be*. We know that, when [Jesus] is revealed, we will be like [Jesus] and that we will see [Jesus] as he is. And *everyone having this hope* in [Jesus] *makes himself holy as that one [Jesus] is holy."*

The author makes three remarkable statements in these verses. First, he asserts that the believer is a genuine child of God in the present. Yet he also makes clear that there is a difference between the believer's present state and the person's future state ("it has not yet been revealed what we will be"). Third, the one who has the hope of being like Jesus at his second coming "makes himself holy as that one is holy." Thus there is an "already" and a "not yet" to the believer's state. The believer is both a child of God and still in need of effort to reach a full realization of that status.

But what is the ethic that the author supplies? It is the root commandment of all ethics: to love one another. While this could hardly be called an ethical "system," we need to remember that early Christianity held to such a commandment as a reflection of the "Great Commandment" that was the root and sum of all proper conduct.

4.4. What about the Gospel's Emphasis on "Knowing"?

As we have seen, throughout the Gospel, "the Jews" had been said to "not know"; Jesus does "know"; all should seek to "know." Although often thought to reflect gnostic-like tendencies, fully "knowing God" is a prerogative of the eschatological outpouring of God's Spirit, as we have seen.

What does 1 John have to say about this? In 1 John it is clear that both the author and his opponents claim the ability to "know" in a way that clearly transcends the ordinary sense of the word. Both the author and his opponents make the claim, but here it is not a matter of the author of 1 John "qualifying" his view with a "yes … but." Rather, the author simply argues that the opponents do not in fact "know" God, whereas the author's followers do indeed know God. In 2:13, the author says:

I write to you, Fathers, that you have known the one [Jesus] from the beginning. I wrote to you, Dear Children, that you have known the Father.

In 2:20, the author explains that the source of this knowing is the anointing the believer has received from God:

> And you have an anointing from the Holy One and you know all. I did not write to you that you do not know the truth but that you know it.

Once again the connection with the prerogatives of the eschatological Spirit could not be clearer. But the opponents do not know God. In 3:1, the author, identifying the opponents with the "world," says:

> Because of this the world does not know us—because *it did not know [the Father]*.

Conversely, the person that truly knows God listens to the author and his followers. As is said in 4:6:

> *The one knowing God hears us*; the one who is not of God does not hear us.

Beyond these assertions, the author provides a test for determining whether a person truly knows God. In 1 John 2:3–4:

> And *by this we are certain that we have come to know* [God]: if we keep [God's] commandments. *The one claiming "I have come to know* [God]" but not keeping [God's] commandments is a liar and in this one the truth is not present.

There can be no doubt that this emphasis on "knowing" derives from the future hopes of the Jews, because there is verbal similarity to the text of Jer 31:34, where it is said that all will know the Lord in the time of fulfillment.

4.5. What Does 1 John Say about the Removal of Sin?

As we saw previously, in the Gospel the dominant view of the death of Jesus is that it is his departure to the Father. There was no soteriological value to the departure of Jesus itself; it was simply the means of his return to the Father antecedent to his sending the Spirit. From a Jewish point of view, there is absolutely no problem with this.

The *real* problem is for the Christian! By "Christian," I mean those persons who believed that the death of Jesus was an atonement for sin. Of course, this is precisely what most Christians believed about Jesus. For two thousand years, Christians have been pointing to Old Testament texts as indications that Jesus's death was an atoning one. But, if you asked first-century Jews whether their eschatological hopes involved a figure that would die, in some sense or other, to bring about the realization of their hopes for the future, they would say no. As Brown (1994, 160) observed: "We have no clear evidence of a pre-Christian description of a suffering Messiah." So we might say that this "dominant" view of the Gospel is more thoroughly Jewish than the paradigm that involves the death of Jesus for sin!

Of course, in the Gospel there are statements about the removal of sin by the death of Jesus, but these are clearly among the "secondary" ("minor") elements that Brown refers to. Moreover these elements are often recognized by redactional critics to be foreign to the contexts in which they appear.[26]

But what does 1 John say about this? There can be no doubt that the author of 1 John is convinced that the death of Jesus was much more than a departure to the Father. The author uses a variety of terms to describe his view of the importance of the death of Jesus: Jesus is an atonement; he came in the flesh; his blood is an atonement for sin.

In 1:7 we read:

> The blood of Jesus his Son cleanses us from all sin.

In 2:1–2 we read:

> We have a Paraclete before the Father, Jesus Christ, the Just One. And [Jesus] is an atonement for our sins and not only for ours but also for those of the entire world.

Again and again the author makes this point. But what is the relation between this and the belief that Jesus came to give the Spirit? The author addresses this issue directly in 1 John 5:6, in a passage that has been one of the most mysterious and frequently discussed passages of the letter.

> This is the one coming through water and blood, Jesus Christ. Not in the water only but in the water and the blood.

---

26. Brown (1982, 73) refused to attempt a discussion of the literary development of the Gospel and simply said that the one group emphasized one thing and the other group emphasized the other.

From the perspective gained in the present analysis, we can see that the author is simply using the "jargon" of his community to address the issue whether Jesus came only to give the Spirit. Just as "(living) water" was used in the Gospel as a symbol of the Spirit, so "blood" was used by the author of 1 John as a symbol of Jesus's atoning death. The author does not deny that Jesus came to give the Spirit, but Jesus did more than this:

> This is the one coming through water and blood, Jesus Christ; not in the water only but in the water and the blood. And the Spirit witnesses to this.

That is, Jesus did not come just to give the Spirit, but also to die as an atonement for sin. Yet another time the author of 1 John has taken a "yes ... but" position. "Yes," Jesus came to give the Spirit, "but" not that alone: he also came to die and to give his blood as an atonement for sin!

Thus we see that all four of the peculiarly distinctive features mentioned at the beginning of this paper (1) can be explained as elements of a coherent theology within the Gospel that focused on Jesus as the herald of the outpouring of God's eschatological Spirit. Moreover, (2) the correctness of this proposal can be corroborated by texts from the Old Testament that show the existence of such a strain of eschatological expectation as well as the prerogatives of that outpouring of the Spirit. Finally, (3) that the description of the dominant strain of the theology of the Johannine Gospel, as I have described it, is correct is confirmed by the way the principal elements of that theology are taken up and corrected by the author of 1 John—a process that is confirmed not only by the ideas involved but also by the verbal echoes of the relevant Old Testament texts.

Before I end, there are two other issues that should be addressed, at least briefly.

First, what about the so-called "denial" of Jesus in 1 John? The author of 1 John repeatedly says that it is necessary to have "the Father and the Son." The opponents claim to have the Father but in fact "have neither the Father nor the Son." How could it be that a group that had suffered expulsion from the synagogue for belief in Jesus now "does away with him" (4:3)? According to the dominant theology of the Gospel, it is clear that Jesus's primary role was to establish his authority as Son, sent by the Father, to give the Spirit. This is the Johannine Christology within that dominant theology.

In the dominant theology of the Gospel, Jesus is the deliverer of the Spirit, but, as any first-century Jew would have believed, it was *the Spirit* that was to be the effective agent of salvation, not the *herald* of the Spirit. The opponents would have believed in Jesus as authentic and so have been expelled from the synagogue for that belief, but later they came to be convinced that Jesus was not himself the effective agent of salvation, and so they differed from the author of 1 John, who believed (as we have seen) that the role of Jesus was both permanent and effective. The opponents' rejection of the role of Jesus is evident from multiple texts within 1 John. Again and again the author asserts that his followers "have" both Jesus and the Father (1:3b; 2:23, 24; 5:10) and "abide" in Jesus (2:27–28). The opponents do not "have" Jesus (2:23; 5:10) and do not "abide" in him (2:27).

To the second point. As should be clear to anyone who is familiar with the Gospel, *there are elements in it that clearly support the thought of 1 John and could have been used to refute his opponents*. I would agree. As we have seen repeatedly, Brown understood the relation of 1 John to the Gospel in terms of *emphasis* on certain notions and *lack of emphasis* on others: the so-called "dominant" and "secondary/minor" motifs. He acknowledged that it would be possible to assign the differences to the editing process, but he pointed out that this could be criticized as being a circular argument.

In my opinion, the approach taken by Brown ultimately does not do justice to the facts. I will choose only one example. I cannot imagine that, if the Paraclete passages were part of the Gospel when the "dominant" theology was developed, they would not have been used to refute the views of the opponents. The Paraclete passages *explicitly* counter the opponents' views. The opponents believed that, once they possessed the eschatological Spirit, the inspiration of that Spirit would be sufficient and they would not need the "revelation" of Jesus. However, the second of the Paraclete passages (John 14:26) makes this view impossible:

> But the Paraclete, the Holy Spirit, whom the Father will send in my name, *will … remind you of all things that I have told you.*

In the third of the passages (15:26), the Spirit's link to Jesus is again clear:

> When the Paraclete comes whom I will send to you from the Father, the Spirit of Truth, that comes from the Father, *he will witness about me.*

The function of the Paraclete is linked to the words of Jesus. The Paraclete is not, as the opponents thought, able to speak on its own and to make the words of Jesus unnecessary. This is clearest in John 16:12–15, where the view of the opponents in 1 John is explicitly denied:

> I still have many things to say to you, but you are not able to bear them now. But when that one comes, the Spirit of Truth, he will lead you in all truth. *For he will not speak on his own but will speak whatever he hears and will proclaim to you what is to come. That one will glorify me because he will take from what is mine and will proclaim it to you.* Everything the Father has is mine. Because of this I said that he takes from what is mine and will proclaim it to you.

Here the limitations imposed on the function of the Spirit are explicit: "He will not speak on his own." His function is linked exclusively to the words of Jesus. Because such passages so clearly contradict the views of the opponents, I believe that they must have been added to the Gospel as part of a modification and clarification of the tradition after the writing of 1 John. I believe that all of the views of the author of 1 John described above were, with modification at times, incorporated into the Gospel in order to have that perspective incorporated into the Gospel. It is not possible to argue that position fully here, but it is spelled out in detail in my commentary referred to above.

Summary/Conclusion

I began my proposal by pointing to several prominent features of the Gospel that have long been recognized as "peculiar." I suggested that the presence of these features is not accidental but in fact is a derivative of what Brown referred to as the dominant theology of the Gospel. However, I also argued that it is possible to go beyond Brown's view of this theology and to show that the dominant theology of the Gospel is more coherent than Brown thought and that this theology conforms to and embodies what might be called the "classical" Old Testament theology regarding the eschatological outpouring of the Spirit and the prerogatives that flow from the possession of this Spirit.

With this as the basis of the investigation, we then looked at this theology from the perspective of 1 John and discovered that not only does 1 John confirm that the view of the dominant theology of the Gospel proposed in sections two and three of this paper is correct, but that it also shows that the author of 1 John could not accept this view as an adequate articulation of the meaning of Jesus's ministry and so corrected or nuanced each major element of this theology in his own tract (1 John). This reading of 1 John has shown that these supposed features are not the product of our imagination or of a misreading of the Gospel. Rather, they are elements of one strand of the Johannine tradition, as this tradition is preserved in the text of the Gospel. But the reading of 1 John is indispensable for recognizing all the dimensions of these features and also for understanding that the author of 1 John could not accept that Gospel presentation completely, simply, and without qualification.

We concluded by reflecting briefly on the relation between the dominant and secondary motifs in the Gospel and suggested that it becomes more difficult to say that the so-called secondary motifs were actually part of the Gospel before the writing of 1 John and that, in the light of this analysis, there appears to be evidence for thinking that 1 John was written to critique the Gospel when it contained *only* the so-called "dominant" theology and that what appears to be "secondary" in the Gospel is actually the result of editorial additions to the Gospel in order to reflect the perspective set forth in 1 John. That is the view that I have presented in more detail in my commentary.

The full reality of Johannine tradition, as the author of 1 John understood it, was greater and was more nuanced than that earlier view. And, it was the work of the author of 1 John that prepared the way for the form and theology of the Gospel as we have it today. In our own time, I believe it is the work of Raymond Brown, more than anyone else, which has paved the way for an understanding of that development.

The Community that Raymond Brown Left Behind: Reflections on the Johannine Dialectical Situation[1]

Paul N. Anderson

Among the paradigm-making contributions in Johannine studies over the last half century, one of the most significant is the sketching of "the community of the Beloved Disciple" by Raymond E. Brown (1979). Extending beyond Johannine studies, Brown's (1984) work on the history of early Christianity and "the churches the apostles left behind" is also among the most practical and interesting of his forty-seven books.[2] Here, Brown's analysis of the unity and diversity of early Christian approaches to leadership and community organization[3] have extensive implications, not only for historical and sociological understandings of the first-century Christian movement, but also for approaches to Christian leadership in later

---

1. An earlier form of this essay was published in *Bible and Interpretation* (Anderson 2013a); see http://www.bibleinterp.com/articles/2013/09/and378030.shtml.

2. Brown also wrote 200 articles and 108 reviews, according to the bibliographic essay by Michael L. Barré in the collection of essays in his honor (Donahue 2005, 259–89). By my count, Brown published nearly 4,000 pages on the Johannine writings; but as impressive as the quantity of his work was its quality. In my review of *Life in Abundance* (2006b), I argue that "I cannot think of a single American New Testament scholar whose work has been more helpful, measured, and significant than Brown's"—period. And, within Brown's extensive number of publications, one of his most enduring contributions has been the sketching of the Johannine situation, based upon his generative analyses of the Gospel and Epistles of John.

3. In addition to Brown's focused works on the Johannine literature, see his edited volumes on the ecclesial implications of Mary and Peter in the New Testament (Brown et al., 1978), as well as his analyses of the strengths and weaknesses in various ecclesial models among the churches the apostles left behind (Brown 1984) and his treatment of Antioch and Rome as catholic origins of the early church (Brown and Meier, 1984).

generations.⁴ In reviewing the impact of the Johannine community that Brown left behind, this paper will assess the perdurance (to use one of his terms) of Brown's overall theory, suggesting also new constructs worthy of consideration by biblical interpreters into the twenty-first century. These issues are especially important in service of interpreting the Johannine writings meaningfully—especially the Epistles.

Brown's Theory on the Community of the Beloved Disciple

Given that Brown was commissioned to write commentaries on the Gospel and the Epistles of John for the Anchor Bible Commentary series, he thus engaged the larger corpus of Johannine literature in his work.⁵ This forced a focus on the Johannine sector of the early Christian movement from which the Johannine writings presumably emerged. Between completing his second Gospel commentary volume in 1970 and his commentary on the Epistles in 1982, Brown sought to answer several questions for himself and the larger community of scholars about the Johannine situation. In his 1979 treatment of "the community of the Beloved Disciple," he laid out his fuller theories of the Johannine tradition and the Johannine situation, which reinforced each other compellingly, and over the next two or three decades, his theory continued to develop.

The Community of the Beloved Disciple (1979)

Within his primary book on the subject, four phases of the history of the Johannine community are outlined, and six groups within the Johannine audience are discerned.

---

4. Following in Brown's wake, applying exegetical insights to ecclesial concerns, an NCCC Faith and Order Commission response was commissioned following Walter Kasper's invitation to engage Pope John Paul II's encyclical, asking if a new day in church unity might be possible (Anderson 2005). I delivered copies of this essay to Cardinal Kasper and Pope Benedict personally in October 2006.

5. Brown's shorter commentary on the Gospel and Epistles of John (New Testament Reading Guide 13), first published in 1960, was revised in 1965 and 1982 and later replaced by the final version in 1988. Note that at the end of the first of his two volumes on the Gospel of John, his word studies include analyses of word-distribution between the Johannine Gospel and Epistles and even the Apocalypse, showing similarities and differences between the Johannine writings (Brown 1966, 497–518).

1. Phase One (Mid 50s–Late 80s CE): A Pre-Gospel Phase

The originating group (in Palestine, including followers of John the Baptist) developed around the Beloved Disciple, who had been a follower of Jesus, although not necessarily a member of the Twelve. They had a relatively low Christology, embracing Jesus as a Davidic Messiah and viewing his signs as fulfillments of prophecy. A second group joined the Johannine community, involving Samaritans with an antitemple bias, a high Christology connecting Jesus with prophets like Moses of Deut 18:15–22, and finally with the preexistent Christology of the Logos hymn. As the addition of this group pushed the Johannine Christology higher, this movement increased theological tensions with local Jewish communities, resulting in accusations of ditheism, which led to the expulsion of Johannine Christians from local Jewish synagogues. This led, then, to taking the gospel to gentile audiences resulting in gentile converts and their joining the Johannine community.

2. Phase Two (ca. 90 CE): The Gospel Was Written Addressing Six Groups within the Johannine Community

The Johannine community has likely moved by this time to a Diaspora setting, wherein the gospel was extended to the Greeks as well as the Jews. Within this new setting, contact with universal understandings of God's redemptive work come into play, and the evangelist constructs engaging dialogues with Jesus as a means of drawing his audiences into an experience of faith. Brown identifies a total of six groups within the Johannine situation that the evangelist targets rhetorically; three groups are nonbelieving, and three other groups are believing.

- "The world" refers to unbelieving gentiles (parallel to earlier unbelieving Jews), whom the evangelist seeks to reach with the gospel of Jesus as the Christ.
- "The Jews" refers to members of local synagogues whom the evangelist seeks to convince that Jesus is the Messiah/Christ, even after the separation from the synagogue.
- "The Adherents of John the Baptist" Brown takes to involve those in Asia Minor who believed John was the Messiah/Christ rather than Jesus.

- "Crypto-Christians" included those who remained in the synagogue as secret believers in Jesus, but who were unwilling to confess openly their belief in him as the Christ.
- "Jewish Christian Churches of Inadequate Faith" involved those who had separated from the synagogue. While believing in Jesus as the Christ, they did not accept his divinity or the Eucharist as the true flesh and blood of Jesus.
- "Apostolic Christians" would have involved Petrine-hierarchical institutional Christian leaders, who did not appreciate the spiritual work of the risen Christ through the Paraclete.

Brown believes that the narrative of the Gospel addresses at least these six groups within its audience, seeking to draw all of them to more adequate faith in Jesus as the Christ, the Son of God.

3. Phase Three (100 CE): The Epistles Were Written

The Johannine community's internal tensions are unfolded more clearly in the light of the Epistles, which Brown takes to be written by the Presbyter (or the Elder). Rather than seeing this person as being the final editor of the Gospel, however, he opts for a Johannine school, in which several leaders may have been involved—the editor being at least a third literary contributor. The primary crisis experienced here is secession, which Brown associates with those who have loved the world and are thus labeled "antichrists." Here Brown wisely dissociates the inferred faith and practice of the secessionists from later second-century heretics and simply constructs a portrait out of a selection of polemical themes in the Epistles, using the letters of Ignatius as a backdrop and building on what may be known of Cerinthus, a known opponent in the Johannine situation in later traditions. In Brown's view, the Presbyter and the secessionists (or "the opponents") were fellow Johannine Christians, who valued the teaching of the Beloved Disciple, but who also interpreted his teachings differently.

In terms of *Christology*, the secessionists denied that Jesus was the Christ, the Son of God, and that he came in the flesh; hence, they possessed docetizing inclinations, also denying the value of the Eucharist. In terms of *ethics*, the secessionists claimed intimacy with God to the point of being sinless, did not put much emphasis on keeping the commandments of Jesus, and thus did not practice sufficiently brotherly love. Therefore, they walk not in light but in darkness. In terms of *eschatology*, while the secessionists probably embraced the evangelist's realized eschatology, the Presbyter appeals to earlier futuristic themes to challenge their beliefs and actions; realized eschatology implies ethical faithfulness. Their errors were alluded to in earlier warnings against false christs and prophets (Mark 13:22) and the man of lawlessness (2 Thess 2:8), and they are challenged by promises of future rewards and accountability; the last hour, warning of antichrists to come, is indeed at hand! In terms of *pneumatology*, the secessionists have distorted the Gospel's teaching on the pneumatic ministry of the Paraclete by forgetting that the teaching work of the Holy Spirit is actually tied to that of the first advocate—Jesus Christ. While guidance by the Spirit should conform to abiding in the teaching about Christ (shared from the beginning), their popular success in the world indicates not gospel faithfulness but worldly compromise. They escape the world's hatred, because they have sided with the prince of this world.

4. Phase Four (Second Century CE): After the Epistles

Following their departure, the Johannine secessionists moved from docetism into the Christian Gnosticism of the mid-second century. Assuming they took the Johannine Gospel with them, Brown infers that this explains how the gnostic-Christian leader Heracleon produced the first commentary on John, why Montanus endorsed women in ministry and came to refer to himself as "the Paraclete," and why Cerinthus evolved a doctrine of the divine part of Jesus having departed before the crucifixion as a factor of his being "lifted up from the earth" in the Johannine witness. Such developments then understandably contributed to why the Johannine writings raised suspicion among some orthodox leaders of the second century church, resulting in their being called *"alogoi"* by Johannine defenders. The rest of Johannine Christianity, on the other hand, was easily subsumed into "the great church," as it was also influenced by the Johannine Gospel (including a movement toward high Christology) and as Johannine leaders resorted to structural leadership (including presbyter-bishops) for the combating of secessionists and intramural adversaries. With the letters of Ignatius (ca. 110 CE) as a backdrop, Brown infers a common high Christology and a prosacramental thrust shared between Ignatius and the evangelist, although Diotrephes who loves to be first (3 John 1:9–10) poses a threat to the Johannine egalitarian and pneumatic ethos. Diotrephes thus demonstrates a movement toward hierarchical leadership supporting the supreme authority of the bishop, even over and against the movement of the Holy Spirit. In the Gospel's being read in orthodox ways, as interpreted by the Presbyter and the Epistles, its message is subsumed into "the church catholic," and John 21, as a plausible later addition to the Gospel, reflects a Johannine embracing of Petrine apostolic leadership.

The Epistles of John (1982)

Over the following years, Brown further developed his theory of the Johannine community in several ways, beginning with his Anchor Bible Commentary on the Johannine Epistles. On *dating*, Brown notes apparent references to themes in the Johannine Epistles by Clement of Rome (ca. 96 CE), Ignatius of Antioch (ca. 110–115 CE), and the Didache (ca. 90–120 CE)—between 90 and 100 CE (Brown 1982, 6–13). On *authorship*, Brown sees John the Elder as the author of the Epistles, who is different from the unnamed evangelist, and whose critiques of Peter and the Twelve exclude him from being among their number (Brown 1982, 14–30). On *composition*, Brown takes the order of 1, 2, and 3 John as they are and sees the first two Epistles as written within a decade of the main part of the Gospel's composition around 90 CE. He also allows for some later material to have been added to the Gospel by the redactor (parts or all of John 1:1–18; 3:31–36; 6:51–58; and chs. 15–17, 21, etc.), perhaps some of it added after the Epistles; although, unlike Bultmann and some others, he does not connect the final redactor of the Gospel with the Elder (Brown 1982, 30–35, 69–115).

Rejecting theories of underlying *sources* in the Epistles, Brown sees behind 1 and 2 John a set of struggles with a single group of adversaries, siding with "Ockham's razor" against multiplying entities unnecessarily.[6] Therefore, (1) *christologically*, the adversaries (called "antichrists") were a threat, because they denied that Jesus was the Messiah/Christ (1 John 2:22–23) and denied that he came in the flesh (1 John 4:2–3; 2 John 1:7); (2) *ethically*, they were a threat, because they were secessionists willing to divide the community, perhaps believing that their high Christology eclipsed the salvific consequences of their less-than-loving actions and attitudes toward the brethren. Flawed theology and ethics impact each other, and the uneven presentation of the adversaries' views and actions

---

6. Interestingly, Brown does not apply the principle of parsimony to the issue of authorship.

has a precedent in the uneven presentation of such heretical/ethical threats as represented by Cerinthus (although Brown notes that little is known about him specifically; Brown 1982, 47–68, 766–771). Brown sees 3 John (between 100 and 110 CE) as a struggle between the Johannine Elder and Diotrephes over church order; the primacy-loving Diotrephes was rejecting Johannine emissaries advocating a Paraclete-centered and egalitarian ecclesiology—on the way to being incorporated into the great church (Brown 1982, 69–115).

The Churches the Apostles Left Behind (1984)

Brown connects his overall theory with more detailed treatments of particular passages in his commentary on the Johannine Epistles, and his book on New Testament models of leadership and ecclesiology carries the ecclesial implications of his analysis further. As the heritage of the Beloved Disciple in the Fourth Gospel presents *a community of people personally attached to Jesus*, the strengths and weaknesses of such an ecclesial model are several. The two major strengths involve: (1) *the priority of individual connectedness to Jesus*, emphasizing relationship with the present Christ effected by the Paraclete; and (2) the *egalitarian character* of such an ethos. Resulting weaknesses thus include: (1) *tendencies toward individualism*, especially if separated from Jewish collectivity; and (2) resulting *questions of authority and accountability* (Brown 1984, 84–101).

Continuing along that trajectory, the heritage of the Beloved Disciple reflected by the Johannine Epistles involves issues related to a community of individuals guided by the Paraclete-Spirit. Building on the strengths of Johannine Christ-centered egalitarianism and spirit-based ecclesial operation, Brown imagines four weaknesses with this model as reflected in the schism and other developments in the Epistles: (1) *dogmatism*—"the one-sidedness of a theology shaped in polemic, ultimately led to exaggeration and division"—that which is fought over in one generation is often what is forwarded to the next, and having split off from the synagogue makes it easier for further schisms to happen; (2) *isolation*—having split off from the synagogue leads to a loss of Jewish religious heritage; (3) *sectarianism*—"extreme hostility toward outsiders" and insular love for "the brethren" leads to a sectarian existence cut off from the world; (4) *unruly pneumatism*—"uncontrolled divisions caused by appeal to the Paraclete" leads to incorrigible pneumatism and ambivalent resistance to emerging Christian structures of authority (Brown 1982, 102–123). Interestingly, Brown notes mostly unfavorable attributes of the Johannine Epistles' ecclesiology, while in his following chapter on Matthean ecclesiology—showing also the rise of hierarchical structure associated with the memory of Peter (Matt 16:17–19) with institutional approaches to accountability and order following (Matt 18:15–18)—Brown mentions primarily strengths and *hardly any* weaknesses.[7]

An Introduction to the Gospel of John (2003)

Following his untimely death in 1998, Brown's revision of his commentary on John was gathered into a new introduction to the Gospel of John by Frank Moloney, nonetheless with implications for the Epistles. In this refinement of his overall theory, several developments can be seen. First, Brown *simplifies his composition theory*, consolidating the five stages of the Fourth Gospel into three (for the "arithmetically challenged"). As he had received a bit of criticism for his theory being too complex, his new approach features (1) "Stage One: Origin in the Public Ministry or Activity of Jesus of Nazareth." The Beloved Disciple was a Judean follower of Jesus—not a Galilean, but someone with perspectives consonant with the dualistic Qumran writings—accounting for his distinctive access to events in Jesus's ministry and different religious interests. (2) "Stage Two: Proclaiming Jesus in the Postresurrection Context of Community History." This tradition-shaping stage features the memory and preaching of a follower of Jesus—not one of the Twelve, but someone having contact with Samaritans and their Moses typology—accounting for differences with Mark, ostensibly based on the memory and preaching of Peter. (3) "Stage Three: The Writing of the Gospel." The evangelist prepares the main body of the Gospel, concluding at 20:31, designed to confirm believers in their faith; the redactor adds other material, including the Logos hymn as the prologue, chapters 15–17 and 21, and other shorter repetitive units in

---

7. Rather, Matthew's "authority that does not stifle" showcases the "great anomaly of Christianity ... that only through institution can the message of a non-institutional Jesus be preserved" (Brown 1984, 124–45). I imagine Diotrephes would have agreed with some of Brown's points, here, especially if he was threatened by Johannine challenges to hierarchical leadership. However, if Diotrephes may have legitimated his high-handed approach to issues of order and accountability on the basis of Matthean ecclesiology, the Johannine leadership would not have agreed with Brown's analyses of Matthean or Johannine ecclesiologies.

chapters 3, 6, 11, and 12—the evangelist and the redactor were followers of the Beloved Disciple in Stage Two. The Johannine Epistles are written by a fourth hand within the Johannine "school" between the first and final editions. Despite this attempt to reconstruct the development of the Johannine tradition, Brown (2003, 62–86) finally agrees with C. K. Barrett and R. Alan Culpepper that the Gospel must be approached as a literary whole.

Second, in his new introduction Brown adds new insights on the relation between the Johannine and the Synoptic traditions, with implications for John's historicity. The value of information found only in John (esp. the archaeological details in chs. 4, 5, 7–8, 9, 10) is significant, and it reflects first-hand knowledge of Palestine before the destruction of Jerusalem in 70 CE. Further, it cannot be said that John is dependent upon the Synoptics or other alien sources; the evidence is too scant. As an independent tradition, Brown believes the Johannine evangelist was familiar with Mark, but not in its written form. Rather, he proposes "cross-influence" between the early Markan and Johannine traditions (giving rise to such details as two hundred and three hundred denarii and "perfume made of real nard")[8] and infers some sort of intertraditional contact on the presentation of Peter in Matthew and John. He is most taken with the distinctive contacts between Luke and John, inferring some sort of cross-influence in both directions. As a result, "John is based on a solid tradition on the works and words of Jesus, a tradition that at times is very primitive. Indeed, I believe that often John gives us correct historical information about Jesus that no other gospel tradition has preserved" (Brown and Moloney 2003, 110).

Third, from the echoes of apologetics and the purpose of the Fourth Gospel, Brown infers several partners in dialogue within the Johannine community, consolidating his earlier six groups into four. (1) *Adherents of John the Baptist* are addressed apologetically during the early stages of the Johannine tradition, seeking to convince them that Jesus (not John) was the Messiah. (2) *"The Jews" who refused to believe in Jesus* (sometimes equated with "the world") are addressed apologetically, reflecting Judeans in Palestine who rejected the northern prophet from Galilee earlier in the tradition and later reflecting synagogue authorities in Asia Minor who

---

8. Over the decade before his death, Brown and I had several discussions of what I would call "interfluence" between the pre-Markan and early Johannine traditions—probably during their oral stages; his input was also helpful to me as I finalized an opening theory of Johannine influence upon the Lukan tradition in Appendix VIII in *Christology of the Fourth Gospel* (Anderson 1996, 274–77).

were resistant to the high Christology of Johannine believers. (3) *Jews who did not confess publicly their belief in Jesus* (in the 80s and 90s). Some Johannine Christians had been expelled from the synagogue for confessing their faith in Jesus openly, but others refused to do so—preferring human praise over the glory of God (such as Nicodemus)—these are addressed as crypto-Christians. (4) *Other Jesus adherents* may also have been seen as *heretics*, such as Cerinthians (with gnostic leanings), Ebionites (with Jewish-Christian leanings), or docetists (with heretical leanings), and other Christians *of inadequate faith,* including Christians of the "larger church who looked on Peter as the most representative figure" and those who may have refused to "eat Jesus' flesh and drink his blood," having a low Christology. Rather than being a missionary document, Brown believes that the narrative of the Johannine Gospel called people to faithfulness to the message they had heard and to abiding with Jesus and his community of faith (Brown 2003, 151–83).

Summary

What one can observe in Brown's larger paradigm is its development over thirty years, integrating in his judgment the best arguments within the secondary literature and the best ways of making sense of the primary texts in the Gospel and Epistles of John. He thus seeks to ascertain three interconnected theories: (1) connecting a two-edition theory of the Gospel's composition with the Epistles' being written in between them, (2) connecting a belief in John's traditional autonomy with a modest inference of its relations to other traditions, and (3) connecting a history of the Johannine community—developing for some time in Palestine and then coming to a fuller presentation in a Diaspora setting—with a variety of apologetic targets as informed by the Gospel and Epistles of John. This is the Johannine community that Brown has left behind, bequeathed to the world of New Testament scholarship as a pivotal contribution in the last third of the twentieth century. That being the case, what has happened to that gift, and how is it faring among its heirs?

Responses to Brown's Theory and Further Developments

While John Ashton considered J. Louis Martyn's 1968 *History and Theology in the Fourth Gospel* "probably the most important single monograph on the Gospel since Bultmann's Commentary," this judgment was made in the mid-1980s, before Brown's commentary on the Johannine Epistles had made its full impact.[9] Indeed, the theory of Johannine-synagogue dialectic has been a pivotal interest in Johannine studies, and while Martyn's theory has been countered by several scholars, I see it as qualified rather than overturned. Still, Martyn's theory would not have fared as well if Brown's complementary theory had not taken it further over the next couple of decades. Put otherwise, it is Brown's more nuanced and extended theory that has made Martyn's general thesis difficult to discredit overall. While Martyn insisted on one primary dialogue—the Jewish-Christian dialogue—Brown's more extensive inference of several sets of dialogues makes better sense of the evidence and is thus more realistic.

A further strength of Brown's theory is that it built not only upon the Johannine Gospel, but it also incorporated the situation of the Epistles in its purview. In my judgment, the greatest weakness with Martyn's thesis is not that it overread the Birkat Haminim (which it did only somewhat); it is that he sought to divorce the Johannine Epistles from the socioreligious situation out of which the Gospel also originated. On this matter, both Martyn and Brown failed to make sufficient sense of Jewish-Christian debates behind the first Johannine Epistle (at least), as it is also discernible behind the Johannine Apocalypse, the Gospel of Matthew, the letters of

---

9. Ashton 1997, 12; While I had earlier agreed with Ashton's naming Martyn's monograph as the most significant single monograph since Bultmann's commentary (Martyn 2003, first appearing in 1968; Anderson 2008a, 367–68), I am coming to rethink that judgment, siding instead with Brown's three Johannine commentary volumes as the most significant contribution (despite being multiple volumes) since Bultmann's commentary. This judgment is arguable, given that: (1) Brown had already laid out a theory of synagogue expulsion, Johannine Jewish-Christian apologetics, and a two-level reading of the narrative (Martyn's seminal work expands upon the approach laid out by Brown two years earlier, although Brown also acknowledges building alongside Martyn's work); (2) Brown's overall approach draws in the larger corpus of Johannine literature, including the Johannine Epistles (whereas Martyn warns against connecting them too closely); and (3) Brown's far more extensive and dialectical model, involving several partners in dialogue over several decades, is more realistic (whereas Martyn focused on a singular partner in dialogue with the Johannine community—the local Jewish presence). Therefore, while I see Culpepper's *Anatomy of the Fourth Gospel* (1983) as the most important Johannine monograph over the last three decades (Anderson 2008b, 95–96), I must side either with Brown's overall set of Johannine writings as the most important contribution since Bultmann's or go with a Martyn/Brown approach to the Johannine situation as the most important development in Johannine studies since Bultmann, rather than Martyn's monograph alone.

Ignatius, and other Christian writings around the turn of the first century CE. Contra Martyn, however, the dialogue with local Jewish communities was not the only dialectical set of relationships within the Johannine situation, and the great strength of Brown's paradigm is its sensitivity to a multiplicity of groups and related crises within the Johannine situation when considered in longitudinal perspective. Therefore, the fuller Johannine dialectical situation involved multiple partners in dialogue, not just the local Jewish sector.

Among the critiques of Brown's theory, at least three deserve mention. First, some have argued against a two-level reading of the Johannine narrative, believing a focus on later levels of history threatens to displace the earlier ones. While something of the Johannine situation history can indeed be inferred by means of a mirror reading of the Gospel's narrative, this does not displace the tradition's originative history. The presentation of Jesus is indeed highly interpreted in John, but that interpretation is still focused on the ministry of Jesus as remembered and recrafted within the oral and written stages of the tradition. For instance, tensions between Jesus adherents and Jewish leaders did *not* begin in 85 CE. Resistance from Jewish and Roman authorities was likely a fact during the ministry of Jesus, and yet many Jewish people, and plausibly some Samaritans and Hellenists, believed in Jesus even during his ministry. Therefore, just because issues with Jews, Romans, and Hellenists developed later within Johannine Christianity, this does not discount earlier engagements with similar groups—perhaps even during the ministry of Jesus of Nazareth.[10] Likewise, just because people are reported as reacting to Jesus in the narrative, this does not prove that such individuals or groups later joined or rejected Johannine Christianity. In particular, just because Samaritans are presented as believing in Jesus in John 4, this does not prove that Samaritans entered the Johannine community, although they may indeed have joined the Jesus movement in general (note the reporting of the successful missions of Peter and John and Philip in Acts 8).

A second critique has to do with the challenging of the Martyn-Brown hypothesis that Johannine Christians were expelled from local synagogues during the post-70 CE Jamnia period in connection with the Birkat Haminim. While such Jewish scholars as Steven Katz (1984), Reuven Kimelman (1981), and Adele Reinhartz (2001) have sought to

---

10. See Klink 2007; also Anderson 1996, 194–250; 1997, 24–57; and esp. 2013b.

overturn the view that expulsions of open Jesus adherents from synagogues were intensive and extensive on the basis that close relations between Jews and Christians during this time were warm and reciprocal, this likelihood may actually prove the opposite.[11] The very fact of close Jewish-Christian relations in the late first-century Asia-Minor situation would have insured fraternal tensions over Johannine christological developments (at least!) rather than alleviating them. Therefore, while the Birkat Haminim may never have involved extensive or thorough excommunications of Jesus adherents from local synagogues, it likely functioned as a means of disciplining those whose monotheistic faith was perceived as being threatened by ascending christological beliefs. If a blessing (or curse) against "the Nazarenes" (followers of Jesus of Nazareth) as heretics was recited in even some synagogues during this time period, open followers of Jesus would have been made to feel quite uncomfortable, forcing a choice between denying or concealing one's belief in Jesus as the Messiah/Christ and being marginalized from the fellowship. The goal of Jewish leaders, however, was probably not to cast out Jesus adherents; it was rather to discipline their perceived ditheism, motivating adherence to the way of Moses and the promise of Abraham. Put otherwise, would a public recitation of the Johannine Logos hymn have been tolerated within *any* orthodox Jewish meeting for worship around that time? Probably not. Therefore, the Martyn-Brown hypothesis regarding the Jewish-Johannine dialectic is qualified, but not overturned.[12]

A third critique has sought to wrest the audience of the Johannine evangelist away from a single community (as well as those of all the evangelists), arguing that the Gospels were written for all Christians, not just a provincial few. Especially sonorous has been Richard Bauckham's (1998) collection of essays arguing that thesis. Given that gospel narratives would

---

11. See analyzes of Katz (1984) and Kimelman (1981) in Anderson 2008a and elsewhere. While challenging the Martyn hypothesis, Reinhartz (2001, 52) nonetheless admits, "Despite their differences, these passages share one central point: the incompatibility of participating in synagogue fellowship while confessing Christ."

12. See, for instance, the pushback by D. Moody Smith (1996) and Joel Marcus (2009) on this issue, confirming support for the impact of the Birkat Haminim upon Johannine believers. In my own view, I see a departure from the synagogue in the Johannine situation (whether forced or consequential) followed by a Jewish recruitment of Jesus adherents back into the synagogue, which is what lay behind the Johannine secession in 1 John 2:18–25 (Anderson 1997, 32–40; 2007a; 2007c).

have enjoyed wide circulation, being transmitted (and crafted) by Christian preachers and teachers traveling among the churches in the larger Mediterranean world, it would have been impossible to restrain gospel narratives from being circulated broadly, and early Christian traveling ministers likely proliferated written testimonies rather than restricting them. Like traveling circulars and letters, gospel narratives were designed from the start to be read and circulated broadly among the churches, so Brown's theory should be qualified as follows: while the canonical Gospels were not written *for* a community and one particular situation alone, they were likely written *from* particular communities and situations. Further, those situations continued to evolve over time, changing locations and complexion at least a couple of times, so the Johannine situation was not always confined to a singular community.

Therefore, the Johannine community that Brown left behind is indeed worth retaining and building upon, but the overall hypothesis has matured in several ways. In my judgment, the most compelling and noncompelling features of Brown's hypothesis are as follows:

Compelling

(1) the Johannine Gospel and Epistles must be read together (contra Martyn) as a means of providing a window into Johannine Christianity, and the four phases put forward by Brown are worthy constructs overall; (2) earlier phases of its history originated in Palestine, and later phases involved a move to Asia Minor, plausibly Ephesus and its environs; (3) the Epistles were written after (most of) the Gospel by a different hand, reflecting a slightly later situation, and within the Johannine school a plurality of leadership (with Culpepper and others) is a likely inference, rather than a single Johannine author, only; (4) different groups in the Johannine dialectical situation included at least followers of the Baptist, Jewish leaders in Palestine and later in Asia Minor, docetizing gentile believers who "loved the world," believers and nonbelievers needing to be reached by the writers, and hierarchical leaders in the "great church" (some of these partners in dialogue, especially those adumbrated by the Johannine Epistles, are confirmed by Revelation and the letters of Ignatius); (5) the docetists took the Gospel with them and later evolved into Montanism and gnostic Christianity of the second century CE.; (6) the Johannine tradition reflects an independent Jesus tradition, which differs with intentionality from the Markan traditions.

Noncompelling

(1) The idea that the Johannine situation was *always* a "community" is flawed; it enjoyed some time as such in Asia Minor or elsewhere, but it might not have been an individuated community during its Palestinian phase (30–70 CE), and it clearly developed into multiple communities in its later Asia Minor phase (85–100 CE) as suggested by the Epistles; (2) Samaritans need not have entered the Johannine community for Johannine Christology to have ascended in its appraisal of Jesus's divinity, and John's prophet-like-Moses Christology would have arisen in Galilee just as easily as in Samaria (it may also have been closer to Jesus's self-understanding than the Synoptic Davidic-king typology); (3) not all adversaries were secessionists, as the term "antichrists" appears to have been used with reference to two distinct threats—the first reflecting a secessionist crisis among those who refused to believe Jesus was the Messiah/Christ in clinging to "the Father" monotheistically (plausibly, Jewish Christians returning to the synagogue), while the second and third references involved an invasionist crisis (likely, gentile Christians advocating assimilation in the world) spreading such false teachings as the refusal to believe Jesus came in the flesh; (4) there is no evidence at all that the docetists rationalized their assimilative teaching on the basis of Spirit-led pneumatism, as they more likely were gentile believers who simply were not convinced that divergences from Jewish-Christian moral standards were to be regarded as "sin"—claiming to be "without sin" thus related to disagreement over what was permissible for believers and what was not (mortal and venial sins) in the context of required emperor laud arising under Domitian (81–96 CE) rather than claims of perfection-status proper; (5) in challenging Diotrephes and his hierarchical kin in the name of a more inclusive and egalitarian form of ecclesiology, the evangelist and the Elder were not opposing apostolic leadership from the outside; they were defending its more primitive articulations over and against proto-Ignatian movements toward institutionalization; (6) Brown's basis for excluding the Johannine evangelist from the apostolic Twelve more plausibly argues *for* his inclusion among them, as an apostolic challenge to rising institutionalism in the late first-century Christian situation adheres more closely to inferences of the charismatic and itinerant ministry of the historical Jesus several decades earlier (while Johannine theology is highly developed, its ecclesiology, sacramentology, and presentation of women in leadership are more primitive than Synoptic parallels).

With these assessments in mind, and in making the best sense of ancient texts and building upon what I feel are the strongest of proposals in the secondary literature, a constructive appreciation of Brown's work leads to proposing the following paradigms: (1) a two-edition model of composition, seeing the Epistles as written between the first and final editions of John; (2) an interfluential theory of gospel relations—I call it a "bi-optic hypothesis"; and (3) a sketching of the Johannine situation in longitudinal perspective—seven crises over seven decades. I call this new overall theory *the dialogical autonomy of the Johannine tradition*.[13]

The Dialogical Autonomy of the Johannine Tradition

Many errors of interpretation have resulted from failing to consider John's autonomy as a self-standing tradition, as well as the multiple ways in which its material originates, develops, and is delivered dialogically. *Theologically*, the Johannine evangelist thought dialectically about his subject, Jesus, who came as the Revealer to humanity, inviting a response of faith to the divine initiative. *Historically*, intratraditional dialogue can be seen as earlier memories are refined in the light of subsequent discovery and reflection, intertraditional dialogue can be seen between varying renderings of Jesus's ministry, and the history of the Johannine situation can be inferred by a two-level reading of the narrative text in the light of the Johannine Epistles. *Literarily*, the narrative invites the hearer/reader into an imaginary dialogue with Jesus by means of constructing dialogues rhetorically within the story, the compiler speaks of the author as the apparently deceased source of the Gospel, and the prologues of both the Gospel and 1 John draw later audiences into transformative engagement with what has been "seen and heard" from the beginning. The failure to appreciate Johannine polyvalence has led

---

13. Other elements of John's dialogical autonomy are spelled out in chapter 6 of *The Riddles of the Fourth Gospel* (Anderson 2011, 125–55) and elsewhere (see also Anderson 2006a, 37–41), and they include: (1) the Fourth Evangelist as a dialectical thinker, (2) the prophet-like-Moses agency schema as the foundation for John's Father-Son relationship and agency motif, (3) the Johannine Gospel's narrative as a knowing alternative to (an augmentation and modest correction of) Mark, (4) revelation and rhetoric—two dialogical modes within the Johannine narrative, and (5) Acts 4:19–20 as an overlooked first-century clue to Johannine authorship. The three described in the present essay are central to the history of the Johannine tradition and its emerging situation.

to more than one interpretive error based upon what can and cannot have been a possibility.[14]

A. An Overall Theory of Johannine Composition

With Brown, on John's *origin and composition*, John's is an autonomous tradition, developing alongside other traditions but not dependent on any of them. Rightly rejecting alien source theories due to their lack of evidence, Brown also finds no evidence for Synoptic dependence theories.[15] Rather, John's distinctive material and familiarity with pre-70 CE Palestine are more explicable as factors of the Johannine tradition's representing an autonomous memory of Jesus and his ministry than of a theologized narrative with fictive origins. Brown also rightly notes homiletical developments within the Johannine tradition, as stories of Jesus's works and teachings are narrated by the evangelist as elements of his own ministry before being gathered into a written narrative. This accounts for the distinctive features of the Johannine tradition as an independent perspective on Jesus's ministry.

While Brown's inference of 90 CE is a good guess regarding the first edition's completion, it could just as easily have been completed a few years earlier (say, 80–85 CE). If the evangelist had indeed moved to Ephesus or one of the other mission churches (and, with Brown, no site is superior to the traditional Ephesus as a choice—including Alexandria and Antioch) after the fall of Jerusalem in 70 CE, this would explain the translation of Aramaisms and Jewish customs for a Hellenistic audience. As tensions between the Jesus movement and Judaism would have been experienced long before the Jamnia councils between 70 and 90 CE, the Birkat Haminin is more likely to have been a codification of existing practices among some synagogues rather than a jump-starting of an innovated practice. Therefore, tensions with local synagogues did not begin in 90 CE; if anything, they were probably cooling as the Jesus movement transitioned (using

---

14. For a fuller treatment of Johannine polyvalence and differing types of Johannine dialogism, see Anderson 2008a and 2011.

15. This was my conclusion also, as I tested all of Bultmann's stylistic criteria for distinguishing disparate sources underlying and overlaying the Fourth Evangelist's work, using John 6 as a case study. Likewise, of forty-five similarities between John 6 and Mark 6 and 8, there are zero identical similarities, thus disconfirming theories that the Johannine tradition is a derivative one (Anderson 1996, 72–109).

Martyn's language) from being Christian Jews to becoming Jewish Christians.[16]

We do have a reflection of an anti-Domitian thrust in the first-edition narrative material, challenging empire worship demands, which is echoed in 1 John 5:21 (leveraged soon after his becoming emperor in 81 CE and beginning construction of the Domitian temple in Ephesus shortly thereafter); the confession of Thomas—"My Lord and my God!" (John 20:28)—argues for a date around that time. Thus, having heard the Gospel of Mark delivered among the churches, John's first edition is likely to have been the *second* gospel, designed to augment and complement Mark.[17] This is why a date of 80–85 CE for the first edition of John seems most plausible.

A strength of Brown's composition theory is that he allows the Epistles to follow the main edition of the Gospel, while still allowing later material to have been added after the writing of the Epistles. A weakness, however, is that he leaves considerable ambiguity regarding what sort of material is likely to have been added as part of the final edition of the Johannine Gospel. On this matter, the theory laid out by Barnabas Lindars (1972) is far clearer, and they agree on many of the particulars.[18] It is also not

---

16. The cooling of tensions between Johannine communities and local synagogues is also apparent in the supplementary material as inferred by Barnabas Lindars (1972), which John Ashton (1991, 124–204) and I came to embrace independently as the most plausible and simplest approach to resolving the major Johannine aporias and riddles. In John 6, 15–17, and 21 the animosity with Jewish leaders is fairly muted, and other issues, such as the incarnational suffering of Jesus and the Holy Spirit's guiding the community of believers are far more pronounced.

17. In Bauckham's (1998) essay on John written for readers of Mark, he notes several instances in which the Johannine narrative appears to set things straight in Mark. For instance, the Baptist is involved in ministry *before* he was thrown into prison (John 3:24; contra Mark 1:14), and I might note that the reference to Jesus's having testified regarding the dishonored hometown prophet in John 4:44 seems to be a direct reference to his having done so in Mark 6:4. A general familiarity with "performed Mark" (as suggested by the important monograph of Mackay 2004) might also account for John's differences with Mark, not just distinctive parallels. A general familiarity with Mark might thus explain John's differences from Mark as an intentionally crafted alternative presentation of Jesus's ministry.

18. Lindars (1972, 46–54) identifies the supplementary material to have been added (by the evangelist) as consisting of John 1:1–18, chapters 6, 11, 15–17, and 21, as well as Beloved Disciple and eyewitness references; in his treatment of composition theories in his new introduction, Brown does not seem to be aware of Lindars's theory—which also is constructed upon aspects of Brown's. I take exception, though,

certain (versus Brown, followed later by Urban von Wahlde) that variations and repetitions (John 3:31–36; 6:51–58; 12:44–50, for instance) were added by the redactor as leftover units of tradition rather than reiterative emphases of the evangelist. More likely, these repetitions represent material within the earlier and later editions, as the recapitulation of themes is a common feature of oral delivery and its consolidation in written form.

On *the identity of the evangelist and the redactor*, two exceptions must be taken regarding Brown's view. First, while the evangelist deconstructs the roles of Peter and the Twelve and includes a good deal of Judean/Jerusalem material, these features do not imply that the author was not one of the Twelve and from Galilee. Rather, the opposite is more plausibly argued, at least on the first point. As most Jesus scholars over the last century or more have concluded, Jesus of Nazareth was a charismatic leader, who challenged institutions and cultic rites rather than establishing them. Therefore, Johannine critique of such in the late first-century situation appears to be challenging institutionalizing innovations in the name of apostolic memory and Jesus's original designs for his followers. Given that Acts 4:20 has been totally overlooked by critical and traditional scholarship alike, connecting John the Apostle with a Johannine phrase (John 3:32; 1 John 1:3), we may well have in the Johannine tradition an apostolic corrective to the perceived hijacking of apostolic authority by Diotrephes and his institutionalizing kin.[19] Therefore, Brown's earlier conviction that the Fourth Evangelist bore considerable overlap with what we know of John the Son of Zebedee, or another first-hand apostolic witness, seems bolstered *because of* John's critique of Peter and the institutionalizing coopting of the Twelve.

On requiring the evangelist to have been a Judean resident on the basis of his familiarity to the high priest and addition of Judean material, this is weak argumentation. If the evangelist was not a Galilean, why does

---

to the inference that John 11 was added later, as it seems to fulfill the words of the steward in John 2:10 regarding saving the best for last.

19. In my conversations with Brown before the publication of *Christology* (1996), he was quite sympathetic with my treatment of Acts 4:19–20 and apparent Lukan dependence on the Johannine tradition in Appendix VIII (pp. 274–277). Since then I have discovered over six dozen cases where Luke departs with Mark and sides with the Johannine rendering of Jesus's ministry—likely a factor of the Johannine witness (probably in its oral forms) having been one of Luke's sources, which he acknowledges in Luke 1:2 (expressing gratitude to eyewitnesses and servants of the Logos; 2010a).

he apparently know so much about Galilean places of origin for Jesus's followers (Bethsaida, Cana, Magdala), and why would travels through Samaria (as well as knowledge of archaeological details) be so prominent in the Johannine narrative? So, inferring a Judean author rather than a Galilean author has its own set of new critical problems. Further, assuming that leading Galilean families would not have traveled to Jerusalem at all is a terribly weak hypothesis. If devout families traveled to Jerusalem two or three times a year for the pilgrim festivals, a young adult from Galilee would have visited Jerusalem some fifty times by the time he was twenty years of age. Judean material does appear to be included in John with intentionality, but such a feature more likely reflects an interest in augmenting Mark's northern presentation of Jesus's ministry rather than the non-Galilean origin of the evangelist.

As the later material added renderings of scenes in Jesus's ministry that were already a part of the Synoptics (John 6—the five signs in the first edition are precisely the ones *not* included in Mark), expanding the material developed in John 13–14 (John 15–17) and restoring dialectically the memory of Peter alongside that of the apparently deceased Beloved Disciple (John 21), distinctive purposes are evident between the earlier and later editions of John. The first edition indeed is apologetic in its purpose (contra Brown), seeking to convince hearers and readers that Jesus is the Jewish Messiah/Christ. Five signs of Jesus, along with five "I am" discourses (rhetorically echoing the five books of Moses), pose a presentation of him as the prophet like Moses (Deut 18:15–22), whose words come true, confirming the authenticity of his mission—worthy of belief (John 2:22; 4:53; 13:19; 14:29; 18:32; 20:31). If the first antichristic threat in 1 John 2:18–25 evidenced a questioning of whether Jesus was indeed the Jewish Messiah/Christ, the first edition of the Johannine narrative would certainly have set that issue straight.

The later material, however, includes nearly all of the incarnational (antidocetic) themes in John (Lindars 1972, 63), suggesting a later rhetorical concern—reflected also by the second and third antichristic references in the Johannine Epistles. For those questioning Jesus's coming in the flesh (the antichristic false teachers of 1 John 4:1–3 and 2 John 1:7), the later Johannine narrative material would certainly have challenged those views. Given the splits and challenges evidenced by the Epistles, the main thrust of the evangelist's continuing preaching (between the first and final editions of the Gospel) and the compiler's finalization of the narrative, show acute concerns for abiding with Jesus and his fellowship. On that point,

Brown would agree—to believe in Jesus is to abide in him and within his community of faith.

Given, though, that the compiler adds the Johannine Logos hymn (echoed in 1 John 1:1–4), adds the water-and-blood theme (John 19:34; echoed in 1 John 5:6–8), and asserts that "his testimony is true" (John 19:35; 21:24; echoed in 3 John 1:12), the author of the Epistles quite plausibly could have been the final compiler/redactor of the Gospel (with Bultmann and others). Rather than multiplying authorial/editorial entities, Ockham's razor also slices against the proliferation of Johannine authors and editors, connecting the multiply-attested claims of Eusebius regarding "two Johns buried at Ephesus" with the Johannine evangelist (John the Apostle) and author of the Epistles/compiler of the Gospel (John the Elder). In the light of Acts 4:19–20, such is not an implausible critical inference.[20]

Between the first and final editions of the Gospel (roughly 85–100 CE), several things appear to be happening within the Johannine situation (involving several communities, not just one)—the time during which the Epistles likely were written. First, the Beloved Disciple continues to teach and preach about Jesus and the relevance of his words and works for later generations. This can be seen in the later Johannine material (1) as the Mosaic agency schema—the *Leitmotiv* of the main narrative—is recrafted

---

20. Anderson 2010a; 2011, 95–124. Here the so-called "confusion of Johns at Ephesus" has itself confused the second-century memory as reported by Eusebius, Irenaeus, and other ancient witnesses. Just because Irenaeus may have confused Papias's reference to John the Elder with John the Apostle, this does not mean he and all other second-century authorities were wrong about two leaders named "John" buried at Ephesus. Given that Eusebius is unequivocal about connecting John the Apostle with an extended ministry in Ephesus, living into the reign of Trajan (98 CE) and being buried in Ephesus along with John the Elder (*Hist. Eccles.* 3.1, 18, 21, 23, 24, 29, 31, 39; 4.14; 5.18, 20, 24), and that John the Apostle's ministry in Ephesus is also attested by Polycarp, Irenaeus, Polycrates, and other second-century authorities, attempts to remove him from the scene entirely are frail. The point is not to assert who the Johannine authors must have been; it is to question whether their nonidentity is as much of an open-and-shut case as critical scholars have recently claimed. One more point: on the so-called "memory of the early death of John," both Philip of Sidetes (fifth century) and George Hamartalos (ninth century) assert that he died in Ephesus around the time of Domitian's reign, despite Jesus's prediction in Mark 10:38–39 that he and James would suffer martyrdom. Therefore, neither Philip nor George claimed or believed their deaths happened at the same time, and modern scholars asserting that John died early have not consulted the primary sources on the matter. Such is a modern myth, not an ancient view.

into a worship hymn to Christ the Logos using terms and language friendly to Jewish and gentile audiences alike (John 1:1–18); (2) as the call to costly discipleship and martyrdom willingness is levied around the call for solidarity with Jesus and his community in the face of growing hard times (John 6); (3) as the call to abide in Jesus and to demonstrate his costly love for community is delivered alongside the prayer of Jesus that his disciples be in the world but not of the world—affirming that Christ would continue to lead his flock by means of the work of the Paraclete (John 15–17); and (4) as the character of apostolic leadership is sketched as a reminder to both love the flock agapeically and to retain an intimate relationship with the Lord (John 21). Some of the Beloved Disciple's continued spoken (and perhaps written) ministry is thus preserved by the compiler and added to the finalized Gospel after his apparent death (John 21:20–24).

These themes, however, can be seen to be addressing several acute crises experienced by Jesus adherents in Asia Minor during this period, echoed in the Epistles. First John is written around 85 CE as a circular and plausibly circulated among several Christian communities in the region. While at least one Johannine community had experienced a schism (1 John 2:18–25), other threats are on the way: (1) debates over mortal and venial sins are finally addressed in the last word as the first word—little children, *stay away from idols!* (1 John 5); (2) just as the water and blood from Jesus's side testify to his suffering humanity, false teachers teaching doctrines of assimilation and easy discipleship ought to be eschewed and resisted (1 John 4); (3) to abide in Christ is to have nothing to do with sin—to walk as he walked—therefore, love not the world and its ways, but stay true to Christ and his sacrifice (1 John 2–3); and (4) in doing so, the love command that has been heard from the beginning (in the gospel narrative) is fulfilled, and walking in the light goes hand-in-hand with abiding in love (1 John 1–4). While less dialectical in his theology than the evangelist, the Elder nonetheless appeals to the self-perception of his audience as the basis for his appeals to loving behavior—*if you claim to love God whom you have not seen, you must also love one another, whom you have seen.*[21] In his

---

21. I find no basis for inferring a difference in authorship between the three Johannine Epistles; the vocabulary and syntax of 3 John is somewhat distinctive, but the subject and purpose are also different. While 3 John was finally accepted into the canon on the basis of 1 and 2 John, this does not mean that its having been questioned was a factor of authorship; more likely, its critique of hierarchical leadership would have posed an ample basis for its uneven reception *whoever* the author may have been.

letters to the chosen lady and her children (2 John) and to Gaius (3 John), the Elder addresses more particular issues related to hospitality and its denial—on both ends of equation. As a means of dealing with Diotrephes and his hierarchical kin, the Elder compiles and circulates the testimony of the Beloved Disciple, whose testimony and first-hand representation of Jesus and his view of the church is *true*.

Within a larger view of Johannine dialogical autonomy, the following three outlines contribute to a paradigm building on the strongest features of Brown's overall theory, as well as those of other scholars, serving to provide a grounded basis for interpreting the Johannine Gospel and Epistles.

Outline A: A Two-Edition Theory of Johannine Composition[22]

The Johannine tradition develops as an independent Jesus memory in its own right, somewhat in dialogue with the pre-Markan oral tradition. A Palestinian setting is reflected, including northern (Galilean) perspectives on southern (Judean) religious/political practices and familiarity with Jerusalem. Sometime between 55 and 70 CE (probably closer to the latter, although an earlier visit cannot be ruled out), the Johannine evangelist relocates among the mission churches (plausibly Asia Minor and even Ephesus) delivering the story of Jesus's mission to Jewish and gentile audiences alike. Both Luke and Q appear to have had access to the Johannine tradition in its oral stages, suggested by Luke's departures from Mark and siding with John and by the "bolt out of the Johannine blue" in Matt 11:27 and Luke 10:22. The Johannine narrator hooks the hearer/reader into an imaginary dialogue with Jesus as a means of engaging later audiences and drawing them into the original story.

1. The First Edition of the Johannine Gospel (80–85 CE)

Following several decades of Johannine preaching (and perhaps some writing), *a first edition of John is completed* by the evangelist or an amanuensis

---

Nor does the difference in form between the first letter and the two shorter ones imply anything about a difference of authorship. To require identical forms of delivery of all authors, ancient and modern, is not exactly a scientific approach to authorial inferences. Therefore, I stand with Brown on the common authorship of the Johannine Epistles and also their order.

22. This outline is an adaptation of Table 1.4 and Appendix I in *The Fourth Gospel and the Quest for Jesus* (2006a, 40 n. 19; pp. 193–95).

between 80 and 85 CE, to some degree as an augmentive and corrective response to Mark. This "second" gospel (chronologically) is not distributed widely, but it begins with the ministry of John the Baptist (John 1:15, 19–42) and concludes with John 20:31, declaring the evangelistic purpose of the Johannine Gospel: inviting hearers/readers to *receive Jesus* as the Jewish Messiah/Christ and Son of God.

2. The Writing of the Johannine Epistles (85–95 CE)

The teaching/preaching ministry of the Beloved Disciple (and possibly other Johannine leaders) continues over the next decade or two, and during this time (85–95 CE), *the three Johannine Epistles are written* by the Elder (85, 90, 95 CE). What was "seen and heard" from the beginning is taken further in terms of community implications, and the "new commandment" of Jesus to love one another (John 13:34) is now become the "old commandment" (1 John 2:7). First John is written as a circular to the churches in the region, calling for Christian unity in loving one another; 2 John is written to a particular church and its leadership: the "chosen lady and her children," exhorting them to remain together in love and to ward off docetizing preachers; 3 John is written to a particular leader: Gaius, exhorting him to extend hospitality, despite its having been denied to Johannine traveling ministers by Diotrephes.

3. The Finalization of the Johannine Gospel (100 CE)

After the death of the Beloved Disciple (around 100 CE), who reportedly lived until the reign of Trajan (98 CE), the Elder *compiles the Gospel*, adding to it the worship material of the prologue (John 1:1–18), inserting the feeding and sea-crossing narrative (John 6) between chapters 5 and 7 and inserting additional discourse material (John 15–17) between Jesus's saying "let us depart" (John 14:31) and his arrival with his disciples at the garden (John 18:1). He also apparently attaches additional appearance narratives (ch. 21) and eyewitness/Beloved Disciple passages (esp. John 19:34–35) and crafts a second ending (John 21:24–25) in the pattern of the first (John 20:30–31). Then, he circulates the finalized witness of the Beloved Disciple, whose "testimony is true," as an encouragement and challenge to the larger Christian movement, inviting hearers/readers to *abide in Jesus* as the Son of God.

After the finalization of the Johannine Gospel, now the fourth among the finalized Gospels, it garners a new set of hearings and readings. It quickly becomes a favorite among gentile Christians, but it also takes root within Jewish and mainstream Christianity. By the end of the second century CE, more surviving Christian citations are connected to the Johannine Gospel than any other piece of Christian literature. The *purposes* of John, both *apologetic* (in its first edition) and *pastoral* (in its final edition), thus appear to have taken effect, despite some breaches in community (suggested by the Epistles). The Johannine Gospel becomes a pattern for the apologetic work of Justin and others, and the rhetoric against the Johannine antichrists becomes a prime source of Christian polemics from the second century to the present.

B. A Theory of Johannine-Synoptic Relations

While Brown's (2003, 90–111) analysis of the relations between the Johannine and Synoptic traditions shows some development in his new introduction to John, he largely leaves unspecified the particular relationships with each of the Synoptic traditions. What he rightly does, though, is to consider the particular connections (or lack thereof) between the Johannine and each of the Synoptic traditions instead of assuming that they were gathered into a collection (along with a hypothetical Q source). To assume that "the Synoptics" as a gathered set of traditions was known by anyone in the late first century is a fiction; it is also probably not true. John's relation to each of the traditions must be assessed individually.

Particular elements of Brown's overall theory worth building on, however, include the following. First, he rightly sees John and Mark as two individuated traditions with their own perspectives on Jesus's ministry. I might call them "the bi-optic Gospels"—posing distinctive views of Jesus's ministry from day one.

Second, Brown correctly infers some level of interaction during the oral stages of their traditions, explaining the presence of common details and buzz words (not taken up by Matthew or Luke)—thus likely characteristic of oral stages of traditional development (such as green grass/ much grass, two hundred and three hundred denarii, etc.).[23] While it is

---

23. Note Brown's consideration of "cross-influence" between John and Mark (2003, 102–4), as well as my inference of "interfluence" between the early oral stages of these two traditions (Anderson 1996, 170–93).

impossible to know whether the claim of Papias—that Peter was one of Mark's primary sources—is correct and whether John or another eyewitness was the source of the Johannine tradition (although some first-century evidence for John's connection with Johannine themes in Acts 4:19–20 has been overlooked on all sides of the debate), Brown notes that Peter and John are reported as preaching and ministering together in Acts 8 (also in Acts 3 and 4). Therefore, something like this could explain some of the nonidentical similarities in the pre-Markan and early Johannine traditions.[24]

Third, Brown notes similarities between John and Luke, although he fails to address Luke's departures from Mark in favor of Johannine detail, ordering, and presentation. Rather than opt for a hypothetical (and unavailable!) common source explaining similarities between Luke and John, more plausible is the possibility that Luke has borrowed from the Johannine tradition, probably during the oral stages of its development. This may also have been the case with Q, as Matt 11:27 and Luke 10:22 bear a distinctively Johannine ring.

Fourth, Brown rightly notes "cross-influence" between the later stages of the Matthean and Johannine traditions over aspects of church governance and the function of Peter's memory organizationally, and some of this dialogue is suggested by the third Johannine Epistle. While I have developed this theory in greater detail elsewhere,[25] following is a synopsis of my second paradigm within an overall theory of Johannine dialogical autonomy.

Outline B: A Bi-optic Hypothesis

While John's material appears to reflect an independent Jesus tradition developing in its own distinctive way over seven decades before its final-

---

24. While Brown (1979, 36–40) makes sense of the mission of Peter and John through Samaria (Acts 8) as a factor in the narration of John 4, involving Samaritans joining the Johannine community, I see the presentation of two Christian leaders traveling together in ministry (whoever they might have been—whether or not they were Peter and John in particular) as a plausible explanation for interfluence between oral stages of gospel traditions and their human purveyors.

25. For more detailed developments of this larger theory of Johannine-Synoptic interfluentiality, see Anderson 2001; 2002; 2004; 2006a, 101–25; 2007b; 2007d; 2010a; 2010b; 2014, 102–26).

ization, it does not appear to be isolated or out of contact with other traditions. Contact, however, does not imply dependence, nor does influence imply a singular direction of movement. Likewise, familiarity may have evoked dissonance as well as consonance, and it is highly unlikely that the timing and manner of the relation between John's and all other traditions were uniform. John's intertraditional contact may have even been different between distinct phases and forms of a particular tradition, such as Mark's. Therefore, the following components are integral elements of a new synthesis regarding John's dialogical autonomy and interfluential relationships with other gospel traditions. In that sense, John represents a "bi-optic" alternative to the Markan Gospels (Mark, Luke, and Matthew), as both complementarity and dialogical engagements may plausibly be inferred as follows (cf. Anderson 2010b).

1. John's Dialogical Autonomy Develops in Ways Parallel to Other Traditions

Parallel to the pre-Markan tradition, the early Johannine tradition developed in its own autonomous set of ways. First impressions developed into Johannine paraphrases, crafted to meet the needs of early audiences (including tensions with Judeans and Baptist adherents) and suited to the personal ministry of the Johannine evangelist, developing parallel to the human source(s) of the pre-Markan tradition.

2. Interfluential Contacts between the Pre-Markan and Early Johannine Traditions

Early contacts between these two traditions created a set of commonly shared buzz-words, references, and themes, explaining their nonidentical similarities in the later texts. Especially within the oral stages of their traditions, influence may have crossed in both directions, making "interfluence" during the oral stages of the Johannine and Markan traditions a plausible inference.

3. Augmentation and Correction of Written Mark

After Mark was written, at least some of it became familiar to the Johannine evangelist, evoking a complementary project. This explains some of the Markan echoes in John and also some of John's departures from Mark.

Some of them may reflect knowing intentionality (John 20:30), as the first edition of John was plausibly the *second* written gospel, though enjoying primarily local circulation. Therefore, Johannine-Synoptic differences are not factors of a three-against-one majority; rather, John and Mark deserve consideration as "*the bi-optic Gospels.*"

4. John's Formative Impact upon Luke

During the oral stages of the Johannine tradition, some of its material came to influence Luke's tradition. This explains the fact that at least six dozen times Luke departs from Mark and sides with John. Because many of John's features are not followed, the Johannine influence upon Luke is unlikely to have taken place in full, written form but probably reflects Lukan familiarity with the Johannine oral tradition. This explains also why Luke does not follow the Johannine ordering of the temple cleansing and why Luke places the great catch of fish at the first calling of Peter and the disciples, rather than at their re-calling. Does mention of what has been received from "eyewitnesses and servants of the Logos" in Luke 1:2 imply acknowledgement of the Johannine tradition as a source?

5. John's Influence upon the Q Tradition?

Not implausible is the likelihood that the contacts between several Q passages and John imply early Johannine influences upon the Q tradition. Especially the "bolt out of the Johannine blue" (Matt 11:25–27; Luke 10:21–22) points to such a possibility, as the Father-Son relationship is a distinctively Johannine theme. Or, these motifs linking the Father and Son together may go back to the historical Jesus, or to earlier tradition, but the more plausible inference is that Q, if there was a Q tradition, was influenced by early Johannine tradition, given that the Father-Son relationship is so distinctively Johannine. Some interfluentiality may also have been involved regarding other Johannine and Q parallels exhibiting less distinctively Johannine features.

6. Johannine Preaching (and Some Writing) Continues

Following the first edition of the Johannine Gospel (80–85 CE), the Beloved Disciple continues to preach and teach and possibly even to write. The fleshly suffering of Jesus becomes an example to emulate for Christians facing hardship under the reign of Domitian (81–96 CE), and the sustaining/guiding work of the Holy Spirit addresses new crises: dialogues with the synagogue, the Roman presence, gentile docetizers, and institutionalizing tendencies.

7. Matthean and Johannine Traditions Engage in an Interfluential Set of Dialogues

Especially on matters of church governance, the Matthean and Johannine traditions appear to have been engaged in a series of dialogues over how the risen Lord continues to lead the church. They also reinforce each other in their outreach to Jewish audiences over Jesus's agency as the Jewish Messiah/Christ. Might we have two ecclesial models in parallel gospel traditions in dialogue with each other in the late first-century situation?

8. The Johannine Epistles Were Written by the Elder

During this time (85–95 CE), the Johannine Elder writes the Johannine Epistles, calling for loving unity, corporate solidarity, willingness to suffer for the faith, and challenging the inhospitality of Diotrephes and his kin. The Johannine Epistles were thus written *before and after* the Johannine Gospel.

9. The Johannine Gospel Was Supplemented and Finalized by the Johannine Elder

After the death of the Beloved Disciple, the Elder adds the prologue and other material (chs. 6, 15–17, 21), circulating it around 100 CE as the witness of the Beloved Disciple, whose "testimony is true." As the first edition calls for belief in Jesus as the Jewish Messiah, the final edition of John calls for believers to abide in Jesus and his community, posing also a corrective to rising institutionalism in the name of the original intention of Jesus for his church. Acts 4:19–20 provides a hitherto overlooked first-century clue to Johannine authorship, calling into question the modern certainty of John's non-apostolic derivation.

10. The Spiritual Gospel Poses a Bi-optic Alternative to the Somatic Gospels

While Matthew and Luke built *upon* Mark, John built *around* Mark. As an independent Jesus tradition developed theologically, however, the

Johannine and Markan traditions all contribute to Gospel christological studies, as well as quests for the historical Jesus in *bi-optic* perspective.

11. The Second Markan Ending Bears Johannine Echoes within It

Interestingly, Mark 16:9–20, while betraying a distinctively non-Markan style and vocabulary and not found in earliest manuscripts, suggesting a later addition—probably in the early-to-mid second century CE—shows familiarity with particular details in the other Gospels and Acts, *including Johannine themes and presentations of events. Interfluentiality continues!*

While some might complain about the complexity of this overall paradigm, it is actually too simplistic, as intertraditional relationships over nearly a century were undoubtedly more complex than the basic set of inferences listed above and sketched diagrammatically below. The following model builds on a basic Synoptic Hypothesis, assuming that Matthew and Luke built upon Mark and Q. Of course, additional traditions are likely besides the four Synoptic traditions and John, and while the oval shapes reflect largely oral traditions and the rectangles reflect written ones, it is not implausible to infer that earlier traditions may have included some written as well as oral material. As all five gospel traditions (including hypothetical Q, if there was a Q source) likely had at least some contact with the historical ministry of Jesus, they also reflect individuated developments with particular situation histories. Among these, the development of the Johannine tradition is the most individuated and autonomous, and yet it is also the most illuminated longitudinally because of the Johannine Epistles. Therefore, a two-edition model of the Fourth Gospel's composition, informed by a charting of Johannine-Synoptic relations, contributes to a larger bi-optic hypothesis.

C. The History of the Johannine Situation

Within the Johannine situation, we have more than just one community, although there are signs of at least one community of believers involved. With Brown and Martyn, three phases of Johannine Christianity are discernible, followed by post-Johannine influence and the reception of its material. Within each of these phases two major crises are evident, with Johannine-Synoptic dialectic spanning all three phases. While these crises are largely sequential, they are also somewhat overlapping, as an emerging

A Charting of Johannine-Synoptic Interfluential Relations

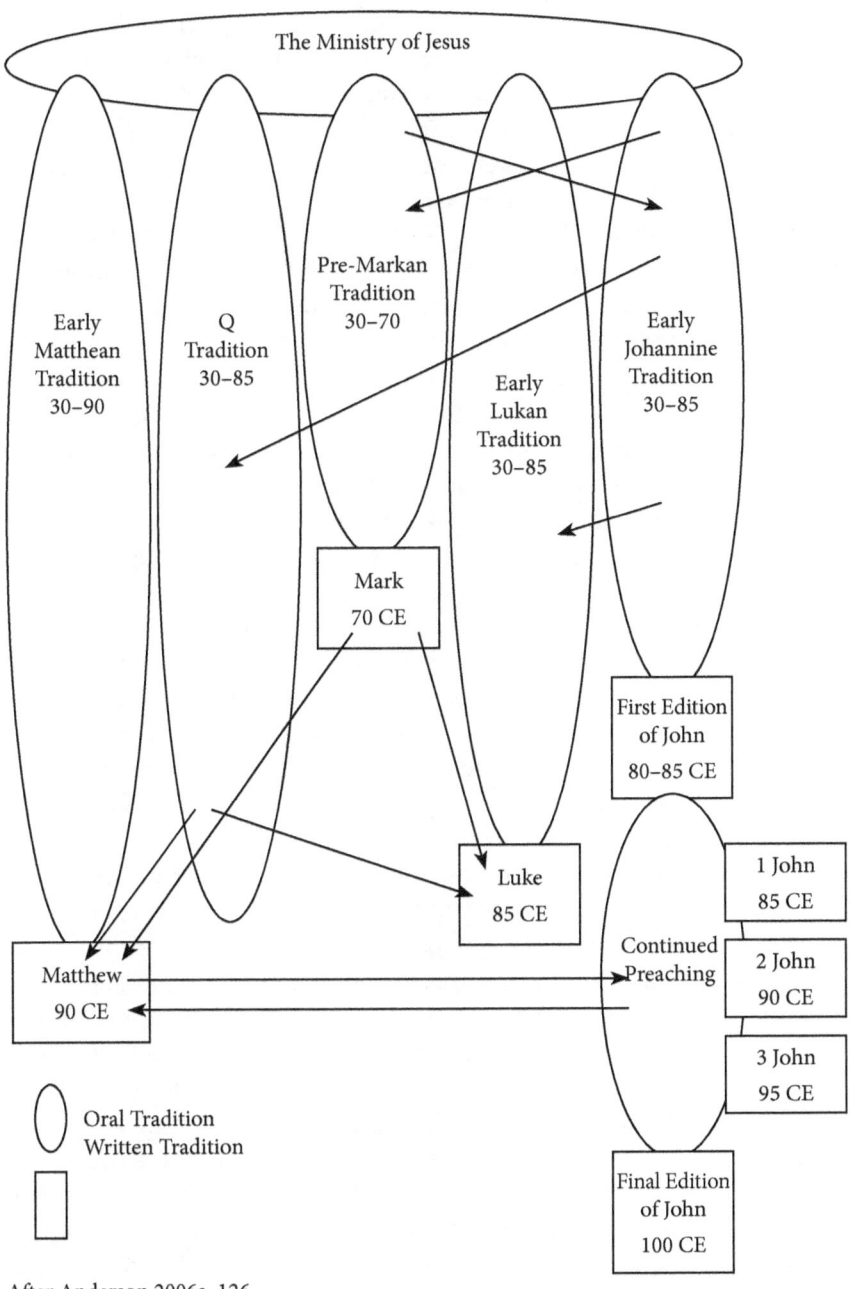

After Anderson 2006a, 126.

crisis rarely waits until previous ones have subsided before rearing its head. And, most controversies never disappear entirely; they simply are crowded out by more pressing ones, although their memory still informs later stances. Brown is indeed correct to infer the Palestinian origin of the Johannine tradition, and for several decades there would have been an ongoing set of debates between southern religious authorities (*hoi Ioudaioi* = "the Judeans"), challenging the movement of the northern (Galilean) prophet.

While some contact with Samaritans is plausible, such is not a necessary basis for the ascendency of Johannine Christology; it was already emerging within the Jesus movement in Palestine and also among the mission churches in Diaspora Judaism. Some high christological memory was also a part of the Johannine tradition from the beginning, as spiritual encounters associated with the man Jesus also have an established place within the Johannine tradition. Agency-schema connections with the prophet-like-Moses (Deut 18:15–22) also could have been Galilean in their origin and development (not particularly Samaritan), likely reflecting a closer fit with the self-understanding of the prophet from Nazareth than king-like-David associations also emerging within the early Jesus movement. Much of John's high christological material is a factor of the Mosaic agency schema rather than a gnostic redeemer myth (versus Bultmann). Brown also correctly infers dialogues with followers of the Baptist, and either in Palestine or Asia Minor, the evangelist is keen to present the Baptist as pointing to Jesus as the Messiah, not himself. Therefore, these two dialogical partners (Judean religious leaders and followers of the Baptist) were likely primary dialogical partners within the first phase of the Johannine situation between 30 and 70 CE.

With the Roman invasion and the destruction of Jerusalem (67–70 CE), however, large numbers of Judeans and Galileans were forced to relocate. Resettling within Jewish communities in such places as Jamnia, Antioch, Alexandria, and Rome, there is no reason to doubt the tradition that the Johannine evangelist relocated in Ephesus, lending his support among the Pauline mission churches. Within Asia Minor between 70–85 CE, a primary community is a plausible inference, with some give and take from members of local synagogues. When the evangelist came to Ephesus, the mission to the gentiles had certainly already begun; therefore, Jewish followers of Jesus probably worshiped with Jewish family and friends in the synagogue on Sabbath days, and they probably shared first-day fellowship with gentile believers in homes. With the Birkat Haminim, some Jesus adherents likely left the synagogue and joined local gentile believers for worship and fellowship. Not unlikely also is the possibility that some Jesus adherents stayed behind in the synagogue (whom Brown calls "crypto-Christians"), and that some who felt excluded from the synagogue were proselytized back into Jewish communities after their departure. This can be seen in the first antichristic crisis in 1 John 2:18–25, where the secessionists had renounced their belief in Jesus as the Christ—ostensibly as a factor of monotheistic commitment to the Father. The Elder clarifies that if they reject the Son they will lose the Father; the only way to preserve their union with the Father is to receive also the Son.

A second crisis during this second phase is one that Brown largely missed but that has emerged as a significant factor in Johannine-situation studies over the last two decades—namely, the problem of the Roman presence and increasing pressure to demonstrate loyalty to Rome by offering the emperor laud. If Jewish Christians were no longer able to claim a Jewish dispensation (paying two drachmas to Rome instead of having to confess Caesar as Lord or being forced to offer incense or a burnt offering in Caesar's honor) having been distanced from the synagogue, they were now subject to harassment and even capital punishment if they did not confess Caesar as Lord.[26] Further, if Ignatius of Antioch is any indicator of their practice, the Romans sought to make examples of Christian leaders, seeking to influence their followers accordingly. Ignatius himself was taken to Rome and executed around 117 CE. The restoration of emperor worship was instituted by Domitian in 81 CE, and he even required his Roman lieutenants to regard him as *dominus et deus* (lord and god). Therefore, one can imagine the confession of Thomas in John 20:28 to have anti-imperial overtones (let alone the dialogue between Jesus and Pilate) for audiences in the late first century, and the clear admonition at the end of 1 John 5 puts directly one of the main themes of the letter—*stay away from idols!*

---

26. See the treatment given to two young women and others by Pliny, governor of neighboring Bithynia, in his correspondence with Trajan a couple of decades or so later (around 110 CE, *Ep. Tra.* 10.96–97). Any who were accused simply of bearing the name *Christiani* were charged with a crime worthy of torture and death. If accused of such a crime, subjects (now rampant in the villages and towns as well as the cities, according to Pliny) were brought to trial and exhorted to denounce Christ and his movement and to offer incense or wine to an image of Caesar, confessing loyalty to Caesar. If they refused, they were executed. The works of Richard Cassidy (1992) and Warren Carter (2008) here are important.

While such an admonition would have applied to Roman imperial worship, it would also have included festivals related to fertility, prosperity, and guild cults clustered together within virtually every major metropolis in the Greco-Roman world. In Pergamum and Ephesus, in particular, many different temples are located together so that local residents could offer sacrifices and engage in festivities in an inclusive fashion. Ephesus and Pergamum competed with each other for *Neokoros* status (Friesen 1993), seeking to be the favored center of emperor worship in the region, so civic leaders and city residents who did not show public support for the empire and its beneficence could jeopardize favor from Rome, including the civic grants and construction projects it bestowed upon its favored cities. With Domitian's high-handed approach, however, came resentment and hostility because of his sometimes violent capriciousness.

In the Domitian temple in Ephesus, there are holes in the marble wall engraving announcing his name; a metal plaque is thought to have been placed over the name as a means of effecting *damnatio memoriae* (the damnation of his memory), as local residents—no doubt *with* Trajan's imperial blessing after the end of Domitian's reign (96 CE)—sought to blot out its memory. This sentiment would have been especially true of Christians, who had resisted both pressures and enticements to participate in local festivities surrounding the emperor cult. Therefore, the admonition to love not the world in 1 John 2:1–17 and the mortal/venial sins distinctions of 1 John 5:16–21 should be seen in this light. If denying that one was a follower of Jesus and a member of the Christian fellowship (as some before Pliny had done—claiming they used to be a Christian several years ago, but no longer were), this was another way of not loving the brethren (not simply secession); if participating in local cultic festivities in celebrating the emperor's birthday or making offerings of incense to Caesar or declaring "Caesar is Lord" was done in public, this would be seen as a death-producing sin and loving the world instead of Christ and his followers. The overall implication here is that the Johannine community during this phase was *not* sectarian; it was cosmopolitan.[27] Jewish Christians had

---

27. Here I take issue with the longstanding judgment of Meeks and others, seeing the Johannine situation as highly sectarian (for instance, Johnson 1993), which Robert Gundry (2002) carries to an extreme. Rather, I see Johannine Christianity as less sectarian than established Judaism in Asia Minor at the time and certainly not as sectarian as Qumran Judaism—cutting itself off from "the world" in the desert. Johannine leaders were experiencing tensions with "the world" precisely because community

no dispensation from Rome, as did members of the synagogue, and while most of them were likely willing to suffer and die for their Lord, gentile Christians might not have been troubled by the festivities; they were likely more assimilative in their new-found faith. Such tensions were brought on by the local Roman presence under Domitian, forcing debates within the Christian movement on several levels.

The third phase of the Johannine situation would have involved the developing of new Christian communities, roughly from the mid-80s until the Gospel was finalized around 100 CE. It was during this phase that the Epistles were written, say, between 85 and 95 CE as a plausible estimation. As 1 John 2:18–25 shows a community split, wherein former community members withdrew and plausibly rejoined the synagogue (diminishing their commitment to Jesus as the Messiah/Christ), and as emperor worship with its associated implications was a growing problem, the acute threat now involved a fifth crisis in the Johannine situation: docetizing gentile Christians, who were teaching a doctrine of cultural (and perhaps cultic) assimilation, advocating grace, and motivated by an interest in less costly discipleship. As in the letters of Ignatius, the Judaizing threat was followed by the docetizing threat, and the Johannine Elder, within his Christ-centered setting, levies the ultimate charge against both problems, calling their instigators "antichrists."

It is important to note here that the targets themselves would not have been comfortable with such titles. These were pejorative labels intended to disturb, and they were also used as a disincentive to others who might be tempted to join their ranks. While Brown does note differences between the antichrists of 1 John 2:18–25 and 4:1–3, he does not take full notice of how different the presentations of the two groups really are. First, there is a difference of *timing*: the first crisis has happened, and the next one is on the way but not fully realized. Second, there is a difference of *action*: the first crisis involved secession (they went out from us), but the next one involves an impending invasion (they have gone out into the world—not necessarily from us, but beware, lest they come to *our* or *your* community—keep them out). Third, the *content* of their doctrinal beliefs is entirely different: the secessionists do not believe Jesus *was the Christ* (let alone divine), and the false teachers deny that Jesus *came in the flesh* (if he was divine, he did

---

members were questioning the Jewishness of the community's standards of faith and practice. They were less sectarian than diaspora Judaism, which is why they struggled with "the world."

not suffer as a human). Therefore, the second antichristic threat involved traveling gentile Christian ministers in the area, who may have been soft on certain elements of Jewish faith and practice. These were not gnostics, and on such an assumption many an interpretive approach has foundered. Further, docetizing Christology might not even have been their primary interest; it became for the Elder a means of testing traveling ministers to see if their overall doctrine was rooted in a suffering Jesus, and the implications for Christian living are what was at stake.

Again, in noting the correspondence between Pliny the Younger and Emperor Trajan (*Ep. Tra.* 10.96–97), two decades or so after the writing of 1 and 2 John, several issues become apparent. First, the governor says that he was charging people of simply bearing the name "Christian," and if found guilty, they were liable to be executed unless they recanted. If they reviled the name of Christ and/or worshipped the idol of Caesar, they were acquitted; even Pliny declares that such could never be guilty of being a Christian if they were willing to perform such actions. Second, he notes some who were brought in denied being Christians even though they met with believers before the dawn on a given day of the week, ate common food, and sang a hymn to Christ "as though he were god." Such were judged innocent of the crime, as well. Third, pressures were being felt from the merchants whose living depended upon the idol-worship trade, because of the effect these Christians were having on the pagan cultic enterprise. Pliny expresses some relief that some of that has begun to be corrected and that the adverse impact of the Christian movement is not as severe as it once had been.

Therefore, inferring two distinctive antichristic threats makes the best sense from the evidence within the first two Johannine Epistles, as informed by the backdrop availed by the letters of Ignatius and the Pliny-Trajan correspondence. The first antichristic crisis was a schism, wherein some Johannine community members of Jewish origin likely rejoined the synagogue, and the Elder surmises somewhat poignantly, "they never really were a part of us" (1 John 2:19). Following the increased pressures toward empire and cultural assimilation under Domitian, the second antichristic threat is labeled as such, because gentile Christian teachers had apparently advocated assimilation in worldly directions, and they resisted costly implications of Christian discipleship by affirming a nonsuffering Jesus. Opponents of Ignatius reflect the same tendency a decade or two later. These crises precipitate a sixth, involving Diotrephes and his kin.

Within the third phase of the Johannine situation, the second crisis was one precipitated by rising institutionalism in the late first-century Christian movement, as third-generation leaders sought to discipline problematic traveling ministers and other centrifugal tendencies by means of a proto-Ignatian monepiscopal (single bishop) approach to leadership. Seeing that the Johannine familial approach to governance and discipline had somewhat failed, Diotrephes and other institutionalizing leaders may even have felt claiming the authority of Petrine keys to the kingdom (Matt 16:17–19) was an advance over less effective (and primitive) organizational structures. Therefore, the opposition of Diotrephes to the Johannine traveling ministers was less likely a feature of their encroachment (versus Lieu 1986) and more a factor of their egalitarianism—a direct threat to his hierarchical approach to holding his community together. The fact that Diotrephes is reported as willing to cast out members of his own community who refused to heed his commands shows that hospitality was an incidental matter rather than the central one. This may be why the Elder then circulates the testimony of the Beloved Disciple, adding the passages affirming the accessible leadership of the Holy Spirit, available to all believers. "His testimony is true!" not only signals a belief in the evangelist's historical witness among the Gospels; it also affirms his conviction that the ecclesial thrust of his witness is apostolic and authoritative for believers and other church leaders.

Outline C: The Dialectical Johannine Situation— Seven Crises over Seven Decades[28]

The early Johannine situation develops in Palestine, reflecting northern perspective (likely in Galilee with Samarian sympathies) and southern familiarity (with Jerusalem and Judea). Within this setting, an autonomous Jesus tradition develops, to some degree in dialogue with Petrine (or other pre-Markan) oral traditions, but also in dialogue with other groups, including political/religious leaders in Judea and followers of John the Baptist. Palestinian archaeological and topographical references reflect historical realism, betraying knowledge of the area before its destruction by the Romans in 70 CE.

---

28. This outline is an adaptation of Table 2.5 and Appendix II in *The Fourth Gospel and the Quest for Jesus* (2006a, 64 n. 19, pp. 196–99).

1. Phase 1 (ca. 30–70 CE): The Palestinian Period, the Developing of an Autonomous Johannine Jesus Tradition

> Crisis A: Dealing with North/South Tensions (Galileans/Judeans)
> Crisis B: Reaching Followers of John the Baptist
>   (The oral Johannine tradition develops.)

The Johannine evangelist and perhaps other associates relocate to one of the mission churches—plausibly Ephesus or another mission setting in Asia Minor—some time before or around the Roman destruction of Jerusalem in 70 CE. There contacts with the local synagogue eventually become strained (the Birkat Haminim is a codification of Jewish resistance to the Jesus movement), leading to an individuated Johannine community composed of Christian Jews and gentile Christians. While appealing for Jewish family and friends to receive Jesus as the Jewish Messiah, members of the synagogue also exhort those with Jewish backgrounds to return to the way of Moses and the household of Abraham. This leads some to abandon the new community and rejoin the synagogue, while Jesus adherents who never left, and perhaps others who did, sought to straddle the two communities. During the reign of Domitian (81–96 CE), the increased expectation of public emperor worship and participation in pagan festivals and civic life creates a crisis for Hellenistic followers of Jesus, especially gentile Christians with non-Jewish origins.

2. Phase 2 (ca. 70–85 CE): The First Asia Minor Phase, the Forging of a Johannine Community

> Crisis A: Engaging Local Jewish Family and Friends
> Crisis B: Dealing with the Local Roman Presence
>   (The first edition of the Johannine Gospel is prepared.)

The Johannine sector of the early church grows, both by the starting of new communities and by establishing contact with other Christian communities in Asia Minor and beyond, leading to correspondence and intervisitation between the churches. Some gentile teachers/preachers comfort their audiences with a teaching that allows some worldly assimilation, including softening the stand on forbidding emperor worship and participation in Hellenistic festivals, arguing a nonsuffering Jesus. Rising institutionalization among neighbor churches reflects a proto-Ignatian means of addressing similar issues, but it also becomes a strident matter as expressed by Diotrephes and his kin. Dialogues with Synoptic traditions continue, now with a focus on Matthean-Johannine dialogues regarding church leadership and how Christ continues to lead the church.

3. Phase 3 (ca. 85–100 CE): The Second Asia Minor Phase, Dialogues between Christian Communities

> Crisis A: Engaging Docetizing Gentile Christians and Their Teachings
> Crisis B: Engaging Christian Institutionalizing Tendencies (Diotrephes and His Kin)
> Crisis C: Engaging Dialectically Christians' Presentations of Jesus and His Ministry (actually reflecting a running dialogue over *all three* periods)
> (The evangelist continues to teach and perhaps write; the Epistles are written by the Johannine Elder, who then finalizes and circulates the testimony of the Beloved Disciple after his death.)

The post-Johannine situation reflects the spurned docetizing preachers' taking the Johannine Gospel with them, leading into what eventually became some parts of second-century Christian Gnosticism (including eventual Johannine influences upon Heracleon, the Gospel of Truth, and the Gospel of Philip, among other texts). The Johannine Gospel becomes a favorite among orthodox Christians in the broader Mediterranean world, and Montanus and his followers in Asia Minor are moved by its influence to seek to restore the spirit-based vitality of the church. John's dialectical Christology becomes a source of debate among Christians, and eventually the Johannine Gospel is employed to combat gnostic influences (Marcion and Valentinus) and to challenge those who would reject the Johannine writings (referred to pejoratively as the *alogoi*) for secondary reasons (references to the Paraclete, differences with the Synoptics, confusion over the Apocalypse, advocating a particular paschal calendar, etc.). By the turn of the second century CE, the Fourth Gospel has become the "spiritual" gospel (alongside the somatic gospels) written by "John the Theologian," a great source of debate within Christology studies and Jesus studies to the present day.

Summary

Within this overall theory, the preaching and teaching of the Beloved Disciple is taken to represent the constructive work of the Johannine evangelist, whoever he might have been. And the author of the Epistles—the Johannine Elder—is taken to be the compiler, who edited at least the final edition of the Johannine Gospel after the death of the Beloved Disciple. I use the term "compiler," because (with Brown) the editor's work seems conservative—trying to preserve the testimony of the evangelist—rather than innovative (even leaving rough transitions in the text, here and there). Of course, he could have played a role in recording earlier editions of the Gospel as well, so that possibility could account for some linguistic similarities—as well as differences—between the Johannine Gospel and Epistles. Other leaders may have also contributed to the Johannine corpus, but such an overall theory is arguable *whoever* these figures might have been. With Culpepper and others, one's interpretation of the Johannine writings must be based on the literary anatomy of the texts themselves rather than risk getting mired down in particulars of authorship or composition inferences.[29]

Conclusion and Implications: Interpreting the Johannine Epistles in the Light of the Dialectical Johannine Situation

In the light of an overall theory regarding the Johannine situation and the composition of its literature, a suitable foundation is laid for interpreting the Johannine Epistles. The first two Epistles of John especially show evidence of building on some of the teaching that has been a part of an earlier edition of the Johannine Gospel, as a "new commandment" of Jesus has become an "old commandment" that has been heard from the beginning—providing the centripetal means of holding the commu-

---

29. As differing approaches to the origin and development of the Johannine tradition hinge upon three premises—who the author must have been, who the author cannot have been, and inferences from literary phenomena whoever the author(s) might have been—the latter (as advanced especially by Culpepper 1983, 1998) is the strongest way to proceed (Anderson 2011, 93–124). Therefore, the above three paradigms are arguable, regardless of who the Johannine evangelist and Elder might have been, despite the fact that the extensive and diverse second-century testimonies to "two Johns at Ephesus" deserves renewed, critical consideration.

nity together against centrifugal forces (John 13:34 → 1 John 2:3–7; 4:21; 2 John 1:5–6). Further, the appeal to abide in Jesus has changed into an exhortation to abide in *the teaching about Jesus*—communicated by the Elder and others. In addition, the extensive appeals to consider Jesus as the Christ and the Son of the Father in the central part of the gospel narrative have shifted in their thrust to a warning to secessionists—if one does not receive the Son, one will indeed forfeit the Father (John 3:31–36; 5:19–27; 12:44–50 → 1 John 2:22–24). And, emphases on the Holy Spirit's being in and with Jesus's followers are echoed by the Elder's reminder that believers have no need for anyone to teach them outwardly, as they possess the inward guidance of the Spirit. In these ways, the Epistles reflect upon and develop further particular themes in the Gospel.

If the inference of supplementary material added to the Gospel is correct, however, later material in the Johannine Gospel also reflect some of the issues in play as presented in the Epistles. The emphasis on the guidance of the Holy Spirit is expanded, then, to affirm the work of the Paraclete in convicting believers of sin and of righteousness and guiding them through a hostile situation in the world. Further, challenges to the docetizing tendencies of the false teachers' precipitating the second antichristic threat are countered by emphases upon the Word-become-flesh, ingesting the flesh and blood of the Son of Man, water and blood flowing forth from the side of Jesus, and the sure martyrdom of Jesus's followers (1 John 4:1–3; 2 John 1:7 → John 1:14; 6:51–58; 19:34–35; 21:18–24). In addition, emphases upon first-hand relationship with Jesus and one's witness being "true" become asserted with reference to the eyewitness and Beloved Disciple, whose "testimony is true" (3 John 1:12 → John 19:35; 21:24). And the prologue of 1 John has become expanded into a full-fledged worship hymn, recapitulating the main themes of the Gospel's earlier rendering and serving as an engaging introduction to the finalized circulation of the Johannine evangel (1 John 1:1–4 → John 1:1–18). Of course, some of these connections could be envisioned as the influence flowing in the other direction, or even both, but the value of seeing the Epistles as being produced before-and-after the Gospel fits well with the textual evidence.[30]

In addition to noting possible interfluence between the Gospel's narrative and the Epistles, interpreting the Johannine Epistles in the light of

---

30. In addition to Brown, the view that the Epistles are written between an earlier and final edition of the Johannine Gospel is shared by Kenneth Grayston (1984) and Von Wahlde (2010a), among others.

the Johannine dialectical situation clarifies several issues regarding its content. First, *claiming to be "without sin"* is less likely to be a factor of gnostic perfectionism and more likely to reflect disagreement within the Johannine community over what is sin and what is not. Despite the fact that most Christian gnostics would have been docetists, it is not the case that all docetists were gnostics. Thus, in the light of discussions over which sins were death-producing, in contrast to less momentous ones, the emphasis of the Elder in 1 John 1 was most likely a challenge to members of the Johannine situation who disagreed that what they were doing was sinful. Therefore, disagreements between community members of Jewish and gentile origins over assimilative issues were most likely the backdrop for controversies over sin and sinlessness in 1 John.

Second, the exhortation to *love not the world* in the Johannine Epistles reflects not the sectarian stance of an ingrown community, but groups attempting to straddle Jewish and gentile understandings of faith and practice, having been largely separated from the synagogue while still seeking to maintain a basic set of Jewish values. In that sense, Johannine Christianity in Asia Minor faced multiethnic, interreligious, and cross-cultural tensions, making it far more cosmopolitan than sectarian. If one were to consider the second generation of what Wayne Meeks (2003) describes elsewhere as "urban" Christianity, seeing the Johannine struggles with loving "the world" as factors of civic engagement in tension with markers of Jewish ideals, things become a bit clearer. Johannine Christianity thus had more in common with the other mission churches in Rome, Corinth, Thessalonica, and Galatia than with Qumranic Judaism.

Third, the secession of Johannine Christians in 1 John 2:18–25 reflects not the departure of Cerinthian protognostics, but of Jewish family and friends, who refused to remain committed to the teaching that Jesus was indeed the Messiah/Christ and who likely returned to the local synagogue whence they had been distanced. As the appeal for their return to the synagogue was likely motivated around loyalty to "the Father," family relationships, and Jewish monotheism, an emphasis upon forfeiture of the Father if they denied the Son can be seen to be challenging such investments directly. In the light of plausible appeals to Jewish loyalties, rhetorical echoes advocating being "children of Abraham" and "disciples of Moses" in the Gospel's narrative make the attraction of synagogue appeals palpable. In disciplining Jesus-related perceived "ditheism" by means of the Birkat Haminim and other religious emphases, Jewish leaders in Asia Minor might not have intended synagogue expulsions; the departure of

Jesus adherents from Jewish worship settings may have been the unintended consequence of disciplinary measures. As distanced Jewish members of Johannine Christianity were then proselytized back into the Jewish community of faith, it is now the Johannine Christians who feel abandoned, expressing their disappointment with the conjecture that "they never really were a part of us" (1 John 2:19). Therefore, the first antichristic threat involved the appeal of religious certainty over and against faith in Jesus as the Messiah/Christ within a fledgling community of faith.

Fourth, the last word of the first Johannine Epistle is likely the first word in terms of its acute religious concern: *little children, stay away from idols!* (1 John 5:21). Given the rising requirement of emperor worship under Domitian (81–96 CE), a new set of crises presented themselves for Jesus adherents in the Greco-Roman world. (1) As Jesus adherents could no longer claim Jewish identity if distanced from the synagogue, whether on their own or by synagogue leaders, they were no longer under the dispensation for the Jews allowing them to forego the demands of emperor worship if they "tithed" two drachmas to Jupiter's temple in Rome each year—the exact amount traditionally required as the expected tithe to the temple in Jerusalem before its destruction. Therefore, Christians of Jewish origin were forced to commit loyalty to Caesar, as they could no longer claim the dispensation as Jews. (2) The expectation that gentile believers were to forego public demonstrations of emperor laud, potentially risking life and limb, must have introduced a momentous crisis among the mission churches. As some Roman officials may have invited superficial though insincere ways of meeting the minimal imperial requirement, some gentile believers saw no conflict between inward loyalty to Jesus as the Christ and the demonstration of outward loyalty to Caesar. (3) Lest it be construed, however, that emperor worship was the only issue operative, a longstanding practice of empire expansion in the Mediterranean world was to coopt other religious and civic customs in order to diminish local resistance to the imperial presence. As a means of subverting Jewish monotheism and its ethical demands, Antiochus Epiphanes (nearly three centuries earlier, ca. 167 BCE) is reported in 2 Macc 6:1–9 not only to have set up a statue of Zeus in the Jerusalem temple, but also to have filled its corridors with cultic prostitution, to have commanded monthly celebrations of the emperor's birthday, and to have required sacrifices and participation in the Dionysius cult announced by the wearing of ivy garlands and wreaths. As a means of instilling Antiochine Hellenism, members of other Greek cities were encouraged to institute such practices and to kill Jews who did not participate in regional civic culture. Therefore, the admonition to stay away from idols must have carried extensive cultural implications not only involving outright emperor worship but also participating in local civic celebrations as a means of vying for *Neokoros* (temple-keeper) status, in competition with Pergamum for imperial honors in the region.

Fifth, it is against this backdrop that the assimilative teachings of the second antichristic threat should be understood. The antichrists of 1 John 4:1–3 and 2 John 1:7 were not secessionists but invasionists. The perception of false teachings by gentile Christian traveling ministers probably revolved around discussions of what was allowable in terms of faith and practice, with an acute emphasis on the latter (Jude 4). If gentile Christian leaders disagreed with ethical and religious standards advocated by Jewish-Christian leaders regarding how "Jewish" followers of Jesus needed to be, they may have argued something parallel to the earlier Pauline debates over grace-redemption over and against works-righteousness. On this note, the Elder may be seen to be coopting the propitiation theme (1 John 2:1) and pushing the implications of the costly sacrifice of Christ toward an emphasis upon costly discipleship among his followers. As gentile Christian preachers probably were more liberal in their teachings on cultural assimilation (i.e., less insistent upon forsaking Hellenistic cultural and festive practices in exchange for Jewish religious standards), they probably resisted Jewish-Christian challenges with the appeal that abundant life through Christ was intended to make things better, not to invite suffering. When reminded that Jesus suffered on the cross, the Hellenistic response was likely that he, if he was indeed divine, could not have suffered—thus, neither need his disciples do so in order to be faithful in the world. Therefore, docetizing Christology may not have been their lead thesis; it may have posed as a means of legitimating greater laxity regarding Christian lifestyle expectations around the turn of the first century CE. As with most debates, it is often not theory (or theology) that drives the consternation, but praxis (or ethical dimensions). As in the letters of Ignatius, the docetists' denial of a suffering Jesus and reminders of his suffering via eucharistic practices had to do primarily with the moral implications involved. If Jesus did not suffer, his followers need not do so in their assimilating existence in the world. Therefore, like the eyewitness testimony at the cross, water and blood and the Spirit testify to the implications of discipleship. Grace is not cheap, and following Jesus in the world implies being willing to suffer with him on the cross if one expects to be raised with him in the afterlife. Solidarity with Jesus and his community implies the willingness to ingest his flesh and blood; without faithfulness, one's faith is of no avail.

Sixth, the moral exhortation to love one another becomes the organizing means by which the Elder seeks to hold his community together in the face of its intense and divisive debates over lifestyle, faith, and its implications. Here the "new commandment" of Jesus to love one another has become the "old commandment" that has been heard from the beginning (John 13:34–35; 15:12–17; 1 John 3:11–4:21; 2 John 1:5). While some interpreters have distanced the appeal for love within community from the exhortation of the Synoptic Jesus to love one's enemies (Matt 5:44; Luke 6:27–35), in addition to loving God and neighbor (Matt 19:19; 22:39; Mark 12:31–33; Luke 10:27), the difference is directional rather than qualitative. Indeed, it can be more difficult to love those with whom one is close than to love a more distanced adversary, although the latter is also a challenge. It could also be that the Johannine emphasis on loving one another may have grown out of impatience with believers who felt they had been successful in their love for God and neighbor, but who had been impatient or even strident within the community of faith. Therefore, to hold community members accountable to the implications of their self-identifying priority of loving God (whom one has not seen) as the greatest of commandments, a reminder of the need to love brothers and sisters (whom one has seen; cf. Anderson 2012) poses a reminder to be faithful to the central teachings of Jesus as well as their implications. Reflecting again a general appeal to order rather than a more specific disciplining of particular irritating actions within the community, the Elder's love-oriented appeals were relatively unsuccessful, as community members split off in Jewish directions (the first antichristic crisis) and as false teachers advocated problematic assimilation in the world (the second antichristic crisis).

Seventh, as a means of staving off docetizing teachings, assimilative tendencies, and schismatic developments, Diotrephes appears to have been asserting monoepiscopal authority in an effort to foster Christian unity and to ward off threats to the movement. In doing so, he seems to be following the counsel of someone like Ignatius of Antioch, who slightly later calls for the appointing of a single bishop in every church—one who will maintain unity within the community as a function of being entrusted with Petrine keys to the kingdom (Matt 16:17–19). Just as Ignatius also dealt with a Judaizing crisis, imperial Roman hegemony, docetizing teachers, and questions of authority, Diotrephes appears to have embraced the monoepiscopal approach to addressing these issues. In doing so, however, he seems threatened by Johannine Christian leaders, and not only does he forbid them from visiting his church, he also intends to expel any from his own community who take them in. Plausibly, he was threatened by their egalitarianism, especially if Johannine claims to Spirit-based and inclusive governance bore apostolic claims, challenging his own authority claims within a Petrine trajectory. Note that the Elder has written to Diotrephes directly, has also written to "the church" (plausibly a Christian center, such as Antioch, whence Diotrephes may have been deriving his authority), and is promising to come for a visit—resembling the accountability procedures of Matt 18:15–17. In contrast to institutionalizing developments in the third Christian generation, the Johannine tradition challenges such innovations in the memory of an earlier, more primitive approach to organization and governance, rooted in the memory of more familial and egalitarian approaches of the charismatic prophet from Nazareth. In terms of historicity, the Johannine trajectory here, critically, bears considerable weight.

Eighth, this may also explain why the Elder finalized and circulated the Johannine Gospel as an appeal to an apostolic and eyewitness memory of Jesus and his intention for the church. It is not hierarchical innovations that bear the seal of apostolic authorization alone, but the risen Christ seeks to lead his church by means of the Paraclete, the Holy Spirit, accessible to all believers, and directly so. This is not an exclusively Johannine motif; it is foundational within the memory of Jesus's teachings in all the gospel traditions, including Q (Matt 10:16–20; Mark 13:11; Luke 12:11–12; 21:12–15; John 14:26; 16:2–13), and in the material added to the Johannine Gospel, Peter even affirms such (John 6:68–69). Upon the aging and eventual death of the Beloved Disciple, the Elder continues to face increasing challenges of holding communities together, staving off false teachings, and challenging abrupt implementations of institutionalizing innovations among the churches of Asia Minor. In addition to dealing with Diotrephes and his kin directly and appealing to centralizing innovators within the region, the Elder finalizes and distributes the testimony of the Beloved Disciple, witnessing not only to the ministry of Jesus but also to the ongoing leadership of the risen Lord through the Holy Spirit. In that sense, the Johannine Gospel and Epistles were not backwater compositions taking place in a cul-de-sac (with Käsemann 1968). No. They were produced in the thoroughfare of traveling ministries throughout Anatolia and Asia Minor, directly between Antioch and Rome, and at the center of the Pauline Mission a generation or two later. That being the case, they came to influence both orthodoxy and heterodoxy in second-century Christianity precisely because of their use and prominence among the churches. And, they have continued to influence Christian movements in every generation hence, contributing to dialogue over governance issues within the church and beyond (Anderson 2005).

Therefore, in reflecting on the Johannine community that Raymond Brown left behind, we indeed see not only the larger perspective of the Johannine eagle—soaring above the other New Testament writings in transcendent perspective; we also get a sense of the eaglets (building on Brown's imagery) scrapping and vying for order and place within the nest, as threats were being faced from without and from within. While most of Brown's inferences remain worth building upon for future interpreters, alternative insights along the way suggest new venues worthy of consideration within future commentaries and treatments of the Johannine Epistles.[31]

In the light of the Fourth Gospel's dialogical autonomy, this new overall theory also has extensive implications for interpreting the Johannine Epistles within their highly dialectical situation. Bringing Roman imperialism into the picture, identifying the antichrists as two different threats, seeing docetizing tendencies of gentile Christians being more of an issue than full-blown Gnosticism, and noting debates over particularities of what should be considered "sin" add new insights into the contexts and crises faced by audiences to whom the Epistles were written. Given his untimely death in 1998, one wonders how Brown would have responded to this alternative approach to an overall theory. Whatever the case, the Johannine community of scholars today shares with and learns from one another in ways that not only seek the truth, but at times might even further it. And, as is ever the case, the truth—even when it is only approximated—is always liberating.

---

31. One of my current projects is writing the Eerdmans Two Horizon Commentary on the Johannine Epistles (anticipated in 2015), and that study will build on the above analyses in ways I hope will contribute to both theology and exegesis. This overall theory is laid out in relation to the larger set of New Testament writings and their contextual histories in Anderson 2014.

The Relationship between the Gospel and 1 John

R. Alan Culpepper

In 1975 Rudolf Schnackenburg (1992, 34) observed that "the question of the relationship between [the Gospel of John] and 1 John was much discussed in the past, but today it has lost its interest." In recent decades, the issue of the relationship between the Gospel and the Epistles has been tied to the history of the Johannine community, and the Epistles have been interpreted as a response to dissension over the interpretation of the Gospel. Judith Lieu has challenged the prevailing approach, offering an alternative reading of the Epistles as more pastoral than polemical and independent of the Gospel, drawing instead on common Johannine tradition.

The question of the relationship between these documents has therefore returned to the forefront of scholarship on the Johannine Epistles. The discussion, moreover, has also evolved, with interest shifting from the verbal, grammatical, and stylistic evidence for and against common authorship to historical reconstructions based on theological and polemical elements in the Epistles.

The growing influence of theories regarding the history of the composition of the Gospel of John, especially following the publication of Rudolf Bultmann's commentary in 1941, its introduction to English speaking audiences by D. Moody Smith in 1965, its translation into English in 1971, and the work of Robert Fortna and Urban von Wahlde have also shifted the grounds for discussion of the relationship between the Gospel and the Epistles. Indeed, Howard Marshall (1978, 39) observed that "until there is some degree of consensus regarding the composition of the Gospel, there is little progress that can be made with regard to the relation between the Gospel and the Epistles."

I am concerned principally with the issue of sequence and relationship, although the question of authorship cannot be avoided.[1] The issue is important, because it is pivotal for the interpretation of the Epistles and it is wonderfully complicated. The relationship of one or more of the Epistles (e.g., 1 John) might be judged to be different from that of the other Epistles. In addition, alternatively, the earlier writing may or may not be judged to be a source or basis for the later, and the later may or may not be viewed as an exposition, clarification, or advance over the earlier. The variations are numerous if not limitless. I will therefore focus my concern to the relationship, especially the sequential relationship, between the Gospel and 1 John.

My intent is to survey recent developments in this discussion, clarify the issues that impinge on this question, and offer some modest suggestions regarding how these issues are interrelated and how they may be evaluated.

1. Background

C. H. Dodd's article on the "The First Epistle of John and the Fourth Gospel" in 1937, in which he compared the style, language, and thought of the Gospel and 1 John and concluded that they were written by different authors, is a touchstone for English scholarship on this question. Dodd observed that the Epistles diverge strikingly from the Gospel in their eschatology, the significance of the death of Jesus, and the doctrine of the Holy Spirit. Dodd (1937, 156) added that the author of 1 John was "quite possibly a disciple of the Fourth Evangelist, and certainly a diligent student of his work. He has soaked himself in the Gospel, assimilating its ideas and forming his style upon its model." The year following the publication of Dodd's (1946) commentary on the Epistles, in which he reiterated the conclusions of his earlier article, Wilbert Howard (1947, 12–25) attempted to refute Dodd's position point by point and thus to reassert the common authorship of the Gospel and the three Epistles. W. G. Wilson (1948) and A. P. Salom (1955) examined the linguistic data and reached the same conclusion. German scholarship of the mid-twentieth century maintained the view that the Epistles, or at least 1 John, were written after the Gospel.

---

1. Kim 2003, 307: "Dabei muss die Reihenfolge des JohEv und der JohBr, die auch für das Verhältnis zwischen dem JohEv und der JohBr erforderlich ist, getrennt von der Frage der Verfasserschaft erörtert werden."

Drawing on Ernst Haenchen's (1960) "Neuere Literatur zu den Johannesbriefen," Bultmann offered the following synopsis of the issue:

> The question of the relationship of the Epistles to the Gospel is basically the question of how 1 John is related to the Gospel. The close affinity in language and content between the two books makes it understandable that the identity of the authors has often been asserted and is frequently asserted even today. I cannot agree with this supposition. The decisive argument against this identification, as Haenchen has correctly observed, is the following: the Gospel of John and 1 John are directed against different fronts. Whereas the Gospel is opposed to the "world," or to the Jews who are its representatives, and therefore to non-Christians, the false teachers who are opposed in 1 John are within the Christian community and claim to represent the genuine Christian faith. This shows that 1 John originates in a period later than the Gospel.... The relationship between 1 John and the Gospel rests on the fact that the author of 1 John had the Gospel before him and was decisively influenced by its language and ideas. (1973, 1)

The magisterial commentaries of Raymond Brown and Schnackenburg took radically different positions on these issues. Schnackenburg treated 1 John as essentially independent of the Gospel:

> The comparison of the two writings yields one positive result. It is impossible to regard the epistle merely as a companion piece to [the Gospel of John]. It is a completely independent literary product. It neither presupposes the existence of the written Gospel, nor does it leave the reader to expect such a work dealing with the earthly life of the Son of God to follow. This means that the question of the priority of the two writings is unanswerable. (1992, 39)

On the other hand, Schnackenburg (1992, 39) adds, "Most scholars today agree about the priority of the Gospel. Menoud's suggestion that the Letter was composed between the dissemination of the gospel tradition in oral form and its completion in writing, has much to commend it." In the preface to the English translation, however, Schnackenburg praised Brown's commentary on the Epistles, calling the publication of Brown's commentary "the most important event that has occurred" since the original publication of his own commentary. Given the centrality of Brown's theory that 1 John is a response to the secessionists' interpretation of the Gospel, it is somewhat surprising to see that Schnackenburg (1992, xi) adds that

"Brown's interpretations are usually close to mine, though he sometimes takes a line of his own. It has not been possible for me to enter into a detailed discussion of his view. His commentary represents a definite advance and is a high point of contemporary scholarship."

In Brown's (1982, 35) view, the debate between the Elder and the opponents is an intra-Johannine debate. First John is modeled on the literary structure of the Gospel, and the setting of the Epistles was an outgrowth of tendencies already at work in the Johannine community at the time the Gospel was written. Both the Elder and the opponents were influenced by the earlier stages of the Johannine tradition, evident in the Gospel, so both the issues and the avenues of response open to the Elder were conditioned by this shared tradition. Nevertheless, Brown (1982, 91 n. 210) nuances his position by asserting that the redactor worked on the Gospel after 1 John was written. Influential as this view has been, the sequence of the Johannine Epistles and their relationship to the Gospel continues to be debated.

Given the intractability of this issue and the diversity of perspectives in contention in current scholarship, I propose to survey recent scholarship, taking particular notice of the evidence and arguments adduced with the hope that doing so will clarify the debate and advance the conversation.

2. Survey of Recent Scholarship

The bibliography is extensive. While noting the classic, older statements, I have focused on the scholarship of the past generation. Before offering this list, however, it is important to remember that historical knowledge is not established by popular vote, even among scholars. New data and new arguments can overturn long-established positions. In reading through a sample of the relevant literature, however, I found that the conclusions on this question fall into five general categories:

> (1) *1 John was written after the Gospel.* The conclusion of Alan Brooke (1912), Dodd (1937, 1946), Hans Conzelmann (1954), and Bultmann ([1967] 1973) has, not surprisingly, continued to claim the broadest base of support since 1970.
> (2) *1 John was written before the Gospel.* Although this remains a minority position, it has been affirmed in recent decades by Ekkehard Stegemann (1985), Georg Strecker (1986), Udo Schnelle (1992), Allen Dwight Callahan (2005), and Charles Talbert (1992), who allows it as a possibility.

(3) *1 John is independent of the Gospel.* Lieu (1986, 2008a) has defended the view that 1 John is independent of the Gospel and needs to be interpreted on its own terms. Strecker (1989) affirmed this view, as does Peter Rhea Jones (2009). This position also requires us to distinguish the issues of sequence and dependence or independence. It is at least theoretically possible, for example, that 1 John was written after the Gospel but by someone who, contrary to Brown's view, did not reference, depend on, follow the structure of, or seek to clarify the Gospel. In other words, sequence and dependence or independence are separate issues.

(4) *The sequence cannot be determined.* Schnackenburg (1992, originally 1953) and Marshall (1978) claimed that we cannot now determine whether the Gospel or 1 John was written first.

(5) *1 John was written sometime during the period of the composition of the Gospel.* A significant cadre of scholars now claims that the Epistle was written late in the process of the composition of the Gospel: Georg Richter (1968), Hans-Josef Klauck (1991a), Fernando Segovia (1982), Kenneth Grayston (1984), Martin Hengel (1989), von Wahlde (1990 and 2010a), Walter Schmithals (1992), Colin Kruse (2000), Theo Heckel (2004), and Paul Anderson (2011). Others recognize this as a possibility: Talbert (1992), Thomas Johnson (1993), and John Painter (2002). This view is predicated on the now commonly accepted premise that the Gospel was composed over a period time, probably decades, during which one can speak of stages or editions of the Gospel.

The primary arguments are as follows:

2.1 Arguments for the Priority of the Gospel

The arguments for the priority of the Gospel are generally more numerous and more diverse than those advanced for other positions.

2.1.1

The Gospel addresses the conflict that led the believers to separate from the synagogue, while 1 John addresses an intracommunity conflict. As Smith (1991, 12) noted, "the Jews" are not mentioned in the Epistles. Since it is scarcely possible that the dissension reflected in 1 John occurred prior to the separation of the Johannine believers from the synagogue, the Gospel was composed before 1 John.

2.1.2

The prologue of the Gospel can be understood on its own terms, but the prologue of the Epistle is difficult to understand apart from knowledge of the prologue of the Gospel. Heckel (2004, 435) states the argument as follows: "Ich meine allerdings, dass der Prolog des Briefes ohne den bereits vertrauten Prolog des Evangeliums nicht verstehbar ist, dass also der Prolog eine Leserschaft voraussetzt, die das Evangelium bereits kennt."

2.1.3

First John follows the structure of the Gospel. Brown (1982, 122–29) proposes the following analysis of the structure of the Gospel and 1 John.

John	1 John
Prologue 1:1–18	1:1–4
Part 1: Theme: "God is light" (1 John 1:5) 1:19–12:50	1:5–3:10
Part 2: Theme "God is love" (1 John 4:8) 13:1–20:29	3:11–5:12
Statement of Purpose 20:30–31	5:13
Epilogue 21:1–25	5:14–21

The parallel statements of purpose and their comparable positions in the two writings are particularly telling.

> Now Jesus did many other signs in the presence of his disciples, which are not written in this book. But *these are written so that you may come to believe* that Jesus is the Messiah, *the Son of God*, and that through believing *you may have life* in his name. (John 20:30–31)
>
> *I write these things to you who believe* in the name of *the Son of God*, so that *you may know that you have eternal life*. (1 John 5:13)

Both statements contain three elements: (1) a statement of the purpose of the writing, (2) the title "Son of God," and (3) a reference to the ultimate goal of having life or eternal life. The question of whether John 20:30–31 places priority on leading readers to believe or confirming their faith is debated. Nevertheless, as Painter commented:

> If literary dependence is suspected, this evidence implies the use of the Gospel by the author of 1 John. The placing of 1 John 5:13 prior to the end of the Epistle seems to presuppose the comparable conclusion of the Gospel prior to its actual end. Because ch. 21 appears to have been added by a hand or hands other than those of the evangelist, this implies that 1 John presupposes the final form of the Gospel including ch. 21. (2002, 71)

We may also note that if this analysis of the parallel structures of the Gospel and 1 John is accurate, it supports a closer rather than a more independent relationship between the Gospel and the Epistle and a dependence of the Epistle on the Gospel rather than on common Johannine tradition. Painter (2002, 73) also contends that "the similarities between the two endings may imply that the Gospel was known complete with ch. 21. Thus 1 John 5:14–21 follows the conclusion in 5:13 just as John 21 follows the conclusion of John 20:30–31."[2] This is a crucial point, because it has implications for both the composition of John and the argument that 1 John was written late in the composition history of the Gospel. On one hand, it means that John 21 was added fairly soon after John 1–20 or that it was part of the Gospel from the beginning. Alternatively, if the author of 1 John was the redactor who finished the Gospel and added John 21, Painter's argument would have to be modified. Either way, the author of 1 John is responsible for the parallels in the conclusions, either by imitation or by writing double conclusions for both the Gospel and 1 John.

2.1.4

Brooke (1912, xxvii) concluded the section of his introduction to the Epistles with the comment: "The impression left—the more clearly the longer the Epistle is studied—is that it was written to help and to warn those for whom the teaching of the Gospel, or 'a body of teaching like' it, had not accomplished all that the writer had hoped." This observation can be seen as foundational for much of the more recent scholarship on 1 John's polemical response to dissension in the Johannine community between

---

2. Zumstein (1996, 398) also advances this argument as evidence that 1 John imitates the structure of the Gospel. The evidence is not incontestable, however. Citing his commentary on 1 John 1:1–4 and 5:13 specifically, Strecker (1996, xl) contends that "no sufficient evidence can be presented to show that the author of the Johannine Letters used the Fourth Gospel."

the writing of the Gospel and the writing of 1 John. On the other hand, Lieu (1986, 210) has maintained the cogency of Brooke's caveat, "or a body of teaching like it" (i.e., the Gospel), contending that the "links 1 John has with the Gospel" may actually be "links with the community traditions behind the Gospel."

2.1.5

Conzelmann (1954, 194–201) noted that the phrase "from the beginning" is not used in an ecclesiastical sense in the Gospel, as it is in the Epistle, and that the tradition had become set in the interval between the writing of the two documents.

2.1.6

The realized eschatology of the community in the Gospel of John had been historicized so that in the Epistle it is being realized. The author of the Epistle is therefore an "imitator" of the Gospel. This argument was advanced by both Conzelmann and Günter Klein (1971, 261–326).

2.1.7

Brown's commentary develops the view that the positions of both the Elder and those who have left the community can be understood as divergent interpretations of the Gospel, especially in the areas of Christology, eschatology, pneumatology, and ethics. Consequently, "The thrust of I John is intelligible as a reaction to an *overemphasis* on high Christology, on death as glorification, on the activity of the Paraclete-Spirit as teacher, and on final eschatology" (1982, 35).

2.1.8

Tobias Nicklas shows that much of 1 John can be read as an attempt to answer a question suggested by the Gospel prologue, namely: What does it mean to be "children of God"? (see 1 John 3:1). "Meine These ist nun, dass sich nicht nur der Prolog des 1. Johannesbriefes auf den des Evangeliums beziehen lässt, sondern dass sich vielmehr grosse Teile des 1. Johannesbriefs (ja im Grunde die drei Johannesbriefe) als Antwort auf eine Frage lesen lassen, die sich im Johannesprolog ergibt: Was bedeutet es, 'Kinder Gottes' zu sein?" (Nicklas 2006, 61; see also Rusam 1993).

2.1.9

David Reis found that the author of 1 John imitates the voice of Jesus in the farewell discourse:

> By applying Jesus' words in the Farewell Discourse to his present situation, the author of 1 John seeks to construct a model for a Johannine identity.... Finally, addressing his community with these terms suggests that the presbyter had cast himself in the role of Jesus and was engaged in instructing and exhorting in the same way that Jesus did in his final message to his disciples. By becoming the 'mimetic voice' of Jesus, the author thus appears to be experimenting with a subtle and sophisticated technique that might circumvent the constraints that the Paraclete's importance had placed on Johannine leadership. (2003, 54)

2.2 Arguments for the Priority of 1 John

Support for the priority of 1 John is generally based on arguments regarding the prologue, the Paraclete, the Epistle's theology, especially its Christology, ecclesiology, eschatology, and its theology of Jesus's death.

2.2.1

The prologue of 1 John is less polished and hence probably earlier than the prologue of the Gospel (Robinson 1962–1963, 120–29; Miller 1989, 4 n. 7). As we noted in the previous section, proponents of the priority of the Gospel in relation to 1 John have argued that the prologue of the Epistle assumes knowledge of the prologue of the Gospel, so the evidential value of the relationship between the two prologues is debated and has been claimed for both positions.

2.2.2

Brooke (1912, xx) cited the astute observation that "the ἄλλος παράκλητος of Jn. xiv.16 was suggested by the doctrine of the Epistle, which presents Christ as the Paraclete (ii. 1)."

2.2.3

The theology of 1 John is closer to traditional early Christian perspectives on the significance of Jesus's death and future eschatology. Grayston (1984, 12), for example, commented: "When the Epistle is placed after the Gospel, it is necessary to explain why so much in the Epistle seems to reproduce ideas that belong to an earlier phase of Christian awareness."

2.2.4

Similarly, Brown (1982, 33) cited the argument that "terminology in I John reflective of Jewish apocalyptic (Antichrist, *anomia*, or 'Iniquity,' false prophets) and the warning against idolatry in 5:21 have been cited for the thesis that I John is more 'Jewish' than [the Gospel of John]." Brown responded, however, with the axiom that "early contents can *prove* no more than that the author knew old traditions, so that a date of writing (or at least of final editing) must be judged from the *latest* contents of a work" (34).

2.2.5

Schnelle turns the argument regarding controversy with docetism in 1 John on its head, arguing forcefully that it points to the priority of the Epistle:

> Because this conflict with docetic opponents is the only methodologically secure point from which to proceed in determining the time sequence of 1 John and the Gospel, 1 John is seen to have temporal priority, in that the Gospel evidently presupposes the acute conflict reflected in the letter and deals with it in theological terms. The fundamental and broadly conceived argumentation of the evangelist against a docetic Christology reveals a distance in time and subject matter from 1 John, which is still engaged in acute controversy. The letter names the problem, but a theological answer is found only later, in the Gospel. (2010, 228)

2.2.6

Strecker (1986, 47 n. 50) argued that the Gospel contains an ecclesiological perspective, so it cannot be placed early in the development of the Johannine tradition: "Die spezifische ekklesiologische Perspecktive im Johannesevangelium verbietet es, das vierte Evangelium an den Anfang der Enkwicklung der johanneischen Schule zu stellen." Moreover, contending that the early date of p^{52} (around 125 CE) is not secure and a date later in the second century is possible, Strecker says, "Diesem Ansatz entspricht die sachlich begründbare Feststellung dass der erste Johannesbrief eher noch vor dem Johannesevangelium abgefasst worden ist." Note, however, that in his commentary on the Epistles, Strecker (1989) argues that because the Johannine writings originated in the Johannine school, where there was vigorous engagement with the developing Johannine tradition, we should not think in terms of linear development or dependence of one writing on another (see below).

2.2.7

Callahan (2005) developed an interpretation of the history of the Johannine tradition based on the priority of the Epistles. The "root conflict" of the Johannine tradition is Diotrephes's rejection of the Elder's appeal for him to work with the Elder. In 2 John the Elder addresses a woman, "the elect lady," who leads a group that may collaborate with him. Then the Elder wrote the discourses that subsequently formed 1 John 2–5. An anonymous "editorial board of disciples" collected these discourses, composed 1 John 1, and disseminated the Epistle among the circles that had received the Elder. The themes and vocabulary of 1 John mark the Gospel—a narrative representation of Jesus, the "archetypal life of love" (Callahan 2005, 2–3).

2.3. Arguments for the Independence of 1 John

Lieu (2008, 8), who has championed the view that 1 John should be read on its own terms, independent of the Gospel, contends that "1 John nowhere appeals to or assumes knowledge of the Gospel, and indeed that the latter seems unlikely; rather each writing is, largely independently, reworking common or shared traditions." In passing we may note that Brooke (1912, xxiii), while he did not affirm the independence of 1 John, observed that "in none of these instances do we find any thought or expression in the Epistle which is obviously, and beyond all doubt, borrowed from the Gospel." C. Haas, Marinus de Jonge, and J. L. Swellengrebel recommended this position in their United Bible Societies handbook on the Epistles published in 1972 (p. 5). Wendy E. Sproston North (2001, 14–15) and Terry Griffith (2002, 5, 162, 209) have added further support for this position in their dissertations, and Jones (2009, 9) affirms what he calls "Lieu's Law." The following three arguments are advanced by Lieu.

2.3.1

First John may draw on community tradition rather than the Gospel: "Even if it can be shown that I John is dependent on the Gospel, this need not mean that the author has understood or followed it fully nor deny that where he differs, rather than showing a development from the Gospel he may be continuing the original thought of the community or developing an independent reflection on it" (Lieu 1986, 167). Strecker carried this point a step further, tying the origin of the Johannine writings to a Johannine school. Moreover, "the thesis of a Johannine school tradition is opposed to a linear literary analysis of the text.... Such a thesis is in danger of underestimating the liveliness of the discussions that are presumed by the Johannine writings and that shape their content" (Strecker 1996, xl).

2.3.2

The theological focus of 1 John is different from that of the Gospel:

> For while the fourth Evangelist builds his theology within an understanding of reality centred on Christ, I John makes his response using the community and the believer's experience as his theological interpretive key. If this fundamental difference of theological focus means that I John cannot be interpreted as a (one-sided) development of the theology of the Gospel, neither need it be the next stage in the history of the Johannine community following the Gospel. (Strecker 1996, 207)

2.3.3

The verbal, stylistic, and exegetical differences between the Gospel and 1 John also point to independent development of common tradition:

> The position taken here is that there is no compelling evidence of a direct literary relationship between 1 John and the Gospel in anything like the latter's current form; on the contrary, the consistent subtle differences of wording, inference, context and combination even where parallels appear close suggest that both writings draw independently on earlier formulations. Good examples are the way that 1 John 2:11 draws on a similar exegesis of Isa 6:10 to that found, more extensively, in John 12:40, or the different settings in which the formula 'because his/their/its deeds were evil' appears (1 John 3:12; John 3:19; 7:7; cf. 2 John 11; 3 John 10). (Lieu 2008, 17–18)

2.4. Arguments that the Sequence Is Indeterminable

The conclusion that the writings are independent from one another is a variation of the position that the sequence of the writings cannot be determined. By the nature of the case, it is difficult to frame an argument that the sequence of the writing of the Gospel and 1 John cannot be determined. It is a judgment based on the perceived lack of evidence for the relationship between the two writings (see Schnackenburg 1992, 39, quoted above).

2.5. Arguments for the Writing of 1 John during the Process of the Composition of the Gospel

The thesis that 1 John was written late in the period during which the Gospel was composed has attracted able advocates in recent years. The general acceptance of the view that the Gospel was composed over a period of time, through various stages or editions, opened the possibility that 1 John was written at some point during the composition process rather than before or after the Gospel was written. Grayston (1984, 10) commented that "the question has become 'where does the material of the Epistle stand in relation to the process by which the Gospel came into being and exercised its influence?'" Furthermore, "if the composition of the Gospel was the work of several hands it is possible to ask whether questions debated in the Epistle made some contribution to the Gospel in one of its stages of formulation." The obvious advantage of this solution is that it can account for the arguments that have been advanced by both those who conclude that the Epistle was written before the Gospel and those who hold that it was written after it. Grayston (1984, 10) contended that "passages in the Epistle often look like first attempts at material which later appears in the Gospel, where its presence can be justified if it began from the situation for which the Epistle was the earlier written response."

Not everyone has agreed, however. Marshall, writing a few years before the publication of Brown's commentary, rejected the view that the theology of the opponents in 1 John arose from their interpretation of the Gospel or an earlier version of it:

> We may well ask whether such views could have arisen out of a reading of the Gospel of John. Certainly in its present form the Gospel could not have been interpreted in this fashion. Suppose, however, that we

assume an earlier form of it, one in which it lacked the prologue (Jn. 1:1–18), references to the last day and the final judgment, such passages as John 6:51b–58; 19:31–37; and 20:24–29, the 'variant' form of the farewell discourse in John 15–16 (and 17), and the epilogue (Jn. 21); could a heretical interpretation be placed on what is left? Even in this form it is hard to see how the Gospel could have given rise to the heresy…. All this suggests that it is impossible to explain the theology of John's opponents as arising from a misreading of the Gospel. (1978, 40–41)

2.5.1

Attention has often focused on the relationship between the farewell discourse and 1 John. William Loader explained the unique proximity of John 15–17 to 1 John:

> The density of parallel motifs here is not to be explained only by the fact that similar concerns are being addressed. It reflects a similar origin. The parallels in John 15-17 are closer to I John than any other part of the gospel. This becomes all the more significant when we recognize that these chapters belong to the more recent stages of the gospel's composition and have been interposed to break the natural sequence between 14.31 and 18.1. They represent an expansion of Jesus' words to his disciples, the Christian community, probably in the light of a new situation which has arisen. (1992, xx)

Critical assessment of the relationship between the farewell discourse and 1 John has been divided, however. Grayston (1984, 14), who judged passages in the Epistle to be earlier than parallels in the Gospel, claimed that "the composer of Jn 13–17 took more seriously than I Jn the experience of the Spirit to which the dissidents bore testimony, but made sure that whole-hearted acceptance of the Spirit could never undermine the human existence of Jesus but always reinforced it." Brown (1982, 109), on the other hand, held that John 15–17 must have preceded 1 John: "John 15–17 contains ideas that would have been most helpful to the secessionists…. The least one may conclude is that, if chapters 15–17 and I John were written by the same man, they were written at very different stages in his life, and that the [Gospel of John] chapters were written before the secession occurred." David Rensberger (1997, 20) dismisses the argument that John 15–17 were added at the time the Epistles were written: "These passages are consistent with the rest of John, however (Rensberger 1992, 298–302); and 1 John's pattern of ascribing to God attributes that the Gospel ascribes to Jesus … applies to all literary levels of the Gospel, including these."

Early in his career Segovia examined the relationship between the farewell discourse and 1 John and concluded that a redactor added verses to this section of the Gospel at the time the Epistle was written:

> At some point along the line, either the author of I John or someone who shared his exact situation (an ultimate decision on this point is impossible to make) decided to incorporate his specific point of view into what appears to have been an already redacted form of the Fourth Gospel (e.g., vv. 3:31–36; 12:44–50). No doubt convinced of the rightness and traditional nature of his position, the individual inserted vv. 13:34–35 and 15:1–17 into their present context in the Gospel. (1982, 202)

Richter (1968, 36) took a further step by identifying the redactor of the Gospel as the author of the Epistles: "Wir im Verfasser von I Jo auch den Redacktor oder Herausgeber des vierten Evangeliums zu sehen haben" (see also Kruse 2000, 3). In doing so, he was following the proposal advanced by Emanuel Hirsch (1936, 170–79).[3] Hartwig Thyen (1971, and more recently Anderson 2011, 142–44) agreed. Since both the redactional material in John 13 and elsewhere in the Gospel (1:14–18; 5:26–29; 6:48–58; 15–17) reflects the same ecclesiastical concerns as the Epistle, Thyen (1971, 350 n. 19) concluded that the author of the Epistles was also responsible for the redaction of the Gospel. Segovia, however, disagreed, maintaining that at most one can only speak of "the same *Sitz im Leben*." If the author of 1 John were the redactor of the Gospel, one would expect to find overt or concealed references to the christological controversy in John. Nevertheless, Segovia concludes:

> It appears, therefore, as if the redactor that has been traced to the *Sitz im Leben* of I John has "sprinkled" that part of Jesus' life which immediately precedes his death with insertions designed to assert the centrality of that death in the life of the community and to trace the origin of the love command to the lips of Jesus himself as he prepared the disciples for his coming departure. (1982, 219)

---

3. See Hengel (1989, 88), who summarizes Hirsch's view: "An anti-Gnostic ecclesiastical redactor, who was at the same time the author of 1 John, revised the Gospel severely and by adding ch. 21 attributed its composition to the beloved disciple, whom he identified with John the Son of Zebedee. The letters also come from this redactor."

In his later work, we should note, Segovia (1991, viii) rejected both his earlier "excavative" analysis of the farewell discourse and the need to posit a variety of authors.

2.5.2

In addition to the farewell discourse, the place of the prologue and John 21 in relation to the composition of the Gospel and the relative dating of 1 John have been debated. Heckel argues that

> Exegesis of 1 Jn 1:1–4 shows that 1 John anchors the Johannine tradition in past history and presupposes a reader who knows John 1–20. Like its prologue the rest of 1 John ties its Christology expressly to the earthly Jesus and anchors its pneumatology historically. The complete collection of Johannine writings corresponds to this historicizing program in which the Johannine tradition finds its conclusion after 1 John in John 21. (2004, 425–43)

The resulting sequence of composition is therefore John 1–20, 1 John, and then John 21. Brown (1982, 111) rejected the theory that John 21 was added by the author of 1 John: "This reading of John 21 [Brown's] posits that the redactor-author of 21 and the epistolary author were different writers with a different opinion as to how the Johannine churches should proceed with regard to structure." Heckel agrees that John 21 was not written by the author of 1 John:

> Waren die Auseinandersetzungen im Brief noch innerjohanneisch, setzt das Nachtragskapitel eine Begegnung der johanneischen Überlieferung mit anderen *christlichen* Traditionen voraus. Und Joh 21 stilisiert sich als letztes Wort der im Evangelium bereits eingeführen Gestalt des Lieblingsjüngers. Nicht das Zeugnis eines immer wieder wirkenden Parakleten, sondern das vergangene Zeugnis des Schulgründers fixiert das Nachtragskapitel. (2004, 442)

Adding to the debate over authorship, Heckel (2004, 442 n. 55) identifies the Beloved Disciple as the Presbyter and concludes that the term "Beloved Disciple" was introduced into the Gospel by his disciples.

2.5.3

Decisive for Klauck (1991a, 47) is the recognition that the view of community and office are so different in John 21 and 1 John that the author of the Epistle could not have known John 21.

2.5.4

The most recent and detailed argument for placing 1 John during the latter stages of the composition of the Gospel has been developed by von Wahlde (2010a) in his three-volume work on the Gospel and Epistles of John, which is actually a history or "stratigraphy" (according to Smith) of the writings of the Johannine tradition. His work is the culmination of decades of reflection on these issues, and it is consistent with conclusions he formulated over twenty years ago. In *The Johannine Commandments*, von Wahlde (1990, 266) tentatively proposed that "the conclusions reached here would seem to suggest that those theories which suggest that the redaction of the gospel was performed to meet the issues confronted in 1 John would seem to be at least partially correct." Later on the same page, he added, "It is unlikely that the person responsible for the epistle is the same person responsible for the redaction of the gospel.... Nevertheless … it certainly seems appropriate to speak of the redaction of the gospel as being done from the same theological viewpoint and by someone who attempted to both confirm the theological position of the author of 1 John and who wrote to deal with a similar set of historical circumstances" (266). Now, twenty years later, in his *The Gospel and Letters of John*, von Wahlde places the writing of 1 John in response to the theological formulations of the second edition of the Gospel but prior to the third (and final) edition.

> When one studies the views of the opponents in the First Letter, it becomes clear that those opinions echo the theology of the second edition. Moreover, the views of the author of 1 John are similar in many ways to those of the author of the third edition. Yet it is clear from a detailed comparison of the material of the third edition of the Gospel with that of 1 John that 1 John comes from a period in the history of the community *after* the composition of the second edition of the Gospel but *before* the composition of the third. (2010a, 1:49)

Von Wahlde proposes eight factors that indicate that 1 John was written prior to the final edition of the Gospel.

(1) "First, in John 14:16, Jesus says to his disciples that he will send them 'another' Paraclete.... On the other hand, the statement in John 14:16 can only be understood once one reads 1 John to discover that the community also looked upon Jesus as a Paraclete. Thus, while 1 John 2:1 does not need John 14:16 in order to be understood, John 14:16 presupposes the existence of the material in 1 John 2:1 for full intelligibility." (2010a, 1:377–78)

(2) "Much the same can be said of the designation of the Paraclete as 'Spirit of Truth.' While this term appears three times in the Gospel (14:17; 15:26; 16:13), its full significance and the worldview within which it is conceptualized are not fully evident until one reads 1 John 4:1–6." (2010a, 1:378)

(3) "Third, in the third edition of the Gospel the commandment of mutual love is described as a 'new' commandment. This is said only once (13:34), and no explanation is given why it should be called 'new.' However, in 1 John 2:8, there is a discussion of the notions of 'new' and 'old' as they apply to the commandments." (2010a, 1:378)

(4) "Fourth, there is a peculiar shift in the source of the witness to the flow of blood and water from 1 John to the Gospel.... I would suggest that it is because the author of 1 John *is* the [Beloved Disciple] and does not want to attribute any special attention or validity to his own witness.... But the best explanation of 19:34 is that it is later than 1 John 5:6–7 since the author of 1 John could not be referring to the text of 19:34 as the explanation of 'coming in water.' Rather, 19:34 is included by the author of the third edition as an affirmation *within the narrative of the Gospel* of what was expressed theologically in 1 John." (2010a, 1:379–80)

(5) "Fifth, we have alluded above to the fact that in the Gospel there is a clear interest in the authoritative office given to Peter. This is evident from the portrayal of the [Beloved Disciple] as superior to Peter spiritually yet cognizant of the authority given to Peter.... This would indicate that at the time of the First Epistle the issue of ecclesiastical authority and the community's relation to the Petrine churches was not yet a reality." (2010a, 1:380–81)

(6) "In the third edition of the Gospel, future eschatology involves bodily resurrection (5:28-29; 6:36, 40d, 44c, 54b).... Given the lack of reference in 1 John we must conclude that the need to affirm a belief in bodily resurrection arose *after* the composition of 1 John." (2010a, 1:381)

(7) Von Wahlde examines "eleven major elements of Johannine theology, sketching the development of these concepts throughout the history of the tradition. *In every case where there are differences, 1 John shows development over the second edition and the third edition shows development over 1 John.*" (2010a, 1:382, emphasis original)

(8) "Eighth, and finally, other aspects of the Gospel make more sense if they are seen to be developments subsequent to the writing of 1 John" (2010a, 1:384). Here von Wahlde analyzes references to righteousness and petitionary prayer.

At the end of the third volume, von Wahlde (2010a, 3:423) asserts that "the third edition does not simply and wholly represent the theological perspective of 1 John. There are a number of differences in the third edition that take the viewpoint of 1 John a step further." Von Wahlde therefore contends that the author of the third edition identifies "the Elder" of 2 and 3 John, who was also the author of 1 John, as the "Beloved Disciple" (see the views of Hirsch, Richter, Thyen, Hengel, and Heckel above). The author of the third edition was not the Elder and not the Beloved Disciple. Neither the earlier editions of the Gospel nor 1 John defend the authority of an ecclesiastical leader or shepherd. The author of the third edition, however, refers to the Elder, the apostolic eyewitness of the Johannine tradition, as the Beloved Disciple (von Wahlde 2010a, 3:417–28).

Analysis and Conclusions

It is worth noting that, although their views are different, Segovia, Brown, Hengel, and von Wahlde agree that the author of the Epistles was not the redactor of the Gospel, in opposition to Richter, Thyen, and Anderson, who argue that the author of 1 John was indeed the redactor of the Gospel. I agree with the former; it is unlikely that the Elder was the redactor. Painter (2002:69) contends that while Brooke's interpretation of the setting of 1 John accounts for its difference in viewpoint from the Gospel, "it does not adequately take account of the tangled Greek of 1 John and its consequent lack of clarity. This, more than differences of thought in the Gospel and 1 John, poses a problem for the view of common authorship." Anyone who has attempted to translate 1 John recognizes the force of Painter's observation, and it is also a difficulty for the view that the Elder was the redactor of the Gospel, unless the redaction is confined to only a few passages. The difference in the use of particles in the two documents is also telling (e.g., οὖν occurs 194 times in the Gospel but never in 1 John). It is unlikely that the Elder was the redactor.

On the other hand, von Wahlde's reconstruction, while attractive, is not without problems. On his theory we have three editions of the Gospel, each by a different author: a first edition; a second edition that is theologically daring and innovative, the work of the Beloved Disciple/Elder in the Epistles; and a third edition that is the work of one of his disciples, whose additions and glosses in the third edition make theological advances over the Beloved Disciple/Elder. The third author also added all the Beloved Disciple references in the Gospel. Von Wahlde (2010a, 1:224–25) comments that the relationship of the second edition to the Beloved Disciple is "a trying question." Ultimately, he finds that the author of the second edition is otherwise unknown and that the author of the third edition identified the Elder (the author of the Epistles) as the Beloved Disciple. But if the author of the second edition is not the Beloved Disciple, then the Beloved Disciple is not the creative literary and theological author of the Johannine tradition. Following von Wahlde's view, the Johannine school would presumably be honoring the Elder as the Beloved Disciple, because he was an eyewitness and because he was their connection with Jesus, but the literary and theological genius of the Gospel remains unnamed and unrecognized. This is possible, but I think not likely. It places the influence of the Beloved Disciple late in the composition history of the Gospel rather than early and continuous through it. If the Beloved Disciple/Elder wrote the Epistles in response to the second edition of the Gospel (which was written by someone else), then the Beloved Disciple actually had little or no role in the composition of the Gospel and only a late influence, through the third author, on its content.

Another issue to be considered is that of the parallel structure of the Gospel and 1 John (see above). If the author of 1 John imitated the structure of the Gospel, as is widely held, then the Gospel had to contain John 21 before the Epistle was written. Alternatively, one would have to conclude that the Gospel imitated the structure of 1 John. Brown holds that the structure of 1 John was influenced by the structure of the Gospel, but John 21 may have been added to the Gospel by the redactor under the influence of the structure of the conclusion of 1 John (Brown 1982, 91 n. 210, 125, 128; see also Painter 2002, 73–74). Against Brown, I find the reverse much more plausible. One can readily understand why someone might find it necessary to add John 21 to the Gospel in order to bring various elements of the narrative to a satisfactory conclusion, quite apart from the structure of the conclusion of 1 John. On the other hand, the place of the purpose statement in 1 John 5:13 is striking when placed in context with the other structural parallels between the Gospel and the First Epistle. If there is imitation, it more likely that the Elder was influenced by the model of the completed Gospel than that the redactor was influenced by the structure of 1 John. The question of the relationship of 1 John to the Gospel, therefore, has implications for the place of John 21 in the Gospel's composition history and may argue that John 21 was originally part of the Gospel or, following von Wahlde's theory of three editions, part of the second edition of the Gospel (Thyen 1977, 259–99).

My review of these issues, and in particular von Wahlde's lucid delineation of the verbal, stylistic, and theological features of the Gospel and 1 John, has persuaded me of the advantages of placing the writing of 1 John late in the process of the composition of the Gospel rather than after the Gospel was completed. Nevertheless, I am not convinced that the Elder is the figure referred to in the Gospel as the Beloved Disciple. It still seems more plausible that the author of the first and second edition of the Gospel is the one named as the Beloved Disciple. Paradoxically, locating the writing of 1 John late in the composition history of the Gospel may be more important for understanding the Gospel than 1 John. This chronology allows interpreters to see the issues reflected in the Epistle in the late sections of the Gospel also, such as the prologue, John 6:60–66; 13:34–35; 15–17; and 21. Continued attention needs to be given to these passages with this view of the relationship between the Gospel and 1 John in mind, however, because there is still little agreement regarding how much of the Gospel should be assigned to this final stage in its composition.

Several points have emerged from this review of the debate over the relationship between the Gospel and 1 John:

(1) Whereas the debate over common authorship focused primarily on linguistic and stylistic data, much of the discussion now focuses primarily on theological development and what they reflect concerning the history of the Johannine tradition/community/school.

(2) The issue of the relationship between the Gospel and 1 John is now closely tied to one's interpretation of the opponents about whom the author of the Epistle warns his readers.

(3) Recognition that the Gospel is the product of an extended process of composition has opened consideration of the place of the writing of Johannine Epistles in this composition history.

(4) In addition to the diversity of opinion regarding the sequence of these writings, one also finds differences regarding the degree of dependence on (e.g., Brown) or independence (e.g., Lieu) of the Epistles from the Gospel, which in the latter case diminishes the importance of the question of sequence.

(5) This debate has implications for the composition history of the Gospel, in particular the authorship of John 15–17 and John 21, the origin of the references to the Beloved Disciple, and the identity of the Beloved Disciple and the redactor.

(6) The delineation of stages of composition of the Gospel and the differences between the Gospel and the Epistles continue to make the theory of a Johannine school, in which various authors wrote Johannine materials under the influence of the Beloved Disciple, an attractive solution to the complexities of the relationship between the Gospel and the Epistles.

(7) The view that 1 John was written during the composition of the Gospel, which has gained support in recent decades, offers variations that will have be sorted out in future investigations. At least the following variations must be considered further:

> (a) The work of the redactor/third author and the Elder reflect the same stage in the development of the tradition.
>
> (b) The author of the Epistle also wrote parts of the Gospel (e.g., John 15–17).
>
> (c) John 15–17 follows and reflects 1 John, but the two were written by different authors.
>
> (d) John 21 precedes 1 John (because the structure of 1 John imitates the structure of the Gospel, including the epilogue) and hence may have been an integral part of the Gospel from the beginning, or John 21 follows 1 John and reflects a view of community leadership not evident in the letter.
>
> (e) The author of the Epistle was, or was not, the final redactor of the Gospel.

While we may be making progress in understanding these issues, there is obviously much that remains to be resolved.

Composition of 1 John Relative to the Gospel

	Before	During	After	Independent	Indeterminable
1910					
1912			Brooke		
1920					
1930					
1936		Hirsch			
1937			Dodd		
1940					
1946			Dodd		
1950					
1954			Conzelmann		
1960					
1967			Bultmann		
1968		Richter			
1970					
1971			Klein		
1972				Haas et al.	
1973			Houlden		

	Before	During	After	Independent	Indeterminable
1974			Culpepper		
1953					Schnackenburg
1977			Bogart		
1978					Marshall
1980					
1982		Brown	Schunack		
		Segovia	Whitacre		
1984		Grayston	Smalley		
1985	Stegemann				
1986	Strecker		Kysar	Lieu	
1988			Stott		
1989		Hengel		Strecker	
		von Wahlde	Vouga		
1991		Klauck	du Rand		
			D. M. Smith		
1992	Schnelle	Schmithals	Kysar	Sproston [North]	
	Talbert	Talbert	Loader		
			O'Day		
1990					
1993		(Johnson)	Johnson		

	Before	During	After	Independent	Indeterminable
1996			Rusam		
		Edwards	Zumstein		
			Edwards		
1997			Rensberger		
1999			Köstenberger		
2000					
		Kruse	Beutler		
2001			Akin	Sproston North	
			Rensberger		
2002			Painter	Griffith	
2003			Reis		
2004		Heckel	Thomas		
2006			Nicklas		
2007			Slater		
2008			Mitchell	Lieu	
2009			Jones	Jones	
2010		Anderson			
		von Wahlde			

Part 2

The Church in the Johannine Epistles

Central to interpreting the Johannine Epistles is garnering an understanding of their context: Who were their audiences? What sorts of issues were they facing? Were their adversaries internal or external to the Jesus movement (or both)? How do these texts address these issues with implications for later generations? These questions revolve around the character of the church-situation as reflected in the Johannine Epistles, and their relation to issues reflected in the Johannine Gospel, of course, are extremely relevant. Then again, what if constructions of larger overall theories—for all their glory and value—actually distort one's understanding of the Johannine Epistles, especially the two shorter ones? The application of inductive analyses to the Johannine Epistles themselves is what the authors of this section perform, but note also the differing results that emerge, even when focusing on 2 and 3 John in particular.

Whatever the case, players and issues that emerge when seeking to understand the religious and social context of the Johannine Epistles will inevitably engage the following questions: who was the Elder, and what was he trying to accomplish with his writings? And, who were the "antichrists" labeled as such in 1 and 2 John (*not* mentioned in Revelation!)? Did they call themselves such a title, or was the appellative a pejorative label ascribed by the Elder? What were their actions—were they leaving or coming; and what were their beliefs—did they refuse to believe Jesus was the Christ, or did they refuse to embrace his fleshly humanity; and were they one group or different groups threatening the Johannine community? If secessionists, why did they leave; and if invasionists, what were the false teachings they espoused? Another question involves the identity and concerns of Diotrephes, who loves to be first. Was he simply a selfish person, or was he advocating positional primacy as a means of dealing with disputes and challenges within the church? The Elder has written to "the church" about his inhospitable behavior, but why? Was his authority coming from an emerging church center, or is it his own church-community that holds him accountable?

In addition to these questions, a broader understanding of Johannine Christianity's relations to local Jewish communities, the Roman presence within this gentile-mission setting, the presence of traveling ministers labeled false prophets by the Elder, and issues related to not loving the world must be considered. Johannine believers are indeed engaging other believers, but they also are engaging other groups within their contexts, so understanding the larger church setting of the Johannine Epistles is essential for appreciating their content. Note also the fact that the emphasis upon denying hospitality to false prophets (labeled "antichrists") in 1 and 2 John is mirrored by hospitality being denied now to Johannine traveling ministers by Diotrephes in 3 John. The question is why? The authors in this part of the collection address these sorts of issues in their treatments of the church in the Johannine Epistles, albeit in different ways and yielding distinctive results.

The Audience of the Johannine Epistles

Judith M. Lieu

It is a widespread convention that the identification of the initial audience is a necessary preliminary to the proper understanding of New Testament texts and so belongs to the introductory matter, for example, of a commentary. With regard to the Johannine Epistles, two elements in such an identification have achieved an unusually high degree of consensus. The first is that the letters are addressed to "the Johannine community" (or, less commonly now, the Johannine circle), a conviction that has played an important role in resisting, at least for the Fourth Gospel, the contention that the "Gospels [were] for all Christians" (see Sproston North 2003 against Bauckham 1998). The second area of broad agreement has been the sociological character of that community; here the key debates have centered around the terminology of "sect," sometimes applied with reference to the internal ethos of the "community," sometimes signaling its relationship with other forms of Christianity, and (or) with its "parent," Judaism. Reading such accounts, it would be easy to suppose that a great deal more is known about the audience of the Johannine Epistles than is, for example, about the church at Corinth, the model of reading a text (1 Corinthians) against an account of its audience. The widespread consensual account has been reached through an iterative process: the Epistles provide much of the rationale for the existence of a distinctive "Johannine" community or group of communities—in particular through the network of visits and letters implied by 2 and 3 John, with the latter's references to "the church." Once so located, the Gospel becomes the primary resource for further scene-setting and especially for providing the initial episodes in the community's history (so, classically, Brown 1979a; Martyn [1968] 2003; and many others since). Without this history, it is assumed, it would not be possible to make sense of the allusions in the Epistles, or one might easily make the wrong sense. Yet this mutually confirming edifice is constructed, despite the fact that the Epistles give no location and no clear account of a past history of relationships and despite the only proper names being the otherwise unknown Gaius, Diotrephes, and Demetrius, whose places within the community (or communities) remain a challenge to the imagination. In what follows, the question of audience shall be addressed by treating the Epistles on their own, and specifically as letters, without reference to the Gospel—a position that is rarely adopted but surely defensible, at least on principle. If, indeed, it is the existence of these letters that secures the idea of a Johannine community, what can be discerned from them alone about their intended audience?

Early Christian Letters

Preliminary to an analysis of content must be a decision as to genre, for it is within the conventions of genre that the impact of the audience will be felt. The conventional label "letters" locates these texts within a genre that has been much studied within the ancient world (Klauck 2006). Across a significant span of time and location, letters retained a remarkable consistency of formal characteristics and perceived function. In particular, it is a commonplace that letters represent the writer, "as if present"; they are frequently described as a conversation or "half a dialogue." Thus, they signal the absence of the writer at the same time as seeking to overcome that absence, although in so doing they acknowledge that they cannot overcome it entirely. Letters create and sustain relationships, although they do this often in the hope that this relationship will be superseded by a more immediate one. Ancient epistolary handbooks also subdivide letters into various types according to their specific function, such as consolatory letters, paraenetic letters, or letters of recommendation, although such rigorous classification may belong more to the sphere of school exercises than to daily practice. Such handbooks tend to focus on letters between individuals and as such have been richly complemented by the analysis of myriad letters surviving on papyrus; but the letter genre was also used for formal and official purposes, for example, from an army commander to the senate or from an emperor to a city. Yet alongside these, letters were also widely used as literary devices both within historical narratives as well as within fictional ones—although even in the former, as with speeches, they might owe more than a little to the imagination of the writer. Moreover, the letter format, whether fictional or based on actual experience, offered a malleable genre for philosophical teaching as well as for practicing *prosopopoeia*—namely, for exploiting the possibilities of characterization. Bridging such divisions, letters were also easily imitated or invented, whether out of an intent to deceive or as an exercise in fictional skill, so that debates about pseudepigraphy do, or should, take a particular form in relation to letters. The various attempts to divide all these possibilities into clear types—"epistles" *versus* "letters," "real" *versus* "literary" letters, "private" *versus* "official" letters—have proved unconvincing and are probably misjudged. Yet, as we shall see, each of these possibilities still demands a different model of envisaging an audience.

First, however, it must be recognized that although the models on which they drew are disputed, the production of letters and the importance of these in establishing networks is one of the most striking characteristics of the early Christian movement. It is widely agreed that the activity of Paul was fundamental in this development and it swiftly provoked imitators. There are also other clusters which have their own tendencies to generating imitation—the Petrine tradition, the letters associated with Ignatius, letters between churches such as 1 Clement and the epistolary accounts of the Martyrdom of Polycarp and of the persecution of the churches of Vienne and Lyons (Eusebius, *Hist. eccl.* 5.1.1–5.2.8). To these must be added "fictional" letters such as those which introduce Revelation (Rev 2–3). It is highly possible that all these owe something, whether or not directly, to the Pauline model, not least as shaped by his distinctive formula of greeting—"grace and peace to you"—as opposed to the conventional Greek "greetings" (χαίρειν). Certainly, early Christian letters have been studied fruitfully in relation to the real and theoretical epistolary conventions of the time; however, a stronger impression is left of the idiosyncratic and creative uses to which the genre is put in early Christian circles and of the undoubted lines of implicit and even of self-conscious imitation.

Characteristic also of these trajectories and of the process of imitation is the collection of letters into a corpus, which might then be treated as a unity. The earliest stages of the formation of a Pauline collection are unknown, but Ephesians probably presupposes an earlier grouping; in turn, a ten-letter Pauline collection was soon extended by the Pastorals, and in some areas by Hebrews. An original core of letters ascribed to Ignatius similarly attracted imitations, which created a larger corpus, although the details and dates of all these are still disputed. As a result of this process, individual letters came to be read very differently as part of such a collection than when sent and received on their own; differences were easily submerged in favor of intertextual "gap-filling," and the specifics of the particular were ignored, or in a number of cases, textually erased.

The Johannine "Letters"

Against this background certain questions arise: where, within the spectrum of ancient letters and specifically within that of early Christian letters, are the Johannine Epistles to be located? What lines of conscious or unconscious dependence do they betray? What lies behind their now conventional collection and sequence? Over the last century, debate has flowed without certain resolution, first as to the genre of 1 John and secondly as to the character of 2 and 3 John. The issues regarding 2 and 3 John are more straightforward, although here too unanimity is not to be found. Responses have ranged from enthusiastic references to these letters as "gems of personal privacy" similar to the personal letters among the papyri to their dismissal as works of novelistic imagination (Harris 1901; Hirsch 1936). Few would hold either position now, at least in their most bald form, but both positions contain elements of truth.

As has been repeatedly noted, 3 John of all the letters preserved in the New Testament, and indeed from Christian circles in the first two centuries, follows most closely the pattern of the private letters preserved on papyrus; its length perhaps is due to the restrictions of a papyrus sheet, although like many it pleads the inadequacies of the letter format, while the greeting, the expression of pleasure at good news, the scene-setting which leads to a specific request, and the concluding sharing of messages could be paralleled countless times (Klauck 2006, 27–40; Lieu 1986, 37–52). The consequence may be that we cannot expect to know any more about the audience of 3 John than we do about those of such other letters, with their allusive references to names, situations, and anxious hopes or fears (see Lieu 2008a, 283 for an example). What is certain is that 3 John is a letter to an individual (Gaius) from an individual (the Elder): the vocative or second person singular pronoun is used twelve times, and there are eleven first person singular verbs from ten different roots. Undoubtedly this creates a strong sense of "presence" such as was conventionally expected of a letter; however, although the Elder implicitly counts Gaius among his "children" (3 John 4), he nowhere explains why he can do so and he approaches him with some circumspection (vv. 5–6). Although the author operates within a context where people ("brothers") visit and report, and although he closes the letter with shared greetings to and from "the friends," he does little to set Gaius himself within a communal context. Gaius is treated as separate from both "the brothers" and "the church"; at the end of his letter the Elder reinforces this: he writes to and he hopes to see Gaius, and Gaius alone—"you" singular (vv. 13–15). The other early Christian letters to individuals, those by Paul (to Philemon), by his imitators (1 and 2 Timothy, Titus), and by Ignatius (to Polycarp) are very different from this: they consciously identify their recipients as community figures. Certainly many reconstructions of events behind 3 John, and therefore of the identity and role of Gaius, do locate him within a communal context, perhaps as a leader of a different group or house-community. But these are works of the imagination and necessarily rely on reading into the letter information or elements that have been further imaginatively reconstructed from elsewhere. On the contrary, from a straightforward reading of 3 John there is nothing to suggest that its audience is any other than whom it claims to be.

Second John is much more complex; even on a superficial reading it is an oddity, poised between the undoubtedly self-conscious elements, such as the extended and elaborate greeting (2 John 1–3), and those features that it shares with 3 John, not only its length but in particular the closing pleasantries (vv. 12–13). These latter may carry with them the guarantee of authenticity, but it is equally possible that they are evidence of imitation—as we have seen, a common epistolary phenomenon (Lieu 2008a, 18, 239–45 in contrast to the caution of Klauck 2006, 40). Moreover, in 2 John the author's relationship with his audience is more distant: he does not speak of them as, or as among, "his children," a difference underlined by the otherwise close similarity between 3 John 4 ("my children") and 2 John 4 ("your children"). Neither does he use any form of address that would establish any mutuality of obligation: he does not address them as "beloved" (as in 3 John 2, 5, 11), and the only vocative, itself used just once, is "lady" (κυρία) (2 John 5), a term of wide applicability. Here for most interpreters the central question is the identity of the "elect lady"; a hidden personal name, "lady *Electa*" or the "elect *Kyria*," seems unlikely, not least because of the presence of her equally elect sister at the end of the letter (v. 13; but see Edwards 1996, 28–29, for a defense of the possibility). A widespread conclusion, often reached with minimal discussion of any alternative, is that the "lady" is a personification of a church, or of *the* church, part of the metaphorical trajectory of the woman Zion (Isa 54:1–6) or of the bridal church (Eph 5:29–32; Rev 21). However, such supposed parallels are far from satisfactory; in each of these cases the nature of the personification is explicit and is integrated into an associated set of images which carry the primary meaning—barrenness, fecundity, virginal purity, exclusive dedication, or belonging—as well as being located in a broader literary context which relies heavily on figural language. The conventional controls of the epistolary genre, reinforced by its isolation and brevity in the case of 2 John, on the one hand, and the apparent specific references to past or projected "real-time" events on the other, provide an unlikely setting for metaphor or personification, and persuasive parallels are hard to identify—although "the fellow elect (woman) in Babylon" who sends greeting together with "*my* son Mark" in 1 Pet 5:13 may be a distant relative. It is these difficulties which have led some to preserve the possibility that the "elect lady" combines in herself both real woman and communal location; she is the woman leader of a community located in her "house" (v. 11; Edwards 1996, 26–29). Yet, this explanation may still be too impervious to the striking tension in the letter: on the one hand, the careful albeit formulaic use of the singular "you" in the framing verses creates for readers the picture of the sisters and their children (vv. 4, 5, 13) and extends beyond what would be needed for a metaphor or even for a communal leader; on the other hand, the body of the letter consistently addresses "you" plural without any attempt at the pretense of their dependency (vv. 6, 8, 10, 12). It is "you" plural who must be encouraged, who may be the recipients of undesirable visitors, and to whom the author has chosen not to write much more since he intends to visit them. The implied audience of the *substantive content* of the letter is treated as a group of equally responsible adult members; the implied recipient of the letter is a woman and her family, who are in epistolary contact with her sister and cousins.

The individual address and the familial language invite a comparison between 2 and 3 John and the Pastoral Epistles. Second (but not 3) John shares with 1 and 2 Timothy the distinctive greeting, "grace, mercy, peace from [2 John: the Johannine "παρά"] God (the) Father and Christ Jesus [2 John: "from Jesus Christ"]"[1]; strikingly it exhibits some of the same modifications as do such distinctive greetings apparently coined by Paul, from which they are surely derived, as "grace to you and peace from God our Father and Lord Jesus Christ" (1 Cor 1:3). Unlike the Pastoral Epistles, 2 John provides a verb, "there shall be," in telling contrast to the semitic

---

1. Unless otherwise noted, the translations of biblical texts are my own.

wish, "be multiplied," adopted by 1 and 2 Peter and Jude. It is improbable that these parallels are entirely fortuitous; yet locating 2 John among these neighbors within early Christianity inevitably raises the specter of pseudonymity, a remarkably persistent characteristic of the early Christian letter trajectory, Pauline, Petrine, and Ignatian. The apparent anonymity of "the Elder" and the difficulty modern scholarship has in agreeing his intended identity might seem incompatible with pseudonymity, which usually relies on claiming the authority of a known significant figure, but it should not be ruled out. As a minimum, a reasonable argument can be made that 2 John is derivative from 3 John (Lieu 2008, but contrast Schnelle 2011, 97 who revives an older view that 2 John is the letter of 3 John 9), but it is also possible that the epithet draws on the tradition of a foundational figure as often imagined by scholarly reconstructions. Pseudonymity of author most naturally carries with it pseudonymity of audience and hence of the situation implied: if the Pastoral Epistles were not authored by Paul, then it is unlikely that they were actually directed to his coworkers Timothy or Titus. Is the "elect lady" any more precise than the "all those who follow the equally valuable faith as us" of 2 Pet 1:1, or than "those called who are beloved in God and preserved in Christ Jesus" in Jude 1? Although 2 John more directly invites such questions, it cannot be ruled out that the characters of 3 John, Gaius, and in the background Diotrephes and Demetrius, may be no more historically secure than Hymenius and Alexander whom the fictionalized Paul "handed over to Satan" in 1 Tim 1:20, namely, individuals drawn from story and legend. The supposition of pseudonymous authorship must also extend to questions as to the nature of this "letter": if 2 Peter, and perhaps Jude, and the Pastoral Epistles are indeed pseudonymous, then they are only formally letters, but they are unlikely to have functioned as such. Unlike a "real" letter, such as 1 Corinthians, they were probably not sent by someone to an audience separated by distance as part of a continuing relationship of direct and indirect communication. This means that the intended audience is hidden and can only be guessed at once the strategy of the letter and of its fictionality is uncovered. For example, in the case of the pseudonymous Jewish letters of Jeremiah or of Baruch, it seems probable that the situation of the audience is not that described in the letters although it may be like it in some respects; indeed, in this case the letters serve to give the audience members a new framework for viewing their actual situation. The combination of pseudonymous author and fictional address is not readily compatible with the suggestion that 2 John can still be understood as an actual, perhaps circular, letter (see Bultmann 1973, 107–8).

First John presents a different set of problems. It provides no names, no location, either for sender or for recipients; it appeals to no events identified by shared referential knowledge such as might provide the persuasive foundation of the epistolary rhetoric. First John lacks almost all the generic qualifiers that mark a letter—it has no greeting formula and no opening health wish or thanksgiving; it contains no direct requests; and it includes no messages to or from third parties. Most of the other labels that have been given to 1 John, such as a sermon or a homily, are at best approximate descriptions rather than based on clear generic identifiers; to the extent that these can be described as a genre, 1 John equally fails the test. Such labels also ignore the repeated references to this as a written document and to this writing as being intentional and not a secondary inconsequential stage; the verb "to write" (γράφειν) is used thirteen times and is followed on three occasions by ἵνα and on seven by ὅτι, both expressing purpose (1 John 1:4; 2:1, [7, 8], 11–14, 21 [26]; 5:13). Yet these alternative suggestions as to its genre do recognize the character of address and of argument in 1 John, and to this extent they also serve to sharpen the question of audience. An oral address such as a sermon or homily has—or according to both ancient and modern convention should have—its immediate audience firmly in view. Once such an address is written down and sent, presumably to be read by a third party, it cannot function in the same way as it did when first produced; the audience of the letter in all probability will not be the same as that of the original addressees, and to some extent, they may be outside the precise knowledge of the original speaker/author, and certainly they will be outside the author's ability to shape their response. A letter functions in a different way from a persuasive direct address, and *as a letter* 1 John must apply to the situation of its audience in a different, and perhaps less direct, way than any oral substratum would have done.

The audience addressed by 1 John is simply "you" (plural), without any further specification. In 1 John there is no suggestion that author or authors and audience have had any association in the past, and the prologue would seem to exclude this (see also 1 John 2:21). It is true that one goal of the 1 John is "fellowship," κοινωνία (1:3), a common epistolary topos, and, as shall be seen, one that is fundamental to the rhetorical strategy of 1 John. Yet there is little to suggest what form any future or continuing relationship might take. Even Hebrews, with which 1 John is sometimes compared because of its equally nonepistolary opening and sermonic style, closes with the author's fervent wish to see his audience (Heb 13:23). Indeed, even to speak of "an author" or "sender" in the case of 1 John is problematic. The writer is almost exclusively singular (except at 1:4), but we hear his voice only in the affirmation, repeated twelve times, "I write." Other than the explanatory "I do not say" in 5:16, the author does not do anything other than *write*, and he does this without any self-referential explanation of his authority to do so. This is in startling contrast to the range of first person verbs in 3 John. Yet if "authorial voice" is taken to identify the authoritative voice heard through the text, then this is exclusively plural, "we," established particularly but not exclusively in the prologue; there is something of a gap between the "I" who writes and the "we" who authoritatively address the audience. In the same way, the audience is also always addressed in the plural, "you," and yet is treated throughout as a unified body, with no suggestion of internal division. Any difference, any alternative way of being, is not part of "you," but belongs either to the indefinite third person singular, "the one who" (2:4–6, 9–11, etc.), or to the potentially equally indefinite first person plural, "if we" (1:6–10). Rhetorically, these are carefully distanced from anything "you" might do. Such a corporate undifferentiated authorial and recipient identity might seem to be more characteristic of letters between churches than those involving an individual. Yet even 1 Clement, traditionally attributed to one author writing on behalf of a community or authoritative group, lacks the singular first person voice, as too do the Letter of the Churches of Vienne and Lyons and the Martyrdom of Polycarp. More important, unlike 1 John, these other community letters use a variety of explicit strategies that establish the relationship between these ecclesial communities as a framework for communication; the "you" of the audiences are identifiable communities, with identifiable concerns.

The Johannine Epistles have often been brought into proximity with the letters of Ignatius, as best illustrating the disputes over the nature of Jesus Christ, the warning against contacts in response, and the tensions over patterns of church authority. Some of Ignatius's letters address churches he had visited; others address those without direct knowledge of him, although the tone he adopts toward them betrays little variation. Yet the differences between the strategy of Ignatius and that of 1 John are more striking than any parallels: Ignatius uses personal names where he can (*Eph.* 2; *Magn.* 2); he makes references to details important to the individual communities (*Eph.* 9); he acknowledges the presence of dissentient voices among those to whom he writes (*Phld.* 2, 8). Like Paul, he also consciously uses epistolary conventions to reinforce his own authority (*Eph.* 12; *Trall.* pref. 12)—something absent from 2 John as well as from 1 John.

The process by which the Johannine letters were collected is less easily traced than that of the Pauline or Ignatian corpus. There are traces of a one-letter collection (1 John), of a two-letter collection (1 and 2 John), and of an alternative two-letter collection (2 and 3 John) set alongside or even in opposition to the single letter; only at a later date does a three-letter collection become standard (Lieu 1986, 5–36). Unlike the Pauline and Ignatian corpora, too, the Gospel and even Revelation, two texts of very different genres, might further complicate the possible permutations of association and so also complicate the literary contexts within which any one text could be read. Tertullian's phrase "Johannine document" in the context of a reference to Revelation may point to one such collection, but its other components cannot be known (*Res.* 38). It would be as mistaken, if not more so, to take the subsequently dominant three-letter, four-text, or even five-text collection as a starting point for the interpretation of any one member, than it would be to similarly treat the fourteen-text Pauline or thirteen-text Ignatian collections.

The Narrative of Letters

As has been already noted, one feature of the majority of early Christian letters is that they embody a narrative. They refer to past events or they anticipate future events, but, in addition, they themselves play some role within the link between past and future. This is a widespread characteristic of letters more generally, which is why they can be used as narrative devices in other settings, whether historical or fictional. Even the so-called "philosophical letters" often achieve their goal in the form of a response to an actual or imagined event. Consequently, studies of the "audience" of letters usually focus on their place within such a broader narrative. In 1 Corinthians, a model of letter-reading, the narrative is unusually clear, in part because of the explicit references to previous communications from the recipients; other than comments on the history of Corinth or on the characteristics of a sea port, few introductions say any more about the recipients of 1 Corinthians than what can be deduced from it. Other letters are more ambiguous; in Galatians the boundary between the narrative of Paul and the narrative of the Galatian believers is porous, particularly in chapter 2, allowing some debate as to where there are continuities or discontinuities in their respective situations. The same is even more the case with Ignatius of Antioch; here scholars continue to debate whether the "heresy" and the threat of schism, against which he so energetically warns his readers in Asia Minor, were in fact to be found in Antioch. Perhaps they represented the situation which had provoked his arrest, and it is he who projects them onto the situation of his audience, reading his brief experiences at some of the churches, as at Philadelphia, through that lens. First Clement presents a different problem; the situation at Corinth—the young having overthrown the established authorities—seems clear, and yet this does not resolve the question as to how the author's perspective on events relates to how they may have been perceived within the church of Corinth itself, nor indeed its significance for the Roman community. In part this is because the narrative of letters, even when apparently descriptive, is designed to persuade, and so may be very different from the narrative told by other participants or by the recipients.

Again, 3 John suggests a fairly specific narrative, by implication largely transparent to its recipient, if not to subsequent readers. The primary narrative events, however, are not those experienced by that recipient, Gaius. Formally they are those of the author (vv. 3–4, 9–10), but no less important is a third party, "brothers" (vv. 3, 5–7, 10). Indeed, even what Gaius has done is only known and related through the testimony of the brothers in the presence of, if not personally to, the Elder (vv. 3, 6), and the Elder himself is largely characterized by a set of relations that pivot around these brothers (vv. 9–10). The focus of the narrative is on the past: the coming of the "brothers," their going out for the sake of the name, the Elder's failed letter to "the church," and Diotrephes's refusal to accept not just the Elder but the brothers and any who associate with them. Gaius is exhorted to continue acting as he already has been doing "toward the brothers," but he has no narrative profile beyond that. To that extent, any role or action ascribed Gaius is determined by that of the brothers and then by that of the Elder, and it is contingent upon them; on the other hand, called to imitate the good, his model is not the Elder but the otherwise unknown Demetrius (v. 12). The Elder's own coming is uncertain, as is its destination and possible effectiveness (v. 10); the Elder hopes to see Gaius, but how this might be achieved and what effect a visit might have is unexplained; unlike 2 John, which otherwise uses closely similar language, a visit is not presupposed (v. 14; cf. 2 John 12). The narrative of 3 John is episodic rather than linear, and the writing of the letter is only indirectly and partially effective within it, namely, to provoke Gaius into continuing his current activity.

Second John is strikingly different. Any past narrative is largely conventional—the Elder's discovery of the true behavior of some of the lady's children (2 John 4), the command which they and "we" have had from the beginning (vv. 4–6), some unspecified labor by "us" (v. 8), perhaps the going out of the deceivers (v. 7, although their effect apparently is still only potential for the recipients of the letter, vv. 8, 10). Instead, the primary focus is on what has yet to happen and quite precisely so: the future coming of Jesus—if the participle "coming" (ἐρχόμενον) is taken seriously—which the antichrists fail to acknowledge, and the possible future loss of reward (vv. 7–8). Most important is the potential coming of someone not bearing the authorized teaching who is to be denied a welcome (v. 10); by contrast, the planned coming of the Elder, also "to you," will be a certain source of joy (v. 12). The letter anticipates and negotiates these possible future advents, and it seeks to determine their outcome with four explicit instructions or promises (vv. 5, 8, 10, 12). Nevertheless, the language in which it does so is so highly stylized that it contributes little to providing a structured profile of the recipients.

First John also looks both to the past and to the future, although here the letter plays less of a role in determining the future. The past dimension of the imagined narrative has three elements. The first of these pertains to the activity of the Son; it is relevant for our purposes, because this activity is largely directed to "us" and not to "you" (1 John 2:1–2; 4:9–10). Despite the promise to "proclaim *to you*" (1:3, 5), the audience is not constructed as the direct beneficiary of the Son's activity in the evangelical message now proclaimed by the author. Moreover, the story of the Son stands outside the immediate defining time-frame of the letter. Second, there is the past expressed most clearly in the prologue, "we have heard, seen, and our hands have touched." As noted by all commentaries, the precise object, and therefore the actual moment, of this past is notoriously imprecise, impossible to anchor. Although in the prologue the audience of the letter appears to be excluded from this past, dependent on "us" for its impact, in the rest of the letter audience members at least have an analogous past: they (or "you") have heard something "from the beginning," have "known," have had sins forgiven, have conquered (2:7, 12–14, 20, 24; 4:14). The third narrative element is usually seen as pivotal: the going out of the many antichrists. This is decisively an experience that only the authorial "we" have undergone: "you have heard" about the coming of *the* antichrist; "you" have an anointing; they went out "from *us*" (2:18–20; see Lieu 2008b). Although this differentiation of narrative history has often been blurred in reconstructions of the epistolary audience, it is central to the narrative and to the function of the letter.

The future dimension has two aspects; one lies in the distant future when "we" may have boldness at his coming and not fear and when we shall be like him (2:28; 3:2, 21; 4:17–18). If the letter achieves its goal, more immediately in the future will be the responses to the exhortations to abide, not to be deceived, and, by implication, to express right belief and love. However, there is no suggestion that any of these will involve a major change for the audience members; they already are doing everything that they are being encouraged to do. Even the apparently anxious "I write to you concerning those who are deceiving you" or "are trying to deceive you" is countermanded by the earlier "I write to you because … you know the truth and that no falsehood is of the truth" (2:21, 26). First John does not locate its audience within a continuous dynamic narrative, neither does it act as a catalyst within such a narrative. This conclusion, shared to a lesser degree by 2 and 3 John, sharply differentiates 1 John from most other New Testament letters. However, it does not disqualify them as letters, many of which do little more than maintain communication.

The Rhetorical Strategy of the Letters

Beyond the overt narrative function of the Johannine Epistles, which turns on the explicit statements within them, like many letters they also have a rhetorical function: their task is not merely to give information or to secure certain stated goals, but to shape the audience. The rhetorical function of 1 John has been analyzed from a number of perspectives, but with results that are largely coherent. It is here that the striking anonymity of 1 John, and in particular the persistent use of "we" and "you" comes into its own (see further Lieu 2008b). The careful interplay between "we" and "you" reaches something of a crisis in 1 John 4:4–6, which itself follows a stern exhortation to discrimination. In verses 4 and 5, an emphatic "you" is set in uncompromising opposition to an equally anonymous "them." The reference is presumably to the "false prophets" of 4:1, although that term is itself more of a mythicized label than a real description of activity, and they have themselves been subsumed into the more recent naming of "*the* antichrist" (sing.; 4:3). This opposition is not something yet to be achieved but is already secured in the past both by "your" achievement, "you have conquered *them*," and by a state of affairs that continues to be true, "the one in you is greater than the one in the world." Verse 6 introduces the emphatic first person plural "we." Throughout the letter up to this point, the identity of this "we" has fluctuated between the authoritative "we," who are, as noted above, separate from and able to address the audience as "*you*" (1:1–3; 2:19), and an inclusive "we" amongst whom the audience members are invited to identify themselves: "he is the means of forgiveness for *our* sins" (1:7–9; 2:2). That invitation now reaches its apex: "*we* are of God" (4:6), just as two verses earlier "*you* are of God"; "the one who knows God listens to *us*, the one who does not know God does not listen to *us*." Is the audience being positioned as the one who by listening declares whether or not they know God, or are they positioned amongst the "us," distanced irrevocably from the "they" to whom the world listens (4:5)? The apparent choice of where to stand is by now hardly a genuine one; inevitably the audience, "you," is interpolated as "us." From this point on, the letter does not again address its audience as "you" until the final affirmation of the single author's (not "our") intention in writing (5:13); instead, the audience loses any separate identity or possibility within the encompassing "we." At this level, the rhetorical strategy of the letter to create fellowship, κοινωνία, has been achieved, although this fellowship has no stated physical or social expression.

Other approaches to 1 John have focused attention on the conceptual world it presupposes; here the emphasis is usually on the dualism of light versus darkness, love versus hatred, the world versus what is of God or us, being children of God versus being children of the devil. Overlapping with this, at least in chapter three, is the possibility, or even the imperative, of not sinning (3:4–10). The world constructed by such language is a closed one, almost entirely coherent and self-sufficient—"almost" because of the troubling possibility of sinning earlier in the letter (1:8–2:2). To leave this circle in any manner—namely, by not believing or by not loving—would be a complete and perhaps irreversible act. Since there can be no meaningful conversation outside—the world neither listens to us nor realistically can do so—there is no conceptual room for dialogue or even for mission. Further, "we bear witness" not because of what others have witnessed to us but solely because "we have seen," even when that "we" embraces (the former) "you" (4:14). There is no sense of any time having elapsed since the foundational event or of a pattern of transmission to be tested or legitimated: "we" ourselves and "you" yourselves have heard what is from the beginning (2:7, 24). Since the circle is complete, there is no space for change or for growth; the call is to abide. Although the future may hold out the unknown, "what we shall be," it is not unpredictable (3:2). Neither is there any consequent sense that in the present we only "see in part."

It has been argued that the warnings against the antichrists function in the same way (so especially Schmid 2002). They represent the archetypal "other," simultaneously mythicized by their label and demythologized by the appeal "as you have heard, so now" (2:18). These antichrists have no substance in themselves; they espouse no active doctrines or practices, in contrast to the long heresiological tradition even from its infancy in 2 Peter and Jude. They are defined only be their absence ("going out") and by their act of denial (2:19, 22)—and even this latter is only indirectly attributed to them ("who is the liar?"; cf. 4:3, "every spirit … is not from God"). Neither do they have a future: there is no promise of condemnation or of final judgment for them. Instead, they are defined only in relation to "us": they "have gone out"; they "do not confess." The world into which they have gone and to which they belong (4:1, 5) is one in which the author has no interest. The world, therefore, has no substantive existence in the symbolic universe that the author constructs. Thus the antichrists embody the specter of failing to remain true: they police the boundaries, rather like gangs of youths—or, more properly, fear of them—police a no-go area for the inhabitants of a more respectable suburb.

Given their brevity and allusiveness, it is more difficult to assess the rhetorical strategy of 2 and 3 John, and much depends on how their authenticity as letters is judged. Certainly, in comparison with 1 John, 2 John apparently represents a different and more immediate scenario: "they" may invade our suburb and knock on our door, an even more disturbing possibility (2 John 10–11). Here, fraternization is a potential option and so it has to be vigorously excluded; the merging of eschatological and real futures (vv. 8, 10–11, and perhaps the "coming" in v. 7) serves to reinforce such exclusion. However, if 2 John is deemed to be pseudonymous, thus implying an element of fiction in the scenario it paints, it would be equally possible that it is designed to explain and justify a pattern of behavior that was already being practiced.

As has already been seen, 3 John works effectively to create a sense of "presence." The initial relationship between Gaius and the Elder is not immediately clear—the epithet "beloved" need not indicate close intimacy (cf. 1 John 4:1, 7, 11). The opening verses establish Gaius's autonomy of action, and although verse 4 implicitly identifies him as among the Elder's children, in contrast to 1 John (2:1, 28; 3:7), he is not directly addressed as such. The first person plural is not introduced until verse 8.

Yet, when picked up in verses 9–10, it invites Gaius to identify himself with the Elder's interests, though he himself is not included in that "we." Indeed, such identification remains something to be secured, and in verse 12 Gaius is still being encouraged to recognize and to affirm his independent loyalty to "us." This encouragement is buttressed by the invitation to position himself with the good and not the evil, but while Diotrephes represents the latter at least by implication, it is the unknown Demetrius (and not the Elder) who represents the former. Our ignorance of Demetrius hides the rhetorical intention and the likely success of this appeal. This unexpected feature may thereby also give the letter its strongest note of authenticity—although such inconsequential details can be the marks of fictional imagination. Nonetheless, by the end of 3 John a strong impression has been created of a network of identification and loyalty that may not have been obvious from the start, and there is no ambiguity as to where the right belongs.

The Johannine Context

The analysis carried out so far has deliberately ignored the "Johannine" character of these documents. Yet, even if the Gospel did not survive, it would be necessary to make some judgment about the interrelationship between these letters: 2 and 3 John share the identification of the author and the closing pleasantries; 1 and 2 John share the threat of the antichrists, defined in terms of a failure to confess Jesus's coming in flesh, as well as the emphasis on the command to love one another, defined as heard from the beginning. Those commonalities are open to a number of explanations. For some they might suggest that the relative passivity of the relationship between sender(s) and recipients in 1 John should be modified by the implied activity of the Elder in 3 and/ or 2 John; for others that difference will appear the more striking. However, conventionally it has been the Gospel that has contributed most to fill the vacuum in which our authors and presumably our audiences might otherwise seem to exist. There is good reason for this, regardless of the sequence in which the writings are put, something to be treated as a separate issue. There is no need, or space, here to trace the numerous similarities, echoes, and possible cross-references between these writings. At its very simplest this broader context provides additional, and otherwise not anticipated, resonance for the antithesis between the one who is of God and the one who has not seen God in 3 John 11 (cf. John 8:47). Equally unexpected, the assertion that "we have borne testimony and you know that our testimony is true" (3 John 12) cannot help but evoke John 21:24, particularly since both are followed by a deprecatory reference to the "many things" that could be written (see Lieu 2008a, 281–84, where it is suggested that 3 John 12 may be primary). More generally, a hinterland of shared language, of exegesis, and of homiletic and paraenetic formulation is betrayed by the multiple but far from simple echoes between 1 John and the Gospel. Any account of an audience will need to include these, while avoiding foreclosing on how they are to be explained.

The Church in the Johannine Epistles

This paper took as its starting point such an avoidance, namely, of the pervasive idea of "the Johannine community." Yet, it has become evident that the idea of "community" cannot be avoided, indeed it is central. Even so, the letters do little to determine the choice of appropriate terminology. On a minimal or formal base, the church, as represented by any unmistakable designation like ἐκκλησία, is limited to 3 John; to this might be added "the Elder," and even "the friends" (3 John 15), although these do not demand an ecclesial definition. If scripturally metaphorically determined, "the elect lady" and her "sister" could be added to the lexicon, and perhaps also "the house" (2 John 10); however, as has been seen, there is nothing internal to the letter that demands such a definition, and all these terms have a natural literal reference whether or not they are fictional. Yet even if included as descriptors of "the community," "the church" appears only as a place for teaching and for the giving of testimony. It is also a place to which people might come and from which they might be excluded. However, the manner of such exclusion and its wider effect are obscure; the author of 3 John's understanding of it as the effect of ambition is unlikely to have been that of Diotrephes, while Gaius is in no way disadvantaged by apparently being independent of the "church." Similar personal rivalries and attempts to win support could be replicated many times over, even from other secular contemporary letters, and they do little to create a distinctively "Johannine" community.

First John undoubtedly does project a "community," although it does so without using any distinctive vocabulary. This emerges as a cohesive, undifferentiated body, which possesses no distinguishing characteristics of status, of ethnicity, of religious background, or of historically shaped self-consciousness that might connect its members with any other sets of structures in society. Even structures based on gender appear to be absent—although the exclusively male language of 2:13–14 is striking and not counterbalanced by other more inclusive terminology. This is remarkable, particularly when compared with other early Christian letters, which regularly address issues provoked by gender, social status, and ethnic background and which often self-consciously mimic or distance themselves from the structures of contemporary society, or from a scriptural past. The audience of 1 John has no personal or communal history, and any allegiance beyond that to Jesus Christ is entirely anonymous—in sharp contrast to the situation in 3 John. Through the language of "children," they are encouraged to see themselves in a relationship of dependency, but other aspects of the author's address to them qualify this. The love for one another to which they are called makes no judgment on the values adopted outside of the community and to that extent they do not project a reactionary sectarian consciousness. Similarly, they do not see themselves as in competition with others over a shared (perhaps scriptural) heritage, another "sectarian" characteristic.

This brief sketch reinforces what has emerged from the analysis of the letters here undertaken. It is a picture that in multiple ways is diametrically opposed to that which is conventionally drawn by the approach based on the "history of the community of the Beloved Disciple," with its complex history, its sense of "tradition" and of inherited authorities or revered personalities, its clearly identified opponents, its strongly defined communal identity, and, most of all, its firm anchoring in time and place. To recognize this does not mean that the latter approach is wrong. It does act as an important reminder that that community is a construct, a production of scholarly imagination upon the texts—and not a foundation in the texts for scholarly erudition—just as much as is the community projected by the Johannine Epistles themselves and explored in this paper.

The Missional Role of ὁ Πρεσβυτερος

Peter Rhea Jones

Time and space have chastened me to limit my topic considerably from the ecclesial role of ὁ πρεσβύτερος to the missional role. This latter choice pressed upon me by the texts themselves, particularly in 1 and 2 John, is itself a rather large focus upon which I can only make a modest and introductory comment. When approaching either the presumably larger topic or the rather more restricted topic, two courses of action commend themselves: first, to do an analysis of the title itself and then, more promisingly, to do an inductive analysis of the actual action implied in the two shorter letters. Due to constraints, I put the title search to one side. Raymond Brown (1982, 647–54) offered an admirable treatment of the title with particular conclusions as well as an inductive portrayal.[1] Judith Lieu (1986) also did a rundown on the title, disclaiming the possibility of definitive results and then proceeding to do an inductive analysis throughout the text with which we will dialogue at the outset and along the way. I register my indebtedness to her both where we concur and diverge.

Is 1 John Missional?

While most of my now more modestly limited paper will focus upon 2 and 3 John, I commence with the mystifying anomaly of the exordium in 1 John as a telling place to open discussion. I suggest we see missional

---

1. Brown analyzed five possible explanations and concluded that the term in the Johannine community designated honor for the tradition bearers and the writer of 2 and 3 John may have been an elderly tradition bearer. "His influence would have been that of a prophetic witness rather than flowing from jurisdiction or structure" (651). Would an elderly presbyter be as itinerant as implied in 2 John 12 and 3 John 13? Possibly.

leadership by letter not only in 2 and 3 John but in the opening sentences of 1 John 1:1–4. While this familiar text parallels the famous prologue of the Gospel, it was not primarily an imitation but rather was crafted for the crisis that beset the Johannine communities in schism (2:18–27). Furthermore, it credentializes those eyewitnesses from the beginning for whom the author speaks. At verse 3 one finds the writer seeking to firm or forge a fellowship (see Jones 2009, 17–24). The anomaly results from the appeal to those already believers to join in fellowship with them, as though they were not Christians, and to participate in their own privileged fellowship with the Father and the Son (1:3b). Though addressed to believers, this text is quite *invitational*—what we might almost call the evangelism of believers and their churches, what Brooke Westcott (1966, 12) took as intending that they "may be united with us, the apostolic body, in the bonds of Christian communion." The author (likely the common author of 1, 2, and 3 John) reveals that his purpose was "that our joy might be complete" by their inclusion (v. 4), significantly reminiscent of 3 John 4.[2] The purposive ἵνα at verse 3c is far from incidental (cf. John 17:20–24). Presumably the acceptance of the offer of fellowship lay in the offing, the outcome in the balance. Brown posited an audience of Johannine Christians he wishes to bind in communion, a threatened communion. The secessionists also claim communion (1:6; 2:6). Brown (1982, 187n) stated that communion among believers "becomes a *sine qua non* of being united to God."[3] The Elder boldly reaches out to include more congregations in a competitive and polarized environment. Of course, anomalously the Elder affirms later in the same letter the recipients as forgiven of sin (2:12b), abiding in the Word of God, anointed and knowing the truth (2:20–21), as having no need to be taught (2:27), as conquerors (2:13d, 14h), and including assurance of eternal life (5:13). Brown (1982, 186) himself posits an older and a newer group being united with each other and with the Father and the

---

2. The reading "our" (ἡμῶν) enjoys considerable support textually, but the Textus Receptus reads ὑμῶν. See Metzger 1994, 709. The writer may speak for a group such as the Johannine school and mission. Unless otherwise noted, all translations of biblical texts are my own.

3. Brown notes how this ecclesiastical tone was taken further by Ignatius, *Magn.* 7:1; Cyprian, *De ecclesiae* 6, 149–50 (CCSL 3:253): "One cannot have God for Father who has not the church for mother." Johnson (1993, 26) minces no words in seeing an invitation to join the "circle of salvation."

Son.[4] One does not find here an antipathy to mission in 1 John. Indeed, 1 John can be read missionally, as can the entire corpus of letters, especially if 1 and 2 John were sent in tandem (see Lieu 2008a, 252).[5] The exordium provides a clue to all the Epistles and to the mission. It sets direction.

One does well to take note also of the famous 2:19 passage associated by Brown with the term *secession*. The text is open to more than merely the church leader's invalidation of the departees.[6] It may well suggest that those leaving did so with a sense of intent, of mission on the part of the departing. The Greek word used to characterize their departure is ἐξῆλθαν. Rudolf Bultmann (1973, 36) took the position that the opponents did not organize themselves; they remain in the congregation but are a present danger.[7] Brown (1982, 338) rightly suggests that they thought of themselves as the true Johannine community and could even have looked upon the Elder's community as a sect.[8] They have become a communal and theological alternative and may well be on mission themselves as suggested by the possibly missional "went out." At Mark 1:38, in a missional context, Jesus spoke purposively of the mission in Galilee as the rationale for his going out (ἐξῆλθον), a departure with purpose (see Taylor 1959, 184).[9] Furthermore, those exiting from the Elder's community broke fellowship, as did Judas (John 13:30–31a; so Schneider 1965, 2:678). Also, in

---

4. F. F. Bruce (1970, 38) saw in the opening lines the voice of a surviving member of the first generation of Christians offering what the community had seen and heard, because the recipients had not seen and heard. I. Howard Marshall (1978, 105) concluded, partly on the basis of the continuous ἔχητε, that verse 3 is "not necessarily prescribing the condition for entry to fellowship, but for continuance in fellowship."

5. Lieu notes that 2 John 7 is so succinct that a reader has difficulty interpreting it without recourse to 1 John 2:18–19, a subtle argument that could favor 1 and 2 John sent simultaneously.

6. The text is layered with the author's critical interpretation of the departee's invalidity all along, because they were exposed by their failure of the pivotal test of *abiding*. Nevertheless, they left voluntarily, and the verb "went out" in other usages is missional. There is more here than apostasy to the world.

7. Bultmann was quite right that they remained a present danger but not concerning their remaining in the congregation. The five appearances of ἐξ at 2:19 preclude remaining.

8. In regard to 2 John 7, Lieu (2008a, 253) comments that what matters is that they are active in the world.

9. Though the sending of Jesus represents a major thematic in John, the concentrated segment in 1 John interestingly appears at 4:9, 10, 14. By implication this strategic text speaks to mission.

the text at 1 John 4:1d, false prophets, who have gone out into the world (ἐξεληλύθασιν), continue as false prophets active and persuasive in the world (4:5).[10] This confirms the reality of a competitive mission. First John not only alerts the recipients to the threat of a rival mission but is itself missional. This continues apace in 2 and 3 John.

THE ROLE OF THE ELDER IN 2 JOHN

One of the ways to work towards discerning the role of the Elder centers upon an inductive reading of 2 John. What does the author of the letter presume and do? He presumes to be an elder that could write a church and advise it. Identifying himself with a church-leader title, whatever the precise parameters, he presumes to lead by letter, writing to a church and as though understood mutually as appropriate (v. 1). If 2 John was in fact a circular letter, then he assumes the privilege of addressing numerous churches in a region (Painter, 2002, 333). He can be a spokesperson for all who know the Christian truth (v. 1c). He can speak definitively and theologically regarding the truth abiding forever in a believer (v. 2). He can even speak for God and offer a pastoral blessing from God (v. 3). He feels competent to summarize the vital essence of faith in two words: truth and love (v. 3c), as perhaps did the Johannine school.[11] He can identify personally with those who have received a commandment from God (v. 4b), make a request of the church (v. 5a), urge obedience to a commandment (v. 5d), have no reservations defining ἀγάπη authoritatively (v. 6), make "the beginning" a baseline of unimpeachable truth (v. 6d), and aver that the lifestyles of the recipients belong to his purview (v. 6e). Furthermore, he takes it upon himself to designate the deceiver and the antichrist (v. 7) and to castigate freely those who do not confess Jesus as come in the flesh (v. 7bc). In his purview as the Elder, he can issue an authoritative warning in the imperative, "Be on your guard" (βλέπετε, v. 8a), and express concern that his readers not lose their full reward (v. 8b). He can tell who

---

10. Of course, if the same group at 2 John 7–9, they travel and proselyte. They did not abide in the doctrine of Christ at the departure or since. Texts in 1 John reflect a threat greater than merely a choice. Rather many have gone out into the world; they are deceivers and have a greater cause (4:1). The departees were prophets, false they may have been, but they were prophets! Hence likely they were impressive advocates.

11. This tends to demonstrate the key role of 3:23 in 1 John.

does and who does not have God (v. 9);[12] he can make or strongly suggest stern policy concerning acceptable recipients of hospitality (v. 10),[13] also justifying it by appeal to the prominent Johannine core value of abiding (v. 9; cf. 1 John 2:23; 4:15);[14] he can announce an intended site visit (v. 12)[15] and speak a greeting on behalf of his church (v. 13)[16] as Clement, though a decidedly authoritative voice on his own, spoke in the name of the church in Rome ("First Epistle of Clement to the Corinthians" in the salutation). The Elder, too, given verse 13, may have been spokesperson for the congregation and not entirely unilateral.

The cumulative effect of this listing forces one to take the measure of the initiating author. He does not hesitate to address his recipients with imperatives (vv. 8, 10), is obviously convinced of his cause, and is very likely a strong personality who felt it quite appropriate to intervene in another congregation of which he was not a "member." This being the case, despite his title as "the Elder," is his ecclesial role here exercised that far removed from a bishop's letter?

On the other hand, the first impression is tempered by the evidence of a characteristic effort at persuasion, at least justification, throughout 2 John (vv. 4, 5, 8, 9, 11, 13). Early on, he also establishes and acknowledges common ground (vv. 2, 4, 5), making references to common Johannine tradition, and recognizes the authority of all believers (v. 1c). He utilizes the inclusive "us" liberally (vv. 2bc, 3a, 5d) as well as "our" (v. 12)

---

12. On the striking emphasis upon "having" in 1 John, see Jones 2009, the sidebar at 234.

13. Verses 10–11 strongly imply that the "deceivers" also traveled, as argued on the basis of other texts above. See Painter 2002, 354.

14. On abiding see the older classic studies by Heise 1967 and Malatesta 1978. See more recently a full blown study by Scholtissek 2000. See also Schnackenburg 1992, 63–69; Strecker 1996, 44–45; Hauck 1967, 4:574–76; Huebner 2:407–08; Painter 2002, 100–102; Pecorara 1937, 159–71. I was unable to obtain Pecorara. On abiding in John, see also Talbert 2010, 133–46; and on 1 John in the same Festschrift Jones 2010, 179–94. The shift toward perseverance is more pronounced in the Epistles.

15. If 2 John were a letter circulated with 1 John, then this virtual promise of a site visit would include numerous churches and imply further the wide missional role undertaken by the Elder. Painter (2002, 356), influenced by Houlden and modifying his theory, makes the capital suggestion that though 1 John was written first and then 2 John, 2 John was intended to be *read* first. See also Houlden 1973, 140. Allow me to add that I take v. 13 as more than "an epistolary commonplace," though it was that. See Kruse 2000, 216; also Stowers 1986, 60.

16. Note the interesting textual variants.

along with "we" (vv. 4b, 8b).[17] Furthermore, in his use of the maxim (v. 9), he places himself under the same measure, a "test" in the venerable taxonomy of Robert Law (see Law 1909, 258–78).[18] He evinces genuine pastoral concern for the recipients (vv. 1, 4, 8, 11). Thomas Johnson (1993, 20) describes the Elder as expressing himself "democratically."[19] Furthermore, 2 John contains an element of defense (vv. 8–10), while 3 John includes an aspect of offense, though both with the missional agenda. The Epistle reflects a definite and pastoral respect for fellow believers, an egalitarian strain still operative.

The cause of the inhospitality urged by the Elder (vv. 10–11) can also speak to the particular missional role of the Elder as *shepherd of the flocks*.[20] He protects the flock against those he perceives as deceivers and antichrists (2 John 7) and a threat to the believers of falling under the baleful influence of deceivers (v. 7).[21] He takes seriously the role of shepherd (cf. John 10:2, 11, 14, 16) and the injunction to tend the sheep (cf. John 21:16, 17) and protect them.[22] The Elder makes crystal clear the staunch rationale for the stern refusal of hospitality or even so much as the civility of a greeting. To offer hospitality means to participate in their evil deeds (v. 11) and to become personally involved in an evil cause. The Greek word utilized here, πονηροῖς, is often associated with the demonic in Johannine parlance, which may well be in the background. John Painter (2002, 355) observes that in John "the judgment brought by Jesus is in conflict with this evil and is depicted in terms of the struggle between the light and the darkness …

---

17. There are textual issues, however.
18. Of course v. 9 is an antithetical couplet.
19. Johnson listed only 2 John 12 under this category but could have included more.
20. See the so-called Asia Minor tradition, noted by Weiss 1937, 774–817. Weiss included the five Johannine writings, the letters of Ignatius of Antioch, Polycarp's *Letter to the Philippians*, 1 Peter, Pliny's *Epistulae ad Trajanum*, Ephesians, and the Pastoral Letters. Of course, there is not consensus that all these works had their provenance in Asia Minor.
21. Lieu (1986, 78) observed astutely that it would be quite difficult to interpret v. 7 without background passages such as 1 John 2:18–27 and 4:1–6.
22. In the Miletus speech, which belongs to the Asia Minor tradition ostensibly, the elders are responsible to watch over all the sheep, to shepherd the church of God (Acts 20:28), and to be alert (v. 31) because of savage wolves from without (v. 29) and some from within who will distort the truth (v. 30). At 1 Peter 5, elders tend the flock of God and have oversight responsibilities.

(John 3:19–21; 7:7)." Here the reference is to evil works or deeds; in 3 John, Diotrephes is accosted for evil words (v. 10b).

The objection to the rival missioners is christologically doctrinal: a failure to persevere in the teaching of Christ (v. 9b) and to teach it (v. 10b). Of course, the teaching of Christ could be a subjective genitive, corresponding to the commandment to love one another.[23] In the Gospel, reference is made to the teachings of Jesus (John 7:16, 17; 18:19). More likely, however, it is an objective genitive contextually and represents a christological criterion,[24] the true disclosure that Jesus Christ came in the flesh (v. 7b; see also 1 John 1:1–3). Hence the Elder bases his firm injunction against providing hospitality on christological orthodoxy. At 1 John 5:11–12, the text assures that those who persevere in the teaching of Christ have both the Father and the Son (cf. John 7:16; 18:19). In the Didache 11:1–6, the guidance laid down was to not listen to a traveling teacher if he or she taught another gospel (ἄλλην διδαχὴν, 2a), a similar prescription. In Ignatius's *Letter to the Ephesians* 7:1, in a christological context, critical mention is made of some who bear the name but with wicked guile who should be shunned as though wild beasts.

What is clear policy, held in common by 2 John, the Didache, and the later writing of Ignatius, is very likely the interpretation of hospitality Diotrephes also held in 3 John, or so I will contend in the final section.

---

23. So argued Rudolf Schnackenburg (1992, 286), on the grounds that the subjective genitive is more profound theologically, closer to Johannine thought, advocated by recent commentaries, and more frequent. Alan Brooke (1912, 177) vigorously denied anything in the context to support an objective genitive, stating that such an interpretation only reflected preconceived notions and that all true teaching derived from Jesus's word. See Brown 1982, 674. John Polhill (1970, 465n) stated that it was "characteristic of Johannine thought to equate Christ with his teaching." Archibald Robertson (1933, 254) stated that it was "not the teaching *about* Christ, but that *of* Christ which is the standard of Christian teaching" (emphasis added). Westcott (1982, 230) said it was "the doctrine which Christ brought." Bruce (1970, 142) argued that there was "a strong balance of probability" in support of the subjective genitive.

24. According to Robert Kysar (1986, 130), the objective is used because it reflects "the proper belief regarding the incarnation-Christ's full humanity." Painter (2002, 354) states that both 1 and 2 John teach about Christ. Lieu (2008a, 258) argues that it shows "faithful allegiance to an inherited body of instruction that is becoming authoritative." See also Loader 1992, 95. Bultmann (1973, 113) argues this "since the author hangs everything on his Christology."

The Missional Role of the Elder in 3 John

Third John contains grist for advancing an inductive analysis of the role of the Elder. The Elder classically utilizes praise (1–7, 12) and blame (9–11), honor (1–7, 12) and dishonor (9–11; see, for example, Neyrey 1998, 1–34) impactfully. This drama of extremes, measure and countermeasure by opponents in 3 John, reflects a challenge to the authentic authority of the antipodal missions. The impression that the NRSV gives of Diotrephes's challenge to the personal authority of the Elder, "does not acknowledge my authority" (v. 9c), is rather misleading. The critical issue centers in opposition to the mission, not just the Elder, though they are bound up together as the Elder identifies himself profoundly with the undertaking. An inductive analysis can nuance the role of the Elder as reflected in 3 John.

Exercising leadership by letter, the Elder identifies himself (1) by ecclesial title rather than name even in this personal letter, because it concerns church issues (v. 1a) and (2) set as theological standards the two pivots of Johannine faith, love (6x) and truth (7x), near code words (see 2 John 3), the strategic place of hospitality and true Christology relevant for the mission. He did speak paternally of his children (v. 4) and of pastoral satisfaction in their walking in the truth (v. 4). He uses the language of obligation (v. 8) and motivated toward becoming coworkers in mission (8b).[25] Urging Gaius to outfit the missioners, he spells out two justifications for sending, hence defining the nature of the mission (v. 7a, "on behalf of the name")[26] and disclosing the missional policy of accepting no

---

25. He did include himself.

26. The Elder himself attributes very high value to the missioners themselves as well as the mission. The preposition ὑπὲρ often rendered "for the sake of," can be "for," "on behalf of" with the genitive. So BDF §231. Brown (1982, 711) names three interpretations: (1) the name of God (Johann Bengel, Joseph Bonsirven, Bernhard Weiss), supported by the absolute tone and the definite article and the previous sentence; (2) the name of the Johannine brotherhood or the Christian cause (James Houlden) or believers as Christians (Acts 11:26); and (3) the name carried by Jesus as states in Rom 1:5 (see 1 John 2:12; John 1:12; 3:18). Brown prefers "Jesus as God's presence in the flesh" (712). Lieu (1986, 107) notes that the absolute use is unusual in the New Testament and recognizes that the name as the presence and power of God was transferred to Jesus. Nevertheless, differing with Gilles Quispel and Brown, she connects the "worthily of God" in the immediate context and "for the sake of the name"; thus the name is that of God. In her later work, Lieu (2008a, 272) reckons with both options but inclines still toward the name of God. The Johannine Jesus reveals the true nature

support from the gentiles (v. 7b), eschewing the methods of mendicants. He confides that he had written a previous letter to a church (v. 9a), most likely concerning the mission, hence his letter to Gaius, a follow-up letter, going around his resistance. He references strong opposition to the mission from Diotrephes,[27] taking the liberty to criticize categorically a local leader (v. 9b). The Elder did not simply register a personal slight or simply a jurisdictional dispute but a full blown attempt to block the mission. Note that the Greek speaks of not receiving *us* (ἡμᾶς), not "did not acknowledge *my* authority."[28] From the vantage of a missional leader, he had sized up Diotrephes as loving to be first.[29] He announces the possibility of a site visit (v. 10a), coming on the scene personally, to deal directly with this missional problem. He dissects the policy issues reflected in the actions of Diotrephes: (1) discrediting the mission (v. 10b); (2) refusing hospitality to

---

of God (John 5:43; 17:6, 11, 13, 26). Schnackenburg (1992, 295) took the position that it designated Christ, not likely God. He calls attention to the impressive parallel at Rom 1:5. Other relevant parallels include Acts 5:41, 28, 40; 1 Pet 4:14, 16; Ignatius, *Eph.* 3:1, 7:1, and Barn. 16:8.While either is possible, I think the parallel at Acts 5:40–41 is the strongest evidence and favors the name of Jesus or Christ. Note also γάρ, a causal coordinating conjunction, is rare in the Johannine Epistles. So BDF §452. This postpositive clarifies the cause for the mission, the passion for "going out." The reference to not receiving from the ἐθνικῶν (v. 7b) is likely to those nonbelievers who "are not newly converted Christians but the general public who listen to their preaching." So Schnackenburg 1992, 295. Brown (1982, 713) took it as referring not to the non-Jew per se but to the non-Christian gentile. This raises the issue of the degree to which the mission was evangelistic, a reading presumed by many but emphasized by Ernst Haenchen: "He is a church leader who pleads in 3 John for a mission to the Gentiles" (cited by Schnackenburg 1992, 272). Verses 6, 7, 8, incidentally, are logically unfolded in a way that is worthy of the rhetorical style of 1 John, reflecting the commitment to persuasion rather than edict.

27. See Richard Bauckham (2006, 373), who recognizes that the literal translation is "does not receive us" (3 John 9b), acknowledges that the NRSV is indeed giving an interpretative translation, and admits that ἐπιδέχεται does not in itself imply acknowledgment of authority. Nevertheless, he prefers "we" as a substitute for "I." While differing as to 9b, I agree that the "we" of authoritative testimony is at play in 1:1–4 and 4:14–16.These latter two cases relate authoritative testimony to the beginning.

28. Of course it could be so interpreted, but it tends to obscure the corporate dimension.

29. This disposition was already present and previously noted by the Elder but possibly activated in the wake of division. The fact that the Elder risks this assessment of Diotrephes, with Gaius evidently able to concur or reject, speaks to its probable accuracy.

the missioners, crippling the undertaking (v. 10c); (3) disallowing others to be logistical support for the missioners (v. 10d); and (4) excommunicating any supporters of the mission (v. 10e).[30] Furthermore, his projected site visit would apparently press for a change in missional policy, reinstating the excluded members who are supportive, reclaiming the provision of hospitality and reprimanding or replacing (?) Diotrephes (cf. 1 Clement). He did utilize the tone of the imperative (v. 11a).[31] He includes a warm and skillful certifying introduction and affirmation of Demetrius (v. 12). He not only expects Demetrius to be housed and provisioned but likely to be heard, even to be a local influence. The expressed hope to see Gaius "very soon" (v. 14), not in the parallel text at 2 John 12, implies a follow-up to his request and a probable encounter with Diotrephes. He sends greetings from the friends, because Gaius had become a missional model, the believers knowing of the letter to Gaius most likely and in support, could even have authorized or encouraged the letter. This church of friends itself held an ecclesiology that was missional. His requesting that Gaius salute the friends by individual name suggests that (1) the Elder knew them, (2) that there were other supporters of the missioners in the church, and (3) that he wants the others apprised of his view of Diotrephes and wants to keep them involved in the mission.

As in 2 John warmth, appeal, persuasion, and common ground obtained in the letter. One finds the presumption of a common mission in which the Elder shares some responsibility himself (v. 8a). Indeed he took considerable responsibility for the logistical support of the missioners. He motivates (v. 8b), appeals, and seeks to convince. He expresses warmth in his address to Gaius (v. 1) and what reads as a spontaneous expression of joy at the news about the faithfulness of Gaius (v. 3bc). He compliments faithfulness (v. 5).

Clearly this elder does not have control of a ministerial personality like Diotrephes but remains resolute to see the furtherance of the mission. He brought forward personal diplomacy and considerable powers

---

30. Clearly some of the church disagrees with the policy of Diotrephes and agrees with the Elder's group.

31. The antithesis at vv. 11bc could be a preexisting truism in the community and in the Johannine school. It bears some affinity to 1 John 2:29. See also 3:6, 9. Most notably it parallels in function 2 John 9, the two of them giving some index as to how these texts were used in the Epistles and likely in the Johannine school and community. They speak to the power of an aphorism, particularly in an oral culture.

of persuasion. He did not possess the formal powers of a regional bishop as commended by Ignatius and Clement. The Elder did feel free to intervene as a hands-on, regional, missional leader. If he could have removed Diotrephes by fiat, he likely would have, particularly if a public encounter proved ineffectual, underlining the limits of his authority. He lacks that formal authority and censures him as it was. He apparently does see his own actions, some rather aggressive, as a part of his "portfolio" as elder.[32]

There seems to be evidence for a missional group of which the Elder was a participant and a leader and a facilitator.[33] There is evidence of itinerants elsewhere, at least an itinerant stage in evolving church organization, as in the Didache. Michael Thompson (1998, 55) speaks of the hospitality system as "a holy Internet" since communication depended on this "protocol software."[34] Furthermore, the missioners reflected in the Johannine Epistles may have been influenced by the dominical model (Mark 3:13–14) and even a Q community and mission.[35] The Elder admires these missioners and is committed to their mission and participates in it. This group, whether very formalized or not, had established missional policies and purpose and depended upon a network of churches for logistical support. These missioners report to one or more churches regarding their outcomes. Was the church of the Elder the missional hub that sent out missioners (see Acts 13:1–3)? They certainly had at least one missional elder in the forefront writing missional letters, exercising leadership by letter. We have seen evidence of a competitive mission holding a contrasting Christology.[36] At least we find missioners, a mission, a missional elder,

---

32. Of course, Diotrephes would have seen the entire enterprise quite differently, likely viewing the Elder as an interloper. The Elder had called him pejorative names like "loving to be first," an accusation that Diotrephes doubtless would have reversed! The Elder had implied also that he was a liar and a deceiver. If he read the letter to Gaius, he would have taken umbrage at 3 John 11. If they were theological opponents, he would have seen the mission the Elder sought to foist on his church as misguided by a faulty Christology.

33. Kümmel (1966, 314) took the position that "there is not even a clue to a provincial missionary organization or something similar."

34. Thompson notes that hospitality became so important that it "became a *paraenetic topos* (Rom 12:13; 1 Pet 4:9; Heb 13:2; etc.), and a requirement of *episkopoi* (Titus 1:7–8)."

35. For a critical evaluation, see Tuckett 1996, 355–92.

36. The missional term ἐξῆλθον has been a thread throughout the argument of this paper.

missional letters and policies and reports, and a network of churches providing logistical support.

Scholars differ on the question, as it relates to 3 John, whether a theological conflict in addition to a power struggle, was at play. Lieu (1986, 160) took it that "only to a marginal extent does the Elder see the struggle in theological terms," rather more parties or sides. Diotrephes, on the other hand, may "have found the Elder doctrinally suspect in Johannine terms" and "may represent the continuation of the independence and antipathy to mission of 1 John" (163). She carefully notes that the Elder did not accuse Diotrephes of failure to confess and toys with the possibility that if there were doctrinal issues Diotrephes thought that the Elder did not understand them (Lieu 2008a, 278).[37]

Building upon Lieu's recognition of a theological conflict, albeit marginal, I mention succinctly considerations in favor of a theological fracas reflected in 3 John and its further definition of the role of the Elder, at least to open the question.[38] First, the prominence of "truth" in 3 John (vv. 1, 3, 4, 8, 12, and "true" at 12), which creates a virtual halo for Gaius and credentializes Demetrius, but which is conspicuously absent from Diotrephes.[39] Gaius and Demetrius are juxtaposed to Diotrephes in a tableau of truth

---

37. As to Ernst Käsemann's (1951, 292–311) inversion of the roles of the Elder and Diotrephes, Lieu finds it unpersuasive, because the Elder would have rejected the alternative witness as antichrist. Käsemann suggests that the Elder's views were deviant.

38. On the basis of 1 John 1:5, one could even argue that the *author* was gnostically inclined.

39. Truth has become a distinctively Christian term. See Spicq 1994, 76. See a wealth of bibliography on pp. 76–81. The first use of truth (v. 1) may well be sincere, as Bultmann (1964, 1:243) argues; but it can be right doctrine, as in 3 John 12, where it "denotes the way of life determined by revelation" and in v. 12, where "revelation is the power that determines the community" (1:247). Lieu (1986, 102), observes that "whom I love in truth" actually exceeds epistolary courtesy and convention. She took it as "not sincere affection so much as a relationship determined by membership of the Johannine circle for which 'truth' was a characterizing term." Stephen Smalley (1984, 347) reads it as "faithfulness to the truth" in v. 3, faithfulness to the truth of the gospel on the part of Gaius himself as perpetuated by orthodox members of the Johannine community. Heinrich Seesemann (1968, 5:945) took "walking in the truth" to mean the whole stance of the believer or faith itself, but in 3 John 3f as "to act uprightly." More inclusively and rightly, Schnackenburg (1992, 293) took it as not just concerning his orthodoxy but also his perseverance in love. It seems to me that Gaius is the very emblem, the personification of the positive fulfillment of 1 John 3:23.

and the lack thereof.[40] Secondly, the use of evil as a critical assessment both in 2 John 11 and 3 John 10, in the former of the evil works of the false missioners and in the latter of the evil words of Diotrephes, is suggestive. In Johannine thought evil is traced back to lineage from the evil one (as 1 John 3:12).[41] Furthermore, the Elder's accusation that Diotrephes's slandering with evil words (3 John 10b) can conjure up the image of lying and deception, and the demonic associated with the secessionists (1 John 2:21, 22, 26, 27) deserves consideration.

Additionally, the missional policy of rejecting representatives not bringing the true doctrine in 2 John 7–11 very likely played in the decision of Diotrephes as well; that is, he probably interpreted incoming intruders as theologically inimical just as the Elder. Also, the similar form of 2 and 3 John suggest proximity in time (see Kümmel 1966, 314). The actions and countermoves of the Elder and Diotrephes are extreme enough to suggest if not demonstrate a deep-seated theological difference. The Elder took a very hard line regarding hospitality in both 2 and 3 John.

These beginning arguments and others at least keep open the disputed question whether theological conflict informs 3 John.

Provisional Conclusions Regarding the Role of the Elder

Scholars have answered the question of the role of the Elder with a variety of images. Brown (1982, 647) identifies the Elder as a prophetic witness and as one who could speak authoritatively for the tradition. He certainly was a prophetic witness, indeed an apostolic witness either in the sense of an actual eyewitness or a tradition bearer, but this does not exhaust his distinctive role, not sufficiently addressing the missional. Burnett Streeter (1929, 84–89), in a famous proposal, saw Diotrephes as a monarchical bishop while the Elder was a bishop of Ephesus and, in practical but not official terms, an archbishop. In the sense of being a regional leader, some support for Streeter's view can be marshaled, but it was in the apostolic sense of mission rather than ecclesiastical authority. Painter (2002, 333) reads the Elder as influential but with "no suggestion of something like

---

40. It must also be recognized, however, that orthopraxy is quite prominent in 3 John both in the antithesis (v. 11) and the gracious hospitality of Gaius. Truth and love are not separable, however.

41. See 1 John 2:13, 14; 3:12; 5:18, 19. In the Gospel 3:19, 20, 21; 7:7; 17:15. See Kretzer 1990, 3:135.

episcopal authority," which can be substantiated by the Elder's dependence on persuasion rather than constitutional power. Georg Strecker (1996, 219) considers him "the principal authority of the Johannine circle,"[42] which he likely was, but we have questioned personal authority as the central issue in 3 John 9. Duane F. Watson suggests that the community regarded him as "a friendly superior" (quoted by Kruse 2000, 303), a characterization that accentuates ecclesiastical office. The characterization "friendly" could pick up on the warmth and personal involvement of the Elder and the way he created common ground.

Our question of the Elder's role is best conceived not as a static quandary but as evolving. It may well be that the crisis of schism and competitive missions called forth a more involved elder as regional leader, and the Elder responded. We see in process an elder in the midst of the fray, embattled but convinced of his cause, and on offense as well as defense. The Elder emerges from inductive observations as a theologian, a pastor caring for and protecting his flocks, an authoritative spokesperson from the beginning, a policy maker, spokesperson, and facilitator for the missioners, a spokesperson for christological doctrine, a missioner himself who may have converted some.

The Elder was above all a missional leader who belonged to a church whose ecclesiology was missiological. He took responsibility for the "brothers" on mission he held in high repute and facilitated support. The missioners and the churches must be factored into any construction of the role of the Elder. We do well to think in terms of a missional system.[43] He made site visits to other churches and acted sternly in furtherance of the mission. As a classic elder by his lights, he protected the flocks. Furthermore, the Elder had an invitational posture and projected a vision of fellowship among Johannine churches.

---

42. Was he the principal of a Johannine school? See Hengel 1989, 109–35.

43. On networking and mobility among the churches, see Bauckham 1998, 30–44. On mobility, see Malherbe 1983, 64–68.

Part 3
The Theology and Ethics of the Epistles

Having addressed the literary composition and historical-situation features of the Johannine Epistles, their theological and ethical content becomes more readily accessible and understandable. In addition to an adequate understanding of their composition and context helping the reader get the content right, however, misconstruing such features may impede one's adequate understanding of their message, so a good deal of modesty is required in any approach to the Johannine Epistles, as one must remind oneself that evidence can sometimes be seen as pointing in more than one direction.

Nonetheless, while the theology of the Johannine Epistles bears similarities with that of the Johannine Gospel, it also bears distinctive features, which are likewise worth noting. That being the case, the following themes present themselves in the Epistles in robust ways. First, the gift of eternal life is a primary-featured promise, a gift to be received through the atoning work of Christ and availed to those who abide in the Father and the Son, empowered by the Spirit. Second, discussions of sin and sinlessness present themselves, raising questions as to whether discussions revolved around perfectability or disagreement over which particular deeds might be sinful or not. A third feature involves the commandment to love one another—the very measure of one's love for God. And yet, how is that communal love to be understood? Are these love appeals aimed at challenging potential defectors, motivating caring for the physical and social needs of others, or a calling to embrace the ways of the community and not the ways of the world? A fourth set of concerns has to do with the labeling of adversaries as "antichrists," signaling the coming of the "last hour" and the need for vigilance. Here especially the need to understand the implications behind, and contexts of, these disparaged believers' actions and teachings is essential for inferring correctly the theological and ethical concerns being advanced. Fifth, note the dualistic constructions of the Elder's rhetorical appeals—his audiences should choose life, light, and love over death, darkness, and hatred. Again, contextual questions emerge: what does walking in the light involve, and what is meant to love not the world but the way of the faithful? Sixth, the extension and denial of hospitality is a central theme in these letters—albeit one that is slanted in opposing directions. On one hand, the Elder admonishes his audiences to deny hospitality to teachers and prophets who deny that Jesus came in the flesh; on the other hand, he confronts Diotrephes for denying the Johannine brothers and friends hospitality within his own community. The questions in each case are how so and why? Seventh, we also have a strong set of appeals to witness and testimony—harkening back to what has been "seen and heard," while also affirming the testimony of the water, blood, and the Spirit. Eighth, the Elder calls for the discernment of truth, distinguishing it from error, and calls for community members to abide in the teaching about Christ that they have received from the beginning. Is this qualitatively different from the call in the Gospel to abide in Christ or simply a difference of nuance?

Again, dealing with any of these issues implies a consideration of the Epistles' relation to the Johannine Gospel, as well as some thought about the socioreligious situation in which they were written. And that's precisely what the four authors in this section carry out. In focusing on particular themes as developed within their particular contexts, clearer insights emerge as to what the message of the Johannine Epistles is claiming—in terms of theology and ethics—and perhaps just as importantly, what it is not. Note again the multiplicity of approaches taken here, as well as the rich yield of this combination of distinctive inquiries.

The Cosmic Trial Motif in John's Letters

Andreas J. Köstenberger

The cosmic trial motif is one of the most important yet often neglected overarching themes in the Johannine corpus. This neglect is particularly regrettable, because the cosmic trial motif provides an overarching framework for John's entire theology and is able to serve as the integrative framework for many other Johannine motifs, such as those related to witness, the world, truth, and judgment.

Further, the cosmic trial motif provides a perspective that is shared among the Gospel, Epistles, and book of Revelation, transcending their differences in genre. In the Gospel, it flavors John's presentation, which is cast in the form of a cosmic drama pitting God and his Christ against Satan. In the Epistles (especially 1 John), it shows believers in a world that is currently controlled by the devil but that presents faith in Christ as assured of ultimate victory. The Apocalypse, for its part, depicts the final battle between the forces of God and his Christ and of Satan and his minions, issuing in God's ultimate triumph and the vanquishing of all his foes.

Thus the cosmic trial motif provides a comprehensive interpretive framework for the entire Johannine corpus on a deep worldview level that should inform and constrain individual exegetical judgments on a smaller scale. In light of this constraining role, it is fitting to turn, first, to a brief study of the main planks in John's *Weltanschauung*.

The Johannine Worldview

The Gospel and Epistles of John are written from a worldview predicated upon at least six foundational beliefs.[1] On the most basic level, John's out-

---

1. For more on this section, see Köstenberger (2009, 275–98); see also Klink (2008, 74–89) to which some of the following material is indebted.

look is controlled, first, by the characteristic Jewish belief in the one God, Yahweh, who is the Creator of the world (John 1:1–4) and the Redeemer and Lawgiver of Israel (John 1:17).[2] Second, John believed that the Messiah promised in the Old Testament had now become flesh, walked the earth, and died vicariously on the cross in the person of Jesus. To show this connection between the Creator God and the equally divine Messiah and Son of God-made-flesh-in-Jesus, John wrote his Gospel (John 1:1, 14; 10:30; 20:30–31) in the conviction that God's glory was revealed both in Jesus's messianic signs and in his vicarious death on the cross (John 1:14; 2:11; 12:23, 28; 13:31–32). Third, John affirmed the possibility and reality of the supernatural revealing itself in word and deed in the person of Jesus Christ. Consequently, he presented both Jesus's body of teachings (in the form of extended revelatory discourses) and a selection of Jesus's most startling messianic manifestations (his "works" and in particular his "signs").

Fourth, the entire Johannine corpus is predicated upon the notion of universal human sinfulness (e.g., John 3:9–12; 8:34–47). John believes that Satan is "the prince of this world" (John 12:31; 14:30; 16:11) and that the world is in moral and spiritual darkness from which people can escape only by coming to Jesus as "the light" (John 1:4–5, 7–9; 3:19–21; 8:12; 9:5; 11:9–10; 12:35–36, 46) and by thus themselves becoming "children of light" (John 12:36).[3] In John's worldview, there is ultimately no middle ground between life and death, between trust and unbelief. John therefore calls his readers to choose between life and death, because, he believes, fifth, that God is a God of judgment and that this judgment will be executed in and through his Son, Jesus Christ (John 5:22–27, 30; cf. Exod 34:6–7). Finally, the exhortation to choose life (John 20:30–31) indicates the strong missionary thrust of the Gospel,[4] driven by a desire to convey the expression of God's redeeming love to a sinful humanity in the person and work of Jesus Christ. This missionary thrust works to overcome the apparent dualism between light and darkness and between life and death.

This set of polarities is thus a distinctive part of the Johannine worldview.[5] Especially in the Gospel and in 1 John, we find contrasts between

---

2. See House (1998, 57) on Jewish monotheism as a "centering theme" of the Old Testament.

3. Unless otherwise noted, all biblical translations follow the NIV.

4. See Köstenberger (1998) and Volf (2005, 193), contra Meeks (1972).

5. Klink (2008, 75) cites Bultmann (1951, 1955, 2:21); Ashton (1991, 206–08); Brown (1979a, 63–66); Neyrey (1988); and Malina and Rohrbaugh (1998, 245ff.).

light and darkness, life and death, flesh and Spirit, above and below, truth and falsehood, love and hate, and trust and unbelief. These contrasts are significant for our purposes as they betray the overarching Johannine perspective of a cosmic conflict between God and his Messiah, on the one hand, and Satan and the world, on the other.

The contrast between light and darkness, for example, is first and foremost a symbol of the struggle between God and Satan. This cosmic conflict is present in the Gospel, the Epistles, and the Apocalypse. What is more, this essay will aim to show how the conflict builds in intensity from the Gospel to the Epistles to the Book of Revelation. The cosmic conflict between God and his Messiah and Satan and the world, in turn, unfolds on a salvation-historical plane: first in the life, death, and resurrection of the Messiah, Jesus Christ; and second in the ministry of the Johannine churches and their relationship with the world as represented by the false teachers. In this way, the very existence of Johannine congregations and their victory over the world (see 1 John 5:4–5) particularizes the cosmic trial between God and Satan (see 1 John 4:4–6).

In the context of this overall framework, then, I will proceed by first briefly surveying the cosmic trial motif in the Gospel since in my judgment the writing of the Gospel precedes the composition of 1 John and is thus presupposed by it. After this, I will examine the cosmic trial motif in 1 John in greater detail and conclude with a few programmatic comments on the cosmic trial motif in the book of Revelation.

In this regard, my approach will be primarily literary, that is, I will seek first to trace the various component parts of the cosmic trial motif in the Johannine writings to some extent independent of their presumed historical setting. I will do this on the basis of my conviction that the cosmic trial motif is a legitimate and exceedingly important motif regardless of one's reconstruction of the historical setting of the various Johannine writings, a matter on which there continues to be a considerable range of views. For this reason, any such presentation would quickly become rather unwieldy, if not entirely unmanageable, if certain constraints were not imposed on historical questions. That said, I will discuss the matter of historical background, specifically with regard to 1 John, for the Johannine trial motif in a final section on history, sociology, and theology at the end of this essay.

The Cosmic Trial Motif in John's Gospel

The cosmic conflict depicted in John's Gospel centers squarely on the question of the true identity of Jesus Christ. John's entire Gospel is written to demonstrate that Jesus is the Messiah and Son of God (John 20:30–31). To this end, John narrates the story of Jesus, the Word made flesh, who came as the Messiah to Israel but who was rejected by his own people. As John makes clear, Jesus was condemned to die on the cross but subsequently rose from the dead and repeatedly appeared to his followers and commissioned them to continue his mission in the world.

The question of truth, christologically focused, in John's Gospel is perhaps epitomized most memorably and poignantly by Pontius Pilate, the Roman governor. At the final trial, Pilate asks, against the backdrop of massive Johannine irony, "What is truth?" with truth incarnate standing in front of him in the person of Jesus. This ironic reference to truth culminates a string of as many as forty-eight instances of the ἀληθ- word group in John's Gospel, a number that is all the more striking when compared with a combined total of ten for all the Synoptics.[6] With laser-like focus, John keeps the question continually before the reader's eye, whether Jesus is the Son of God or whether he is an impostor guilty of blasphemy. John insists that Jesus himself claimed to be the Messiah and that his claim was accurate; the Jewish leaders, on the other hand, rejected Jesus as a blasphemer (see esp. John 5:18; 8:59; 10:33–36; 19:7).

Extending far beyond Jesus's trial before Pilate, the cosmic trial motif in John's Gospel encompasses Jesus's entire ministry, which is cast against the backdrop of the universal spiritual conflict in which Jesus and the world are engaged. Years ago, Rudolf Bultmann spoke of the great trial between God and the world, which provides the larger backdrop against which Jesus's Jewish and Roman trials are conducted.[7] Yet while Pilate judges Jesus according to the world's standards, the reader knows that, in truth, it is Jesus who is the judge who decides over eternal life and death (John 5:19–29).

More recently, Andrew Lincoln (2000; 2004, 128) has argued that the "witness" and "judgment" word groups are part of a cosmic trial or law-

---

6. The breakdown is as follows: ἀλήθεια: twenty-five times in John, seven times in the Synoptics; ἀληθής: fourteen times in John, twice in the Synoptics; ἀληθινός: nine times in John, once in the Synoptics.

7. See Bultmann's (1971, 653–57) penetrating discussion of Jesus's trial before Pilate.

suit motif in John's Gospel "in which Jesus as God's uniquely authorized agent acts as both witness and judge." According to Lincoln, the lawsuits between God and Israel and God and the nations, respectively, in Isaiah 40–55, form the background against which the Johannine lawsuit motif should be understood. In the context of the lawsuit, truth stands for the whole process of judging, culminating in the verdict. At the heart of John's Gospel is the question of whether or not the crucified Jesus is the Messiah and whether or not he rightly claimed to be one with God. "Truth," in essence, is an affirmative answer to these questions. The reason why John does not record a Jewish trial is because his ministry is conceived as a trial in its totality.

In Jesus's trial before Pilate, therefore, the reader is shown that after having been rejected by the Jews. Jesus, the Truth, has now come before Pilate, the Roman, gentile governor, in keeping with the universal message of the Gospel. As in Luke-Acts, there is therefore a salvation-historical movement from Jew to gentile in John's Gospel.[8] In the context of the entire Johannine narrative, similar to the ending of Luke-Acts, Pilate's question, "What is truth?" continues to resound through the ages, calling for an affirmative or negative answer from every reader of the Gospel.[9]

The Cosmic Trial Motif in John's First Epistle

John's Epistles contain virtually all the same ingredients of the cosmic trial motif as does the Gospel. One finds terminology related to witness, the world, and truth, all within the context of the cosmic battle between God's Christ and Satan. While focused on Jesus, who has "overcome the world" (John 16:33) and has destroyed "the devil's work" (1 John 3:8), this cosmic conflict has also engulfed believers, who are assured of victory by their faith in the victorious Son of God (1 John 5:4–5) who has broken the power of the evil one. First John therefore particularizes, at the ecclesial level, the universal cosmic trial of the Gospel. Indeed, with Edward Klink (2008, 88), we may perceive 1 John as "continuing the cosmic drama of

---

8. See John 3–4; 10:16; 11:49–52; and 12:20–50, esp. 12:32, 37–40; see also Acts 1:8; 13:46–48; 28:17–31; and Rom 1:14–16.

9. In another sense, while John "records no answer in words," Morris (1995, 682) is surely correct that "the whole of the following narrative of the death and resurrection of Jesus is John's answer in action. On the cross and at the empty tomb we may learn what God's truth is."

the Fourth Gospel." Thus John's opening words in the Gospel are proven true: "The light shines in the darkness, and the darkness has not overcome it" (John 1:5). The cosmic trial motif in 1 John is integrally related to John's depiction of the world, witness, judgment, Satan, the antichrist, and truth.

The World

The "world" (κόσμος) is mentioned in 1 John first at 2:2, where reference is made to the sufficiency of Jesus's atoning sacrifice "for the sins of the whole world." The term is used in a different sense in its six instances in 1 John 2:15–17, where the readers are warned not to "love the world or anything in the world." The threefold reference to "the lust of the flesh, the lust of the eyes, and the pride of life" (1 John 2:16) echoes the scenario at the fall (see 1 John 3:12) and affirms the world's sinfulness, denied by the world (1 John 1:5–2:2). In its sinfulness, the world is antagonistic, even hateful, toward believers in the Messiah (1 John 3:1, 13).

By this time it is likely that the "world" includes not just gentiles, but Jews who have rejected the Messiah. On the basis of the fact that the phrase "his own" in John 13:1 refers to the Twelve, subsequent to the rejection of Jesus as Messiah by the Jewish authorities (John 12:37–50; see Köstenberger 2004, 389–98; 2009, 233–35), the world has accordingly been redefined in 1 John along christological lines. Those who are of the world in the negative sense are those who do not receive Jesus as Messiah (see John 1:10–12). Hence, much of the rhetoric about the world in 1 John echoes the negative statements found in the Gospel regarding the Jewish authorities representing the Jewish nation.

The world is also the sphere of operation of many false prophets (1 John 4:1), deceivers who exhibit the "spirit of the antichrist" (1 John 4:3; see also 1 John 2:18, 22; 2 John 7). Yet the Holy Spirit, the "Spirit of truth" (1 John 4:6; see also John 14:17; 15:26; 16:13) who dwells in believers, is greater than "the one who is in the world" (1 John 4:4), "the spirit of falsehood" (1 John 4:6; see also 1QS III,18; IV, 23–26; Köstenberger 2004, 437–38). This sinful world is also the place where God sent his Son as an atoning sacrifice for sins (1 John 4:9–10; see also 1 John 2:2; John 1:29, 36; 3:16–17) and as the Savior of the world (1 John 4:14; see also John 4:42).

John observes that "in this world we are like Jesus" (1 John 4:17), "for everyone born of God overcomes the world" (1 John 5:4–5; see also John 1:5; 16:33). In fact, "the victory that has overcome the world" is "our faith"—the only instance of the noun "faith" (πίστις) in John's Gospel and Epistles—in Jesus the Son of God (1 John 5:4–5). The last reference to the world in 1 John is found in 5:19: "We know that we are children of God, and that the whole world is under the control of the evil one." This again underscores the necessity of a new, spiritual birth and asserts that the world is controlled by "the evil one," the devil or Satan.[10]

Witness

Like the Gospel, 1 John claims to represent eyewitness testimony.[11] The author bears witness concerning "the Word of life ... which was with the Father and has appeared to us" (1 John 1:1–2) and testifies "that the Father has sent his Son to be the Savior of the world" (1 John 4:14). The point of this testimony is to elicit confession of faith in the Son (1 John 4:15). Ten of the twelve instances of "witness" terminology in 1 John (μαρτυρέω, "testify"; μαρτυρία, "testimony") appear in 1 John 5:6–11, the passage concerning the three witnesses regarding Jesus, namely, the Spirit, the water, and the blood. This passage is especially significant for the grounding of the Epistle's main claim that "God is light" (1 John 1:5), for it describes the historical and theological ground of faith—Jesus Christ—and the required human faith response.

Verses 6 to 9 of 1 John 5 focus on the object and content of the faith. In verse 6, the object is identified as "Jesus Christ." This usage is John's preferred title for the "historical person of Nazareth ('Jesus'), as well as to the anointed Son of God ('Christ')."[12] This Jesus is "the one who came [ὁ ἐλθών] by water and blood." Most likely, the aorist participle ὁ ἐλθών points back to Jesus's incarnation, while "water" in this instance refers to Jesus's baptism and "blood" to the crucifixion, the beginning and end points of his public ministry.[13] So as not to base his argument on his own words

---

10. See the references to the "ruler of this world" in John 12:31; 14:30; and 16:11; see also 1 John 4:4.

11. For a helpful treatment on the eyewitness nature of the Gospel of John and 1 John, see Bauckham (2006, 358–83).

12. Yarbrough 2009, 281, who notes that "Christ Jesus" is used ninety-five times in the New Testament, but never in the Johannine corpus. For Johannine usage, see John 1:17; 17:3; 1 John 1:3; 2:1; 3:23; 4:2; 5:6; 5:20; 2 John 3, 7; Rev 1:1, 2, 5.

13. So rightly Yarbrough (2009, 282–83) and the majority of commentators; see also R. Alan Culpepper (1998, 272), who argues that the incarnation is the referent for the "water." Yarbrough cites the following New Testament passages as associating

alone, but also to appeal to God's own testimony, John then states that the Spirit also "testifies [μαρτυρέω], because the Spirit is the truth." In the Fourth Gospel, the Spirit is intimately linked with truth. He is the "Spirit of truth" (John 14:17; 15:26; 16:13; see also 1 John 4:6) who bears witness to the sonship of Jesus Christ who himself is the truth (John 14:16; see also 18:38). First John 5:7–8 then serves to clarify and support verse 6. The three witnesses all "testify" and agree in their testimony, because they bear witness to the same truth: Jesus Christ, who is God incarnate.

The presence of three witnesses, for its part, may be in keeping with the "two or three witness" requirement in Deut 17:6 and 19:15, which was also upheld by Jesus (Matt 18:16) and Paul (2 Cor 13:1).[14] In his important study of the "opponents" of 1 John, Daniel Streett (2011) recently argued that 1 John employs the Jewish legal tradition, not to oppose specific docetic, Cerinthian, or antisacramental tendencies in the Johannine community, but rather to point to Jesus as Messiah and Son of God. If so, 1 John is not primarily a polemical but a pastoral letter that uses truthful witnesses to elicit a true confession (1 John 1:1–4; 2:18–27; 4:1–6; 5:1–13).[15]

Verse 9 of 1 John 5 thus argues *a fortiori*, reinforcing the thought of verses 6–8.[16] If humans are willing to accept the testimony of other humans, as they regularly do in court, what then of the testimony of God, who is greater than humanity?[17] What is more, John argues that God's testimony is greater also because of the content of his testimony, which pertains to his Son. Just as Jesus taught that God the Father "has testified [μεμαρτύρηκεν] concerning [Jesus]" (John 5:37), so John passes on that teaching here ("has borne witness"; μεμαρτύρηκεν; 1 John 5:9). Therefore, as Donald Carson (1994, 228) states, "it is God himself who stands behind the three witnesses." Verses 6 to 9, then, emphasize the public verifiability of the incarnation, baptism, and death of God's Son, Jesus Christ.

Jesus's atoning death with "blood": Matt 26:28; Acts 20:28; Rom 3:25; 5:9; Eph 1:7; Col 1:20; Heb 9:12; 13:12.

14. There may also be a link with the Trinity—Father, Son, and Spirit.

15. See Schmid 2004, 24–41; Griffith 2002, 108, 119.

16. So Carson (1994, 229); see also Streett (2011) on 1 John 5:6–12 and his extensive bibliography.

17. But note Lincoln's (2000, 342) analysis of Paul Ricoeur's hermeneutics of testimony: "Testimony is not confined to the courtroom but can occur in any dispute between two parties with conflicting claims and in which a decision or judgment must be made."

First John 5:10–12 then proceeds to focus on the proper human response to this threefold testimony to Jesus Christ.[18] The testimony concerning the truth regarding the Son of God, Jesus Christ, must be appropriated personally by faith. Hence, in verse 10 "the one who believes in the Son of God has the testimony in himself [ἐν ἑαυτῷ]" (NASB). The one who believes thus not only agrees with the three witnesses of verses 6 to 9 but appropriates this agreement internally. This is in keeping with the truth not only because Jesus Christ is the truth (John 14:6) but also because the opposite is true as well: to reject the testimony is to make God a liar (see 1 John 1:6, 10). There is either true or false testimony about God and his Son, Jesus Christ.[19] To deny the publicly verified incarnation, baptism, and death of Jesus Christ is to reject its positive implications—eternal life—and to welcome its negative implication: divine judgment.

As Robert Yarbrough (2009, 285) rightly states, by marshaling the three witnesses, "John's point is that given this wealth of irrefragable testimony, readers are logically, historically, and theologically bound to receive his message as binding" (see also Kruse 2000, 183–84). Although it brings judgment (1 John 5:12) upon those who bear false witness about God in Jesus Christ, the thrust of the Johannine testimony is to bring life (1 John 5:11; see also John 20:30–31). That is, those who have been "born of God/again/from above" (1 John 3:8–10; see also John 1:12–13; 3:1–8) stand on the side of God and his Son, Jesus Christ, in the great cosmic trial against Satan and the world. By their faith in the Son, they testify to the one who came to defeat Satan and his works, thus overcoming the world (1 John 3:8; 5:4–5). As Hansjörg Schmid (2004, 35) states, "The victory is not only promised, it is also proclaimed. It is the victory over the opponents (4,4) and finally, over the whole cosmos (5,4.5), reflecting the universality of the final struggle." In 1 John, therefore, the cosmic trial is progressing toward the goal of Christ's final victory over Satan. The church exists as the earthly witness to this cosmic goal (1 John 3:1–3; see also Rev 19:6–9; 20:7–21:4).

---

18. Thompson (1998, 138) states the point succinctly: "This passage presents the content of the confession about Jesus Christ that believers are to have and to hold."

19. Ricoeur (1980, 128–30), cited in Lincoln (2000, 342), states "false testimony is a lie in the heart of the witness."

Judgment

In addition, John makes reference to his expectation of a future "day of judgment" (1 John 4:17; see also John 12:48). As John's Gospel makes clear, this judgment (κρίσις) has already confronted people in the form of the person and work of Christ (John 3:19). It can be averted only by believing in Jesus the Son (John 5:24). Those who believe have fellowship "with the Father and with his Son" (1 John 1:3) and "life" (1 John 5:12), because they know and abide in the love of God (1 John 4:13–21). Moreover, believers have confidence (παρρησίαν) on the day of judgment, for as they abide in Christ, so they may be confident (σχῶμεν παρρησίαν) at his coming (1 John 2:28; Kruse 2000, 167). Conversely, those who reject the Son will be subject to divine judgment, to be executed by the Son himself (John 5:22, 27, 29; Yarbrough 2009, 258).

Satan

"World," "witness," and "judgment" terminology thus shows jointly that the world is a place under the dominion of Satan, inhabited by the "children of the devil" (1 John 3:10). Indeed, as Clinton Arnold (1997, 1078) states, "according to John, evil behavior finds its paternity in Satan." This comports with Jesus's assessment of the Jewish leaders in the Gospel of John who rejected him (and his Father) in keeping with the will of their true father, the devil (John 8:39–44). These "children of the devil" hate the things of God, most pronouncedly his Christ, and for this reason also the followers of Christ who are gathered in the new messianic community. Yet Jesus gave himself up as an atoning sacrifice for the whole world, and it is incumbent upon believers, the "children of God," to bear witness to Jesus the Son of God.

Third John 7 indicates that there was indeed active missionary work being carried out by the Johannine churches, bearing witness to their role in the cosmic overcoming of Satan and his works. Rather than pull back from the world, which was persecuting them, the network of Johannine churches[20] worked together in overcoming Satan and the world by their proclamation of "the name" (see John 17:11–12). These active missionaries were thus to be supported, because they were co-laborers in the truth (3 John 8). Just

---

20. On the nature of first-century church networks, see Thompson (1998, 49–70).

as Jesus sent out his disciples in the battle against Satan, so the Johannine churches came out against Satan as well.[21] Believers, therefore, are in the thick of intense spiritual warfare, thrust into a cosmic conflict that came to a head when Jesus and Satan squared off at the cross. Satan intended Jesus's demise, but in the predetermined will of God, the cross served as the place where the obedient Son was glorified at the completion of his mission, prompted by divine love.

Antichrist(s)

Believers encountered the presence of Satan in this world, as mentioned, through the spirit of the antichrist which pervades it in the persons of the "many false prophets" who "have gone out into the world" (1 John 4:1, 3; see also 2 John 7). The "antichrist" is first mentioned in 1 John 2:18, where John writes that just as "the antichrist is coming, even now many antichrists have come." The antichrist figure in 1 John, then, serves to highlight Satan's connection to false teachers in the community as a precursor of the coming of the antichrist which is depicted in the book of Revelation.

The word "antichrist" (ἀντίχριστος) appears only in 1 John 2:18, 22; 4:3; and 2 John 7, but the same figure appears elsewhere in the New Testament as well (Watson 1997, 51). The antichrist is likely the incarnation of the evil one mentioned in the teachings of Jesus (Matt 6:13; John 8:44; 17:15) and Paul (2 Thess 2:1–12; 3:3), with the Old Testament false prophet tradition (see Deut 18:18–22) and the apocalyptic of Dan 7 as likely backgrounds (Yarbrough 2009, 143–144; Watson 1997, 51). This figure is prominent in Revelation as the great beast (Rev 11:7; 13:1–10; 16:12–16; 17; 19:20–21). His activity focuses on the denial of Jesus Christ as the Son of God and his persecution of the "saints" who worship him as Lord (see Dan 7:23–25).

The "many antichrists," then, were likely subversive members of the Johannine churches who did not abide by the teaching that Jesus is the Christ, the Son of God (1 John 2:18; 4:3), a teaching that, in turn, was accompanied by lax ethical standards (Yarbrough 2009, 143; Rensberger 1997, 78; Akin 2001, 115). In short, these opponents were false teachers (1 John 4:1), minions of Satan, the chief deceiver and false teacher.[22] As

---

21. Yarbrough (2009, 373) cites Matt 10:1–40; Mark 6:7–13, 30; Luke 9:1–6, 10; 10:1–20 as instances when Jesus taught his disciples of God's provision for their needs as they went out. Note, e.g., Luke 10:17–20 and the cosmic implications of this activity.

22. For a recent study on the Second Temple background, see Lorein (2003).

Yarbrough (2009, 144) states, therefore, "John's distinctive 'many antichrists' apparently refers to forerunners of this end-time figure." Again, the cosmic trial motif is evidenced on the local level, as the true children of God—those who confess Jesus as the Christ—encounter persecution from Satan through his "antichrists."

Truth

This cosmic conflict, in turn, is in essence a battle concerning truth. The centrality of truth—christologically-focused truth—was already observed with regard to John's Gospel. First John, likewise, exhibits a rich "truth" vocabulary, including the noun "truth" (ἀλήθεια; 1 John 1:6, 8; 2:4, 21 [2]; 3:18, 19; 4:6; 5:6); the adjectives "true" or "real" (ἀληθής; 1 John 2:8, 27; and ἀληθινός; 1 John 2:8; 5:20 [3]); and the adverb "truly" (ἀληθῶς; 1 John 2:5). This "truth" language contrasts with the use of falsehood language (see 1 John 4:6). If, as Yarbrough (2009, 46–51) has argued, 1 John 1:5 expresses the central burden of the letter, then "light" and "darkness" likely reflect the conflict between "truth" and "falsehood."[23] Truth, in turn, must also characterize the manner, or "walk," of life of the believer in both word (1 John 1:7–9) and deed (1 John 3:18).

According to John, no one who denies his own sinfulness lives in truth. With a denial of one's sin also comes a disregard for God's remedy for sin, the atoning sacrifice of Jesus Christ (1 John 1:5–10). Another sign of a lack of truthfulness is a person's disobedience to God's commands (1 John 2:4–6). Thus anyone who claims to love God while hating one's brother is a liar, demonstrating his or her disregard for truth (1 John 4:20; see also John 13:34–35). Yet believers "know the truth," namely, that "Jesus is the Christ" (1 John 2:22). In this central contention, John's Epistles and Gospel utterly concur. To this also the "Spirit of truth," who stands opposite the "spirit of falsehood" (1 John 4:6), testifies, because "the Spirit is the truth" (1 John 5:6).

Truth is therefore intimately linked to witness in both John's Gospel and 1 John. Those who confess the truth in 1 John do so on the basis of the eyewitness testimony of the group of apostolic eyewitnesses (including John) mentioned in 1:1–4 ("we"), which likely corresponds to the vari-

---

23. Klink (2008, 79) states, "The bipolarity of truth and falsehood is intimately connected to the bipolarity of light and darkness."

ous witnesses to Jesus's messiahship in John's Gospel. The messianic signs (John 5:36–37; 20:30), the ministry of John the Baptist (John 1:32; 5:33), God the Father (John 5:32, 37), and the beloved disciple (John 21:24; see Bauckham 2007, 78–91) all bear witness to the messianic identity of Jesus. Jesus Christ himself came to bear witness to the truth (John 18:37; see also 1:14; 14:6). Hence, the cosmic trial motif is encapsulated in this witness to the truth revealed in Jesus Christ, and the three witnesses (1 John 5:6–11) testify to the same truth. Only those who confess this truth enter into fellowship with God, Jesus Christ, and fellow believers. The true identity of Jesus Christ as God's Messiah is the demarcation line of truth in the Johannine churches.

The suffering of Johannine believers is therefore part and parcel of the truth and witness themes in the cosmic trial motif.[24] As the notion of "world" has become almost wholly negative (1 John 2:15–17), 1 John depicts true believers as those persecuted, indeed put on trial, by the world (1 John 3:13). The emphasis on knowledge in 1 John thus is tied to persecuted believers' witness to the truth (1 John 2:21; 3:19; 5:18–21). What is more, the call to "abide" (μένω), likely emphasized in 1 John due to this persecution setting, represents the Johannine call to faith in the Messiah—which is the will of God (1 John 2:17, 24)—in keeping with the truth. The exhortation to faith in Christ in the face of increasing persecution is in keeping with the testimony of John's Gospel (e.g., John 9:24–31; 15:18–27) and anticipates the same, further intensified, reality in the book of Revelation.

The Cosmic Trial Motif in the Book of Revelation

Perhaps most obvious of all the Johannine writings, the book of Revelation is thoroughly saturated with the notion of cosmic conflict. In keeping with the apocalyptic genre[25] of Revelation, the book features the culmination of the cosmic conflict between God and his Christ on the one hand and Satan and his demons on the other. Revelation thus shares many terms and themes with 1 John, especially Satan, the antichrist, and false teaching (see esp. Rev 2–3; see Yarbrough 2009, 16–21). At the heart of the second

---

24. See Streett (2011) and Stegmann (1985, 284–94).

25. On the Old Testament apocalyptic genre, see Bernhard Anderson (1999, 305–9). On the genre of Revelation, see Aune (1997–1998); Caird (1966); and Beale (1999). On the cosmology of Revelation, see McDonough (2008, 178–88).

and third visions of the book are thrice-repeated scenes of seven escalating judgments of the unbelieving world which occupy the bulk of the book (Rev 4–20). Again, the motif of reversal is apparent: while in the world, which is controlled by Satan, believers in the Messiah are put on trial; yet three interludes within the second vision (Rev 7:1–17; 10:1–11:13; 12:1–15:8) depict the role of the saints as prophetic witnesses against the dragon and the beast (Bandy 2007).

By way of example, the two witnesses of chapter 11 likely correspond to Old Testament judicial requirements for true testimony (Deut 17:6; 19:15; Num 35:30) indicating the truthfulness with which God and his saints will carry out the cosmic conflict. Acting as God's prophets before the evil world, the witnesses face hostility (see Rev 13:1–18) and even death because of their testimony (Bandy 2007; see also Bauckham 1993b, 85, 120).[26] Yet in the end, the saints are vindicated by God in resurrection (Rev 11:7–12; see DeSilva 1998), and Satan and his demons are judged. This eschatological reversal, in turn, has the purpose of reassuring believers and of calling them to perseverance until the end.

Throughout the course of the book, one finds numerous instances of "world," "witness," and "judgment" terminology, fleshing out the cosmic conflict perspective underlying the entire series of apocalyptic visions.[27] As in the case of the Gospel and the Epistles, the Apocalypse is placed under the rubric of witness (Rev 1:2, 9; 22:16, 18, 20). Witness, truth, and cosmic terminology converge when Jesus is identified as "the Amen, the faithful and true witness, the ruler of God's creation" (Rev 3:14). Again and again, the writer affirms that God's word, and all of his promises, are true (e.g., Rev 19:2, 9, 11; 21:5; 22:6). Significantly, this affirmation also includes the assertion that God is right to judge the unbelieving world. This judgment is executed in keeping with God's justice and with the participation of those who were given authority to judge (Rev 17:1; 18:20;

---

26. On the identity of the witnesses, see, e.g., Turner (2004); Bauckham (1993); and Jauhiainen (2005).

27. "World" (κόσμος) is used in 11:15; 13:8; and 17:8; "witness" terminology is rich throughout (μαρτυρέω: 1:2; 22:16, 18, 20; μαρτυρία: 1:2, 9; 6:9; 11:7; 12:11, 17; 19:10; 20:4; μαρτύριον: 15:5; μάρτυς: 1:5; 2:13; 3:14; 11:3; 17:6); "truth" terminology is represented by ἀληθινός (3:7, 14; 6:10; 15:3; 16:7; 19:2, 9, 11; 21:5; 22:6; though ἀλήθεια is not found); and "judgment" terminology is pervasive as well, including κρίμα (17:1; 18:20; 20:4), κρίνω (6:10; 11:18; 16:5; 18:8, 20; 19:2, 11; 20:12, 13); and κρίσις (14:7; 16:7; 18:10; 19:2).

20:4). Subsequent to Christ's millennial reign, both Satan and unbelievers are judged (Rev 20).

In providing the closing bookend to the entire canon, the book of Revelation completes the story that commenced at the beginning of time as recorded in the first canonical book, the book of Genesis. The cosmic drama that pits God and his Christ against Satan and the other fallen angels is thus shown to culminate in a giant courtroom drama in which the truth of God and his righteous purposes in Christ are utterly vindicated and all forces opposing them are decisively defeated. God's truth prevails, his righteousness triumphs, and his redemptive purposes in Christ receive final consummation. This universal, global, forensic perspective encompasses the totality of outlook adopted in the Johannine writings—the Gospel, the Epistles, and the book of Revelation—testifying to the unitary worldview underlying the entire corpus. Our study of the *Weltanschauung* underlying these documents can now form the basis for a brief discussion of the historical, sociological, and theological settings of the Johannine literature.

History, Sociology, and Theology in 1 John

In the foregoing examination of the Gospel, 1 John, and Revelation, I have argued that the cosmic trial motif provides a comprehensive interpretive framework for the entire Johannine corpus on a deep worldview level that should inform and constrain individual exegetical judgments on a smaller scale. To this point, historical matters have been largely excluded. However, the literary examination of the cosmic trial motif does not preclude treatment of historical and sociological matters. To the contrary, while 1 John reflects real sociological conflict in the Johannine churches (e.g., 2:19), this conflict is not merely sociological but reflects a spiritual, cosmic conflict between God's Christ and Satan working out in real time and space between faithful believers on the one hand and false teachers on the other. In what follows, I will briefly outline the roots of the Johannine community hypothesis and its sociological concerns and then offer four reasons why an alternative explanation is preferable.

In keeping with Gospel scholarship at large, many scholars have seen the Johannine corpus as the product of a "Johannine community."[28]

---

28. See the summary discussion in Köstenberger 2009, 55–60. The following sketch is a general survey of the roots of the sociolinguistic interpretations of the Johannine literature. I recognize the variegated approaches within this method, yet for

According to this view, John's Gospel and the Johannine Epistles reflect the experiences of a rather isolated community of Christians at the end of the first century CE. J. Louis Martyn's (2003) two-level hermeneutic serves as the interpretive framework for this approach, contending that the Gospel should be read as a story which is every bit as much about the Johannine community and its expulsion from the synagogue as it is about Jesus. Thus the blind man's synagogue expulsion narrated in John 9 becomes paradigmatic for the community's own experience (see esp. John 9:22).[29]

On the basis of Bultmann's (1951; 1955) work on myth in the New Testament, Wayne Meeks applied Martyn's hermeneutic to the ascent/descent motif in the Gospel. For Meeks, the Son of Man's descent to earth and ascent back to heaven (John 3:13) established his strangeness and thus persecution and crucifixion by "the Jews." Hence, in Meeks's view, the ascent/descent motif is a language pattern which in effect was meant "to provide a reinforcement of the community's social identity, which appears to have been largely negative" (1972, 69). Again, the Gospel is the product of a Johannine community, perhaps even a single author in that community (see Brown 1979, 94), written to describe the community's *Sitz im Leben* at the time of writing and thus to reassure the members of the community of their sectarian ideology and theology.

Raymond Brown developed this approach further and applied it to the Epistles as well. Brown's landmark work, *The Community of the Beloved Disciple*, reconstructed multiple phases in the Johannine community's history, which consisted of competing groups of Johannine Christians (Brown 1979, 22–24; 166–67; see also 1978, 5–22). According to Brown (1979, 106; see also 17), "both parties knew the proclamation of Christianity available to us through the Fourth Gospel, but they interpreted it differently." Therefore, 1 John was written to settle areas of dispute indicated by social disruption (see 1 John 2:19) and thus correct opponents, and the language betrays this concern (Brown 1979, 96, 109–144). Such language may be regarded as "antilanguage," which functions to maintain the solidarity of an insider, antisocietal[30] group and helps the group interpret their new

---

the purpose of brevity I make some generalizations which, I trust, accurately reflect the overall scope and nature of this method.

29. The first edition of Martyn's *History and Theology in the Fourth Gospel* was published in 1968. See also Martyn (1979, 90–121).

30. Malina and Rohrbaugh (1998, 7), citing Halliday (1978, 171), explain: an antisocietal group as "a society that is set up within another society as a conscious

sectarian reality (Malina and Rohrbaugh 1998, 9–15). According to this view, the Gospel and Epistles (especially 1 John) primarily reflect a sectarian outlook on part of a "Johannine community." Theological meanings, for their part, are predicated upon these sociolinguistic findings.

This approach to the Johannine literature, however, is reductionistic on account of its failure to account for four features which intersect in the above-surveyed cosmic trial motif: its underlying worldview; its missionary thrust; its spiritual orientation; and its salvation-historical point of reference. First, the Gospel and Epistles of John, as argued above, are written from a first-century CE Jewish monotheistic worldview, best characterized by the cosmology and theology of the Old Testament. Scholars have long discerned a dualism in 1 John, which some argue has affinities with the worldview of the Qumran literature; light and darkness is of special concern (1QM, *passim*; 1QS III, 21; IV, 9–14).[31] Yet, as Hoffman (1978, 122) argues, the Qumran literature and 1 John share "concerns common to all religions." Other scholars, typified by Bultmann (1925, 100–46; see also Meeks 1972, 44–72), maintain that a gnostic worldview stood in front of or behind the Johannine literature. However, Gnosticism was more than likely never a coherent worldview or thought system and almost certainly had not coalesced to form a coherent thought structure by the time John's Gospel and Epistles were written (Carson 1994, 229; see also Streett 2011).

A more adequate approach to understanding the worldview of 1 John involves looking at the Old Testament. If 1 John was written subsequent to the Gospel of John and shares its worldview (on which see further below), then 1 John likely shares the source of that worldview as well. Hence "light," for example, has a prominent place in the Old Testament in connection with God's creation (Gen 1:3), preservation of his people (Exod 13:21), and spiritual light (e.g., 2 Sam 22:9; 23:4; see also Ps 119:105; Yarbrough 2009, 49). Therefore, John's affirmation that "God is light" (1 John 1:5) reflects God's character as truthful and as opposed to any form of darkness, whether ethical or spiritual. What is more, Jonathan Pennington (2004, 260–277) has insightfully argued that the Old Testament presents a dualistic cosmology, summarized in the frequent merism "heaven and earth" (e.g., Gen 1:1; Deut 4:26). According to Pennington,

---

alternative to it. It is a mode of resistance, resistance which may take the form either of passive symbiosis or of active hostility and even destruction."

31. Schnackenburg 1992, 75; Brown 1982, 242–45. See also Price 1990, 9–37; Boismard 1990, 156–65.

the epithet "heaven and earth" describes the Old Testament's worldview, and this "dualistic *Weltbild*, in turn, undergirds a dualistic *Weltanschauung* or worldview" (Pennington 2004, 262). If this is the case, then John's so-called "dualism" does not derive from a Qumran or gnostic-style sectarian worldview. Rather, John's way of viewing the world has been shaped and is continuous with the cosmology of the Old Testament. It follows that Jesus Christ is the fulfillment of underlying Old Testament realities and symbols (Köstenberger 2009, 155–67), and Old Testament cosmology informs Johannine cosmology and Christology in the revelation of the gospel that gives life in Jesus's name (John 1:14, 18; 20:31; 1 John 5:13).

Second, the missionary thrust of the Johannine literature, in keeping with its worldview, arguably does not support a wholly sectarian view of John and his writings (see esp. Köstenberger 1998, 203–06). Even if the Gospel had been redacted, the Gospel's evidence—especially the large swath of mission material throughout the Gospel (see esp. 3:16; 17:18; 20:21)—militates against the notion that the Gospel's author or final redactor espoused a sectarian outlook; to the contrary, he demonstrably advocated a mission to the world. What is more, the Gospel's portrayal of the new messianic community is rooted in the Old Testament metaphors of God's "flock" (John 10) and "vineyard" (John 15). According to John, there are other sheep to be gathered into the fold (John 10:16; see also 11:51–52); outward movement is required (4:38; 15:16). It is therefore considerably more plausible that salvation-historical, not sectarian-sociological, purposes drove the author(s) of the Fourth Gospel. In keeping with this outlook, therefore, the new messianic community will partake in the worldwide mission of the Messiah, Jesus (see Köstenberger 1998, 45–197).

An important, related point is the intended audience of John's Gospel. While the Gospel was likely intended initially for a specific audience, its implied readership was more than likely a universal reflection of the worldwide nature and mission of first-century Christianity (Bauckham 1998, 9–48; see also Klink 2007; 2010). Many (if not most) versions of the "Johannine community hypothesis" are unable to account for the mission motif of the Fourth Gospel, especially when its audience is held to be the community itself (see Köstenberger 1998, 206). On the contrary, John's Gospel makes clear that it was the very "world" that stood opposed to both God and his Christ (see John 3:16) that became the primary intended recipient of the gospel message proclaiming Jesus as Messiah and Son of God (John 20:30–31; see Carson 1987, 639).

The Epistles of John, therefore, should be regarded as particular, pastoral applications of the universal mission of the Messiah and his messianic community. Jesus's disciples are those who "overcome the world" by their faith in him while renouncing teaching that is from the devil, the *antichristos* (1 John 3:8; 5:4–5; see Kruse 2000, 123; 173–74). Such faith is evidenced in true confession (1 John 2:21–22; 4:14–15) and ethical behavior, the keeping of his commands (e.g., 1 John 3:4–10; 4:20–21). Moreover, the Johannine churches evince an active involvement in, and obedience to, the salvation-historical mission of Jesus (3 John 7). Their missionary work in the service of truth, and against false teaching and concomitant conduct (see 2 John 7–11; 3 John 10), was, in turn, to be supported by a network of churches (3 John 8, 11; see Thompson 1998, 49–70).

Third, the regeneration language of 1 John—namely, that one must be "born of God" (1 John 2:29; 3:9; 4:7; 5:1, 4, 18)—coheres with that of the Fourth Gospel (John 3:3, 5; see also 1:12–13) and further indicates that the cosmic trial motif is a universal reality with particular spiritual implications. The author of 1 John thus addresses spiritual "children" (e.g., 1 John 2:1, 12, etc.) and how they ought to relate to supernatural realities manifested in the many antichrists and their false teaching. Hence only those "born of God," in keeping with the apostolic and triune witness to Jesus's life and ministry (1 John 1:1–4; 5:6–11), will be protected from Satan, the antichrist(s), and the world (1 John 5:18). No doubt there was concrete conflict in the Johannine congregations, as indicated by passages such as 1 John 2:19 (see also 2 John 7). However, the analysis above suggests that John would have viewed any local church conflict against the larger backdrop of the cosmic conflict between Christ and Satan. For this reason it seems precarious and foreign to the Johannine mindset to interpret the cosmic conflict motif in 1 John as a projection of the local conflict in the Johannine churches onto a cosmic scale. More likely, John viewed the cosmic spiritual conflict between God and Satan as primary and believed that this conflict is only secondarily played out at the social, ecclesial level.

The issue of the "opponents" in 1 John, then, as Streett (2011) has argued, should be connected primarily to broad salvation-historical rather than narrow sectarian concerns. As John observes in his Gospel, the Messiah was rejected by his people (see also John 12:37–50) in keeping with Isaiah's prophecy concerning Jewish resistance to the Messiah (Isa 53:1; 6:10; see Köstenberger 2007, 477–83). Thus, John's negative depiction of "the Jews" corresponds to the polemical references in Rev 2 and 3. For example, as Yarbrough (2009, 19) points out, the church in Smyrna is said to be persecuted by "those who say they are Jews" but whom he calls "a synagogue of Satan" (Rev 2:9). In Thyatira, false teaching is associated with the deep things of Satan (Rev 2:24).[32] Hence in Rev 2-3, as in John 8 and 1 John, the opponents of Messiah are associated with Satan. This demonstrates that John is moving along first and foremost a salvation-historical, not sociological, plane: whether Jew or gentile, those who have set themselves against Jesus the Messiah are on the wrong side, salvation-historically speaking, of the cosmic spiritual conflict centering on the true identity of Jesus as God's Messiah.

Fourth, at its root, therefore, the cosmic conflict deals with the life of Jesus. The Gospel primarily narrates the history of the Messiah, Jesus, and his gathering of a new messianic community. The Epistles testify to the implications of the life and work of Jesus Christ upon those who do or do not confess him as Christ. The book of Revelation anticipates the culmination of the cosmic trial and its consequences for those who have sided with the Messiah or Satan, respectively. Hence, contrary to Martyn's (2003) two-level drama proposal, the primary point of reference in the Gospel's narrative in keeping with the Gospel genre, is the earthly ministry of Jesus, whereas the primary point of reference of the Epistles is the situation of the Johannine churches toward the end of the first century CE. The issue of which document was written first, for its part, must be decided largely on the basis of the internal evidence.

On balance, as mentioned, it is more likely that John's Epistles were written after the Gospel.[33] Though it is possible that some of the connections in 1 John are based on a common tradition (see Brooke 1912, xix-xxii; Grayston 1984, 12-14), in a few places the Gospel seems to be assumed. For example, 1 John 2:7-8 refers to and explicates the new commandment of John 13:34-35 without naming it. Also, as was argued in some detail above, 1 John 5:6 likely uses "water and blood" to refer to the baptism and crucifixion of Jesus Christ, encompassing his earthly ministry. Thus, the historical claims of the Fourth Gospel seem to be assumed in 1 John. On this basis, and in view of the lexical and thematic links with Rev 2-3, it appears that 1 John (as well as 2-3 John) operates in a salvation-historical vein and exhibits a theology and purpose consistent with

---

32. Yarbrough (2009, 18-21) ably demonstrates the lexical and thematic links between Rev 2-3 and John's Epistles.

33. Much of this paragraph is indebted to my previous work (Köstenberger 2009, 93).

the Fourth Gospel: life is found in the name of Jesus Christ as portrayed in the Gospel's narrative (John 20:30–31; 1 John 5:13). Yarbrough's statement (2009, 21) is worth quoting in full:

> All three [letters] are frank, realistic, but positive pastoral missives (not congregational creations) seeking to affirm and reinvigorate doctrinal direction, ethical urgency, relational integrity, and a forward-looking faith in God, generally in a geographical setting and temporal era in which relatively young churches were facing the challenges of longer term existence.

The cosmic trial motif therefore provides an interpretive framework on a deeper worldview level that informs not only our literary and thematic analysis but also enables us to arrive at informed judgments regarding the historical and sociological setting of the Johannine churches as reflected in the Johannine corpus and especially 1 John.

Conclusion

In this paper I have sought to establish that the cosmic trial motif constitutes a shared framework for interpreting all five documents making up the Johannine corpus of writings. John's Gospel narrates Jesus's story as the account of the Word made flesh that took up temporary residence in the universe he created yet that was rejected by the very world he made (John 1:10–11). At the same time, John also records Jesus's establishment of his new messianic community, made up of the Twelve, who were also the recipients of three of Jesus's resurrection appearances (see John 21:14) and his commission to receive the Holy Spirit and to pronounce forgiveness in Jesus's name (John 20:21–22).

First John conveys the notion of cosmic conflict to his readers in a similar fashion. The world is under the dominion of the evil one; believers are not to love the world and the things in the world; and the Spirit, together with Jesus's baptism and the cross, serve as a threefold witness testifying to the truthfulness of the Christian claim that Jesus is the Messiah. In this, 1 John serves as the pastoral application of the Johannine Gospel drama, of which the book of Revelation constitutes the final consummation. The Apocalypse also comports closely with the Gospel's realized eschatology by showing the end-time consummation of God's righteous purposes in

Christ, a consummation that includes the final judgment of Satan and of the unbelieving world and the vindication of Christ and of his followers.

In my judgment, the material presented in this paper adds plausibility to the view that one and the same author was responsible for the Gospel, the Epistles, and the book of Revelation, whether John the Apostle or John the Elder or a Johannine school or community subsequent to John's death.[34] Regardless of the identity of its author or authors, all of the Johannine writings provide a unified witness to the truthfulness of the claim that Jesus is the Messiah, testifying to the universal need for people to believe in him in order to receive the gift of eternal life and expressing the firm expectation of Jesus's return and of the final consummation of God's redemptive and judicial purposes.[35]

---

34. Again, see the important recent treatment of the opponents in 1 John by Streett (2011).

35. Many thanks to Culpepper for his kind invitation to participate in the 1 John symposium and for his formative influence in my own work, particularly through his landmark study, *Anatomy of the Fourth Gospel*. See also my related study, "Heaven in John's Gospel and Revelation," in *Heaven, Theology in Community 6* (ed. Christopher W. Morgan and Robert A. Peterson; Wheaton, Ill.: Crossway, 2014), 139–57.

Spirit-Inspired Theology and Ecclesial Correction: Charting One Shift in the Development of Johannine Ecclesiology and Pneumatology

Gary M. Burge

The work of Raymond Brown in the study of the Johannine literature has been nothing short of remarkable. When he died in 1998, many of us felt a great light had passed from the church and the academy. Brown made Johannine studies fascinating, and I can tell you from one vantage anyway, his work inspired my career as well as a host of others.

Urban von Wahlde and Paul Anderson have given us a helpful evaluation of Brown's "Johannine Community" hypothesis. As we know, the ongoing discussion through the 1980s and 1990s weighed it carefully. Brown (1979a, 7) called this effort "detective work" and hoped that if only sixty percent of it was correct, he would be satisfied. For myself, I think he may have achieved his goal.

I am interested in one feature of his hypothesis that I believe has withstood the test of analysis. Brown first offered this idea in Matthew Black's 1979 *Festschrift* (Brown 1979b) and then went on to give it full expression in his well-known *Community of the Beloved Disciple* (Brown 1979a). He also gave it thorough exegetical support in his Anchor Bible Commentary on the Johannine Epistles three years later (Brown 1982). Today it is overlooked by many commentators, but in my mind it is one of the vital clues to understanding 1 John.

Brown believed that a number of theological themes found in the Gospel of John became the source of considerable theological divisions in later stages of the community's life and that 1 John provides significant evidence of this problem. He felt, for instance, that the high Christology of the Gospel may have contributed to what seemed to be a debate centered on docetism and a denial of a full incarnation. He also felt that the dualistic language of the Gospel and its perceived tensions with the "world" laid the groundwork for the ethical dualism that may have divided the community. He famously said that the weapons of conflict that the Gospel aimed at the world later were turned back on the community members who used them.

In 1 John 4, the author (and here I will simply use the name "John" for convenience) warns about deceitful teachers. "Beloved, do not believe every spirit, but test the spirits to see whether they are of God; for many false prophets have gone out into the world" (4:1).[1] In the immediately following verses, we learn that the test of a spirit which has come from God is that it embraces a correct Christology: "By this you know the Spirit of God: every spirit which confesses that Jesus Christ has come in the flesh is of God, and every spirit which does not confess Jesus is not of God" (4:2–3a).

Two ideas seem clear: (1) we can fairly assume that these false teachers were prophets who were claiming some spiritual authority to lead the church in new theological directions. And (2) we can assume that they were successful. In 1 John 4:5, the letter says with a hint of despair that "the world is listening to them." The congregation was listening to these novel teachers, they were doubting what they had heard "from the beginning," and now they were ready to claim that the Spirit of God had given them these new insights into life and belief. And this is one of the concerns that prompts the writing of 1 John. The recipients are torn between what has been taught in the tradition and what is being revealed by these new teachers.

The question is simply this: What ecclesial and theological environment would lend itself to this sort of pastoral crisis? And this is where Brown's thesis becomes a useful tool. [As an aside, when I explain these sorts of issues with pastors in the charismatic-Pentecostal world who know the Johannine literature, they feel right at home. They have an immediate answer, and it is a close echo of Brown's proposal.]

Brown's thesis is simple: the pneumatology of the Gospel of John gave rise to the pastoral crisis we later see in the Epistles. Or we might put it another way: A community deeply invested with spirit-experience found itself in jeopardy because of the very intense spirituality it had so eagerly promoted.

---

1. Each citation is taken from the RSV.

The prominence of the Spirit in the narrative of the Fourth Gospel is well-known. Jesus's own identity is presented with reference to the Spirit (1:34; 3:34; 6:27; 7:37–39; etc.), and in this gospel we not only hear Jesus promising and describing the coming Spirit-Paraclete for his followers (14:17, 26; 15:26; 16:13) but also delivering it on Easter (20:22). Perhaps the most interesting metaphor for the Spirit is given in the living-water imagery of the Gospel. The Samaritan woman is offered this water (4:10), the worshipers at the tabernacles hear about it (7:37–38), and water mysteriously flows from Jesus's side on the cross (19:34). John tells us that this is the Holy Spirit (7:39), and it is a signal marker of the gift that Jesus is bringing to the church. For some interpreters the dialogue with Nicodemus in chapter 3 is a template for what it must have meant to belong to the community formed by John.

No other Gospel quite compares to all this. Moreover, in the Farewell Discourse we learn that the promised Spirit will sustain the presence of Jesus within his disciples. In 14:17 this Spirit is with them (presumably in the presence of Jesus) and will be in them (presumably in the coming of the Spirit-Paraclete). This teaching even resolves the eschatological crisis: Jesus will return to them but in a manner that they need to appreciate: the resurrection-return will provide the gift of Jesus's own Spirit-return, which will be breathed into them. This is why they are not orphans (14:18). Jesus never leaves them. As many have pointed out, the tasks of the Paraclete parallel the tasks of Jesus signaling that the indwelling of the Spirit will sustain Jesus's own life in the world. This fits well with the way in which discipleship is described in 1 John 4:13. We know we abide in him and he in us, because he has given us "his own Spirit."

What will this Spirit-Paraclete do? It will dwell in them (John 14:17), teach them everything (14:26), and lead them into truths that they have not yet heard (16:13). Simply put, the Spirit-Paraclete will be the resumption of Jesus's life in the church and thus continue the revelatory work that Jesus brought to the world. As Jesus came to reveal the Father (17:6), so now Jesus-in-Spirit will continue to reveal the deeper truths about God, which the community needs to hear.

Therefore this is what we have: The followers of John are formed by the theology of the Gospel and possess a heightened awareness of the indwelling Spirit. And while this contributes to a community of vibrancy and immediacy (John 3:3; 4:23–24), it spins off prophet-teachers who use this same inspiration to justify their novel teachings. Because they can claim that the indwelling Spirit of Jesus was with them, they can reveal to the church things about a docetic Christ no one had considered before. These controversial teachings are among the things Jesus could not say earlier but now is ready to reveal (John 16:12–13). And as prophets they are ready to supply him with a voice. If challenged, they can even up the ante: Dwelling in them are the *Father and the Son,* who together confirm this revelation of the Spirit (John 14:23).

Brown never saw these prophets as mystics for whom religious ecstasy inspired their following. He saw them as teaching prophets and demonstrated this role from the Didache, where the difference between prophets and teachers is vague (Did. 11–13; see also Eph 4:11).

This explains something else that my charismatic-Pentecostal friends do not think I understand—or at least that good Presbyterians and Baptists do not understand. In this pastoral environment with Spirit-anointed false teachers, there are some things you simply cannot do. In a word, you cannot take the posture of Paul. That is, you cannot appeal to your own authority and believe that the gravitas of your position or the force of your experience will win the day. Ecclesial correction in a spirit-filled setting requires different strategies; just ask anyone at the Society of Pentecostal Studies.

First, notice that in 1 John the author never appeals to any apostolic authority or his authority as a bearer of teaching that cannot be contradicted. He never uses an authoritative "I" statement. Compare this with the approach of Paul in Galatians. His words resound from the first: "I am astonished that you are so quickly deserting him who called you" (1:6), or "As we have said before, so now I say again, if anyone is preaching to you a gospel contrary to that which you received, let him be accursed" (1:9). There is an unmistakable authority there which Paul leverages to his advantage. Paul is deferring to tradition (the gospel "which you received") but considers himself the arbiter of its meaning.

John cannot do this. He does not leverage pastoral authority or power anchored to a position. (If this were an apostolic author, we might expect such an appeal.) He cannot point to the apostles in Jerusalem as if they validated him (as Paul does in Gal 2). John lives in a world where the institutionalization of authority has barely surfaced, and so the correction of misguided teachers cannot be achieved easily.

Second, note what John does do. He must appeal to the discernment of spirits as a chief strategy. He cannot discredit their anointing directly—they would just return the favor. But he can remind his church that the same Spirit-Paraclete dwells in them just as it dwells in the teachers. He does not want them to be intimidated by any who might claim a fuller inspiration. "But you have each been anointed by the Holy One and you know" (1 John 2:20). "But the anointing which you received from him abides in you, and you have no need that any one should teach you; as his anointing teaches you about everything, and is true, and is no lie, just as it has taught you, abide in him" (1 John 2:27). In other words, they each have the same equipment as the secessionists, and their knowledge and inspiration are comparable to these new teachers. They have no need to be intimidated.

Thus, John must propose that they learn to test the spirits. There are spirits of truth and spirits of error (1 John 4:6); even the spirit of the antichrist is now in the world (1 John 4:3). So this is his chief strategy. John cannot deny the Spirit, but he can teach discernment of spirits and urge followers to weigh the claims made by the prophet-teachers.

But the immediate question in such a unique ecclesial setting is this: What is the criterion we use to discern such revelatory spirits? John has his answer, which is tenuous but necessary. The validity of the true Spirit of God is found in ethics and right belief (1 John 4:13–21). Simply put, he appeals to tradition.

John's doctrinal test of true spirits needs to be anchored, and here he makes a final argument that was as risky as it may have been ineffective. John appeals to what had been taught traditionally in the apostolic record. Ten times he refers to "the beginning" or "what you heard in the beginning" and points his followers to the apostolic tradition no doubt presented in his Gospel.

The only problem for John, however, is this: the Gospel enshrined the same orthodox tradition that gave birth to the spirituality that he needs to restrain. Therefore, rather than beginning 1 John with a recital of his credentials (as Paul does in Gal 1:1), he reaches back to how this Christian faith is anchored: in the incarnation that was heard, touched, and seen—and was proclaimed from the very beginning. In other words, what the Spirit of Christ is saying now must cohere with what we understood him to have said during his incarnate life.

First John may represent the early stages of a process that is evident in the New Testament. Prophets were clearly held with esteem in the early chapters of the church (1 Cor 12:28; Eph 3:5; 4:11; 1 Tim 4:14), but their efforts inspired departures from the apostolic tradition and these had to be restrained (Mark 13:32; Matt 24:11; 1 Cor 14:29, 32; 2 Pet 2:1, 16; Rev 2:20). John reflects the same reserve or caution with regard to prophecy as we see in, say, 2 Peter.

I was once speaking at the Society of Pentecostal Studies and mentioned this theological dilemma of 1 John to a friend there in the Assemblies of God. "I get it exactly," he said, "and this is why we now require our pastors to go to seminary." This theological and pastoral tension between inspiration and tradition is timeless. And Brown successfully demonstrated that if we link the Gospel and the Epistles thoughtfully, suddenly new light is shed on what was happening behind the scenes in 1 John. He also demonstrated that this tension continued well into the second century. The opponents of Ignatius, second-century Gnosticism reflected in Nag Hammadi (esp. Hypostasis of the Archons), and what little we know of Cerinthus, all point to the irresistible temptation to an inspiration that in some manner upends tradition and is very difficult to defeat.

One might think that this is an ancient issue or something restricted to Pentecostal settings that might be foreign to each of us, but let me reach as far from these places as I can. However, to tell you this example runs the risk of inspiring the very unhappiness found in 1 John, so please recall those love exhortations in 1 John as you read to this.

In a major fundamentalist church in the United States, a pastor recently spoke to his congregation of fifteen thousand about what God had revealed to him concerning the end of the world. He appealed to spirit-texts of the Gospel of John (such as 16:12) and claimed that the Spirit-Paraclete was revealing to the church things Jesus could never say in his lifetime. His revelation: that war would break out soon in the Middle East, that political support for Israel was God's test of faithfulness in our day, and that all Christians need to become politically active and urge that the United States arm its ally and be ready for a preemptive attack on Iran. It was quite a sermon!

What is interesting here is not the subject itself (Christian Zionism, to be precise). What is interesting is how this was presented. Theology was not a matter of wrestling with tradition or text; it was grounded in the self-validating experience of what someone believed to be the Spirit-Paraclete. The speaker did not even try to do theology: he temporarily joined Montanus, appealed to the Spirit and made a pronouncement.

Now traditionalists in this church have an interesting dilemma on their hands, not unlike that of the author of 1 John—which is why this is an interesting case study and one which appears in many forms in churches today. *When text and tradition are not the basis of theological discourse, when unprecedented revelations are offered with confidence, how does one challenge a new theological teaching?*

Perhaps a sound recommendation would be that they hand this dilemma to the Society of Pentecostal Studies. They seem to know how to address those who claim to speak in the name of the Paraclete thanks to their long tenure living in the world of John. John 16:12 is familiar territory to them, and they (like John) know how to correct teachers who promote things Jesus never said.

The Antichrist Theme in the Johannine Epistles and Its Role in Christian Tradition

Craig R. Koester

Some of the most provocative and influential comments made in 1 and 2 John have to do with the notion of antichrist. These texts contain the earliest known occurrences of the term "antichrist" (or ἀντίχριστος), and they bequeathed it to the generations that followed.[1] By the late second and third centuries CE, the question of antichrist had become the focus of speculation and comment in some Christian circles, and the power of the term to engage the imagination has continued down to the present. Bernard McGinn's (2000) comprehensive study of the antichrist idea in western culture put it well in its subtitle. He called it *Antichrist: Two Thousand Years of the Human Fascination with Evil*.

The usual picture of the antichrist has many sides to it. Writers from antiquity onward have envisioned the antichrist as a singular figure, the consummately evil human being, who is to be the agent of Satan on earth. He is often pictured as a political ruler who will reign during the final years of this present age and persecute those who refuse to worship him. But in the end there will be a cosmic battle in which the returning Christ will destroy the antichrist and bring him to a fiery end.

What is so striking is how little of the traditional scenario has to do with 1 and 2 John.[2] These two letters may supply the term "antichrist," but

---

1. The term ἀντίχριστος appears in 1 John 2:18, 22; 4:3; 2 John 7. The next occurrence is in Polycarp, *Phil.* 7:1, which seems dependent on the Johannine Epistles, since it links the antichrist to those who do not confess that Jesus Christ has come in the flesh.

2. Interpreters are uncertain whether 1 and 2 John were written by the same author. Some consider common authorship plausible, though not certain (e.g., Brown 1982, 16–19; Rensberger 1997, 19). Others think it likely that they were written by different people, though the two works share some common traditions (Lieu, 2008, 6–9;

much of the content comes from elsewhere. One might wonder whether the Epistles might refer so briefly to the antichrist because the tradition about this figure was so well-known. After all, 1 John assumes that readers have already heard that the antichrist is coming (2:18; 4:3). Over a century ago, Wilhelm Bousset (1896) of the history of religions school argued that there was a unified antichrist tradition that circulated in Jewish communities long before the Epistles were written. He thought that it envisioned an antichrist much like that described by Christian writers several centuries later. But more recent studies have shown that Jewish beliefs about an eschatological adversary were marked by variety, not uniformity, and that the notion of an antimessiah seems to have been developed by Christians (Peerbolte 1996; see also Jenks 1991; McGinn 2000, 3).

When I consider 1 and 2 John in light of the later tradition, I do not assume that the later sources reveal the ideas that shaped *the writer* of the Epistles. Rather, the later tradition has shaped many *readers* of the Epistles, and it continues to influence the interpretation of these passages, sometimes in subtle ways. The long history of speculation about the antichrist and the polemical use of antichrist language is difficult to ignore, even when interpreters try to limit their work to the context in which the Johannine Epistles were composed.

Attention to the history of reception of the antichrist idea can make us more aware of assumptions that are often brought to the reading of 1 and 2 John.[3] By comparing later portrayals of the antichrist with passages from the Epistles, we can better discern what the interpretive assumptions are and can ask whether or not we want to affirm those assumptions. Then the study of reception history comes full circle when it brings each interpreter back to a renewed engagement with the biblical text itself. So by giving attention to reception history, I want to consider three questions: First, how do the Johannine Epistles portray the antichrist? Second, how do the Epistles depict the eschatological battle? And third, how do the Epistles encourage or subvert the polemical use of antichrist language?

Painter 2002, 50–51; Strecker 1996, xl). Since the references to the antichrist in 1 and 2 John are so similar, they will be treated together as expressions of a common outlook.

3. For a useful introduction to reception history or *Wirkungsgeschichte*, see Luz 2007, 63. He points out that one never encounters biblical texts in abstract space. Interpreters inevitably have presuppositions that are shaped to some extent by tradition. The interpretive process involves thinking critically not only about the text but about the perspectives the interpreter brings to the text.

The Portrayal of the Antichrist

Two of the principal architects of the antichrist tradition were Irenaeus and Hippolytus, who wrote in the late second and early third century CE.[4] Their approach was to create a unified portrait of the antichrist by synthesizing elements from various biblical passages. The term "antichrist" was taken from the Johannine Epistles and combined with Revelation's description of the tyrannical ruler, who is pictured as a seven-headed beast. According to Rev 13, this beast is the agent of Satan, and it rises from the sea to dominate the peoples of the world. The beast is the center of the ruler cult, so that the beast himself becomes an object of worship. This beast makes war on the saints, while a second figure—known as the false prophet or beast from the land—promotes the ruler cult by working miracles, slaughtering his opponents, and marking people with the name and number of the great beast, which of course is six hundred and sixty-six. This vision from Revelation was fused with 2 Thess 2:8, which warns about the man of lawlessness, whose coming is to be heralded by signs and wonders. In this scenario, the man of lawlessness not only makes himself the object of worship but actually takes his seat in the temple of God. This in turn led to speculation that the antichrist might even rebuild the temple, since the temple had been destroyed by the Romans more than a century before Irenaeus and Hippolytus wrote (Koester 2014, §25E).

When we return to the Johannine Epistles, however, it is remarkable how nearly all of this vanishes. There are no signs and wonders. There is no violent persecution of the saints. And, most significantly, the Johannine antichrist is not a figure who makes himself the object of worship. Instead, the antichrist works by way of negation. In the Epistles, the established confession of the community is that Jesus is the Christ, who has come in the flesh. The work of the antichrist is to negate this. The author of 1 John can ask, "Who is the liar but the one who *denies* that Jesus is the Christ? This is the antichrist, the one who *denies* the Father and the Son" (1 John 2:22, emphasis added). And 2 John will insist that "the deceiver and the antichrist" is the one who does "*not confess* that Jesus Christ has come in the flesh" (2 John 7, emphasis added).

---

4. See especially Irenaeus, *Haer.* 5.25–30 (*ANF* 1:553–60) and Hippolytus's *Treatise on Christ and Antichrist* (*ANF* 5:204–19).

If the confession that Jesus is the Christ constitutes the norm, then the antichrist drains this confession of certain content, but the Epistles do not suggest that the antichrist makes himself an alternative focus for belief as in the scenarios above. To be sure, some have noted that the word "antichrist" begins with the Greek prefix *anti-*, which has multiple meanings. It almost certainly means that this figure is "against" Christ, but the prefix could also suggest that he is a "substitute" for Christ, since the prefix *anti-* can also mean substitution or replacement (Brown 1982, 333). The Synoptic Gospels do warn that in the end times there will be many false messiahs (ψευδόχριστοι), who will come in Jesus's name and say "I am he" (Matt 24:24; Mark 13:6). But significantly, the Johannine Epistles do not picture an antichrist who says, "Believe that I am the Christ and that Jesus is not."

Instead, what the antichrist does according to the Epistles is to offer a substitute form of belief by denying certain claims about Jesus. Interpreters have tried to determine more precisely what this negation might have meant. When read in light of later docetic Christology, it could be taken to mean denying that Jesus was truly human. The idea would be that Jesus appeared to be human, but in reality was not, or perhaps that his divine nature merely took up temporary residence in the body but was not connected to it. The problem is that it is not clear that these later views can be ascribed to the context of the Epistles (Lieu 2008, 169; Strecker 1996, 65–76).

The essence of the antichrist's work, according to the Epistles, is to sever the connection between the title "Christ" and the human being named Jesus. The author of 1 and 2 John sometimes uses the word "Christ" as a title, referring to Jesus as "the Christ," or Anointed One (1 John 2:22; 5:1). He also makes it a part of the name "Jesus Christ" (e.g., 2:1; 5:6; 2 John 7), and links the term to Jesus's identity as "the Son of God" (1 John 1:3; 2:22; 3:23; 2 John 3). Traditionally, the idea that Jesus is the Christ and Son of God drew on Jewish messianic hopes, though in the Johannine tradition the titles came to have an expanded significance, connoting Jesus's unity with God his Father (Koester 2008, 89–107).

For the writer or writers of the Epistles, the Christ is the Son of God, the one through whom God acts. It was out of love that God sent him to bring atonement, life, and salvation to the world (1 John 4:7–14). And Jesus did so in the flesh, so that he conveyed God's truth and love in a manner that could be heard and seen and touched (1:1–2). What the antichrist does is to negate the idea that being God's agent has anything to do with the flesh of Jesus, which meant denying that Jesus's humanity had any salvific significance (Brown 1982, 505).

This dimension has intriguing implications for the Johannine portrayal of antichrist. It means that the antichrist—if he is true to his own character—will not assume his own incarnate form. The later tradition will picture the eschatological adversary as one particular human being, who incarnates evil. But the Johannine antichrist has no flesh of his own. The one who denies the flesh of Jesus does not claim it for himself—at least not directly. Instead, he takes up residence in the people who give voice to the beliefs he promotes. That is why the author warns that "many deceivers have gone out into the world, those who do not confess that Jesus Christ has come in the flesh. *This person* is the deceiver and the antichrist" (2 John 7; see also 1 John 2:22–23).

The Johannine Epistles do not allow readers the luxury of equating the antichrist with one particular tyrant, who becomes the focus of all evil. Instead, they use the term "antichrist" in the singular for any person who denies the value of Jesus's humanity, and this means that the one becomes many. *The* antichrist turns into *many* antichrists.[5] The author of 1 John says that the readers "have heard that antichrist is coming," but then he adds that now "many antichrists have come" in the form of ordinary people, who have now left the author's faith community (2:18–19). Those looking for the miracle-working tyrant may find themselves bewildered, for in the Johannine Epistles the antichrist is not known through signs and wonders or the horrors of persecution. Instead, the antichrist is known by words that negate the significance of Jesus's humanity, words that are spoken by the kind of people the readers might encounter anywhere, including some people whom the readers had previously considered to be their brothers

---

5. Note that those who profess the opponents' Christology become "antichrists" (ἀντίχριστοι), but those who adhere to the author's Christology do not thereby become a multiplicity of "christs" (χριστοί). The difference is significant. The readers have received an anointing (χρῖσμα), which probably refers to the Spirit (Klauck 1991, 168; Strecker 1996, 76). This anointing enables them to confess that Jesus is the Anointed One; the χρῖσμα (1 John 2:20, 27) enables them to confess Jesus as Χριστός (2:22). Yet the author also maintains a critical distinction between Jesus as the Anointed One and those who have received the anointing that enables discernment. Since Christ is not simply equated with the believers, the believers remain reliant on and accountable to someone beyond themselves. This differentiation is integral to 1 John's words of encouragement and rebuke.

and sisters in the faith. So given such a diffused presence of the antichrist, what does this mean for the eschatological battle?

The Eschatological Battle

Christian tradition has often pictured the great battle with scenes of high drama. Writers typically rely on 2 Thessalonians, where Christ comes from heaven with his mighty angels in flaming fire to inflict vengeance on the godless and to annihilate the man of lawlessness with the breath of his mouth. Other details came from Revelation, which portrays the great battle in which the beast and false prophet lure the kings of earth into a futile attack against the returning Christ at the battle of Armageddon. It is there that the beast is defeated and hurled into the lake of fire, while the corpses of his slaughtered allies provide a grisly banquet for the birds of the air, who feast on the carnage of the battlefield (Rev 16:12–16; 19:11–21).

Initially, the Johannine Epistles also seem to hold dramatic promise. They depict a cosmic struggle between God and the devil, who has been sinning from the beginning. As readers we enter the story midway, for God has already taken action by sending his Son to do battle. According to 1 John, the Son of God has taken on a militant role by coming to destroy the works of the devil (1 John 3:8). Yet despite Christ's attack on the devil's realm, the world remains under the power of the evil one (5:19). This situation makes the world (κόσμος) the scene of continued spiritual warfare. The author tells of two spirits, the spirit of truth and the spirit of deceit, which are operative in the world (4:6). And the spirit of deceit is the spirit of the antichrist (4:3). Readers are warned about the antichrist's covert operations, for his agents include the many purported prophets, who have gone out into the world to deceive people into denying the significance of Jesus's flesh (4:1).

This is war, but a war of words. The weapons in the conflict are a claim and a counterclaim: the confession that the human being named Jesus is the Christ versus the conviction that Jesus's humanity has no place in God's designs. For the writer of 1 John, this is not merely the prelude to the final battle; it is the great battle with the antichrist.[6] The combatants

---

6. Some interpreters maintain that 1 John might continue to envision a future and final antichrist (Smalley 2007, 95). Others, however, point out that the epistolary author identifies the eschatological appearance of the antichrist in the many that have left the author's community. See Brown 1982, 337; Klauck 1991, 150–51.

are not a heavenly warrior on a white horse and a seven-headed beast.[7] Instead, the combatants are people like the readers, who find themselves in the middle of the fray, being called to distinguish truth from falsehood. The single antichrist is transformed into many antichrists, and the future becomes present. The writer will insist that "it is the last hour" and that it is precisely the coming of the many antichrists that allows readers to "know that it is the last hour" (2:18; see also 4:3).

In the eyes of many the situation would seem to be a defeat. For the antichrist's many agents, the false prophets, have gone out into the world, where they find a ready reception for their views. The author says, "They are from the world; therefore what they say is from the world, and the world listens to them" (4:5). Yet in the seeming darkness of defeat, the author of 1 John pronounces victory—a victory that is manifest not in fire from heaven but in faith on earth. He insists that where the Spirit of God moves people to confess that Jesus Christ has come in the flesh, there one finds true victory. He tells the readers, "you have conquered them" (4:4). For "whatever is born of God conquers the world. And this is the victory that conquers the world, our faith. Who is it that conquers the world but the one who believes that Jesus is the Son of God?" (5:4–5; see also 2:13–14).

For the writer of 1 John, the cosmic battle between Christ and antichrist is being fought and won in the present. The author does not treat the readers as spectators but casts them in the role of participants, who are called to resist the incursions of falsehood and to overcome them with the truth that fosters faith. According to 1 John, God sent Jesus to destroy the works of the devil, and such works include unbelief and the forms of sin that flow from it. These are marked by hatred and death (3:8, 12–15). The battle against false belief is won when genuine faith is created, and such faith from the author's perspective is manifested in love and is characterized by life (4:7–21; 5:11). This is a battle of the most peculiar sort, for triumph over the antichrist does not come by inflicting death on his followers but by fostering life through the words that express and engender faith.

---

7. It is significant that even in Rev 19:11–21, where Christ is portrayed as a warrior, there is only one weapon: the sword that comes from Christ's mouth, symbolizing his word. The great battle in Revelation is won through the power of the word.

The Polemical Use of Antichrist Language

This brings us to our final question, which concerns the polemical quality of the author's antichrist language. Christ may be the agent of life and Savior of the world, but the way the author castigates the opponents as antichrists certainly sits awkwardly with the reminders about the importance of love (Thatcher 2013). Moreover, the term "antichrist" was frequently used as an epithet by writers of later generations, who found it a convenient way to vilify political and religious figures of their own times.[8] So, as we consider the role of the antichrist in the Johannine Epistles, it is important to ask how the polemics work.

Rhetorically, the author levels the charge of antichrist against those who have left his community. He says "they went out from us, but they did not belong to us; for if they had belonged to us, they would have remained with us. But by going out they made it plain that none of them belongs to us" (2:19). In this conflicted situation, the author draws a sharp line between two groups: those who belong to Christ and those who belong to antichrist. The author seems to recognize that the main reason that people should remain in the community is that they find its confession and manner of life to be compelling. But at the same time, identifying the opposing group with antichrist is rhetorically powerful, because it raises the barrier against leaving the community. The writer insists that joining the other side is more than just adopting an alternative Christology. It means joining the agents of evil (Lieu 1991, 85).

This language seems to leave us with a simple "us versus them" situation in which the author's group belongs to Christ and the other group has become antichrist. Yet having established this clear division, the author also subverts it. The struggle against antichrist cannot be reduced to one group versus another. It is a struggle that goes on within the author's community and, by extension, within each member of that community.

The Johannine Epistles identify the antichrist with the negation of the community's confession of Jesus, and they also recognize that negating

---

8. Identifying the antichrist with figures of one's own time became especially common from the twelfth century onward. Examples included Pope Gregory IX (1241) and Innocent IV (d. 1254) as well as the Emperor Frederick II (d. 1250). During the sixteenth century, many Protestants came to identify the papal office itself with the antichrist. Later candidates have ranged from the emperor Napoleon to modern American presidents. See McGinn 2000, 200–49; Fuller 1995; Koester 2014, §25E.

the confession can occur through actions as well as through speech. The author assumes that if Christ is embodied, then faith must be embodied and conveyed in deeds that are consistent with the words. First John points to the irony that those who confidently confess their faith with their lips can effectively deny it with their lives—and when they do so, even those who belong to the community exhibit the traits of the antichrist. Note how the Epistles use the term "liar." The author can say, "Who is the liar [ψεύστης] but the one who denies that Jesus is the Christ? This is the antichrist" (2:22). But he can also say, "Whoever says, 'I know him,' but does not obey his commandments, is a liar [ψεύστης]," which means that the person takes on the traits of antichrist (2:4; see also 4:20). The same is true with the notion of deception. Second John can say that that if one "does not confess that Jesus Christ has come in the flesh, that person "is the deceiver [πλάνος] and the antichrist" (2 John 7). Yet 1 John also says, "If we say we have no sin, we deceive [πλανῶμεν] ourselves and the truth is not in us" (1 John 1:8).

When the warnings against the deceptive qualities of the antichrist are read in light of the warnings about the readers' own propensities to self-deception, then the antichrist can no longer be comfortably externalized and located only within the other group. When the threat of denying Christ is extended to include not only words but actions that are inconsistent with the words, then it becomes an inducement to self-examination *within* the author's own community. This way of reading the antichrist passages may have been obscured in the later tradition, but it was not lost. It surfaces, for example, in Augustine's sermons on 1 John.[9] He notes that according to this letter, the people called "antichrist" have gone out of the community, but this also means that before going out they were present within it. The antichrist is not purely external. It is a force that operates within the community of faith itself. Therefore, Augustine comments that members of the community must ask themselves whether they might be antichrists. And the criterion that Augustine says they should use? Whoever "in his deeds denies Christ is an antichrist" (*Tract. ep. Jo.* 3.4, 8). And the deeds that most effectively deny Christ are those that violate the command to show love.

---

9. The importance of Augustine's approach and the way similar ideas are reflected in Gregory the Great and others plays an important role in McGinn's work (2000, xv, 77, 82, 278–80). McGinn comments, "Antichrist is meant to warn us against ourselves" (xvi).

The Johannine Epistles have contributed to the highly charged use of antichrist language in western culture. But when that language has been taken more contextually, the Epistles have also played a distinctive and subversive role, which sets them apart from aspects of the later tradition. In the Epistles the one antichrist is transformed into many, the future becomes present, and the enemy cannot be comfortably externalized but is a force that can operate within the believing community itself.

According to the Epistles, the authentic Christ is made tangible in Jesus, and authentic faith is made tangible in love. The term "antichrist" identifies the opposite of this. The Epistles call readers to actively discern where the spirit of the antichrist might be at work in the world and in communities other than their own. But these same texts also call readers to discern their own propensities for self-deception and the ways they negate the work of Christ through acts of hatred, which diminish life. The Epistles may do their most subversive work when they move the readers to say: "We have seen the antichrist, and he is us."

On Ethics in 1 John

Jan G. van der Watt

First John is indeed "the letter of love," and ethical issues are generally regarded as a core focus in this letter. As a topic, ethics are mentioned in virtually all commentaries on the Epistles,[1] with an obvious emphasis upon aspects like the commandment of love, the exemplary requirement to act according to the light, and some interesting references to sin. The pessimistic view of the presence of ethics in the Gospel of John[2] does not apply to the Epistles of John.

The interest in the ethics of John is evident in several articles on the ethics in the Epistles of John that were recently published (see also Snodderley 2008). Udo Schnelle (2010) emphasizes what he calls a theological ethic, while Jan G. van der Watt (1999) and Dirk G. van der Merwe (2005, 2006a, 2006b) focus on the communal basis of ethics in the Epistles. Oda Wischmeyer (2009) differentiates between the situations of the Gospel and the Epistles, arguing that ethics is much more prominent in the Epistles, because of the difference in the situation between the Gospel and Epistles—what Jesus said to his disciples in John 13–16 (i.e., in the Gospel) is applied to a wider audience in the Epistles.

In this article some aspects of the ethics in 1 John will be explored in greater detail. Within the wider context of ethics in the Epistles, three central aspects will receive attention: the ethical implications of fellow-

---

1. See, for instance, relevant sections in Brown 1986, Schnackenburg 1984, Smalley 2002, Klauck 1991, Painter 2002, Lieu 2008, and Menken 2010.
2. See van der Watt 2006, 107–08. Michael Theobald (2002, 565) remarks that "Ein *ethisches* interesse an der Gestaltung der Lebensbereiche der Gemeinde wird im Buch nirgends greifbar." W. Schrage (1996, 302) even includes the Epistles by remarking: "we may ask whether a chapter on the Johannine writings even belongs in a book on the ethics of the New Testament" (297). See also Blank 1981, 69; Gerhardsson 1981, 98; Houlden 1973, 35–36.

198 COMMUNITIES IN DISPUTE: THE JOHANNINE EPISTLES

ship, the family as a social basis for motivating ethics, and following the example of Jesus as the guiding principle for ethics.

The Ethical Implications of Having Fellowship (κοινωνια)

The emphatic statement or maxim that God is light (1 John 1:5, ὁ θεὸς φῶς ἐστιν)[3] formulates a basic "truth"[4] on which the first ethical remark in 1 John (1:6–7)[5] is based. Although this maxim forms part of the tradition (the ὅτι links it to the message preached), it is stated as an accepted fact without contention. This technique of moral argumentation, namely, stating accepted facts as the basis for further ethical argumentation, was common in Greco-Roman moral philosophy (Morgan 2007 argues this in detail), and John uses it elsewhere in moral arguments, for instance, in John 12:24 (see also John 8:38).

In order to grasp the metaphor "God is light" and the consequent argumentation based on this statement, it is important to understand the semantics of this metaphor. In the metaphor God (tenor) is (copulative) light (vehicle), the commonplace(s) or analogy between God and light that could determine the meaning of the metaphor are numerous, of course.[6] However, the uses in the Epistles (1:5–7 and 2:7–11—not in 2 and 3 John) as well as in the Gospel (see also Akin 2001, 64–71) clarify the possible points of analogy.

It is assumed that 1 John stands in the same tradition as the Gospel, although both involve interpretations within specific situations, which of course lead to differences (Brown 1986, 227; Klauck 1991a, 83). Although light could be described as a universal image (see Blumenberg 2010, 3–5, 143), it is developed in a specific direction in several instances in the

---

3. See Brown 1986, 228, for the relationship between God and light in Hebrew Scriptures that could have served as referential framework.

4. The notion that this could have been a slogan of the secessionists is rejected by Brown 1986, 226.

5. Brown (1986, 230) notes that "the first overt attack on dangerous ideas is in the moral sphere," while it could have been expected to be on christological errors.

6. Brown (1986, 194–95) points out that the anarthrous use here might focus more on the quality of God or on the "existential statements about God's activity towards humans" than on his identity, but this does not exclude touching on his mysterious identity. Smalley (2002, 20) like most commentators, interprets light as referring both to the nature and being of God. He even links the image of light in this passage to the glory of God, which seems like an over-interpretation.

Gospel and Epistles so that one can gather a fair idea of the author's specific intention.[7] In John 9:4, Jesus axiomatically states that one cannot work by night, only during the day. Light makes positive action and work possible. The same concept is also found in John 11:9–10: in the light of day one can walk around without stumbling, but at night one stumbles, that is, cannot act properly. In John 12:35, it is noted that a person who walks in darkness does not know where he is going. The trend is clear: one cannot work in darkness; moreover, one cannot walk positively or know where one is going. Ethically meaningful actions are not possible in darkness; they are only possible in the light. Ethically "meaningful action" in John relates to works that are done according to the will or word of God as it is expressed in Jesus (John 3:19–21; 8:12; 12:46–47). Such a person walks in the light (Brown 1986, 198). First John 2:7–10, which says that a person who walks in darkness does not know where he is going since he cannot see, further supports the metaphorical framework for interpreting remarks about darkness and light in 1 John. It serves to "translate" the meaning of the metaphor that a person who walks in darkness is ethically lost.[8]

Returning to our metaphor of "God is light," it could thus be asserted in an analogous manner that just as light illuminates and makes positive ethical action possible, God also illuminates and makes positive (ethical) action, without stumbling, possible. This should not be seen as an "abstract definition but portrays God's identity revealed in terms of function" (Brown 1986, 229; see also Rensberger 2001, 19). Hans-Josef Klauck (1991, 81) sees the expression that God is light as more than a "Funktionsaussagen," since it also expresses something of "Gottes unvergänglichem Wesen" but should not be seen as "einfache Identität." The expression "God is light" is essentially both a theological and a moral statement (Johnson 1993, 28). Thus, God not only makes positive actions possible, but also establishes the principle against which positive actions are to be measured

---

7. Maarten Menken (2010, 27; see also Smalley 2002, 19; Klauck 1991, 86) mentions that light is indeed a universal religious symbol. For the religious background of light and darkness, see Klauck 1991, 81–83; Painter 2002, 138–39; Haas et al. 1972, 23–24. Colin Kruse (2000, 66–67) also gives an overview of the use of light and darkness in the New Testament. Smalley (2002, 19–20) mentions that the imagery of light was part of both the Hellenistic and Jewish worlds, but prefers the Jewish background, and of course the Gospel itself as a framework for the Epistle.

8. Brown (1986, 235) quotes several examples from the intertestamental period linking light with truth, that is, illustrating the metaphorical link between light and ethics.

(Brown 1986, 198; Lieu 2008, 48). As Stephen Smalley (1984, 20) puts it: "'God is light' carries with it an inevitable moral challenge."

The argument goes further: God is light, but God is also in the light (1:7), implying that God's own actions are done in the light, which gives them a quality of meaningfulness. This might have the added value that these actions are visible and clear and can be seen to be good. Raymond Brown (1986, 229) also emphasizes the knowability of God that comes with the expression that God is light. A person in this light will also be able to know God (2:3), a knowledge that will lead to correct behavior (in the light).

Let us now move on to the next phase of our investigation, namely, the argument based on the statement that "God is light." A string of statements is related to this basic statement about God: God is light.... We have fellowship with him—We are in the light.... We walk[9] in this light as God is in the light (1:5–7). By metaphorically identifying God with light, a positive ethical sphere, or space, is described that is qualitatively identified with God.

"Walking in" and "being in" are related: "But if we *walk* in the light, *as* he is in the light, we have *fellowship* with one another" (emphases mine, ἐὰν δὲ ἐν τῷ φωτὶ περιπατῶμεν ὡς αὐτός ἐστιν ἐν τῷ φωτί, κοινωνίαν ἔχομεν μετ' ἀλλήλων).[10] "Walking in" implies "being in" and vice versa. By walking in the light as God is the light, believers are introduced to, and embedded in, the transcendental reality of God as light—the (earthly) person, who is normally ethically determined by his earthly social situation (family, social group, etc.) is "transferred" to the positive divine space that is qualitatively determined by God. God now becomes the point of determination of his or her ethical actions—God who is light and who is in the light, that is, who determines true and correct behavior. This serves as a point of departure in developing any moral argumentation in the Epistle. Any other point of departure is described as a lie or a deception (1:6).[11]

---

9. To "walk" is probably a Semitism (see Prov 8:20; Isa 2:5; Brown 1986, 197; Klauck 1991, 88; Smalley 2002, 23). See also Lieu 2008, 52–54, and Rensberger 2001, 20, for detailed discussions. It is also used elsewhere in John and in the New Testament, though not frequently (for instance, Mark 7:5; Acts 21:21; Rom 14:15; Eph 5:2; as well as 1 John 2:6, 7, 11; 2 John 4, 6; 3 John 3, 4).

10. Unless otherwise stated, translations of biblical material are mine.

11. As is typical for this Epistle, the negative side is also formulated emphasizing the point made (see Brown 1986, 195). This will, however, not receive attention here.

This raises a question: how should the interrelatedness between identity and deeds be understood? The last part of the conditional phrase reads: "if ... we have *fellowship* with one another" (κοινωνίαν ἔχομεν μετ' ἀλλήλων).[12] It is not a philosophical system that frames ethical behavior. Rather it is a personal relationship that is qualified by the concept of κοινωνία.[13] This fellowship (κοινωνία) does not only exist between the Johannine believers (one another); it also exists between believers and the Father and Son

---

12. G. Stählin (1964–1976, 9:152) remarks, "The motif of κοινωνία esp. recurs with considerable monotony" in the ancient literature about friendship (citing Euripides, *Orest.* 735; *Andr.* 376f; and Plato, *Lys.* 207c; *Phaedr.* 279c; *Leg.* 5, 739c; *Resp.* 5, 449c; 4, 424a; Aristotle, *Eth. nic.* 9.11, 1159b, 31f; *Eth. eud.* 7.2, 1237b, 32f; 1238a, 16; *Pol.* 2.5, 1263a, 30; Diogenes Laertius, *Vit.* 6.37 and 72; Philo, *Mos.* 1.156; Muson. frg. 13 [p. 67]). This implies that friends have things in common, even property, according to the variation in the degree of friendship (so also Plutarch, *Flatterer* 24; *Mor.* 65AB; Martial, *Epigr.* 2.43.1–16; Cornelius Nepos, *Vir. Illus.* 15.3.4; Diogenes Laertius, *Vit.* 7.1.124). Plato (*Lysis* 207c) also remarks on this view by describing fellowship within the context of friendship, saying: "And, you know, friends are said to have everything in common, so that here at least there will be no difference between you." Brown (1986, 170) calls it "the dynamic *esprit de corps* that brings people together," including the results of this spirit of togetherness. It has to do with holding things in common, sharing them through active participation (van der Merwe 2006, 542). See, for instance, Aristotle *Eth. nic.* 8–9 for this use of κοινωνία. BDAG (ad loc.) describes it as follows: "close association involving mutual interests and sharing, association, communion, fellowship, close relationship (hence a favorite expression for the marital relationship) as the most intimate between human beings ... the common type or bond of life that unites people ... (harmonious) unity ... attitude of good will that manifests an interest in a close relationship, generosity, fellow-feeling, altruism ... participation, sharing ... the common possession or enjoyment of something ... or the common possession or enjoyment of virtues." I have listed these descriptions by BDAG not to imply that all these meanings are activated with each and every use of the word κοινωνία, but to give some indication of the semantic range of the word.

13. Painter (2002, 151–52) argues that κοινωνία is not part of the Johannine tradition and is also not prominent in the Epistles. He therefore concludes that it was taken from the opponents who used it as slogan: "We have *koinōnia* with him (God)." See also Smalley 2002, 23. He consequently argues against, for instance, Malatesta, that 1 John is constructed around the theme of κοινωνία. He argues that love terminology is more typical of John—"to have *koinōnia*" is expressed in Johannine terms as "to love." It must, however, be said that although love and fellowship semantically overlap to some extent, they are not identical. Fellowship carries more of a denotation of sharing in unity. The prominent place it has in 1 John also gives it special emphasis—it is inevitable that it should be intertextually linked to other expressions of unity following later in 1 John. See also Hauck 1965, 807–8.

making the believer part of a divine transcendental social group (1:3–4). This κοινωνία (fellowship) becomes apparent if people walk in the light by means of "doing the truth" (1:6–7). But how does the author's use of the concept of κοινωνία enrich what he is saying here?

In ancient contexts, this term is used to define an intimate social relationship in which relational borders become porous and sharing and caring take place on a material and a spiritual level (as is appropriate within the context of each relationship) (Klauck 1991, 70–71). For instance, κοινωνία is used of friends who share and participate (Hauck 1965, 797–98) in everything (being one soul). Elsewhere it refers to politicians or statesmen who have close alliances. The term defines the specific nature and quality of the relationship between persons—qualities like goodwill, sharing, openness, belonging, and trustworthiness are part and parcel of the relationship typified by κοινωνία.

Creating fellowship between the author's group (we) and the addressees (you, v. 3) introduces them into the fellowship of the Father and Son, establishing a closed social group in which mutual fellowship, trust, sharing, *et cetera* are characteristics. In this way, social boundaries are drawn, and social expectations are created. For a person to have κοινωνία with the Father and Son as well as with fellow believers implies that such a person is fully integrated into this divine transcendental relationship and is accordingly determined by all that κοινωνία implies, transcending ordinary human relations. The relational borders between God and humans become porous in the sense that the influence and presence of God penetrates the life of the believer, and the believer's identity and actions are integrated with those of God. People should orientate themselves towards, and seek their identity and patterns for behavior within, this transcendental fellowship. This should characterize the nature of the behavior outlined in 1 John.

What should a person walking in the light do? No direct explication is given for what it means to walk in the light in 1:6–7, except that it is linked to fellowship with God. The person should live according to the ethos of God and what God expects, being influenced by the porousness of the relationship. The phrase "doing the *truth*" (1:6),[14] which contrasts with lying (Brown 1986, 198; Menken 2010, 28), also typifies the nature of the correct behavior. The concept of *truth* is central to John and func-

---

14. See Klauck 1991, 89, and van der Watt 2009, 317–33, for the use of "*doing* the truth," an expression that is not common in Greek literature.

tions as a symbolic concept referring to that what is associated and related to God (see van der Watt 2009, 317–33). The only ethical specification is that lying is wrong and that it is not to be associated with God as a point of orientation for the truth. Brown (1986, 199–200) argues that in John lying should be interpreted against a Hebrew background where lying relates to opposition against God (Jer 9:2–3—for a more comprehensive argument on this point see van der Watt 2009, 317–33).

The further reference to light in 1 John—here referring to the presence of Jesus—is found in 2:7–10. Although the image is worked out in a little more detail in terms of stumbling and blindness, emphasizing wrong behavior, the basic structure of the argument is the same: he who claims to be in the light but does not act accordingly remains in the darkness. What is added is the reference to love and hate as criteria for correct behavior in the light. Hating your brother and abiding in the light do not go hand in hand, while loving and remaining in the light do (i.e., in the presence of Jesus and God). This confirms the idea that acting in the light relates to ethical behavior in accordance with love (as determined by God).

Some commentators are quick to point out that κοινωνία is not a typical Johannine word. In contrast to its usage by Paul (see Smalley 2002, 12–13; Klauck 1991, 70; Menken 2010, 24), it is not used as frequently in the Epistles (only in 1 John 1:3, 6, 7, and 2 John 11). Although the word is only used in the beginning of 1 John, the tone is set along the lines of sharing and belonging in an intimate manner. This idea of social interrelatedness, with all the associated implications, remains intact throughout the Epistles. It is further developed by employing related conceptual expressions like filial metaphorical language or through the use of words expressing close union like "being in" (εἶναι ἐν) or "remaining in" (μένειν ἐν) (See Brown 1986, 232). These expressions of unity form a conceptual cluster that expresses the intimate relationship between God and the believer while developing the consequences of such a relationship. Due to space constraints, attention will only be given to filial language as a motivation for ethics.

Filial Imagery as Basis for Behavior

A powerful, even controversial,[15] ethical statement in 1 John 3:9 links birth directly to behavior: "Everyone who is born of God [Πᾶς ὁ γεγεννημένος

---

15. Willi Marxsen (1989, 261–62) maintains that the absoluteness of this state-

ἐκ τοῦ θεοῦ]¹⁶ will not sin, because God's seed remains in him [σπέρμα αὐτοῦ ἐν αὐτῷ μένει]; he cannot go on sinning, because he has been born of God [ἐκ τοῦ θεοῦ γεγέννηται]." Similar statements relating birth with behavior abound in 1 John; for instance, 2:29; 3:10; 4:7; 5:1–2, 18. He who is born of God "does not sin" (ἁμαρτίαν οὐ ποιεῖ) and indeed "cannot sin" (οὐ δύναται ἁμαρτάνειν; 3:9; 5:18). Evil does not touch him (ὁ πονηρὸς οὐχ ἅπτεται αὐτοῦ; 5:18) since he is protected.¹⁷ John also portrays a flexibility of expression in describing the relationship between birth and actions which underlines the closeness between the two: he, for instance, states that a person who is born from God cannot, or at least should not, sin (3:9; 5:18). But he also puts it the other way around, namely, that the righteous deeds of a person prove that he or she is indeed born of God (2:29; 3:10; 4:7; 5:1–2). What are the ethical implications of John motivating deeds by emphasizing *birth*? Within family imagery (van der Watt 1999, 1–21), birth plays a key role on the physical, social, and symbolic levels.¹⁸

---

ment is due to "sorglosen Umgang mit der Sprache" by the author. This cannot be accepted, as will become clear later.

16. Being born out of God (ἐκ τοῦ θεοῦ) indicates *origin*. The particle ἐκ indicates the source and point of origin of the one who is born. According to ancient views, the seed of the man carried character traits that were transferred to the newborn baby. That God is the source or point of origin does not make God the mother, but rather the source and origin of identity. Lexicographically it is possible to use σπέρμα αὐτοῦ to refer to the man's involvement in the birth of a child. It is even said that God's *seed* remains in such a person (σπέρμα αὐτοῦ ἐν αὐτῷ μένει; 3:9), a very concrete picture of what happens.

17. The following statement is made in this context (5:18): ὁ γεννηθεὶς ἐκ τοῦ θεοῦ τηρεῖ αὐτόν. How this should be understood is controversial. Klauck (1991, 334–35) mentions several possibilities: (1) the one born of God (= the believer) keeps himself; (2) the one born of God (= believer) keeps God; (3) the one born of God (= believer), is kept by God; (4) the one born of God (= Christ) keeps them (= believers). He chooses the latter, as does Smalley 2002, 303. It is, however, not certain what is meant. Menken (2010, 115) chooses to see the first part of the phrase as a *casus pendens*, which means that ὁ γεννηθεὶς ἐκ τοῦ θεοῦ and αὐτόν refer to the same person and that the subject of the verb is God—i.e., option 2 above. Smalley 2002, 303, rejects this option.

18. Aristotle (*Ethica nichomachea*) gives due attention to the relationships within households. A father's first care is for the welfare of his children. "The friendship of a father for his child is of the same kind (only here the benefits bestowed are greater, for the father is the source of the child's existence, which seems to be the greatest of all boons, and of its nurture and educational and we also ascribe the same benefits to our forefathers).… These friendships then involve a superiority of benefits on one side, which is why parents receive honor as well as service" (8.xi.2–3). Parents indeed love

In the ancient context, birth was an important way of determining a person's social position, status, and identity. Through birth, a person was introduced into the social dynamics of a family, determining that person's identity and honor and accordingly suggesting appropriate behavior.[19] Who you were was formulated in terms of the social group (family[20]) within which you were born. Birth implied that the child stood in a specific, well-defined, hierarchical relationship to the father of the family. The father was the authoritative head of the family[21] and therefore set the tone for life in the family, both by protecting the family tradition and by educating his children to follow that tradition.[22]

---

their children as part of themselves while children love their parents as the source of their being (8.xii.1). Children love their parents as their superiors on the basis of their birth, upbringing, and education (8.xii.5). In the case of brothers, it is more a matter of comradeship in which both parties are equal. They love each other as "being from the same source, since the identity of their relations to that source identifies them with one another.... They are of the same being, though embodied in separate persons" (8.xii.3).

19. Helmut Schrot (1979, 512) points out that "family" was not only a term referring to people as such, but was also an economical description or "Vermögensbegriff." Being part of a family, means sharing in what that family has. See also Gilbertson 1959, 43–44; de Vaux 1974, 20; Bund 1979, 546; Malina and Neyrey 1991, 28.

20. The family (οἶκος) is generally regarded as the basic and most intimate social structure in ancient Mediterranean (in so far as one can use such a generalization) life; see Stambaugh and Balch 1986, 123, on the Graeco-Roman situation, and Lassen 1992, 247, 254, on the situation in ancient Israel and early Judaism. Beryl Rawson (1987, 7–8) points out that *"familia"* does not only include blood relations, but all people under the control of the *"paterfamilias."*

21. The powers and position of the father within the family differed from area to area, from time to time or from culture to culture (see for instance De Vaux 1974, 23). In Jewish circles the father had no absolute power over his children (as was for instance the case in Roman circles during certain periods), although Roland De Vaux (1974, 20) points out that initially the father had absolute authority. That changed gradually. In cases of serious offenses by children, the father was not in a position to punish the child accordingly, but the matter was to be taken to the other elders for a verdict (Deut 21:18–21; Keil 1888, 177). In the Graeco-Roman world, the father had more, and absolute, powers (Gielen 1990, 147). He could even reject a newborn child, which of course probably meant death for the child. In the second and third centuries, these absolute powers over children were toned down (Gielen 1990, 147; Lassen 1992, 260).

22. See Eva Lassen (1992, 248, 254–55, 258–59) on both the Roman and the early Judaistic situation and De Vaux (1974, 20) on ancient Israel. E. Bund (1979, 547) points out that during the times of the Caesars the responsibility of the father towards

In 1 John there are multiple references to birth (2:29; 3:9, 10; 4:7; 5:1–2, 18), and in most cases they are contextually linked to ethical aspects. For instance, in 3:1–10 particular behaviors are related to birth several times; it is even related to the *seed* of the Father (3:9–10). His children will act according to his will, which has a strong correlation to the words of Jesus in John 8:38, 41: like Father, like Son.²³ This is why sinful deeds identify

---

his family was a matter of ethics and morality. It was however only Antoninus Pius (Ceasar from 138 to 161 CE), who eventually gave a legal basis to the responsibility of the father towards his family. See also Schrenk 1973, 949; Schrot 1979, 512; Malina and Neyrey 1991, 26; Gielen 1990, 135; Christ 1984, 10; Dixon 1991, 131, 138; Rawson 1987, 7.

23. For instance, the parents were (often) regarded as God's agents who must care for the child. The reason for obeying and honoring the father was consequently not just a command, but could also be religiously explained: "For parents are the servants of God for the task of begetting children, and he who dishonours the servant dishonours also the Lord" (Philo, *Decal*.120). "For its children the duty of religiously sanctioned obligations towards the parents corresponded to that of the relations between men and gods. And this duty was designated by the same word, *pietas*" (Christ 1984, 10). The parents were seen as agents of God. By showing honour to them, honour was paid to God and *vice versa*. This was not all. Receiving something from somebody obliges the "receiver" to respond accordingly and fittingly towards the "giver." Because parents cared for their children and gave them what they needed, the children were obliged to return these gestures by being responsive and obedient and thus honoring their parents. As Merrill Gilbertson (1959, 44) formulated it: "The principal duties of the children in this home were obedience and reverence." A child will behave or at least try to behave like his father (Josephus, *Ant.* 4.260–64, 289; Philo *Spec.* 2.243; *Deus* 3.17–18). Gilbertson (1959, 44) and G. Schrenk (1973, 950) points out that in the Greek situation a command to love one's parents was superfluous; it is something natural. Josephus (*Ant.* 4.260–64) clearly links the honor due to the parents to the loving care the parents have shown the children. In *Ant.* 4.289 Josephus remarks that the loyalty a child shows his parents should be the result of his eternal gratitude for receiving life from his parents—this gratitude should never cease. Epictetus gives a penetrating description of the duties of a "son" in 2.10.7 of the discourses reported by Arian: absolute help, respect, protection, etc. are required. See also Keener 1993, ad loc. Philo (*Decal.* 118) argues that children received everything from their parents, and this should motivate them to be loyal to their parents. See also Golden 1990, 102. It also contributes to your honor if you treat your parents well (Philo, *Deus* 17–18). Philo (*Spec.* 2.243, see also 2.236) further emphasizes that if a child treats the givers of his life badly, he should be disciplined. Cicero (*De Officus* 1.17) argues that honor is the obligation parents lay on their children, because they have done so much for them. See also Dio Chrysostom, "The Twelfth Discourse" 43. This was common in ancient Mediterranean thought. Dio Chrysostom ("Twelfth Discourse" 42) says that "the

a person with the devil and make him a *child* of the devil, which in turn places him in opposition to the children of God. The author of 1 John used the socially pregnant imagery of birth to explain and motivate particular behavior.

The ethical implications of the relation between the Father and his children become even more evident in the later chapters of 1 John. Love is of God, as are those who are born of God (ἀγάπη ἐκ τοῦ θεοῦ ἐστιν, καὶ πᾶς ὁ ἀγαπῶν ἐκ τοῦ θεοῦ γεγέννηται; 4:7). Since God, the Father, is love[24] (4:8), people born of God should also love one another. Everyone who loves Him who "begot" also loves him who is "begotten of him" (καὶ πᾶς ὁ ἀγαπῶν τὸν γεννήσαντα ἀγαπᾷ [καὶ] τὸν γεγεννημένον ἐξ αὐτοῦ; 5:1). Practicing righteousness (2:28–29) shows that one is born of God, since one follows the example of Jesus (and the Father), who is righteous. The source and origin of behavior directly corresponds to the birth status of a person. This appears to be ancient convention.

The effect of relating birth to behavior, with all the expectations that went along with it (i.e., behave according to your social position of birth, obey your father, allow your identity to be determined by the group, etc.), is that a person lives within a framework of expected behavior based on his birth. The child is under an obligation to behave according to the will of the one from whom he or she was born. In 1 John, God is the father of the believers, and the devil is the father of those who do not believe in Jesus. These "fathers" determine the nature of the deeds of their children. They become the measurement of, and also explain, the ethics within a particular (spiritual) family.

Closely linked to the concept of birth is that of receiving life.[25] Becoming part of God's family starts with birth from God and continues through life eternal in that family. Having life implies being able to partake in the reality of the family of God.[26]

---

goodwill and desire to serve which the offspring feel toward their parents is … present in them, untaught, as a gift of nature and as a result of acts of kindness received." Children should show their gratitude through their obedience (see Marshall 1987, ad loc.; Haas et al. 1972, ad loc.).

24. Brown (1986, 548–49) sees the use of love here not as an abstract description but as God in relation to humans.

25. ζωή is used in the Epistles only in 1 John and then in 1:1, 2; 2:25; 3:14, 15; 5:11, 12, 13, 16, 20; and ζάω only once: 4:9.

26. See van der Watt 2000, 317–33.

The dynamics of this rhetoric are evident. Certain specific social conventions existed in the ancient Mediterranean world regarding family structures and dynamics.[27] Due to the use of "family imagery," these conventions are associatively activated, in the reader who is familiar with them, during the reading process.[28] Simply stating that a child is born of a father implies (for the "informed reader") sharing these conventions, that he is born into a fixed social structure where it will be expected of him to respect the will of the father and to be loyal to the honor and "character" of the family. Within this context reciprocity and obedience are important ethical values. *Et cetera*. In this way different aspects of family life are interrelated in the interpretation process. This matrix of social information need not be specifically mentioned or stressed in the argument of the Epistle where family imagery is clearly used. In the reading process, this information should be associatively activated and will become a constitutive part of the interpretation process. The family imagery therefore communicatively activates a network of social associations that function in a cohesive manner on the basis of the use of family imagery.

The link between having life and behavior in 1 John becomes evident in 3:11–18, where the major difference between having *life* and being dead is *loving* instead of hating. This is illustrated through the well-known familial story of Cain, who murdered his brother because he hated him (3:14–15).[29] It is also implied in the Cain episode, where a brother kills his brother in hate, something that is not expected of family members. This shows his evilness, both in deed and identity (3:12–13; Painter 2002, 233). His evil identity leads to evil actions. This most probably reflects

---

27. This statement should not be read as if conventions were exactly the same everywhere. The earlier remarks about creating a scenario as a comparative set of material should be borne in mind in this instance. In working with the ancient material, it soon becomes clear that one can only work with "tendencies" and not with strict "rules." There are exceptions on virtually every "rule." This should, however, not discourage us to work with comparative material; rather, it should make us more careful in reaching conclusions.

28. That is either the first readers, for whom these conventions formed part and parcel, or the informed "later" reader.

29. This narrative most probably has the secessionists as second reference (but see Klauck 1991, 209). See Gen 4:1–16 for the Old Testament reference. See a detailed discussion on the interpretation of this imagery in Brown 1986, 441–43; Smalley 2002, 183–84. Painter (2002, 233) is of the opinion that this section does not depend on scriptural quotation, but rather develops John 8:39–44.

on those who left the Johannine group and are now their opponents. The person who loves has life in him or her and has passed from death to life (3:14–15). Loving one another (3:11) is a sign of living as the family of God (3:14). Otherwise one is dead (3:14). Thus love is directly linked to identity by way of obligation (Brown 1986, 473–74), namely, being a child of God. In 4:9 another aspect is described—God's love was shown to us through the sending of his Son so that we could have life through him. We have life, because God loved us and acted accordingly (see John 3:16). Because of this love of God that resulted in life, we should also love (4:7–12).

The significance of moving from death to life (spiritually and not biologically) is that a reorientation of identity takes place in the believer. Believers do not "lose" their ordinary earthly life when receiving "eternal life." However, on a qualitative level being part of, and living in the family of, God completely dominates. Where these two "lives" (i.e., earthly and eternal life) clash on whatever level, the heavenly family must be regarded as the primary family from which one's true identity is determined. Believers therefore have a "double existence" in this sense: they still live as earthly people within their families in this world, but within their determining identity and orientation, they are part of the eternal family of God. The latter is a reality based on a faith relationship (see Schnackenburg 1982, 312; Marxsen 1989, 258–64).

This new identity is socially organized by way of the Johannine group and their actions. This group is ethically determined—they belong to one another, should love one another, should receive missionaries (3 John), should avoid people who bring false doctrines, *et cetera*. The Father, the Son, as well as believers are bound together by this life and show it through love. This life introduces the human believers to a transcendent reality in which they share what God has to offer.

The implication of the above for ethical behavior is that the social dynamics of an ancient family become the matrix within which ethics must be understood (see van der Watt 1995, 71–80). Familial ethical conventions applicable to families are implicit in statements related to behavior.

Following God/Jesus as Exemplary Authority

It becomes evident that deeds are determined by identity and are motivated and inspired from this identity; ethics in 1 John are relationally motivated and are the obvious product of relationships. An important way in which this relational ethics is developed in 1 John is by way of an exemplary standard. A standard is set by God and Jesus, which the believer is obliged to follow—expressions like "as," "like" (ὡς, καθὼς), or "ought to" functionally relate the behavior of Jesus to that of the believers.

The following cases will be treated briefly.

2:6. Walk like Jesus walked
ὁ λέγων ἐν αὐτῷ μένειν ὀφείλει καθὼς ἐκεῖνος περιεπάτησεν καὶ αὐτὸς [οὕτως] περιπατεῖν.

2:29 and 3:7. Being righteous like God and Jesus are righteous
2:29. ἐὰν εἰδῆτε ὅτι δίκαιός ἐστιν, γινώσκετε ὅτι καὶ πᾶς ὁ ποιῶν τὴν δικαιοσύνην ἐξ αὐτοῦ γεγέννηται.
3:7. ὁ ποιῶν τὴν δικαιοσύνην δίκαιός ἐστιν, καθὼς ἐκεῖνος δίκαιός ἐστιν

3:3. Being pure as Jesus is pure
καὶ πᾶς ὁ ἔχων τὴν ἐλπίδα ταύτην ἐπ' αὐτῷ ἁγνίζει ἑαυτόν, καθὼς ἐκεῖνος ἁγνός ἐστιν.

4:11 etc. Love like God/Jesus loved
εἰ οὕτως ὁ θεὸς ἠγάπησεν ἡμᾶς, καὶ ἡμεῖς ὀφείλομεν ἀλλήλους ἀγαπᾶν.

3:16. Die like Jesus died
ὅτι ἐκεῖνος ὑπὲρ ἡμῶν τὴν ψυχὴν αὐτοῦ ἔθηκεν· καὶ ἡμεῖς ὀφείλομεν ὑπὲρ τῶν ἀδελφῶν τὰς ψυχὰς θεῖναι.

These examples cover a wide spectrum. First John 2:6 is a general expression regarding the behavior of believers; the next two expressions (2:29/3:7 and 3:3, regarding righteousness and purity) deal with two aspects related to identity, while the next one (4:11, to love) deals with actions based on attitude—in 3:16 it is more narrowly defined through a reference to the physical action of dying.

1. To Walk in the Same Manner as Jesus

In 1 John 2:6, the exemplary authority of Jesus's behavior as a model is deontologically linked to the behavior of the believer. This is based on an intimate relationship between the two (so Brown 1986, 263; Lieu 2008, 74): "whoever says he abides in him *ought to* walk in the same way in which he walked" (ὁ λέγων ἐν αὐτῷ³⁰ μένειν ὀφείλει καθὼς ἐκεῖνος περιεπάτησεν καὶ αὐτὸς [οὕτως]³¹). This expression occurs in a theologically dense context that brings together several important notions, like knowing and remaining or existing in God/Jesus, keeping the commandments or loving your brothers.

The word περιπατέω (walking) refers to general behavior (moving around) among people during everyday life.³² Believers should thus structure their everyday lives, that is, moving around (= reference to behavior) among people, in the same way that Jesus did.³³ What exactly typifies the "walking around" (περιπατέω) of Jesus which believers are obliged³⁴ to follow? The ample references in 1 John that convey the message, with the assumption that the implied readers knew his message,³⁵ create the impression of a tradition of knowledge within which this community functioned. Somehow people should know what Jesus did and how he behaved. The best assumption of where this knowledge comes from is the Johannine tradition, since it is also expressed in the Gospel, which is probably a reference to the earthly life of Jesus. In that reference, Jesus's example and behavior are primarily defined in terms of unrestricted love

---

30. The reference to "him" is most probably to God but then also implicitly to Jesus. See also Smalley 2002, 50.

31. "The external evidence for and against the presence of οὕτως is rather evenly divided (ℵ C Ψ 81 *al* for; A B 33 2464* *al* against). From a transcriptional point of view, the word might have been accidentally omitted following αὐτός. On the other hand, it might have been added as an emphatic correlative with the preceding καθώς. In light of such considerations, the Committee considered it best to include the word but to enclose it within square brackets" (Metzger 1994, 639–40). Brown (1986, 262–63) and Lieu (2008, 74) give detailed descriptions of the use of the comparative particle in the Gospel and Epistles of John.

32. Liddell and Scott (1996, ad loc.) mention that περιπατέω is often used to refer to the philosophers walking around and talking. BDAG points out that where it is used in the New Testament it is always "more exactly defined." This expression reminds one of similar uses in the First Testament. Painter (2002, 144) notes that John is fond of this expression.

33. "The particular aspect of obedience mentioned on this occasion is Christlikeness" (Smalley 2002, 52).

34. Klauck (1991, 118) speaks of a "Verpflichtung." Haas 1972, 43; Painter 2002, 170.

35. See, for instance, 1 John 2:13–14, 20–21; 3:1, 5, 6, 14–15; 4:7; 5:13, 18, 19, 20; etc.

(for instance, John 13:34–35),[36] as is the case here (Smalley 2002, 52). "The Law is the source of Jewish obligation, while the example of Jesus is the source of Christian obligation" (Brown 1986, 262). Indeed, "the test of our religious experience is whether it produces a reflection of the life of Jesus in our daily life" (Marshall 1978, 128).

Is there any clue in this passage *why* a person should behave like Jesus? The key is found in the concept of "remaining/abiding in him" (*Immanenzformeln*)—the proof of this union between the believer and God lies in the imitation of Jesus, which is also expanded by the references to "knowing God" (ἔγνωκα αὐτόν; 2:3–6).[37] Knowledge does not only imply being aware of, but having and sharing the knowledge of God in such a way that it determines the person's behavior accordingly.[38] Smalley (2002, 50) notes that the expressions "to be or exist in him" (ἐν αὐτῷ ἐσμεν) and "to abide in him" (ἐν αὐτῷ μένειν) are used synonymously and that they should be read in parallel with "knowing God" (ἔγνωκα αὐτόν), since they describe an intense and intimate relationship between the believer and God/Jesus.[39] True behavior thus results from this relationship.

Behavior is further qualified in this context through references to keeping his commandments (τὰς ἐντολὰς αὐτοῦ μὴ τηρῶν) or his word (τηρῇ αὐτοῦ τὸν λόγον), motivated inter alia by the fact that they know God. Thus behavior is defined through God's commandments and word (or revelation). The authoritative or hierarchical nature of the argumentation is clear: behavior in the group (family of God) is determined by God who conveys His commandments through Jesus to the rest of group, who

---

36. Klauck (1991, 119) is of the opinion that the author has the total existence of Christ in mind, but concentrated on his death. The focus for him then falls on John 13 as background. Painter (2002, 178) sees "the grounding of Johannine ethics in God's love revealed in Jesus' as a central theme emerging from this context."

37. Lieu (2008, 75) also underlines that walking as Jesus walked specifies the earlier image of light.

38. Louw and Nida (1988, 27.18) define the denotative meaning of knowledge thus: "to learn to know a person through direct personal experience, implying a continuity of relationship—'to know, to become acquainted with, to be familiar with.'"

39. Smalley (2002, 51) underlines the intimacy of the union between believer and God/Jesus: "The use of μένειν at this point suggests an intensely personal knowledge of God; it presupposes an intimate and committed relationship with him, through Jesus, which is both permanent and continuous. To abide 'in (ἐν) Jesus,' moreover, indicates a close and ongoing relationship between the Father and the Son." See also Haas 1972, 42; Akin 2001, 94.

in turn must obey. This interrelatedness is only possible if they remain in him, that is, in the case of an intimate relationship.[40]

In short, if a person knows God, has fellowship with him, and remains in him and in the light, that person should walk like Jesus walked by keeping his words and commandments, which requires the person to love his or her brothers so that the love of God can reach its aim in him or her.

2. Being Righteous Like God and Jesus Are Righteous

Two expressions encouraged believers to ethically reflect what could be called characteristics of Jesus, namely, to act righteously as Jesus is righteous (δίκαιός; 2:29; 3:7) and to be pure (ἁγνός) like him (3:3). Both God (πιστός ἐστιν καὶ δίκαιος; 1:9) and Jesus are described as being righteous (Ιησοῦν Χριστὸν δίκαιον; 2:1; ἐὰν εἰδῆτε ὅτι δίκαιός ἐστιν; 2:29[41]; ἐκεῖνος δίκαιός ἐστιν; 3:7). Their righteousness is linked to believers in the following ways: (1) In 2:29 it is stated that if you know that God is righteous (an expression of identity), you may be sure that everyone who practices righteousness (an expression of action) has been born of God, in other words, stand in an intimate familial relationship to him (ἐὰν εἰδῆτε ὅτι δίκαιός ἐστιν, γινώσκετε ὅτι καὶ πᾶς ὁ ποιῶν τὴν δικαιοσύνην ἐξ αὐτοῦ γεγέννηται). (2) Whoever practices righteousness is righteous, as God is righteous (3:7: ὁ ποιῶν τὴν δικαιοσύνην δίκαιός ἐστιν, καθὼς ἐκεῖνος δίκαιός ἐστιν).

---

40. Brown (1986, 285) sees the point of this verse to underline the fact that abiding in God or Jesus and the way one lives one's life cannot be divorced. Akin (2001, 95) follows Strecker and formulates it a bit dogmatically: "The indicative and the imperative of the Christian life are joined together as a cause and effect. This union occurs only to the degree that the soteriological significance of the death and resurrection of Jesus the Christ precedes the ethical imperative, so that the indicative of the Christ-event becomes the foundation for and the content of the imperative." It is, however, a question of whether the concepts of imperative and indicative are appropriate analytical categories for the Johannine literature.

41. This reference is most probably to Jesus—Haas et al. 1972, 31, although there is some doubt (Johnson 1993, 66, 72)—it could also refer to God. See Smalley (2002, 133) for a discussion of the different views in this regard. He thinks that this verse is ambivalent on purpose. The "him" that is mentioned in connection with birth later in the verse refers to God, though Smalley (2002, 133) says that Jesus also has something to do with it. G. Schrenk (1965, 189) paraphrases this expression: "The righteous Christ is the Doer of the will of God (his obedience is both passive and active) in the fullest sense." So also Klauck 1991, 175; see Haas et al. 1972, 30; Smalley 2002, 31; Johnson 1993, 32–33.

The word "righteousness" is not only used as a characteristic that expresses status (1:9; 2:1, 29; 3:7), it also refers to the qualitative nature of related actions (2:29; 3:7).[42] The inseparable link between identity and behavior is evident: Jesus (and God) is righteous—a person who acts accordingly is also righteous, because the example set by God and Jesus is followed.[43] Klauck (1991, 211) speaks of Jesus as the "Vorbild und Maßstab." C. Haas, Marinus de Jonge, and J. L. Swellengrebel (1994, 89) note that "the maxim that a person's activity is decisive for his quality: one is what one does" is central. Deeds reveal the inner nature of the one who is acting righteously.

The nature of righteousness is determined by God and Jesus. In both 1:9 and 2:1, the righteousness of God and Jesus are linked to actions related to the elimination of sin and sin's effects (see also 3:7). In this light, it seems plausible to conclude that righteousness in 1 John refers to an opposite position to sin (Lieu 2008, 118–19), namely, where there is no sin, not in a person, nor in his or her actions (Brown 1986, 209). Practicing righteousness[44] refers to acting in accordance with what is right. This righteousness is determined by, and relationally measured against, God who is righteous. Doing what is right is acting according to what God expects, that is, God's will, expressing his ethos (Haas et al. 1972, 31). I. Howard Marshall (1978, 167) describes this righteousness as "correct, moral behavior, acceptable to God," while John Painter (2002, 216–17) and Terry Griffith (2002, 127) relate it to the love commandment.

This interpretation is confirmed in 3:12 (Brown 1986, 441–43). *Deeds*, and not persons, are described as righteous in the story of Cain and his brother (τὰ ἔργα αὐτοῦ πονηρὰ ἦν τὰ δὲ τοῦ ἀδελφοῦ αὐτοῦ δίκαια). Righ-

---

42. See Brown 1986, 209–10 for a detailed discussion of righteousness in 1 John.

43. Lexicographically (BDAG, ad loc.), righteousness in the Greco-Roman world is "being in accordance with high standards of rectitude" or "upholds the customs and norms of behaviour." Newman 1980, ad loc.: "conforming to the standard, will, or character of God." Louw and Nida ad loc.: "pertaining to being in accordance with what God requires." Smalley (2002, 166) speaks of "doing is the test of Being," meaning that "the truly 'right' person is the one who *acts* rightly (cf. Matt 7:16 [Luke 6:44])."

44. For background information, see the following remark by Smalley (2002, 167): "There is a clear [Old Testament] background to the concept of acting 'righteously,' and being 'righteous' (δίκαιος). See Gen 18:23–26; Ps 1:6; Isa 60:21; Dan 12:3. In the [New Testament] this language is particularly associated with Paul (cf. Rom 1:17; 3:21–26; 5:1); but it is also found elsewhere (cf. Matt 23:28; Luke 18:14; 1 Pet 4:18; Rev 22:11)."

teous deeds are contrasted with evil (πονηρὰ) deeds (i.e., they are both *unrighteous* and evil) and are related to love and hate respectively in this context. This qualifies righteous deeds as *good* deeds that, in this context, are identified with deeds that correspond with the requirements and expectations of the family (brothers). Implicitly righteous deeds should be in line with the requirements of the family of God, that is, of God's will which is expressed through love (Haas et al. 1972, 86). Jesus is the prime example of what such deeds involve—he gave his life because of his love for his brothers (3:17). This is in obedience to the will of God, who sent Jesus to die for the sins of the world (3:16; 4:9, 14–16). What Jesus did was the right thing, since it was God's will. This shows that he is righteous. Believers should follow the example of Jesus if they want to do the will of God (3:16). Righteousness (see 2:1, 29; 3:7) and righteous deeds are inseparably interconnected.

The other side of the coin looks similar: two things are said about Cain—he is from (origin; Smalley 2002, 184) the evil one (Κάϊν ἐκ τοῦ πονηροῦ ἦν), and he murdered his brother (3:12; Johnson 1993, 80). "Cain's actions were evil because he was evil, in origin and in character, in contrast to 'the children of God' (3:10)."[45] This echoes John 8:44 (Marshall 1978, 189). Again familial origin determines behavior.

3. Being Pure as Jesus is Pure

In 3:3 it is stated that all who have (this) hope in Jesus purify[46] themselves as Jesus[47] is pure (καὶ πᾶς ὁ ἔχων τὴν ἐλπίδα ταύτην ἐπ' αὐτῷ ἁγνίζει ἑαυτόν, καθὼς ἐκεῖνος ἁγνός ἐστιν). Again we find an exemplary standard (Johnson 1993, 69) that should be followed. Believers should purify themselves[48] by

---

45. Haas et al. 1972, 96; Johnson 1993, 81. Akin (2001, 155) remarks, "In Cain's case the inner nature brought forth the outward action."

46. BDAG (2000, ad loc.) distinguishes three possible usages: (1) to purify and cleanse and so make acceptable for cultic use; (2) to cause to be morally pure; (3) to set one apart in dedication. The term is only used here in the Epistles and once in the Gospel (11:55) where the reference is to the cultic purification of the Jews. Haas et al. (1972, 85) acknowledge the different possible uses, but chooses for the ritual meaning, as do Klauck 1991, 183, and Smalley 2002, 149.

47. Haas et al. 1972, 85: "The pronoun *he*, lit. 'that one,' refers unequivocally to Christ."

48. The present tense seems to focus on the continuous nature of the activity. Haas et al. 1972, 85; Johnson 1993, 69.

means of positive and conscious action according to the example Jesus set, as Smalley (2002, 166–67) indicates: "the believer must keep himself pure; but this can only be accomplished through him whose purity is a model for all Christians." He is the motivation, means, and pattern of righteous behavior. The change from the plural to the singular in this verse emphasizes the personal responsibility a person has in this regard (Smalley 2002, 148).

The term "pure" (ἁγνός) "refers to cleanliness and holiness of life" that has cultic or ritual undertones, but it can also simply be used to refer to moral behavior.[49] It can refer to both a quality and the actions to attain that quality. In 3:3 the requirement is set against the eschatological expectation of the future appearance of Jesus. Then believers will be like him (3:2), something that should already start taking place now. Believers must purify themselves now already as Jesus is pure, bringing them in line with what they are going to be when Jesus is revealed.[50] "The hope of being like Christ in the end, that is to say, should inspire (and can produce) Christ-like behavior even now" (Smalley 2002, 149). The next verse offers a framework for understanding the context of this pureness—the person should not sin—which is equated to lawlessness (ἀνομία)—but should live according to the will of the Father by acting righteously. The whole context is dominated by familial language that explains by convention why a believer should act like Jesus. To live as a true member of the family of God is to renounce sin—Jesus, the Son of God, is without any sin and his aim was to get rid of sin (3:5), which could also be a reference to him being pure. Jesus is indeed the example that they are to follow (Smalley 2002, 149–50). The ethical connotation of the reference to be pure is undeniable—it "denotes a continual moral purification process" (Akin 2001, 137). Implied in the context this means to avoid sin as a quality that belongs to the devil. Those who believe in Jesus should have no part in it (3:5–6), since Jesus destroyed

---

49. BDAG 2000, ad loc.; Louw and Nida 1988, ad loc. Painter (2002, 222) says that "no indication is given as to what purity means." He sees it as a ritual term, though no ritual is implied. Brown (1986, 397–98) argues for a ritual use in the sense that Christians must make themselves holy to encounter the divine. This is done through the cleansing blood of Jesus that is referred to in 1:7, 9; 2:2. The moral use of the word should, however, not be overlooked.

50. Akin (2001, 137) emphasizes the link between eschatology and ethics here: "John joins his previous eschatological thoughts with a moral, practical conclusion. Being born of God creates a vibrant hope for the future, one that motivates pure living in everyday life."

it (3:7–8). This is a continuous process (present tense, ἁγνίζει) that should be seen as the responsibility of the individual.

4. Love Like God/Jesus Loved

God is the source and origin of love (4:7) and *is* indeed love (4:8, 16). He expressed His love concretely by sending His Son (4:9–10) ... and if God so loved us, we also *ought to* love one another and God (4:11, 21). We should love, because God loved us first (4:19). Love indeed cements the relationship of unity between God, Jesus, and believers (4:16). Whoever loves God should also love his or her fellow believers (4:21; 5:1–2). Porousness characterizes the way love functions within interpersonal relationships. The love that "flows from God" reaches and "passes through" a believer as a means of returning love to God, thus fulfilling God's goals regarding love. It penetrates and determines all relationships.

This love is concretized in 3:16–17—Jesus gave his life for us; we ought (are obliged—Brown 1986, 449) to do the same for our fellow believers (Smalley 2002, 244). The love of God through Jesus forms the exemplary standard for the behavior of the believers. If we do not follow the example of Jesus, by helping the needy fellow believer, the question is posed: how could the love of God remain in us? (πῶς ἡ ἀγάπη τοῦ θεοῦ μένει ἐν αὐτῷ; 3:17). The quality of the love of the believer should correspond to the quality of the love God has (i.e., a qualitative or descriptive interpretation of love). Ethically, this means that the actions of believers should create an atmosphere wherever they go that corresponds with the ethos of the life-giving and loving God. Wherever they are present, God's love must be evident. An example of what is expected is given in 3:16.

In 5:1–2, love is also directly related to behavior within the context of familial relationships. It is stated that if a person loves the father, he should love the offspring also. This type of argument can only be valid in a group-oriented society where interpersonal relationships bind people together in unity. Your attitude may not differ in relation to different parts of the unity.

5. Die Like Jesus Died

In 3:11–18, a context with a secondary reference to the conflict with the secessionists, the effects and difference between hate and love are expressed by contrasting the taking of your brother's life against giving your own life for somebody (see Smalley 2002, 195). Loving a person (3:11) will not destroy the person but would mediate life, even though your own life might be required in the process.

Getting to know the nature of God's love was facilitated by Jesus—through his concrete act of laying down his life for our sake (ἐκεῖνος ὑπὲρ ἡμῶν τὴν ψυχὴν αὐτοῦ ἔθηκεν; 3:16). Our actions ought to (in the sense of an obligation or duty) run parallel to his—we should also lay down our lives. In the case of Jesus, laying down his life refers to his death on the cross (see also John 10:11, 15, 17–18; 13:37, 38; 15:38), but what does that imply for his followers? In 3:17 this explanation follows: "But if anyone has the world's goods (τὸν βίον τοῦ κόσμου)[51] and sees his brother in need, yet closes his heart against him, how does God's love abide in him?" This rhetorical question (see Haas 1972, 101; Johnson 1993, 160) emphasizes the positive side: Love for God implies that you should lay down your life for your brother, which is concretized by helping him compassionately when he is in need.[52] In this way life is created and not taken away in contrast to Cain's actions.

True ethical actions involve creating life not destroying it. Through his cross, Jesus mediated eternal life for us; through our deeds of compassion and help for those in need, we create life for them. The basic requirement is clear: a follower of Jesus ought to better the lives of brothers in need in practical ways even if it might require sacrifices from the follower of Jesus, perhaps even to the point of laying down one's life.

Again the question should be posed: why ought a believer to follow Jesus? Why should he or she take his ethical directive from Jesus? Verse 3:14 explains it: "We know that we have passed from death to life, because we love the brothers" (ἡμεῖς οἴδαμεν ὅτι μεταβεβήκαμεν ἐκ τοῦ θανάτου εἰς τὴν ζωήν, ὅτι ἀγαπῶμεν τοὺς ἀδελφούς). Brothers are family, and believers have passed into this eternal life. As we have seen, family conventions require family members to act according to the requirements of the family. God's

---

51. Brown (1986, 475) considers contexts like the apocalyptic last hour, or he reads this saying within the framework of the secession. Smalley (2002, 196) argues that this verse is not addressed to the rich people in the congregation, but to everybody—τὸν βίον τοῦ κόσμου refers to things one needs for everyday life. So Haas 1972, 91; Painter 2002, 242.

52. Brown (1986, 474) underlines the fact that this is not a new command, but is part of Christianity's Jewish heritage—see Deut 15:7. For a discussion of κλείσῃ τὰ σπλάγχνα αὐτοῦ ἀπ' αὐτοῦ, see Smalley 2002, 197. Smalley (2002, 197), therefore, correctly points out that "almsgiving, and the sharing of goods with those in need, was a feature of the early Christian Church inherited from Judaism."

love for us determines the manner of our love for others (Painter 2002, 242). Once again, this forms the heuristic framework of the remark in 3:16.

6. What about Sin?

In Jesus there is no sin (3:5), and the same ought to be true of the child of God (3:6, 9).[53] Children should act according to the requirements of their family. However, 1:7–2:2 indicates that believers do sin. The requirement is, however, that in such a case the personal relationship should be restored through forgiveness, purification, and atonement (1:8–9; 2:1–2). In this manner the ideal is maintained, and where the ideal is broken through concrete reality, the relationship between God and the believer that is spoiled should be restored.

The way ethical behavior is determined is through an orientation toward Jesus and his Father. The exemplary authority lies with them. This forms the basic ethical structure of 1 John. Ethical behavior involves an obedient relational orientation towards Jesus and the Father and not an adherence to a list of "do's" and "do not's." This means that the ethos (i.e., the generally accepted and assumed behavior within the community) became crucial, since life is lived within that ethos. Reciprocity, common in the ancient world,[54] plays a key role in motivating the actions resulting from the interpersonal relationships. In order to maintain sound inter-

---

53. See Brown (1986, 403), who in this context argues that the believer should be like Jesus. This needs more explanation, since in 1:8, 10 it is clear that believers are not sinless, to the contrary. Painter 2002, 227.

54. *Reciprocity* (in the context of such intimate relations as friendship) is described as follows by Aristotle in his *Ethica nichomachea*: "and in all respects either party receives from the other the same or similar benefits, as it is proper that friends should do" (καὶ κατὰ πάντα ταὐτὰ γίνεται καὶ ὅμοια ἑκατέρῳ παρ' ἑκατέρου, ὅπερ δεῖ τοῖς φίλοις ὑπάρχειν; 8.iv.1; 8.xiii.8–9), or "each party therefore both loves his own good and also makes an equivalent return by wishing the other's good" (ἑκάτερος οὖν φιλεῖ τε τὸ αὑτῷ ἀγαθόν, καὶ τὸ ἴσον ἀνταποδίδωσι τῇ βουλήσει; 8.v.5), "in essence friendship seems to consist more in giving than in receiving affection" (8.viii.3); or in the words of Cicero (*Amic.* 14.49; see Konstan 1996, 8–9): "For nothing gives more pleasure than the return of goodwill and the interchange of zealous service." In a real intimate relation, Cicero (*Amic.*16.58) is of the opinion that there will not be "petty accounting," but one would like to give back more than one received. This implies that such relationships were conditional in general, including expectations as well as obligations (Keener 2003, 1008).

personal relationships what is received should somehow be returned. A child should reciprocate the deeds of his parents; children should do that, as well as friends. In relationships between people of unequal status (like fathers and children), what is received cannot necessarily be returned in the same form—it should be returned equally, but not identically. Reciprocity should, however, be maintained by returning the gesture in a comparable, though not necessarily the same, way.[55] For instance, if Jesus dies on the cross, believers should die by helping others. The idea of the believer "returning the love of God" reciprocally underlies the argument in most of the exemplary passages. God loves the believers and in order to reciprocate, they should "return" his love by loving the children of God in a like manner.

---

55. Intimate relationships also exist between people who are not necessarily of the same social status. This may be illustrated by friendship—friendships may exist between members of a family (father-son, son-son, cousins, etc.) or between distinctive social classes (ruler-persons ruled) and even patrons and clients (Keener 2003, 1008, referring to Martial *Epigr.* 3.36.1–3; 3 Macc 5:26). This has implications for reciprocity. How does an inferior "repay" a superior? Aristotle recognized this: "the benefits that one party receives and is entitled to claim from the other are not the same on either side" (*Eth. nic.* 8.7.2). Persons have different excellence and functions and may also experience their relationships differently. Aristotle takes the friendship relationship between father and son as an example: Children render parents services as authors of their being, while parents offer services to them as their offspring—this ensures an enduring and equitable friendship (8.7.2). It remains a requirement that the affection rendered in these various unequal friendships should remain *proportionate* (9.1.1). For instance, the more important party should receive more affection, since for him to be willing to be friends with an inferior person should be compensated by means of additional affection (8.7.2). This additional affection will "make them equal" (8.8.5; 8.13.1). In *Eth. nic.* 8.14.2 Aristotle formulates it thus: "Both parties should receive a larger share from the friendship, but not a larger share of the same thing: the superior should receive the larger share of honour, the needy one the larger share of profit, for honour is the due reward of virtue and beneficence, while need obtains the aid it requires in pecuniary gain" (8.14.2). At least a person should repay what he can (8.14.4). Cicero's view, however, differs a bit from that of Aristotle as to how equality is to be reached: "As, therefore, in friendship, those who are superior should lower themselves, so, in a measure, should they lift up their inferiors" (*Amic.* 20.72).

Conclusion

Some aspects of ethics in 1 John were considered and discussed in order to understand the dynamics of ethics in this letter.

(1) Identity and behavior cannot be separated and should be understood in terms of a continuum with porous borders. Identity is determined by the relationship between the believer and the Father and Son; deeds are an expression of this identity.

(2) Fellowship (κοινωνία) between God and the believer is a framework within which the dynamics of the relationship are explained and motivated. The concept of κοινωνία expresses a form of relational intimacy that has the characteristics of sharing and having things in common; in other words, a dynamic interrelatedness with porous boundaries. The idea of unity is also expressed in familial language and by way of *Immanenzformeln*.

(3) It follows that the essence of ethics in 1 John is relational; in other words, the actions are motivated by, and are performed in terms, of relationships. These relationships are hierarchically dominated by God—behavior should reflect what God stands for. What is expected of the believer is to live in an obedient relationship with Jesus and not merely to live according to a list of expected rules. This is possible when the ethos of the group is clear, which presupposes a clear definition of identity.

(4) The ethical orientation is important. To illustrate this point: the believer does not live with his or her eyes focused upon the situation at hand, rather his or her eyes should be cast in the direction of God and Jesus. Actions are determined by the requirements and maintenance of this relationship. The group ethos must be maintained. Rules related to particular actions are not in focus. Rather the focus rests upon an expression of the relational ethos.

(5) Familial imagery plays an important heuristic role in understanding ethics in 1 John. The motivation is based on ancient family conventions. Because the believer is part of the family, he or she should behave according to the requirements of the family. Since God is righteous, behaving according to God's will is also righteous. This was a social convention in ancient times. No further motivation is needed.

(6) Reciprocity plays an important role. God loved believers, and believers should love God and their fellow believers in return. God loved first (4:19), and believers should therefore reciprocally respond to that love.

(7) The underlying ethical structure in 1 John is theological (its origin lies with God), revelational, and therefore deontological (it is obligatory).

Knowledge of God and God's revelation (involving knowing God)—and not reason (in the sense of human abilities to discover right or wrong within themselves or somewhere else)—is the key to unlocking the ethics of the Epistle. This knowledge is conveyed within a relational framework, expressed with terms like fellowship, familial terms, and *Immanenzformeln*. This relationship must be expressed in actions that reflect the ethos of God.

The Significance of 2:15–17 for Understanding the Ethics of 1 John

William R. G. Loader

My initial reaction in returning to 1 John 2:15–17 after investigating attitudes towards sexuality in the New Testament and early Judaism was to see here a reflection of the view expressed in Mark 12:25 and, I believe, presupposed by Paul, that in the age to come there would be no place for sexual desire and sexual relations, for "the world and its desire are passing away" (ὁ κόσμος παράγεται καὶ ἡ ἐπιθυμία αὐτοῦ, 1 John 2:17).[1] This need not imply a negative stance towards sexual desire in itself as part of God's creation. It is just that in the age to come it will cease to be. I determined then to test this assumption and in the process not only modified it, but found my focus falling on other important aspects of the text and asking what its significance may be for understanding ethics in 1 John.

Examining 1 John 2:15–17

The passage is about more than sexual desire. It may not be about sexual desire at all. Many commentators caution against trying to be specific either way. Thus Judith Lieu (2008, 95) writes: "It is probably unnecessary to identify three separate activities among the three phrases—for example, that the desire of the flesh is sexual, the desire of the eyes is covetousness, and the arrogance of life is wealth" (similarly Schnelle 2010, 97; Klauck 1991a, 141; Brown 1982, 307). My paper will cross that line of caution but with care and on the basis that I believe the triad of vices may have more coherence and specific reference than is usually assumed. I will not revisit

---

1. Unless indicated by an asterisk as the author's own, all biblical translations follow the NRSV.

here the issue of the genitives σαρκός and τῶν ὀφθαλμῶν. With most others, I take them to be subjective genitives (Lieu 2008, 94; Brown 1982, 307, 308; Painter 2002, 194).

While the ἡ ἀλαζονεία may derive from τοῦ βίου, which would give us a third subjective genitive (so Brown 1982, 312), I consider an objective genitive more likely (Painter 2002, 192). Ultimately, it does not make a lot of difference in this third instance (so Smalley 1984, 85). More difficult is the meaning of ἡ ἀλαζονεία. It is certainly negative. Given its meaning in the Septuagint, it is probably more than simply pride, but rather also the kind of pride which boasts and so may carry connotations here of pretentiousness. Raymond Brown (1982, 311) notes that ἡ ἀλαζονεία usually means pretentiousness in classical Greek, but in Hellenistic Greek has more the meaning of ostentation as in Septuagint (2 Macc 9:8; 15:6; Wis 17:7; 4 Macc 8:19; and in relation to wealth: Wis 5:8; see also Jas 4:16). He points also to the link with appetite in Hab 2:5 (Brown 1982, 312; see also Yarborough 2008, 132). I. Howard Marshall (1978, 145) depicts it as pride in possessions exaggerated in order to impress (see also Klauck 1991a, 140; Painter 2002, 194; Witherington 2009, 1:509). I agree with those who see τοῦ βίου here, as in 3:17 (see also Mark 12:44), referring to livelihood, including possessions (Brown 1982, 312; Schnackenburg 1984, 130; Klauck 1991a, 141). Robert Yarborough (2008, 132, 134) writes of vain and ostentatious pursuit of earthly goods and translates: "what the body hankers for and the eyes itch to see and what people toil to acquire." Following the pattern of threes elsewhere, the third item appears to carry special weight. Thus Rudolf Schnackenburg (1984, 130) speaks of it as "noch eine Stufe höher." This coheres with the fact that it alone finds an echo in the author's expressed concerns elsewhere in the letter, to which we shall return.

Klaus Wengst (1978, 95–97) argues for a coherence across all three members of the triad, interpreting all three as referring to desire for wealth. Some suggest that the first item functions as the summary title, which is unpacked in the two vices which follow (so Westcott 1966, 64; Smalley 1984, 83; Marshall 1979, 146; Witherington 2009, 1:509). There are certainly parallels which might support seeing ἐπιθυμία τῶν ὀφθαλμῶν as a reference to greed (Matt 20:15; 6:23; Luke 11:34; Mark 7:22; Eccl 4:8; Sir 14:8), which would sit well with the third item (so Vogler 1993, 89). Ruth Edwards (1996, 84) writes of the triad as "sensual cravings, ruthless greed, and the pretentiousness of material success." Some read "desires of the flesh" as sexual (so Schnelle 2010, 96; Vogler 1993, 88–89; Marshall 1978, 145; Painter 2002, 191; Witherington 2009, 1:509). Horst Balz

(1985, 180) describes the triad as depicting "sexuelles Verlangen, Gier nach macht und Geld."

Many have noted that there is also strong parallel support for seeing a sexual reference in ἐπιθυμία τῶν ὀφθαλμῶν. The evidence is extensive: 2 Pet 2:14; Matt 5:28–30; Gen 39:7; Num 15:39; 2 Sam 11:2; Prov 6:25; Job 31:1; Sir 9:5, 8; 23:4–6; 26:21; 41:20–21; 1 En. 8:1–2; Jub. 20:4; Jdt 10:4; 16:7–9; L.A.B. 43.5; Sus 7–8, 12, 52–53, 57; Pss. Sol. 4:4–5, 9, 12; CD II,16; 4Q435 2 I,1–2; 4QBer[b]/4Q287 8 13; 11QT[a]/11Q19 LIX,13–14; 1QS/1Q28 I,6–7; V,4–5; 1QpHab V,7; 4QInstr[c]/4Q417 1 I,27; T. Reu. 2:4; 3:10; 4:1; 6:1; T. Jud. 17:1; T. Iss. 4:4; T. Benj. 6:2; Philo, *Sacr.* 21; *Spec.* 3.171 (see also Vouga 1990, 40). Schnackenburg (1984, 129–30) sees sexual reference in both the first two items of the triad. Hans-Josef Klauck (1991a, 138–41) notes the broadening of ἐπιθυμία beyond the concern with possessions that it has in the Decalogue, but argues against limiting the eyes to sexual lust on the basis that flesh is not used negatively in Johannine literature. Yarborough (2008, 132–33) sees a range of possible references including the haughtiness of rebellion, blindness, greed, "the moral short-sightedness that obscures higher and better realities," but also "what the eyes itch to see," including pornography (see also Brown 1982, 310). If we do not consider all three as referring to greed and especially if we see here, as many do, a minicatalogue of vices (as Vouga 1990, 40; Klauck 1991a, 137; but see Vogler 1993, 88) or, as I shall argue, an association of vices, then the sexual reference in the second item is likely.

If the first item is not a heading, but one of three vices, then we should at least consider whether it might have been understood as having more specific reference. This seems likely. But first we note that most discussions that see here a reference to three vices make no particular connection between them except for the overall observation that they illustrate, for the author, "all that is in the world." One might even argue with Brown (1982, 310) that neither ἡ ἐπιθυμία τῆς σαρκός nor ἡ ἐπιθυμία τῶν ὀφθαλμῶν is referring to a vice, but simply to an aspect of creation, namely, "all that satisfies the needs and wants of human beings taken as such" of which some are good and some are not. First John criticizes "the desire of the flesh" not primarily because it is sinful in itself but because it is not of the realm of the Spirit (Brown 1982, 311). The three are neutral as part of human nature, part of biological life (Brown 1982, 326), and accordingly the author's point is the transitoriness of these, along with the rest of the current order, in the light of the approaching eschaton (1 John 2:8, 18; see also 1 Cor 7:31) (Brown 1982, 314; see also Smalley 1984, 85; Painter 2002,

194). Similarly, Klauck points to 2:9–11 and the link between 2:8 and 2:18 (Klauck 1991a, 138, 142; see Schnackenburg 1984, 130). That might indeed come close to what my first re-reading suggested in relation to sexuality, assuming that is the reference of the second item. These will pass away, so you should not be attached to them. For some it might inspire asceticism, though that is not a necessary consequence (so rightly Lieu 1991, 54), at least not as a pattern for all, as both Paul and the Jesus tradition about eunuchs for the kingdom of God show (1 Cor 7:7; Matt 19:12).

Since, however, the third item is so clearly negative, it is most unlikely that ἡ ἐπιθυμία τῆς σαρκὸς or ἡ ἐπιθυμία τῶν ὀφθαλμῶν is neutral. They are, after all, "not of the Father," as the creation would be (so Schnackenburg 1984, 128; Lieu 1991, 54). If they are seen as negative, that still leaves the possibility that the author may see all sexual desire negatively, which would drive another path to asceticism. Once again, the third item suggests that the issue in each is a particular response to something. It is the ἀλαζονεία in relation to τοῦ βίου, not βίος in itself. To have livelihood and possessions is not in itself evil; one should share them. Similarly, to be flesh and to have eyes is not in itself evil. Many have noted the distinction between Paul's dualism and that of the Fourth Gospel (so Brown 1982, 309; Schnackenburg 1984, 128), which does not associate flesh with the realm of sin and death, but sees it as a level of the divine creation which has worth, not least as the arena of divine testimony to what is to come, but which should now no longer be determinant for the believer, as it is for "the world." As Georg Strecker (1989, 119) notes, being of the world means being ruled by ἐπιθυμία. Similarly, Lieu (2008, 93) writes: "When the author forbids any love of the world, this is not in itself rejection of the accoutrements of a comfortable life, or of social success and its benefits; neither is it a repudiation of anything associated with human bodily existence as if this was by definition something to be escaped from–although conceivably these might follow." It is weak and transitory, but not evil. It needs to be kept in its proper place. It is this overall view that probably also informs the author of the Epistle, although his concerns are more strongly ethical. Thus when he speaks of the flesh and the eyes, we may assume that he would have seen them as God's creation, including the desires that are naturally part of that creation. What matters is how one responds to them. In 2:16 he addresses inappropriate responses, typical of the world.

Aside from some extreme views and the overstatements which belong to rhetoric, the attitude towards ἐπιθυμία in both Hellenistic philosophy and its Jewish appropriation in writers such as Philo, the author of 4 Maccabees, and also Paul is that ἐπιθυμία like πάθος has its place; it becomes problematic when it is excessive and misdirected. As Gaca (2003, 34; see also 106-7) notes, the Pythagoreans held to extreme positions about sexual desire, influencing both Plato and some Stoics: "Showing proper restraint in dietary and sexual behavior is thus central to Plato's conception of what it means to be morally responsible." Unlike the Pythagoreans, however, Plato set such limits only for the period when couples were childbearing, as little as ten years, and thereafter saw no problem in couples continuing to engage in sexual intercourse right into old age, provided it was not flamboyant or excessive (*Leg.* 783e4-7; 784b1-3; 784e3-785a3) (Gaca 2003, 53, 56, 106). The later, so-called Neopythagoreans, Charondas in *Preamble* (some time prior to mid-first cent CE) and Ocellus in *The Nature of the Universe* (150 BCE), insisted that sex was legitimate only for procreation. Both Seneca (4 BCE-65 CE) and Musonius Rufus (ca. 30-102 CE), the Roman Stoics, appear to stand under their influence, which has led to the widespread misconception that procreationism was a Stoic tenet. Gaca (2003, 97) writes: "Though both Stoicism and ancient society make procreation central, neither of them limits permissible human sexual activity to reproduction, and hence they are not procreationist." Of Seneca, she observes: "Like Ocellus and Charondas, and unlike any Stoic other than Musonius, he presumes an exclusive disjunction between human sexual activity 'for the purpose of pleasure' (*voluptatis causa*) or 'for the purpose of reproduction' (*propagandi generis causa*)" (111). "It is utterly foreign to Stoicism to contend, as Seneca does, that one must do away with the experience of erotic love except for the reproductive urge within marriage" (112).

This stands in contrast to the claims of Dale Martin (2006, 67) that Stoic writers of the time promoted passionless sex, which then had only one justification: begetting children (similarly Fredrickson 2003, 23-30). As a corrective, see also Will Deming (2004, 45), whose assessment of Stoic and Cynic discussion on marriage leads him to conclude that it "is wrong to assert that this excludes love, passion, or romance from marital relations." Similarly, J. Edward Ellis (2007, 95) writes: "Condemnations of sexual desire per se are quite rare. Far more common are, on the one hand, condemnations of sexual immorality (in various forms) and overpowering, excessive, or misdirected desire and, on the other hand, exhortations to self-control." Actual disapproval of sexual desire and sexual intercourse occurs unambiguously only in the Jewish Sib Or. 1 (late first or early second century CE). One should also see Apoc. Mos. 19.3, according to which the poison sprinkled on the fruit that Eve ate was ἐπιθυμία (on this see Loader 2011b, 68–77, 336–40). On Philo, see my earlier discussion (Loader 2011a, 41–45, 56–66, 84–90). Lieu (2008, 94) also writes that it was "commonplace in philosophy that desire threatens to overturn the rational mind, and needs to be controlled with regular practice," citing Thucydides, *Hist.* 6.13; Epictetus *Diatr.* 2.18; also Ps 106:14 (LXX 105:14). As she states:

> First John has brought together the Johannine cosmological dualism and mythologization of "the world," with this separate ethical tradition that also works with a form of dualism, but with one that is more moral and anthropological. However, he does so only here, and it has no further effect on the rest of the Letter: there are limited connections with the other uses of "flesh," "eyes," and "life" (*bios*) elsewhere in 1 John (4:2; 1:1; 3:17). (2008, 94)

Context thus determines whether ἐπιθυμία is to be seen as bad and so translated as "lust," whether in a sexual or nonsexual sense. Brooke Westcott (1966, 64) spoke of being swayed by passion. Similarly, Stephen Smalley (1984, 82) notes that desire like love can go both ways and be positive or negative, and Marshall (1978, 144) states that "anything in the world can become the source of sinful desire, even though it is good in itself" (similarly Lieu 1991, 54). In 2:16 it is clearly negative (as in John 8:44 about the devil's desires). Thus Yarborough (2008, 132) writes of "a quality of desire that is inimical to God's desire," degraded desire (similarly Strecker 1989, 119).

To return to the triad and its first item, if the third item is specific and the second likely to be heard as referring to sexual lust, might ἡ ἐπιθυμία τῆς σαρκός have a more specific meaning than is usually supposed? On its own, ἡ ἐπιθυμία τῆς σαρκός really could be applied to many kinds of desires, especially if we see it simply as one of a list of three. Hence the caution about trying to go further. Most attempts to relate the triad to the world of the time do so by seeking out texts that contain verbal parallels or parallel ideas, none of them particularly convincing (so Schnackenburg 1984, 128). These include occurrence of the concepts, sometimes as triads in Sir 23:4–6; Jub. 7:20–24; CD IV,17; Philo, *Decal.* 28, 153; *Post.* 135; T. Jud. 13:2; 17:1; and Pirke Avot, but only partially corresponding to the content here. Udo Schnelle (2010, 96–97) notes Philo's description of ἐπιθυμία as the source of all evil (*Spec.* 4.84–85); Epicurus's judgment that it disturbs wellbeing (Plutarch, *Mor.* 449D); and Dio Chrysostom, *4 Regn.* 4.84, and cites Rom 7:7, adding: "Darüber hinausgehende Folgerungen lassen sich kaum ziehen, denn die Trias der hier angeführten Laster findet sich auch in der philosophischen Unterweisung." On suggested analogies with the snake's pitch to Eve (Gen 3:6) or Satan's pitch to Jesus in the temptations as no more convincing, see the discussion by Lieu (2008, 95; similarly Brown 1984, 307–8; Smalley 1984, 85).

I want to suggest that we should look beyond literary parallels and analogies to social realities of the time to which authors alluded, especially in their attacks on the evils of their day, and in which they saw all three vices concurrently occurring. C. H. Dodd (1946, 41–12, 46) spoke generally of an attack on pagan society as characterized by sensuality; being captive to external things; and proud humbug, sensuality, materialism, and self-glorification. Klauck (1991b, 138) went beyond Dodd in arguing that 2:9–11 shows that the author saw the world as loveless and dominated by hate. He notes that Christian exegesis associated sexual profligacy with gluttony and drunkenness as in Sir 23:4–6 and saw the pagan world as characterized by lust, avarice, and pride (Klauck 1991b, 139, 143). John Painter (2002, 194) reflects on the social situation of the author when he writes: "the language of this third attitude may well point toward the Greco-Roman cultural challenge to Johannine Christianity ... part of the honour culture with which Johannine Christianity was forced to struggle." Peter Rhea Jones, noting Ephesus as a possible location, writes that the author

> may have been concerned about pagan cults, especially the Egyptian religions of Isis and Serapis as well as imperial cults and activities at the stadium and theatre. Furthermore, the Roman farces in theatres including burlesque revue of song and dance, nudity and obscene subjects (Dio Chrysostom, *Alex.* 32:4; Apuleius, *Met.* 10:29–34), and pantomime often involving obscenity. (2009, 86)

The likely setting which then suggests itself is the culture of depravity present in the banquets of the rich. There, gluttony and drunkenness often went hand in hand with sexual excess. While producing no triadic formulation matching 2:16, Philo cites gluttony/drunkenness, linked with sexual excess and aberration, and the pretentious greed of the wealthy as the three major elements characterizing the depraved lifestyle. He regularly associates gluttony, sexual lust, and profligate feasting, where "drunkenness, daintiness, and greediness ... caus[e] the cravings of the belly to burst out and fanning them into flame, make the man a glutton, while they also stimulate and stir up the stings of his sexual lusts" (*Opif.* 158). "For strong drink and gross eating accompanied by wine-bibbing, while they awaken the insatiable lusts of the belly, inflame also the lusts seated below it, and as they stream along and overflow on every side they create a torrent of evils innumerable, because they have the immunity of the feast for their headquarters and refuge from retribution" (*Spec.* 1.192). "All this the lawgiver observed and therefore did not permit his people to conduct their festivities like other nations, but first he bade them in the very hour of their joy make themselves pure by curbing the appetites for pleasure" (*Spec.* 1.193; see also *QG* 2.12; *Somn.* 2.147; *Mos.* 2.185). He writes of city clubs "with a large membership, whose fellowship is founded on no sound principle but on strong liquor and drunkenness and sottish carousing and their offspring, wantonness" (*Flacc.* 136; similarly *Legat.* 312; *Leg.* 2.29, 33; *Cher.* 92; *Agr.* 37–38, 160; *Spec.* 1.148, 150). He lambasts both Xenophon's and Plato's symposia for sumptuous indulgence, gluttony, drunkenness, and sexual perversion (*Contempl.* 53–56), making similar allegations of the people of Sodom in *Somn.* 1.122–125 and *Abr.* 133–135, where he writes of "gluttony and lewdness" and "every other possible pleasure" as well as greed, "deep drinking of strong liquor and dainty feeding and forbidden forms of intercourse" (*Abr.* 135). Philo basically identifies two levels of lust typically as those of the belly and those below it (*Spec.* 1.192; *Spec.* 2.163, 195; *Leg.* 3.114; *Deus* 15; *Mos.* 1.28; 2.23–24; *QG* 1.12; *Sacr.* 49; *Fug.* 35; *Virt.* 182, 208; *Somn.* 2.147). Excess greed, excess liquor, excess sex go together for Philo (see further Loader 2011a, 2–258).

Philo is certainly not alone. Already in Sirach we see this connection: "Never dine with another man's wife, or revel with her at wine" (Sir 9:9; see also 26:8; 31:25–32:13). Klauck, who mentions Philo's attack on the boastful rich in *Spec.* 2.18–19, also cites Petronius's *Trimalchio* in relation to ἀλαζονεία (Klauck 1991b, 141). Petronius is, however, equally relevant to what I would see as the other two aspects. I cannot here review all the evidence of attacks on such depravity. It is substantial and widespread, including also Wis 2:6–9 (wine and revelry); 1 En. 46:4–5; T. Mos. 7:1–4; Rom 13:13; 1 Cor 6:10 (greedy drunkards); Gal 5:21 (drunkenness, carousing, and things like these); and 1 Pet 4:3. The association of sexual profligacy, wealth, and self-indulgence also informs the image of Rome in Rev 17:1–6; 18:3, 9.

All this renders it very likely that people hearing the triad would have thought of the places where it most obviously manifested itself: the drunken parties of the profligate. It was standard polemical fare. It is what characterized the world's life. New Testament vice lists also regularly juxtapose reference to sexual wrongdoing with references to overindulgence in food and wine (Rom 13:13; 1 Cor 6:10; Gal 5:21; 1 Pet 4:3). Thus rather than attacking only lust for wealth or simply listing three different kinds of vice as separate entities, the author can be seen as depicting life in the world by referring to three aspects which belonged to one of its most commonly attacked settings: the depraved excesses of the rich at their often pretentious banquets. I suggest this as a plausible context for understanding the author's triad in 2:16. It is clear to me that with one foot behind the line of caution, I can go only as far as pointing to this as a very plausible possibility. The strength of the proposal lies in the coherent explanation it can give to the three items and the way it takes into account a widespread social phenomenon of the day and common target of critique. But it remains a hypothesis which at most can claim to make sense of the material but no more.

1 John 2:15–17 and Johannine Ethics

If the triad is attacking the abuses of the rich in particular, how might this observation inform our understanding of the ethics of 1 John? Let me approach this in two ways, first by examining the role of the statement in its context and then by considering its significance for the ethical concerns of the Epistle.

The transition from the twofold set of formally structured addresses to children, fathers, and young men in 2:12–14 to 2:15–17 is not immediately obvious or is at least surprising (see Loader 1992, 24–26). John Stott (1988, 103), for instance, writes of 2:15–17 as "a digression about the world." Why instruct them all not to love the world and its threefold vices, something not repeated elsewhere in a letter which is forever repeating itself? Perhaps the author is drawing on tradition in 2:15–17, his own or that of others. Lieu (2008, 94) writes of 2:15–17 as a "separate ethical tradition," which "has no further effect on the rest of the Letter: there are limited connections with the other uses of 'flesh,' 'eyes,' and 'life' (*bios*) elsewhere in 1 John (4:2; 1:1; 3:17)." Similarly Jones (2009, 85) writes that it "may well be pre-formulated homiletical fragments or even a précis." The Epistle's final statement warning against idols (5:21), ringing similarly odd, is a traditional exhortation. Even so, 2:15–17 reflects elements of the author's style, not least the threefoldness, and of his vocabulary. Lieu (2008, 95) notes the distinctive Johannine use of ἐκ in the expressions ἐκ τοῦ πατρὸς ἀλλ' ἐκ τοῦ κόσμου. The transition to 2:18 appears also somewhat odd and unmediated, warning about antichrists of the last times, people who have left the author and his recipients' community. Both transitions make good sense, however, when we read what is on either side of 2:15-17 in the light of statements which occur later.

The third item in the two formal addresses in 2:12-14 receives special emphasis and addresses the young men. In both instances they are told: "you have overcome the evil one"* (νενικήκατε τὸν πονηρόν). "The evil one" (τὸν πονηρόν) comes to expression in 2:18 as ἀντίχριστος ("the antichrist"), then applied somewhat creatively to the teaching opponents in the plural: ἀντίχριστοι πολλοί ("many antichrists"). Equally significant we find an echo of "you have overcome"* (νενικήκατε) in 5:4-5, "for whatever is born of God overcomes the world. And this is the victory that overcomes the world, our faith. Who is it that overcomes the world but the one who believes that Jesus is the Son of God?"* (ὅτι πᾶν τὸ γεγεννημένον ἐκ τοῦ θεοῦ νικᾷ τὸν κόσμον· καὶ αὕτη ἐστὶν ἡ νίκη ἡ νικήσασα τὸν κόσμον, ἡ πίστις ἡμῶν. Τίς [δέ] ἐστιν ὁ νικῶν τὸν κόσμον εἰ μὴ ὁ πιστεύων ὅτι Ἰησοῦς ἐστιν ὁ υἱὸς τοῦ θεοῦ). Significantly, we have here the language of overcoming the world. Almost certainly, then, we should see the reference to the young men overcoming the evil one as equivalent to their overcoming the world, and furthermore, we have here an explanation of what this means: confessing Christ aright and not, as I think it means, docetically. The intratextual link with 4:1-6 is also important, where addressing the τεκνία, again we have themes of overcoming ("you have overcome them"*; νενικήκατε αὐτούς); "many false prophets" (πολλοὶ ψευδοπροφῆται) recalling "many antichrists" (ἀντίχριστοι πολλοί) and directly connected to "the spirit of antichrist" (τὸ τοῦ ἀντιχρίστου) in 4:3; that they "went out into the world"* (ἐξεληλύθασιν εἰς τὸν κόσμον; similarly 2 John 7); and that the spirit of antichrist is "already in the world" (ἐν τῷ κόσμῳ ἐστὶν ἤδη). Brown (1982, 324) argues that the secessionists loved the world in the sense of John 3:16 and that the author is complaining that in their outreach they have neglected their own (but see Painter 2002, 191). The theme of the world continues in 4:4-5, where the author contrasts "the one who is in you" (ὁ ἐν ὑμῖν) with "the one who is in the world" (ὁ ἐν τῷ κόσμῳ), probably the evil one, and declares that they are "from the world" (ἐκ τοῦ κόσμου) and that therefore "what they speak is from the world"* (ἐκ τοῦ κόσμου λαλοῦσιν) and "the world listens to them" (ὁ κόσμος αὐτῶν ἀκούει). The concern is, as in 5:5-6 and in 2:22-23, with rightly confessing Christ. Such texts make the logic of the transitions from 2:13-14 to 2:15-17 and from 2:15-17 to 2:18-19 very clear, as Strecker (1989, 119) notes in relation to victory over the world and the evil one in 4:4-5; 5:4-5; and 2:14c; similarly Jones (2009, 86), though he misses the connection when he writes of the young men's conquering as "conceivably of the allures of the world and youthful impulses."

These statements suggest that there is a connection between false Christology and the world. That would imply that there is some connection between false Christology and ethics, between 2:12–15 and 2:18–27, on the one hand, concerned with Christology, and 2:15–17, on the other, with its strong ethical focus on what is "of the world." Some have indeed seen a nexus between denying Jesus's full humanity and neglecting the humanity or at least the needs of others. Thus Maarten Menken (2008, 205–6) sees the secessionists as former members who on the basis of their reading of the Gospel had developed a view of Jesus as superhuman, who see themselves as having "already attained full salvation, and who therefore consider the verification of their faith in everyday reality as not very relevant." He notes that in this they exhibit some similarity with the docetists of whom Ignatius writes that they not only denied Jesus bore flesh and really suffered (*Smyrn.* 4:2; 5:2), but also had no interest in love, in the widow, the orphan, the oppressed, the one who is in chains or the one set free, the one who is hungry or the one who thirsts (6:2) (Menken 2008, 207). Klauck (1991a, 154) writes: "Wenn 2,16 die 'Prahlerei mit dem Wohlstand' anprangiert und 3,17 unterlassene Hilfeleistungen anklagt, dürfte das verraten, dass die einflussreichen und begüterten Leute unter den Gegnern zu suchen sind" and of "soziale Misstände in der Gemeinde" (Klauck 1991b, 141). I also argued formerly a connection between neglecting Jesus's humanity and neglecting that of other community members and that the secessionists belonged on the side of the wealthy (Loader 1992, 42, 68).

The nexus may, however, also be sociological, namely, that those who happen to be wealthy happen also to be more open to a docetic view of Christ, perhaps reflecting exposure to intellectual and philosophical perspectives which found a real incarnation offensive. The author does not, of course, equate the opponents with the world, but does claim that the world finds their views more amenable. From the author's perspective to become amenable to the world in developing Christology inevitably makes one amenable to its ethical values, which in 2:15–17 the author deplores. This is probably polemical. The author is not suggesting that 2:15–17 describes the vices of his opponents. There is, however, a connection with 3:17, where he implies that their vice lies in not expressing love for the brothers by not sharing their livelihood with brothers in need. By implication he tars them with the same brush as the self-indulgent rich of his day.

The intensity of this polemic comes to expression also when he confronts their lack of sharing by depicting it effectively as murder in the tradition of Cain. These are very strong statements. Lieu (2008, 152) notes the importance of the reference to Cain in the context of the allegation of neglect, but then, strangely, sees 3:17 as a weak conclusion. If we read 3:17 as the author's focus in developing the allusion to Cain, it is anything but weak and still has the capacity to challenge people today. It is much in the spirit of applying "Am I my brother's keeper?" to the issue of social justice and needs to be read against a likely setting where without the support of their richer members the author's addressees were finding themselves in dire straits.

The likely background for the author's ethical concerns is not the kind of middle class morality of today in which appeals to generosity for the needy have their place along with much else, but a setting where people lived close to the poverty line. Thus Lieu (2008, 151) writes of 3:17 giving us "a glimpse of a real world of poverty and inequality, in the midst of which most early believers lived" and goes on to note the inequalities in the early Roman empire and the dependency on handouts and on voluntary associations for support, citing Heb 13:1–3; Jas 2:1–7 about neglect. Mutual support in Christian communities was probably crucial to people's survival and understood as part of what the good news entailed, including good news for them, the poor. In this situation more wealthy members had a vital role, and this had not been fulfilled. The repeated assertion of the need to love the brothers is likely to have this concern in mind throughout the Epistle and not just in 3:17. It would surely have come high on the agenda had we been able to ask members what loving one another actually meant in their world.

I suspect that references to hate have less to do with offensive emotional attitudes and more to do with not caring for the brothers, which is tantamount to murder, not just in the sense of the original illustration of rage leading to murder, but neglect leading to death. It is, of course, intramural, but this is typical of how the first Christians appear to have understood Jesus's message of good news for the poor. It was a promise to God's people and remains so, and for all who join it, and only in that sense good news for all. The likely social setting which underlies 1 John means that the author can employ formulations which echo those of the last discourses of the Gospel, especially what I see as their latest expansions, namely, John 13:34–35 and chapters 15–17; but unlike there, he focus not on the danger of disunity, but on the danger of neglect of mutual support for survival.

Of course, with regard to ethics, 2:15–17 certainly enables us to say that the author espoused moderate and controlled consumption of food and drink and response to sexual desire and clearly a rejection of boastful pride about possessions, rather than asceticism, including about sex. The author deploys 2:15–17, however, not primarily to address social evils, but to serve a more fundamental concern: to challenge the neglect of the ethical obligation of support for the poor, which appears to underlie the repeated statements about loving the brothers.

Completed Love: 1 John 4:11–18 and the Mission of the New Testament Church

David Rensberger

This essay concerns both the translation and the understanding of the verb τελειόω in relation to love in 1 John 4. The way that τελειόω has traditionally been translated into English, I believe, has in some measure concealed a significant aspect of the point that 1 John 4 is making, and I hope to take a step toward bringing that aspect into the open.

Let me begin by briefly indicating my understanding of the structure of 1 John 4:11–18, which will to some extent guide the discussion (for more details, see my commentary: Rensberger 1997, 116, 118–22.) The address Ἀγαπητοί ("Beloved") at the beginning of verse 11 (parallel to the identical address in v. 7) marks the beginning of a new unit. Verse 11 gives the overall topic of this unit as the relation between God's love for believers and their love for one another: "Beloved, since God loved us so much, we also ought to love one another" (NRSV). Two statements in verse 12 then set up the two subthemes discussed within the unit: "No one has ever seen God; if we love one another, God lives in us, and his love is perfected in us" (NRSV). "God lives in us" introduces the topic of mutual abiding with God (discerned in the presence of the Spirit, true christological confession, and love) treated in verses 13–16. The statement that divine love "is perfected in us" introduces the topic of "perfect love" that is taken up in verses 17–18. The unit is thus neatly and tightly organized, a rather impressive achievement for this particular author. It is the second of the two subthemes that will be the focus of this essay: "if we love one another … his love is perfected in us." What are the implications of this assertion?

Perfect Love?

The first task in coming to a better understanding of 1 John 4:12 and the statements in 4:17–18 that depend on it will be to undo the effect of their traditional rendering on the minds of English Bible readers. The NRSV wording "his love is perfected in us" in verse 12 is identical to that of the KJV, as is the phrase "perfect love" in verse 18. Indeed, most contemporary versions use "perfect" and related words to translate the forms of the Greek verb τελειόω in 1 John 4:12, 17–18. In my view, however, τελειόω in Koine Greek did not mean what "perfect" means in modern English, and we cannot really get at the sense of what 1 John is saying here until we rid ourselves of this particular translation.

One step toward this goal is to consider how the rendering "perfect" arose and has maintained itself in the tradition of English Bible translation.[1] The choice of "perfect" for rendering τελειόω in 1 John (including 1 John 2:5 as well as these verses in ch. 4) goes all the way back to John Wycliffe, or at any rate to the fourteenth-century translation associated with his name. Wycliffe and his colleagues worked from the Latin Vulgate, not the Greek text of the New Testament (Daniell 2003, 66–85; Metzger 2001, 56–58). The Vulgate rendering of 1 John 4:12 reads, "Deum nemo vidit umquam. Si diligamus invicem deus in nobis manet et caritas eius in nobis perfecta est." It is plain that the Wycliffe translation, "No man say [= 'saw'] euer god; if we louen togidre, god dwellith in vs, and the charite of hym is perfit in vs" is based on this.[2] The Vulgate uses similar expressions in 4:17–18 and in 2:5 and so does Wycliffe (see table 1).

William Tyndale, whether adapting the Wycliffe rendering or looking to the Vulgate himself (Daniell 2003, 85–88), reads similarly in 4:12: "No man hath sene god at enytyme. Yf we love one another god dwelleth

---

[1]. Comparison of historical renderings of passages from 1 John into English was greatly facilitated by the use of BibleWorks software and the following websites: http://rockhay.tripod.com/worship/translat.htm; http://www.studylight.org; http://www.biblegateway.com/; and http://www.bible-researcher.com/ (from which I have derived much information about translations in the last century). Without endorsing the critical or theological positions of any of these sites, I have found that they provide ready access to sometimes very obscure English versions.

[2]. Transcriptions of the Wycliffe New Testament are taken from http://www.studylight.org/, with minor corrections based on Wycliffe 1986, 182–83. This represents the later of the two Wycliffe recensions.

in vs and his love is parfect in vs."³ The same wording, with varying spellings, appears in the succeeding English versions, and the KJV modified it only slightly, ending with "his love is perfected in us." (The Douay-Rheims version differs only by using "abideth" instead of "dwelleth" and the Latinate "charity" instead of "love.") The other uses of τελειόω in 1 John are similarly rendered from Tyndale to the KJV. It may be noteworthy that the KJV and Douay-Rheims both shift from the adjective "perfect" to the verbs "perfected" and "made perfect" in these verses, perhaps in an effort to more closely reflect the verbal nature of the expressions in the Greek.

The nineteenth-century English and American revisers, while introducing a number of small changes in these verses reflecting developments in the understanding of the Greek text, were content to retain the forms of "perfect" as their translation of the forms of τελειόω (see table 2). The RSV and the NRSV continued this pattern, though the NRSV shifted from the RSV, "he who fears is not perfected in love," at the end of 4:18 (KJV: "He that feareth is not made perfect in love") to "whoever fears has not reached perfection in love." If anything, this seems to set the standard for love even higher and to intensify the sense that it is the believer's responsibility to meet this standard.

Other major translations through the twentieth and into the twenty-first centuries have seldom deviated from this tradition. This is true of formal-equivalence translations that stand generally in the KJV-ASV line, such as the NKJV, the NASB, and the more recent ESV and Holman Christian Standard Bible. It is also true of the Roman Catholic NAB (including its recently published revised edition). The most recent new version at this writing, the CEB (which seems to seek a mediating position between formal-equivalence and functional-equivalence translation practice), also uses forms of "perfect." The same situation prevails even in many functional-equivalence translations, where we might expect more creativity as the translators seek to render ideas and not merely vocabulary and grammar. A broad spectrum of such versions all continue to use forms of "perfect" to render τελειόω in most of its occurrences in 1 John (see table 3).

The persistence of this legacy translation, even in versions that are beholden to no traditional heritage or explicitly seek to use newer or more broadly accessible language, could perhaps be explained by simply acknowledging that "perfect" is the best way in modern English to render

---

3. Transcriptions of Tyndale come from Tyndale 1938, 488, 491.

forms of τελειόω. We must assume that that is the opinion of these translators at any rate. But I will show reasons to doubt this, and in fact other modern versions have taken different approaches, suggesting that their translators have recognized a difficulty with the traditional rendering.

It was in private translations (by which I mean those carried out essentially by an individual without significant institutional or organizational support) that divergence from the traditional rendering "perfect" first appeared. Though some early private translators (several nineteenth-century versions, and Richard Francis Weymouth and Edgar J. Goodspeed in the twentieth century) retained "perfect," many of these translators have tended to seek out other ways of expressing the meaning of τελειόω (see table 4). The pioneer, very early on, was James Moffatt, who used "complete" rather than "perfect" in his 1913 translation of the New Testament (and "fulness" in 4:18). This was a significant departure: to the modern English ear, to say that something is "complete" is not at all the same thing as saying that it is "perfect." Moffatt's innovation proved to be a fruitful one, especially among functional-equivalence translations. The JB, for instance, used "complete" in 4:12, while retaining forms of "perfect" in the other instances. (The NJB, however, reverted to "perfection" even in 4:12.) More thoroughgoing departures were made by two translations intended for readers with limited reading ability. The BBE used "complete" in all instances except 4:18a. The very free CEV prefers "truly" or (in 4:18) "real(ly)." More recently, the NLT has adopted "completely" in 1 John 2:5 and "brought to full expression" in 4:12, though it falls back on "perfect" in 4:17–18. Among formal-equivalence translations, the NIV followed in Moffatt's footsteps, using "made complete" in 1 John 2:5 as well as in 4:12, 17, though it inexplicably reverted to "perfect" in 4:18; its successive revisions have retained these preferences.

More recent private translations have tended to be more paraphrastic (see table 4). (I am not attempting an exhaustive survey of private versions here, only of those I have seen that diverge significantly from "perfect.") J. B. Phillips translated in terms of growth in love, relating this growth to "perfection" and in 4:18a speaking of "fully-developed love." The LB, an icon of 1970's evangelicalism despite Kenneth Taylor's sometimes theologically tendentious paraphrases, rendered similarly, except in 4:18, which he interpreted in terms of God's love, not that of the believer. The most recent such private translation, Eugene Peterson's *The Message*, which may be on its way to an iconic status of its own, uses a stylistically uneven variety of renderings, ranging from both "complete" and "perfect" to "mature" to "well-formed" to love that "has the run of the house."

Two essentially private translations of the mid-twentieth century took an expansive approach to Bible translation. The AMP, created by Frances Siewert (with the support of the Lockman Foundation), cycled through forms of "perfect," "complete," "maturity," and other terms, both inside and outside of parentheses and brackets, in rendering τελειόω and τέλειος in 1 John. For all its awkwardness, this does succeed in giving a fairly well-rounded representation of the interpreter's understanding of what 1 John is saying. Kenneth Wuest's scholarly but unendingly pedantic expanded translation of the New Testament favored "completion" (but used "fullness" in 4:12), surrounded with qualifiers supposed to bring out for the reader who does not know Greek the full force of the perfect tense (Wuest 1961, x–xi).

I have saved for last what proves to be the most interesting of the private translations of the New Testament for our purposes. William Beck was a Lutheran pastor, editor, and professor who created a version of the New Testament "in the language of today" intended to be accessible to everyday readers (Beck 1963). Whatever the merits of his version overall, his renderings in our verses are of remarkable interest. Rather than using variations on "perfect," "complete," or "mature," Beck gives us in 1 John 4:12 the translation, "If we love one another, God lives in us, and *His love has accomplished in us what He wants*" (emphasis added; similar renderings in 2:5 and 4:17). By referring not only to the end-state of love itself but to God's intentions, Beck potentially opened up a new vista on the meaning of this passage (whether or not he recognized this himself—his "finest love" and "love … at its best" in 4:18 are much less instructive). It is regrettable that his insight has not been taken up by other translators. Indeed, even in the successive revisions of his work that ultimately produced the God's Word translation, Beck's unique renderings in these verses have almost completely disappeared (Bunkowske 1995). Only in 4:17 do we find the same sense: "God's love has reached its goal in us." This particular translation is also to be found in 1 John 2:5 in the NCV: "But if someone obeys God's teaching, then in that person God's love has truly reached its goal"; but this version too stays with forms of "perfect" in all the instances in chapter 4.

The persistent use of forms of "perfect" in rendering τελειόω in 1 John is not surprising. "Perfect love" is an almost irresistible phrase in modern English, and perfection is a theological concept well-known, if sometimes troubling, to scholars, preachers, and ordinary Bible readers alike. But that in itself is precisely the problem: "perfect" raises all sorts of connotations, undertones, and overtones for contemporary users of the Bible, most of them quite unrelated to the Greek word that 1 John actually uses.

Forms of *perfectus* certainly made sense in the Vulgate as translations of perfect passive forms of τελειόω in 1 John.[4] As the passive participle of *perficio*, *perfectus* means finished, complete, perfect, excellent (Lewis and Short 1879, s.v. "perficio"), mature, realized to its full extent, developed or completed so as to have all the desired qualities (Glare 1982, s.v. "perfectus"). *Perficio* itself means to achieve, execute, carry out, accomplish, perform, bring to an end or conclusion, finish, complete, perfect (Lewis and Short 1879, s.v. "perficio"), to bring to its highest point of development, bring to maturity, establish, or settle (Glare 1982, s.v. "perficio"). As we will see below, this is very much the same semantic range as τελειόω; and it is interesting to note that several of these English words are used by contemporary versions to render forms of τελειόω in the Gospel of John.

It is possible that words derived from *perfectus* also made sense as renderings of τελειόω in fourteenth–seventeeth century English. Today, however, "perfect" in English does not mean what *perficio* and *perfectus* meant in Latin, nor does it mean what τελειόω and τέλειος meant in Greek. Webster's dictionary gives definitions of "perfect" in contemporary usage that include "entirely without fault or defect; meeting supreme standards of excellence: flawless"; "satisfying all requirements"; "free from admixture or limitation: pure, total"; "lacking in no essential detail; fully developed: complete, whole"; "being without qualification: absolute, unequivocal" (Gove 2002, s.v. "perfect"). There is certainly some overlap between some of these meanings and the meanings of both *perfectus* and τελειόω. But nothing in Webster's includes or implies "finished," "brought to a conclusion," or "fully accomplished," and on the whole the normal significations of "perfect" in contemporary English are not really a satisfactory fit for τελειόω and τέλειος.

We have continued to use "perfect" to translate forms of τελειόω, not only in the Bible but in classical works as well, without noticing that the meaning of "perfect" in English has slipped significantly from the meaning of *perfectus* in Latin, to the point that we may be confusing ourselves about

---

4. Although as a matter of fact the Vulgate generally prefers forms of "consummo" to "perficio" when translating τελειόω in the New Testament, except in John 4:34; 5:36; 1 John; and Phil 3:12; in Hebrews the two alternate somewhat perplexingly.

what the ancient texts are actually saying. Specifically, "perfect" has been and continues to be used to translate forms of τελειόω in 1 John in most of the English Bible tradition, from Wycliffe to the CEB.[5] I am skeptical of this continuing use of "perfect" in 1 John, but such skepticism can only be justified by examining what τελειόω did mean and how it was actually used, particularly in the Johannine writings.

The Meaning of Τελειοω

The basic meaning of τελειόω, of course, is "to make τέλειος" (Delling 1972, 79), an adjective that is itself usually translated "perfect." These are not terribly widespread words in the New Testament. The verb appears twenty-three times, nine of them in Hebrews, five in the Gospel of John, and four in 1 John. The nineteen occurrences of the adjective are somewhat more broadly distributed, but in the Johannine literature it occurs only in 1 John 4:18.

τελειόω in general: The third edition of the Bauer and Danker *Greek-English Lexicon* (BDAG, 2000) gives two main definitions for τελειόω, the first being quite straightforward: "to complete an activity, *complete, bring to an end, finish, accomplish*" (italics original). Most of the uses in the Gospel of John are placed under this heading. The second definition is rather more murky: "to overcome or supplant an imperfect state of things by one that is free fr. objection, *bring to an end, bring to its goal/accomplishment*" (BDAG, s.v. τελειόω). The uses of τελειόω in Hebrews are given under various subdivisions of this heading, and all the uses in 1 John are placed under its subdivision *e*, "make perfect."

But if we are no longer certain that "perfect" really captures the meaning of τελειόω, this analysis simply raises another question: "What is 'make perfect' supposed to connote in these texts?" Is it really different from "complete, bring to an end, finish, accomplish"—the more so since "make perfect" is presented as a subdivision of "bring to an end, bring to its goal/ accomplishment"? It is particularly noteworthy that the uses of τελειόω with reference to love in 1 John are placed alongside Jas 2:22 (βλέπεις ὅτι ἡ πίστις συνήργει τοῖς ἔργοις αὐτοῦ καὶ ἐκ τῶν ἔργων ἡ πίστις ἐτελειώθη), which the NRSV translates, "You see that faith was active along with his

---

5. It is noteworthy, however, that the NRSV and NIV do not generally render forms of τελειόω with forms of "perfect" elsewhere in the New Testament (except in Hebrews), although they do often use "perfect" for τέλειος.

works, and faith was *brought to completion* by the works" (italics mine). This understanding suggests a weakness in the BDAG classification. The sentence in James quite clearly means that Abraham's faith was finalized, was brought to its completion and full realization, by his actions. This may mean the overcoming of an imperfect state of affairs, but it is hard to see how it could be rendered "made perfect," in the contemporary English sense of that word; and indeed most (though not all) current English versions translate similarly to the NRSV. So then, if τελειόω in James means that faith is brought to its completion, why is τελειόω in 1 John said to mean that love is "made perfect"?

Other lexica confirm the significance of these questions. While Liddell-Scott-Jones (1996, s.v. τελειόω) may use "perfect" or "perfection" at the beginning of a definition of τελειόω, this is immediately expanded with words like "complete," "accomplish," or "consummation." The examples cited there have to do with the completion or conclusion or success of an action, activity, period of time, literary work, and so forth; or with coming to maturity. The article on τελειόω by Gerhard Delling (1972, 80; in Geoffrey W. Bromiley's translation) notes general senses in nonbiblical Greek of "to bring to completeness, wholeness," "to complete," "to do fully." For our passages in 1 John 4, Delling suggests that τελειόω "denotes the completeness or perfection" of love, and in 1 John 2:5 he sees the love of God having "come to entirety" in those who keep the commandment (81–82). In these ways "does the love of God achieve totality in the lives of Christians" (82). He also notes that τελέω and τελειόω "coincide in the New Testament especially in the sense 'to carry through,' 'to complete.'"[6] In the Gospel of John, as we will see, this is very much the case, and this will affect our understanding of 1 John significantly.

Delling points to two texts that are too lengthy to examine in detail here, but which are nevertheless worth noting briefly. The first is a discussion of the meaning of τέλειος by Aristotle in the *Metaphysics* (Delling 1972, 68). Aristotle defines τέλειον as something that has all its proper parts within it, or lacks nothing that it ought to have, or is not surpassed by anything of its class, or has reached its end, its τέλος (*Metaph.* 5.1021b). The basic idea, then, is of wholeness, completeness, and having arrived at

---

6. He goes on to associate τελέω with the senses of τέλος (goal, issue, end) and τελειόω with those of τέλειος (whole, complete, perfect) (Delling 1972, 84). In my opinion, while this may well hold for the particular usage in Hebrews, it does not for the Gospel of John, where τελειόω is used precisely in a sense like that of τελέω.

the utmost possible excellence. The second text is a passage in Philo's *On Agriculture* (147–165) (Delling 1972, 80). Philo is discussing Deut 20:5–7, the law excusing from battle those men who have just built houses, planted vineyards, or become engaged. He interprets these three classes allegorically (in reverse order) as having to do with beginnings (ἀρχαί), progress (προκοπαί), and completion (τελειότητες) in philosophy. Quite clearly τελειόω here means to bring something to its conclusion, after having made a start and then advanced in it.[7] Thus for both Aristotle and Philo, τελειωθῆναι, to become τέλειος in something, means to reach its utmost or topmost level. For both of them, interestingly, it also includes continuing to practice that ἀρετή, that virtue: Philo speaks of the τέλειος philosopher still requiring unremitting practice (*Agr.* 160), and Aristotle allows the possibility of not only the perfect physician but the perfect thief, both of whom obviously continue at their trades (*Metaph.* 5, 1021b 15–19).

τελειόω in the Johannine writings: The most immediate literary and intellectual context for the Johannine Epistles is of course the Johannine Gospel. There we find τελειόω used in a distinctive connection, one that is parallel in important ways to what we find in 1 John. Three times in the Gospel, Jesus speaks of completing the work, the ἔργον or ἔργα, that the Father gave him to do (John 4:34; 5:36; 17:4). This is part of a major theme in the Gospel, in which Jesus does and says what God has commanded him, and so makes God known (see, for example, John 5:19–30; 8:28–29; 9:1–5; 10:37–38; 12:44–50; 14:9–14). To speak of his completion of this revelatory and salvific task, Jesus uses the verb τελειόω, obviously in the sense of bringing a commission to its full and complete conclusion. In none of these instances has the English tradition of Bible translation used forms of "perfect" to render τελειόω, instead generally preferring "finish," "complete," or "accomplish."[8] Here is confirmation of Delling's observa-

---

7. Note also Philo, *Somn.* 1.131: ψυχὴ μεταλαβοῦσα καὶ τελειωθεῖσα ἐν ἄθλοις ἀρετῶν, which BDAG cites for the use of τελειόω in the sense "make perfect" in connection with Jas 2:22 and 1 John 2:5; 4:12, 17. We should note that in its context, this clause is immediately followed by καὶ ἐπὶ τὸν ὅρον αὐτὸν ἀφικομένη τοῦ καλοῦ. Pairing the soul's "perfection" in contests of virtue with its reaching the very limit (or perhaps meeting the utmost standard) of honor makes it clear that τελειωθεῖσα has to do with having reached an ultimate goal.

8. The sole exception is the Douay-Rheims version, which uses "perfect" in John 4:34 and 5:36, following the Vulgate "ut perficiam."

tion about the meaning of τελειόω coinciding with that of τελέω with regard to completing something or carrying it through. This is especially clear in the crucifixion scene, where the work of giving eternal life by making God known reaches its climax. In John 19:28, 30 both the narrator and Jesus himself, rather than continuing to use forms of τελειόω, use a form of τελέω instead: τετέλεσται, "It is finished!" or perhaps better, "It is accomplished!"[9]

The Gospel of John, then, generally uses the verb τελειόω, not in the sense of making something "perfect" (without fault or defect), but in the sense of carrying it through to completion, to its intended goal.[10] It is actually not easy to find exact parallels elsewhere for the specific topic in connection with which John uses τελειόω in these passages. The Gospel does not speak of completing or perfecting human qualities or qualifications, but of a divine activity that is intruded into human life and brought successfully to its intended conclusion by the actions and words of Jesus.[11] This usage with respect to the ἔργα of God in the Gospel of John seems to me highly significant, really almost decisive, for what is said about the ἀγάπη of God in 1 John. The use of the same verb in these closely related

---

9. Wycliffe used "ended" for τετέλεσται in 19:28, following Vulgate "consummata"; this was changed to "performed" by Tyndale and then to "accomplished" by KJV and to "finished" by the ERV. Recent versions use "finished," "completed," or "accomplished." In 19:30, Wycliffe again used "ended" for τετέλεσται, following Vulgate "consummatum"; Tyndale originated "it is finished" there, which has been almost universally followed (Douay-Rheims followed the Vulgate with "consummated"; in modern times, JB, NEB, and REB use "accomplished"; NJB "fulfilled"; NET and CEB "completed"; CEV, "everything is done"; *The Message*, "It's done ... complete").

10. The one other use of τελειόω in John is in 17:23, where Jesus prays, ἐγὼ ἐν αὐτοῖς καὶ σὺ ἐν ἐμοί, ἵνα ὦσιν τετελειωμένοι εἰς ἕν, ἵνα γινώσκῃ ὁ κόσμος ὅτι σύ με ἀπέστειλας καὶ ἠγάπησας αὐτοὺς καθὼς ἐμὲ ἠγάπησας. Given the other usages of τελειόω in John's Gospel, this presumably expresses the wish that the disciples be brought to complete unity, or perhaps to *the desired goal* of unity. Note also John 13:1, where we read that Jesus ἀγαπήσας τοὺς ἰδίους τοὺς ἐν τῷ κόσμῳ εἰς τέλος ἠγάπησεν αὐτούς. Given the uses of τελειόω and τελέω in John, εἰς τέλος here may also have a sense not only of Jesus loving his own completely or to the end of his life, but to the completion of the goal for which he was sent into the world.

11. This may be a further specialization of an already specialized usage of τελειόω having to do with the carrying of words, promises, or prophecies into action, often translated "fulfill." BDAG cites, among others, Josephus, *Ant.* 15.4; Herm. Mand. 9:10; 1 Clem. 23:5; Mart. Pol. 16:2 and compares the use of τελείωσις in Luke 1:45 and Jdt 10:9.

writings with regard to two things that are given by God to be carried out in human life suggests a close similarity of intention.[12]

Let us turn now to look more closely at the specific uses of τελειόω in 1 John, particularly in chapter 4, but beginning with a brief look at the use in 1 John 2:5. There are a number of grammatical and other uncertainties in this verse (Rensberger 1997, 59–62). It speaks of someone who "keeps his word," that is, probably God's word (though perhaps the word of Jesus) and probably meaning the commandment of love, given the surrounding context. The text goes on to say of this person, ἐν τούτῳ ἡ ἀγάπη τοῦ θεοῦ τετελείωται, "in this person the love of God has been made τέλειος," whether we translate τετελείωται in terms of "perfection," with the NRSV, or as "complete," with the NIV, or in some other way. Apart from the meaning of τετελείωται, the other main problem in this clause is whether ἡ ἀγάπη τοῦ θεοῦ, "the love of God," is subjective genitive or objective genitive: does it refer to God's love for humanity or to human love for God? Commentators are divided on this as on the other questions in this passage, but my own inclination is to view it as objective, human love for God, since on the whole God is object rather than subject in the surrounding context.

What does it mean, then, to say that human love for God is made τέλειος in the person who keeps God's word, the commandment to love one another? Perhaps much the same as is said later on, in 4:20–5:3, that those who claim to love God must also love their sisters and brothers, since that is God's commandment, and to love God is to obey God's commandments. Human love for God, then, reaches its ultimate completeness, is really whole, when those who love God obey God by loving one another. If indeed the genitive in ἡ ἀγάπη τοῦ θεοῦ is objective, then we have a use of τελειόω here that is more akin to those elsewhere that discuss the bringing of human qualities and activities to their utmost excellence. This is a different usage from that in the Gospel of John discussed above, and different from the usage in 1 John 4, and therefore less relevant to our discussion.

In 1 John 4, beginning in verse 7, the talk is explicitly about love that comes from God, not our love for God but God's love for us, the love revealed in the sending of Jesus, the love that God *is*. First John 4:12 reads:

---

12. To be sure, it is not hard to list examples in which 1 John's linguistic usage differs from that of the Gospel (Dodd 1937; Rensberger 1997, 18, 39–40). Here, however, the usage is in fact so similar that it seems reasonable to assume a corresponding similarity of meaning.

> θεὸν οὐδεὶς πώποτε τεθέαται. ἐὰν ἀγαπῶμεν ἀλλήλους, ὁ θεὸς ἐν ἡμῖν μένει καὶ ἡ ἀγάπη αὐτοῦ ἐν ἡμῖν τετελειωμένη ἐστίν.
> No one has ever seen God. If we love one another, God abides in us and his love has been made τέλειος in us. (my translation)

In this context ἡ ἀγάπη αὐτοῦ, "his love," is clearly subjective genitive, God's love for humanity. The use of the perfect passive of τελειόω in connection with this love takes us in a different direction from its use in connection with human love for God in 2:5. The topic now is not human love reaching completeness but God's own love becoming τέλειος. What does it mean to say that God's love has been made τέλειος? To answer this question we must return to the somewhat unusual linguistic territory we found in the Gospel of John.

In John, as we saw, τελειόω did not mean to make something perfect or flawless, but to carry a task through to completion, to bring it to its intended goal. The Gospel uses τελειόω to speak of Jesus fully completing the work God gave him to do, the work that is God's own work and glorifies God by making God known. God sends Jesus into the world to carry out not merely a divinely given commission but work that is itself divine, is expressive of the divine nature. The work of God, the actions of God, the reality of God, invades the world in the person, the words, and the deeds of Jesus.

When we compare this to what we read in 1 John 4:12 and its context, the similarity is striking. Here too an activity that is characteristic of God intrudes into the human world, but the activity is identified, not as a broadly inclusive ἔργα, "works," but specifically as love. God *is* love, and the love that God is was revealed when the Son of God was sent into the world to be the atoning sacrifice that would bring human beings eternal life. God's love entered the world and was revealed in the person of Jesus and in his self-giving. These affirmations in 4:7–10 offer a clear parallel to the entry of Jesus into the world in the Gospel of John in order to make God known, climactically by giving his life for the life of the world.

But then 4:12 adds a new twist. There is, in the first place, a new and ongoing phase to the revelation of God's love, God's nature. It is now placed in the hands of ordinary human believers. All they have to do is love one another, and the God whom no one has ever seen abides in them and thus becomes visible. As Jesus made God known as love, so now the believers have the task of continuing this revelation; in a manner of speaking, they also become revealers.

As if this were not enough, the author says that when believers love one another ἡ ἀγάπη αὐτοῦ ... τετελειωμένη ἐστίν, the divine love has become τέλειος. As their mutual love brings about a new phase in God's self-revelation, so it also represents a new phase in the carrying out of God's designs. In the Gospel of John, Jesus *finishes* the divine work that God gave him to do; he carries it through to its intended conclusion. When 1 John uses the same verb to speak of something that is also given by God and actualized in the world by human revealers, surely the verb ought to have the same sense as it does in the Gospel: not "make perfect" but "bring to the intended consummation."

When we try that out in translating 1 John 4:12, we get a result something like this:

θεὸν οὐδεὶς πώποτε τεθέαται. ἐὰν ἀγαπῶμεν ἀλλήλους, ὁ θεὸς ἐν ἡμῖν μένει καὶ ἡ ἀγάπη αὐτοῦ ἐν ἡμῖν τετελειωμένη ἐστίν.
No one has ever seen God. If we love one another, God abides in us and his love *has been brought to its completion in us*.

The point is not that God's love has been "perfected," as if delivered from a flawed condition. Rather, it has been *completed*, carried out, its purpose achieved. Like the works of God in the Gospel, the love of God in 1 John is successfully consummated by the human agency to whom it has been entrusted. Jesus carried out the work given to him by God, and now the believers, by loving one another, carry the love given to them by God to its intended completion.

The difference in focus in such a rendering of τελειόω is significant. The passive participle "perfected" and the adjective "perfect" (not to speak of the noun "perfection") center on the final state of a thing, its condition resulting from a process of activity. To speak of something being finished, brought to its completion, consummated, on the other hand, brings into view not only its final condition but the relation of that condition to an original intention. A τέλος is not merely an end-state, of whatever random sort it might prove to be, but a goal, the result of a deliberated purpose. If τελειόω means to bring something to such a goal (as it does in Johannine usage), then it implies the existence of an aim or intention for that thing. To speak of God's love reaching its τέλος is to think in terms of a divine purpose for which that love was extended. Translating 1 John 4:12 as saying that, in the love of believers for one another, God's love has been "brought to its completion," rather than "perfected," refocuses our understanding of the text toward the implicit *intention* of God in revealing divine love through the sending of Jesus and through the mutual love of those who believe in him.[13]

Turning to 1 John 4:17–18, where ἡ τελεία ἀγάπη becomes the topic again, we can hardly doubt that it is once again God's love that is under discussion, since it is this love that is τετελειωμένη—has become τέλειος—according to verse 12. There are some perplexing grammatical and stylistic questions in verses 17–18, which need not detain us here. The fundamental point of these verses is that, since God's love has been brought to its intended completion among the believers, they are—already in this world—as Jesus is, and therefore have no fear of the final judgment.

This fundamental point, I believe, ought to be understood in the following way. In the light of 4:12, the completion of God's love among the believers obviously consists in their love for one another. First John 4:17, then, coheres with the exhortation in 3:16 to be like Jesus through self-giving love for one another: it is precisely because the believers love one another, as the finalization of God's love, that they are "as he is … in this world." But if believers are like the Messiah, the eschatological Savior, then eschatological judgment is not fearsome to them, because *they are already there*, on the other side of that judgment.[14] The ἀγάπη that is τελεία—the divine love that has arrived at its completion, its goal, in their love for one another—signifies that *God's ultimate plan and desire for the world has been attained in them*. Love brought to its goal drives out fear of eschatological judgment, because believers already live in God's new creation and new world: as Jesus the Messiah is, so they are, already transferred from death to eternal life as evidenced by their love for one another (3:14)—love that is the completion and (at least proleptically) the conclusion of God's creative and eschatological vision.

---

13. One might prefer to think of τελειόω as meaning to bring something to a goal that is inherent within its own nature, as can be the case in general Greek usage. God's love being τετελειωμένη would then imply a quality or characteristic within divine love that tends toward a specified end. But such an understanding in terms of the nature of divine love might in fact differ very little from thinking in terms of the purpose God intended for love, in a context in which God has been *identified as* love.

14. Judith Lieu (2008, 194) remarks not only that completion or perfection is an eschatological concept, but that "it is determined by what belongs on the other side of judgment."

Completed Love and the Mission of the New Testament Church

The obvious point to be made about the verb τελειόω, the adjective τέλειος, and their cognates is that they tend to express things that are *telic*. They point toward goals, or at least toward ends. If τελειόω in general Greek usage has as much to do with completeness as with reaching a goal, it nevertheless implies an end-point, something beyond which further progress or advance is impossible; and it can and often does involve bringing a thing to its natural or desired conclusion. In the Johannine texts specifically, τελειόω is used to speak of someone carrying a divinely given commission through to its proper and intended end or goal. To say that God's love has been brought to its completion in believers' love for one another is to say that in this mutual love the intended aim of God's love has been achieved.

This is not a point that has been widely recognized by commentators, who may discuss various implications of the "perfection" of divine love without questioning the concept of "perfection" itself (Brown 1982, 257–58; Schnackenburg 1992, 98, 218, 222). Several more recent commentators, however, do investigate the meaning of τελειόω and its cognates, generally concluding that they refer, not to flawlessness, but to completion, maturation, realization, or reaching a goal (Klauck 1991, 117, 254; Smith 1991, 110; Thompson 1992, 56, 123, 126; Painter 2002, 177, 281; Culy 2004, 28–29; Lieu 2008, 71–72, 185–86, 194–95).[15] However, they do not draw further conclusions about the significance of God's love having a goal, in terms of what that implies about an *intention* behind this activity of love.

Long ago, Brooke Foss Westcott (1892, 152) spoke of the "full development of the divine gift of love" that results in the obedience, active love, and confidence of 1 John 2:5; 4:12, 17–18, though he understood τελειόω to refer not to reaching a goal but to "love which is complete in all its parts, which has reached its complete development" (159, see also 49–50).

---

15. I. Howard Marshall (1978, 217, 223) already interpreted the perfection or completion of love in terms not only of maturity but of love reaching its full effect or coming to full expression. Stephen Smalley (1984, 49, 257) also saw in these passages love reaching fulfillment, completeness, maturity, and indeed reaching its goal. However, he rather implausibly viewed the perfect-tense verbs as equivalent to a present tense and so representing ongoing fulfillment rather than a (static) termination or completion.

Robert Kysar (1986, 98) developed this insight and gave it, in my view, greater point in saying that when Christians love one another they "bring to completion the loving act of God in Christ" and thus "that redemptive plan is complete." Most recently, Urban von Wahlde (2010a, 3:158) has remarked that in Christians' mutual love, divine love "has reached its perfection (that is, achieved its full effect)," because it "has been recognized and imitated (as God had hoped it would be)."[16]

And that, I believe, is what raises the most interesting question of all. The thought in 1 John 4 is not that God's love ever was "imperfect," but that it only really comes to its intended completion in the believing community, whose acts of mutual love are necessary for God's love to do what God desired it to do. The implication of this is that there was indeed a *plan*, something that God desired divine love to accomplish. The revealing of divine love, and thus of the nature of God, in the sending of Jesus to give life through his death was done with a purpose in mind, so to speak, and that purpose was not exhausted in the death and resurrection of the Messiah. Rather, the intention of divine love "from the beginning" was precisely to create a community of mutual love among those who believe and accept the messianic life-giving. That is the logic of saying that God's love has reached its completion in the believers who love one another. Viewing the Gospel of John and 1 John together, we might say that Jesus's cry from the cross, τετέλεσται, "It is accomplished!" (John 19:30), refers to his completion of what God had given *him* to do, not yet to the accomplishment of God's ultimate goal. That is only achieved when God's love itself becomes τέλειος in the mutual love of those who believe in him.

In these considerations, we are edging toward the language of mission. Certainly the Gospel of John presents Jesus as being on a mission in the literal sense, as one who has been sent from God for a purpose. I have tried to show that 1 John presents the believers in a comparable light, as being entrusted and charged with carrying out the purposes of

---

16. The understanding of the meaning and function of τέλειος in the New Testament developed by Paul Johannes Du Plessis is in general accord with this reading. In Du Plessis's (1959, 168) view, perfection in the New Testament is based on Christ's soteriological and eschatological work: "Christ performs the will of God and carries it to its *telos* (*telein*)." Indeed, "not only did He bear redemptive history to its *telos* by His work, He was its *Telos*" (242). Du Plessis's exegesis of the texts in 1 John, unfortunately, is far from satisfactory in light of this understanding (174–76); but his basic insight seems in line with the interpretation that I am proposing.

God in revealing divine love to the world and in the world. The sense of this in 1 John is clearly eschatological: as in the Fourth Gospel, so here the Messiah, the eschatological life-giver, has come and has inaugurated the eschatological community of those who love one another as he has loved them (John 13:34–35).[17] The realized eschatology of the Gospel is still present in 1 John in this respect at least, that the ultimate aim of God is already being actualized, indeed *has been* actualized among those who share actively in this love. The mission of God's love and the aim of God's eschatological action is to generate love among human beings, not in an abstract way, but by creating concrete relationships and practices of love within a human community (1 John 3:16–18). This mission succeeds (at least in 1 John's terms) when it produces communities of those who believe in Jesus the Son of God and love one another (3:23; 4:7–18).

The Johannine Epistles, in my view, represent a fairly late stage in the development of New Testament Christianity. In their own way, they bear witness to the mission of the church in the late first century, perhaps even the very early second century. Second and 3 John, with their traveling teachers supported by the hospitality of local Christian communities and their controversies over the authenticity of such travelers and the support they do or do not receive, seem to reflect a stage in the church's activity similar (in this respect) to that seen in the Didache (see Did. 11–12). That these Johannine communities were in some way involved in mission activity is thus more than likely. Indeed, one way of viewing the controversy behind 1 John is to see it as being about missional enculturation, the issue being whether the author's opponents had gone too far in accommodating the gospel message to the prevailing cultural and religious patterns of their region in order to win new adherents (Rensberger 1997, 115).[18]

What may be most intriguing about the sense of mission in the Johannine Epistles is not that issues of institutional development are emerging (at such a relatively late date, this is to be expected), but that even in this period the goal of the mission is seen not as establishing the institution on a firm organizational basis (contrast the Pastoral Epistles) but as generat-

---

17. Schnackenburg (1992, 98, 218) denies that "perfection" in the Johannine writings is eschatological, but without adequate grounds. Contrast Lieu (2008, 194).

18. Paul Anderson suggests something similar in regard to assimilation, but with reference to emperor worship and in the framework of a different and much more elaborate understanding of Johannine history (Anderson 2006, 34–35, 194, 198; see also his essay in this volume).

ing communities of love. For the writer of these letters, the Christian mission certainly has to do with what we might call "conversion" to belief in Jesus as Messiah and Son of God, a belief that must be properly nuanced with regard to the real flesh-and-blood humanity of the Savior (1 John 4:1–6; 2 John 7–10). But the mission does not end with conversion to right belief. The divine love that sent the Son into the world has as its aim not only the creation of individual believers, but the formation of them into a community of mutual love. Only when this community exists and maintains its love in concrete daily practice has the mission of God, and therefore the mission of the church, reached its goal. Because this goal is still seen in eschatological terms, as God's climactic intervention in human history and society ("the world"), the creation and continued existence of this community in its members' love and care for one another represents the culmination of God's designs for the human race. For this community to be on mission means for it to be engaged with God in the creation of yet more communities of belief and mutual love. Divine love achieves its aims when human love is fully and vividly exercised, for this is what God has intended for humanity all along.

Table 1: Early Translations

Vulgate

> 1 John 2:5: qui autem servat verbum eius vere in hoc caritas dei perfecta est in hoc scimus quoniam in ipso sumus
> 1 John 4:12: deum nemo vidit umquam si diligamus invicem deus in nobis manet et caritas eius in nobis perfecta est
> 1 John 4:17: in hoc perfecta est caritas nobiscum ut fiduciam habeamus in die iudicii quia sicut ille est et nos sumus in hoc mundo
> 1 John 4:18: timor non est in caritate sed perfecta caritas foras mittit timorem quoniam timor poenam habet qui autem timet non est perfectus in caritate

Wycliffe (1380s)

> 1 John 2:5: But the charite of god is perfit verili in him, that kepith his word. In this thing we witen, that we ben in hym, if we ben perfit in hym.

1 John 4:12: No man say euer god; if we louen togidre, god dwellith in vs, and the charite of hym is perfit in vs.

1 John 4:17: In this thing is the perfit charite of god with vs, that we haue trist in the dai of doom; for as he is, also we ben in this world.

1 John 4:18: Drede is not in charite, but perfit charite puttith out drede; for drede hath peyne; but he that dredith, is not perfit in charite.

Tyndale (1534)

1 John 2:5: Whosoever kepeth his worde in him is the love of god parfect in dede. And therby knowe we that we are in him.

1 John 4:12: No man hath sene god at enytyme. Yf we love one another god dwelleth in vs and his love is parfect in vs.

1 John 4:17: Herin is the love perfect in vs, that we shuld have trust in the daye of iudgement: For as he is even so are we in this worlde.

1 John 4:18: Ther is no feare in love, but parfect love casteth out all feare, for feare hath paynfulnes. He that feareth, is not parfect in love.

Coverdale (1535)

1 John 2:5: But who so kepeth his worde, in him is the loue of God perfecte in dede. Hereby knowe we, that we are in him.

1 John 4:12: No man hath sene God at eny tyme. Yf we loue one another, God dwelleth in vs, and his loue is perfecte in vs.

1 John 4:17: Here in is the loue perfecte with vs, that we shulde haue a fre boldnesse in the daye of iudgment: for as he is, euen so are we in this worlde.

1 John 4:18: Feare is not in loue, but perfecte loue casteth out feare: for feare hath paynefulnes. He that feareth, is not perfecte in loue.

Geneva (1560)

1 John 2:5: But hee that keepeth his worde, in him is the loue of God perfect in deede: hereby wee knowe that ye are in him.

1 John 4:12: No man hath seene God at any time. If we loue one another, God dwelleth in vs, and his loue is perfect in vs.

1 John 4:17: Herein is that loue perfect in vs, that we should haue boldnes in the day of iudgement: for as he is, euen so are we in this world.

1 John 4:18: There is no feare in loue, but perfect loue casteth out feare: for feare hath painefulnesse: and he that feareth, is not perfect in loue.

Bishops (1568)

1 John 2:5: But who so kepeth his worde, in him is the loue of God perfect in deede. Hereby knowe we that we are in hym.

1 John 4:12: No man hath seene God at any time. If we loue one another, God dwelleth in vs, and his loue is perfect in vs.

1 John 4:17: Herein is the loue perfect in vs, that we shoulde haue boldnesse in the day of iudgement: For as he is, euen so are we in this worlde.

1 John 4:18: There is no feare in loue, but perfect loue casteth out feare: for feare hath paynefulnesse. He that feareth, is not perfect in loue.

KJV (1611)

1 John 2:5: But whoso keepeth his word, in him verily is the love of God perfected: hereby know we that we are in him.

1 John 4:12: No man hath seen God at any time. If we love one another, God dwelleth in us, and his love is perfected in us.

1 John 4:17: Herein is our love made perfect, that we may have boldness in the day of judgment: because as he is, so are we in this world.

1 John 4:18: There is no fear in love; but perfect love casteth out fear: because fear hath torment. He that feareth is not made perfect in love.

Douay-Rheims (1610)

1 John 2:5: But he that keepeth his word, in him in very deed the

charity of God is perfected; and by this we know that we are in him.
- 1 John 4:12: No man hath seen God at any time. If we love one another, God abideth in us, and his charity is perfected in us.
- 1 John 4:17: In this is the charity of God perfected with us, that we may have confidence in the day of judgment: because as he is, we also are in this world.
- 1 John 4:18: Fear is not in charity: but perfect charity casteth out fear, because fear hath pain. And he that feareth, is not perfected in charity.

TABLE 2: MODERN FORMAL EQUIVALENCE TRANSLATIONS

ERV (1885)

- 1 John 2:5: but whoso keepeth his word, in him verily hath the love of God been perfected. Hereby know we that we are in him:
- 1 John 4:12: No man hath beheld God at any time: if we love one another, God abideth in us, and his love is perfected in us:
- 1 John 4:17: Herein is love made perfect with us, that we may have boldness in the day of judgment; because as he is, even so are we in this world.
- 1 John 4:18: There is no fear in love: but perfect love casteth out fear, because fear hath punishment; and he that feareth is not made perfect in love.

ASV (1901)

- 1 John 2:5: but whoso keepeth his word, in him verily hath the love of God been perfected. Hereby we know that we are in him:
- 1 John 4:12: No man hath beheld God at any time: if we love one another, God abideth in us, and his love is perfected in us:
- 1 John 4:17: Herein is love made perfect with us, that we may have boldness in the day of judgment; because as he is, even so are we in this world.

1 John 4:18: There is no fear in love: but perfect love casteth out fear, because fear hath punishment; and he that feareth is not made perfect in love.

RSV (1952; 2nd edition 1971)

1 John 2:5: but whoever keeps his word, in him truly love for God is perfected. By this we may be sure that we are in him:

1 John 4:12: No man has ever seen God; if we love one another, God abides in us and his love is perfected in us.

1 John 4:17: In this is love perfected with us, that we may have confidence for the day of judgment, because as he is so are we in this world.

1 John 4:18: There is no fear in love, but perfect love casts out fear. For fear has to do with punishment, and he who fears is not perfected in love.

NKJV (1982)

1 John 2:5: But whoever keeps His word, truly the love of God is perfected in him. By this we know that we are in Him.

1 John 4:12: No one has seen God at any time. If we love one another, God abides in us, and His love has been perfected in us.

1 John 4:17: Love has been perfected among us in this: that we may have boldness in the day of judgment; because as He is, so are we in this world.

1 John 4:18: There is no fear in love; but perfect love casts out fear, because fear involves torment. But he who fears has not been made perfect in love.

NRSV (1989)

1 John 2:5: but whoever obeys his word, truly in this person the love of God has reached perfection. By this we may be sure that we are in him:

1 John 4:12: No one has ever seen God; if we love one another, God lives in us, and his love is perfected in us.

1 John 4:17: Love has been perfected among us in this: that we may have boldness on the day of judgment, because as he is, so are we in this world.

1 John 4:18: There is no fear in love, but perfect love casts out fear; for fear has to do with punishment, and whoever fears has not reached perfection in love.

NIV (1973; 1984)

1 John 2:5: But if anyone obeys his word, God's love is truly made complete in him. This is how we know we are in him:

1 John 4:12: No one has ever seen God; but if we love one another, God lives in us and his love is made complete in us.

1 John 4:17: In this way, love is made complete among us so that we will have confidence on the day of judgment, because in this world we are like him.

1 John 4:18: There is no fear in love. But perfect love drives out fear, because fear has to do with punishment. The one who fears is not made perfect in love.

NIV (2011)

1 John 2:5: But if anyone obeys his word, love for God is truly made complete in them. This is how we know we are in him:

1 John 4:12: No one has ever seen God; but if we love one another, God lives in us and his love is made complete in us.

1 John 4:17: This is how love is made complete among us so that we will have confidence on the day of judgment: In this world we are like Jesus.

1 John 4:18: There is no fear in love. But perfect love drives out fear, because fear has to do with punishment. The one who fears is not made perfect in love.

NAB (1991; revised edition 2011)

1 John 2:5: But whoever keeps his word, the love of God is truly perfected in him. This is the way we may know that we are in union with him:

1 John 4:12: No one has ever seen God. Yet, if we love one another, God remains in us, and his love is brought to perfection in us.

1 John 4:17: In this is love brought to perfection among us, that we have confidence on the day of judgment because as he is, so are we in this world.

1 John 4:18: There is no fear in love, but perfect love drives out fear because fear has to do with punishment, and so one who fears is not yet perfect in love.

NASB, updated edition (1995)

1 John 2:5: but whoever keeps His word, in him the love of God has truly been perfected. By this we know that we are in Him:

1 John 4:12: No one has seen God at any time; if we love one another, God abides in us, and His love is perfected in us.

1 John 4:17: By this, love is perfected with us, so that we may have confidence in the day of judgment; because as He is, so also are we in this world.

1 John 4:18: There is no fear in love; but perfect love casts out fear, because fear involves punishment, and the one who fears is not perfected in love.

ESV (2001)

1 John 2:5: but whoever keeps his word, in him truly the love of God is perfected. By this we may know that we are in him:

1 John 4:12: No one has ever seen God; if we love one another, God abides in us and his love is perfected in us.

1 John 4:17: By this is love perfected with us, so that we may have confidence for the day of judgment, because as he is so also are we in this world.

1 John 4:18: There is no fear in love, but perfect love casts out fear. For fear has to do with punishment, and whoever fears has not been perfected in love.

Holman Christian Standard Bible (2009)

1 John 2:5: But whoever keeps His word, truly in him the love of God is perfected. This is how we know we are in Him:

- 1 John 4:12: No one has ever seen God. If we love one another, God remains in us and His love is perfected in us.
- 1 John 4:17: In this, love is perfected with us so that we may have confidence in the day of judgment, for we are as He is in this world.
- 1 John 4:18: There is no fear in love; instead, perfect love drives out fear, because fear involves punishment. So the one who fears has not reached perfection in love.

CEB (2010)

- 1 John 2:5: But the love of God is truly perfected in whoever keeps his word. This is how we know we are in him.
- 1 John 4:12: No one has ever seen God. If we love each other, God remains in us and his love is made perfect in us.
- 1 John 4:17: This is how love has been perfected in us, so that we can have confidence on the Judgment Day, because we are exactly the same as God is in this world.
- 1 John 4:18: There is no fear in love, but perfect love drives out fear, because fear expects punishment. The person who is afraid has not been made perfect in love.

TABLE 3: MODERN FUNCTIONAL EQUIVALENCE TRANSLATIONS

BBE (1965)

- 1 John 2:5: But in every man who keeps his word, the love of God is made complete. By this we may be certain that we are in him:
- 1 John 4:12: No man has ever seen God: if we have love for one another, God is in us and his love is made complete in us:
- 1 John 4:17: In this way love is made complete in us, so that we may be without fear on the day of judging, because as he is, so are we in this world.
- 1 John 4:18: There is no fear in love: true love has no room for fear, because where fear is, there is pain; and he who is not free from fear is not complete in love.

JB (1966)

> 1 John 2:5: But when anyone does obey what he has said, God's love comes to perfection in him. We can be sire that we are in God.
>
> 1 John 4:12: No one has ever seen God; but as long as we love one another God will live in us and his love will be complete in us.
>
> 1 John 4:17: Love will come to its perfection in us when we can face the Day of Judgment without fear; because even in this world we have become as he is.
>
> 1 John 4:18: In love there can be no fear, but fear is driven out by perfect love: because to fear is to expect punishment, and anyone who is afraid is still imperfect in love.

NJB (1985)

> 1 John 2:5: But anyone who does keep his word, in such a one God's love truly reaches its perfection. This is the proof that we are in God.
>
> 1 John 4:12: No one has ever seen God, but as long as we love one another God remains in us and his love comes to its perfection in us.
>
> 1 John 4:17: Love comes to its perfection in us when we can face the Day of Judgement fearlessly, because even in this world we have become as he is.
>
> 1 John 4:18: In love there is no room for fear, but perfect love drives out fear, because fear implies punishment and no one who is afraid has come to perfection in love.

TEV, 3rd edition (1971)

> 1 John 2:5: But whoever obeys is word is the one whose love for God has really been made perfect. This is how we can be sure that we live in God:
>
> 1 John 4:12: No one has ever seen God; if we love one another, God lives in us and his love is made perfect in us.
>
> 1 John 4:17: The purpose of love being made perfect in us is that we may have courage on Judgment Day; and we will have it because our life in this world is the same as Christ's.

1 John 4:18: There is no fear in love; perfect love drives out all fear. So then, love has not been made perfect in the one who fears, because fear has to do with punishment.

GNT, 2nd edition (1992)

1 John 2:5: But if we obey his word, we are the ones whose love for God has really been made perfect. This is how we can be sure that we are in union with God:

1 John 4:12: No one has ever seen God, but if we love one another, God lives in union with us, and his love is made perfect in us.

1 John 4:17: Love is made perfect in us in order that we may have courage on the Judgment Day; and we will have it because our life in this world is the same as Christ's.

1 John 4:18: There is no fear in love; perfect love drives out all fear. So then, love has not been made perfect in anyone who is afraid, because fear has to do with punishment.

NEB (1970)

1 John 2:5: but in the man who is obedient to his word, the divine love has indeed come to its perfection. Here is the test by which we can make sure that we are in him:

1 John 4:12: Though God has never been seen by any man, God himself dwells in us if we love one another; his love is brought to perfection within us.

1 John 4:17: This is for us the perfection of love, to have confidence on the day of judgement, and this we can have, because even in this world we are as he is.

1 John 4:18: There is no room for fear in love; perfect love banishes fear. For fear brings with it the pains of judgement, and anyone who is afraid has not attained to love in its perfection.

REB (1989)

1 John 2:5: but whoever is obedient to his word, in him the love of God is truly made perfect. This is how we can be sure that we are in him:

1 John 4:12: God has never been seen by anyone, but if we love one another, he himself dwells in us; his love is brought to perfection within us.

1 John 4:17: This is how love has reached its perfection among us, so that we may have confidence on the day of judgement; and this we can have, because in this world we are as he is.

1 John 4:18: In love there is no room for fear; indeed perfect love banishes fear. For fear has to do with punishment, and anyone who is afraid has not attained to love in its perfection.

CEV (1995)

1 John 2:5: We truly love God only when we obey him as we should, and then we know that we belong to him.

1 John 4:12: No one has ever seen God. But if we love each other, God lives in us, and his love is truly in our hearts.

1 John 4:17: If we truly love others and live as Christ did in this world, we won't be worried about the day of judgment.

1 John 4:18: A real love for others will chase those worries away. The thought of being punished is what makes us afraid. It shows that we have not really learned to love.

God's Word (1995)

1 John 2:5: But whoever obeys what Christ says is the kind of person in whom God's love is perfected. That's how we know we are in Christ.

1 John 4:12: No one has ever seen God. If we love each other, God lives in us, and his love is perfected in us.

1 John 4:17: God's love has reached its goal in us. So we look ahead with confidence to the day of judgment. While we are in this world, we are exactly like him *with regard to love.*

1 John 4:18: No fear exists where his love is. Rather, perfect love gets rid of fear, because fear involves punishment. The person who lives in fear doesn't have perfect love.

NLT, 2nd edition (2004)

1 John 2:5: But those who obey God's word truly show how com-

pletely they love him. That is how we know we are living in him.

1 John 4:12: No one has ever seen God. But if we love each other, God lives in us, and his love is brought to full expression in us.

1 John 4:17: And as we live in God, our love grows more perfect. So we will not be afraid on the day of judgment, but we can face him with confidence because we live like Jesus here in this world.

1 John 4:18: Such love has no fear, because perfect love expels all fear. If we are afraid, it is for fear of punishment, and this shows that we have not fully experienced his perfect love.

NCV, revised edition (2005)

1 John 2:5: But if someone obeys God's teaching, then in that person God's love has truly reached its goal. This is how we can be sure we are living in God:

1 John 4:12: No one has ever seen God, but if we love each other, God lives in us, and his love is made perfect in us.

1 John 4:17: This is how love is made perfect in us: that we can be without fear on the day God judges us, because in this world we are like him.

1 John 4:18: Where God's love is, there is no fear, because God's perfect love drives out fear. It is punishment that makes a person fear, so love is not made perfect in the person who fears.

NET (2005)

1 John 2:5: But whoever obeys his word, truly in this person the love of God has been perfected. By this we know that we are in him.

1 John 4:12: No one has seen God at any time. If we love one another, God resides in us, and his love is perfected in us.

1 John 4:17: By this love is perfected with us, so that we may have confidence in the day of judgment, because just as Jesus is, so also are we in this world.

1 John 4:18: There is no fear in love, but perfect love drives out fear, because fear has to do with punishment. The one who fears punishment has not been perfected in love.

Table 4: Private Translations

Webster (1833)

> 1 John 2:5: But whoever keepeth his word, in him verily is the love of God perfected: by this we know that we are in him.
> 1 John 4:12: No man hath seen God at any time. If we love one another, God dwelleth in us, and his love is perfected in us.
> 1 John 4:17: In this is our love made perfect, that we may have boldness in the day of judgment: because as he is, so are we in this world.
> 1 John 4:18: There is no fear in love; but perfect love casteth out fear: because fear hath torment. He that feareth, is not made perfect in love.

Darby (1890)

> 1 John 2:5: but whoever keeps his word, in him verily the love of God is perfected. Hereby we know that we are in him.
> 1 John 4:12: No one has seen God at any time: if we love one another, God abides in us, and his love is perfected in us.
> 1 John 4:17: Herein has love been perfected with us that we may have boldness in the day of judgment, that even as *he* is, *we* also are in this world.
> 1 John 4:18: There is no fear in love, but perfect love casts out fear; for fear has torment, and he that fears has not been made perfect in love.

Young, 3rd edition (1898)

> 1 John 2:5: and whoever may keep his word, truly in him the love of God hath been perfected; in this we know that in him we are.

- 1 John 4:12: God no one hath ever seen; if we may love one another, God in us doth remain, and His love is having been perfected in us;
- 1 John 4:17: In this made perfect hath been the love with us, that boldness we may have in the day of the judgment, because even as He is, we—we also are in this world;
- 1 John 4:18: fear is not in the love, but the perfect love doth cast out the fear, because the fear hath punishment, and he who is fearing hath not been made perfect in the love;

Weymouth (1912)

- 1 John 2:5: But whoever obeys His Message, in him love for God has in very deed reached perfection. By this we can know that we are in Him.
- 1 John 4:12: No one has ever yet seen God. If we love one another, God continues in union with us, and His love in all its perfection is in our hearts.
- 1 John 4:17: Our love will be manifested in all its perfection by our having complete confidence on the day of the Judgement; because just what He is, we also are in the world.
- 1 John 4:18: Love has in it no element of fear; but perfect love drives away fear, because fear involves pain, and if a man gives way to fear, there is something imperfect in his love.

Moffatt (1913; 1926)

- 1 John 2:5: but whoever obeys his word, in him love to God is really complete. This is how we may be sure we are in him:
- 1 John 4:12: God no one has ever seen; but if we love one another, then God remains within us, and love for him is complete in us.
- 1 John 4:17: Love is complete with us when we have absolute confidence about the day of judgment, since in this world we are living as He lives.
- 1 John 4:18: Love has no dread in it; no, love in its fulness drives all dread away, for dread has to do with punishment—anyone who has dread, has not reached the fulness of love.

Goodspeed (1939)

> 1 John 2:5: but whoever obeys his message really has the love of God in perfection in his heart. This is the way we can be sure that we are in union with him;
>
> 1 John 4:12: No one has ever seen God; yet if we love one another, God keeps in union with us and love for him attains perfection in our hearts.
>
> 1 John 4:17: Love attains perfection in us, when we have perfect confidence about the Day of Judgment, because here in this world we are living as he lives.
>
> 1 John 4:18: There is no fear in love, but perfect love drives out fear. For fear suggests punishment and no one who feels fear has attained perfect love.

Wuest (1961)

> 1 John 2:5: But whoever habitually with a solicitous care is keeping His word, truly, in this one the love of God has been brought to its completion with the present result that it is in that state of completion. In this we have an experiential knowledge that in Him we are.
>
> 1 John 4:12: God in His [invisible] essence no one has ever yet beheld, with the result that no one has the capacity to behold Him. If we habitually are loving one another, God in us is abiding, and His love has been brought to its fullness in us and exists in that state of fullness.
>
> 1 John 4:17: In this has been brought to completion the aforementioned love which is in us [produced by the Holy Spirit], which love exists in its completed state, resulting in our having unreservedness of speech at the day of the judgment, because just as that One is, also, as for us, we are in this world.
>
> 1 John 4:18: Fear does not exist in the sphere of the aforementioned love. Certainly, this aforementioned love which exists in its completed state throws fear outside, because this fear has a penalty, and the one who fears has not been brought to completion in the sphere of this love, and is not in that state at present.

Phillips (1962)

1 John 2:5: In practice, the more a man learns to obey God's laws the more truly and fully does he express his love for him. Obedience is the test of whether we really live "in God" or not.

1 John 4:12: It is true that no human being has ever had a direct vision of God. Yet if we love each other God does actually live within us, and his love grows in us towards perfection.

1 John 4:17: So our love for him grows more and more, filling us with complete confidence for the day when he shall judge all men—for we realise that our life in this world is actually his life lived in us.

1 John 4:18: Love contains no fear—indeed fully-developed love expels every particle of fear, for fear always contains some of the torture of feeling guilty. This means that the man who lives in fear has not yet had his love perfected.

Beck (1963)

1 John 2:5: But if you do what He says, God's love has in you really accomplished what He wants. That's how we know we're in Him.

1 John 4:12: Nobody has ever seen God. If we love one another, God lives in us, and His love has accomplished in us what He wants.

1 John 4:17: His love has accomplished what He wants when we can look ahead confidently to the day of judgment because we are what He is in this world.

1 John 4:18: Such love isn't terrified, but the finest love throws out terror. We are terrified by punishment, and if we're terrified, our love isn't at its best.

AMP (1965; 1987)

1 John 2:5: But he who keeps (treasures) His Word [who bears in mind His precepts, who observes His message in its entirety], truly in him has the love of *and* for God been perfected (completed, reached maturity). By this we may perceive (know, recognize, and be sure) that we are in Him:

1 John 4:12: No man has at any time [yet] seen God. But if we love one another, God abides (lives and remains) in us and His love (that love which is essentially His) is brought to completion (to its full maturity, runs its full course, is perfected) in us!

1 John 4:17: In this [union and communion with Him] love is brought to completion *and* attains perfection with us, that we may have confidence for the day of judgment [with assurance and boldness to face Him], because as He is, so are we in this world.

1 John 4:18: There is no fear in love [dread does not exist], but full-grown (complete, perfect) love turns fear out of doors *and* expels every trace of terror! For fear brings with it the thought of punishment, and [so] he who is afraid has not reached the full maturity of love [is not yet grown into love's complete perfection].

LB (1971)

1 John 2:5: But those who do what Christ tells them to will learn to love God more and more. That is the way to know whether or not you are a Christian.

1 John 4:12: For though we have never yet seen God, when we love each other God lives in us and his love within us grows ever stronger.

1 John 4:17: And as we live with Christ, our love grows more perfect and complete; so we will not be ashamed and embarrassed at the day of judgment, but can face him with confidence and joy, because he loves us and we love him too.

1 John 4:18: We need have no fear of someone who loves us perfectly; his perfect love for us eliminates all dread of what he might do to us. If we are afraid, it is for fear of what he might do to us, and shows that we are not fully convinced that he really loves us.

The Message (2002)

1 John 2:5: But the one who keeps God's word is the person in

whom we see God's mature love. This is the only way to be sure we're in God.

1 John 4:12: No one has seen God, ever. But if we love one another, God dwells deeply within us, and his love becomes complete in us—perfect love!

1 John 4:17: This way, love has the run of the house, becomes at home and mature in us, so that we're free of worry on Judgment Day—our standing in the world is identical with Christ's.

1 John 4:18: There is no room in love for fear. Well-formed love banishes fear. Since fear is crippling, a fearful life—fear of death, fear of judgment—is one not yet fully formed in love.

Response

Moving the Conversation Forward:
Open Questions and New Directions

Paul N. Anderson

Given that R. Alan Culpepper has fittingly summarized the essays in the introduction to the present collection, such an overview will not be necessary in this concluding essay. Rather, my charge is to comment on how the above essays move critical conversations forward as well as noting new directions and open questions regarding state-of-the-art understandings of the Johannine Epistles. As such, this essay will progress through the developments achieved in the three parts of this collection, but then return in reverse order, from the third part to the first, considering the open questions and new directions that emerge.

Urban von Wahlde is correct. No part of New Testament studies (and I would extend it to biblical studies in general) is as fraught with differences of opinion—among top critical scholars—as the Johannine writings. And, pivotal within those debates are the origin, character, and meaning of the three Johannine Epistles. A generation or two ago, the conventional understanding among scholars, with some exceptions, might have included the following judgments: the Epistles of John (1) were written either before or after the Gospel of John; (2) reflect Hellenistic Christianity with no connection to Judaism and are out of the mainstream of the developing Christian movement; (3) were written in the light of emerging Gnosticism, where claims of having achieved perfection caused enthusiasts to be incorrigible; (4) reflect primarily theological issues at stake, such as a devaluing of the atonement or aspects of Christology; (5) expose secessionists in every closet; and (6) reflect sectarian idiosyncrasies and are thus devoid of meaningful ethical content or instruction.

In the light of the present collection, however, none of these views are compelling. Rather, (1) it could be that the Epistles of John were written within the process of the Gospel's being finalized, bearing connections with its earlier and later material. (2) Engagement with Jewish neighbors and other partners in dialogue, within a Hellenistic setting, is a more plausible inference for all five of the Johannine writings (cf. the letters of Ignatius), and the presence of Hellenistic Christians does not preclude Jewish or other partners in dialogue. (3) Docetizing tendencies do not imply Gnosticism; the Gospel and Epistles of John may have influenced mid-second-century Gnosticism, but not all docetists were gnostics. Spirit references are also rhetorical and do not imply pneumatism as the source of divisions. (4) Many of the concerns faced were practical rather than theological; an emphasis on the atoning work of Christ does not imply that adversaries devalued it, and christological stances and assertions may have bolstered approaches to more mundane concerns. (5) Secession was one problem, but it was not the only issue faced within the Johannine situation; far more acute were the teachings of false prophets—traveling ministers, with whose doctrines on matters of faith and praxis the Johannine leadership disagreed. (6) Indeed, many of the most intense disagreements appear to have revolved around different stances regarding moral and ethical issues and how to approach them; thus, considering the content of the Epistles themselves is instructive for inferring their contextual situation. Therefore, convergences among the essays above move the conversation forward on several levels.

Literary and Composition Aspects of the Johannine Epistles

On the writing of the Johannine Epistles and their relation to the Gospel, some interesting convergences emerge, reflecting on the composition theories of von Wahlde, myself, and Culpepper.

(1) Rather than seeing the Johannine Epistles as written before or after the Johannine Gospel, a convergence of opinion sees the Epistles as plausibly being written within the process of the Gospel's being produced, sometime between its first and final editions. This makes sense for a number of reasons, as the Gospel itself seems to have undergone an earlier and later set of developments. Thus, some of the material in the Gospel seems to have been developed in 1 and 2 John especially (the love commandments, Jesus's being the Christ, what has been seen and heard from the beginning, tensions with the world, etc.), while some issues engaged in the Epistles (church unity, the fleshly suffering of Jesus as the Christ, issues related to church governance, receiving light and life from the Logos, etc.) seem to

have been developed in the later Johannine material. Raymond Brown was moving in this direction, but others have carried out their own approaches further, beyond his.

(2) Rather than seeing the Gospel as depending on alien sources or the Synoptics, the paradigms put forward by these scholars see the Johannine tradition as an autonomous and individuated tradition, developing alongside others but not derivative from them. In that sense Brown's approach to the origin and formation of the Johannine tradition has largely won the day, although the Leuven School and the Barrett trajectory among some British scholars continue to infer varying levels of Synoptic derivation upon it. For a consideration of two leading examples of John's composition in multiple editions, the reader should follow von Wahlde's advice and review the first volume of his three-volume commentary (2010), where he lays out the bases for a three-edition theory of composition, each having distinctive views on eleven different issues. Even if one might not concur with all aspects of his theory, appreciating the theological tensions he sets in sharp relief will be an aid for interpreting the theology of the Johannine Gospel and the Epistles. Following Lindars and Brown, though, seems simpler: a basic first edition followed later material that could have been added at the same time or at different times, with judgments based primarily on literary perplexities rather than theological tendencies. Such a theory is laid out clearly in a variety of places, especially in my introduction to John (2011). However John's composition may have come together, Culpepper's (1983, 1998) insistence on the final coherence of the text and the need to interpret it as a unity stands. On an overly synchronic view of the composition (not the reading) of the Gospel, the facts that John's final chapter and Logos-hymn prologue encapsulate and introduce its material exceptionally well might not indicate their being written at the same time as the first edition of the narrative (indeed, John 1:1–18 can also be seen as a response to the Gospel's narrative—similar to 1 John 1:1–4, and John 21 affirms what has been said before, even if it was added later), but the emphasis on interpreting the completed Gospel and Epistles as they stand is affirmed by all three paradigms.

(3) An interesting set of convergences here surfaces, as the authors of these paradigms infer a plurality of hands in the production of the Johannine Gospel and Epistles, albeit in differing ways. Von Wahlde sees three different authors involved in the writing of each of the three editions of the Gospel, and while the author of the Epistles concurs with its dominant themes, he also seeks to correct things here and there in a nuanced

way. Therefore, the author of the Epistles operates in a "yes ... but" sort of way, affirming the revelatory work of the Spirit of Christ, but also insisting on faithfulness to the teachings of Jesus and the command to love one another. As such, the dialectical critique of John's Gospel by 1 John opens one to corrective secondary dialectic also in the finalized Gospel. My approach, however, works with these tensions differently. I see the work of the final editor as conservative and not adding theological tension to the evangelist's work (with Brown, here, versus Rudolf Bultmann). Rather, John's theological tensions emerge from other factors: (1) the evangelist was himself a dialectical thinker (with C. K. Barrett and Judith Lieu) looking at things from one side and then another; (2) we have here a highly dialectical situation in which the evangelist engages his audiences according to their needs, which vary; (3) the main thrust of John's Christology is a prophet-like-Moses agency schema (with Peder Borgen and also von Wahlde), featuring the agency of the Son, the Spirit, and believers; (4) the dialogical function of narrative engages audiences by means of irony, double meanings, and rhetorical devices. Culpepper questions my inferring that the author of the Epistles is plausibly the final compiler (with Bultmann) on the basis of stylistic differences (although he may have added the evangelist's work as well as his own, and the characteristic use of οὖν in John's narrative, while absent from the Epistles, is not found in the Gospel's prologue and only three times in John 15–17). Nonetheless, all three of us infer a plurality of hands in the Johannine composition process, although Andreas Köstenberger sees John the apostle as author of the Johannine Gospel and Epistles.

(4) Considerable advances are also made in the present collection in considering the differences in literary function between the three Johannine Epistles, and especially Lieu's work on this subject continues to be strong. As 1 John contains no overt epistolary features, such as a greeting to an audience, asides to individuals, or personal comments at the beginning or the end of the writing, it most likely represents a circular letter that was read in a multiplicity of settings rather than being intended for a particular audience. Second John, however, is written to a particular community from another, and 3 John is written to an individual by an individual. That being the case, considerable advantages follow from understanding the more general message of 1 John after considering the more contextual concerns reflected in the second and third Johannine Epistles. And, the point is well taken that larger inferences as to what might have been going on within a community, emerging from larger theories and interpretations

of the other Johannine writings, may even corrupt one's understanding of what is being said in 2 or 3 John, since especially in 3 John, the Elder's experience alone is implied as a factor in his writing. Then again, the connections between 1 and 2 John are close enough that each of these two texts cannot ignore the other. Therefore, in Lieu's work we see the value of focusing on a text by itself without being swayed unduly by inferences of a community and its features, although such connections and their implications inevitably follow.

Historical and Situational Aspects of the Johannine Epistles

On the historical situation of the Johannine Epistles, Brown's influence still remains, although its influence has varied in terms of reception and development.

(1) First, and continuing with Brown over and against J. Louis Martyn's approach, a multiplicity of crises is apparent within the historical Johannine situation, arguing for the Elder's addressing of not just one issue but several over a decade or two. In addition to Brown's paradigm, which sees Johannine Christians being engaged dialectically with several crises in the second and third phases of the Johannine situation, other targeted concerns surface within the present collection, which are not incompatible with his inferences. These include: (1) dialogues with the local Jewish presence in a Hellenistic setting—apparently involving defections back into the synagogue; (2) somewhat stressed engagements with the Roman presence during the reign of Domitian (81–96 CE) plausibly over the reassertion of the imperial cult and associated issues; (3) challenges regarding assimilative teachings of gentile-Christian traveling ministers—bolstered by a nonsuffering (docetizing) presentation of Jesus as the divine Son; and (4) dialectical engagements with Diotrephes and his kin—proto-Ignatian hierarchical approaches to discipline and order. Here especially, Köstenberger's noting of God's eschatological work challenging worldly powers (Rome's hegemony as outlined in Revelation) and William Loader's inference of sexual and libertine issues as factors of "worldly" concern would fit into several of these dialogical issues. At this point, one might add at least two more crises: (5) tensions with those appealing to pneumatism (as Von Wahlde and Gary Burge might argue)—calling for right action and loving consideration as key; as well as (6) the simple command to love one another (as Lieu, Peter Rhea Jones, and J. G. van der Watt argue) in the face of impending penalties for adhering to Christ and his way.

(2) A second point follows: incipient Gnosticism is no longer seen to be a primary issue in the Johannine situation—either on the part of the evangelist or the author of the Epistles, and likewise not on behalf of the adversaries. With von Wahlde, the agency of the Son in the Johannine Gospel and Epistles is thoroughly Jewish—rooting in the Mosaic agency motif of Deut 18:15–22 and confirmed in the Son's word coming true and returning to the Father who sent him. Therefore, the Johannine Gospel and Epistles (especially 1 John) advocate Jesus's being the Jewish Messiah/Christ, calling for audiences to believe in him as the Son of God. The seceding persons (labeled "antichrists" in 1 John 2:18–25) refuse to acknowledge Jesus as the Messiah/Christ in holding to the Father, and yet, because the Son is sent by the Father, they will thereby forfeit their desired monotheistic goal if they reject the one the Father has sent. The second and third antichristic passages refer a different crisis: those who deny Jesus's having come in the flesh (1 John 4:1–3; 2 John 7), but these are docetizing gentile-Christian ministers rather than mid-second-century gnostics. David Rensberger's devastating analysis of flawed inferences of perfectionism within the Johannine situation makes this all the more clear. Further, if Loader's treatment of sexual mores' being at stake in late first-century Jewish engagements with Greco-Roman culture is any indicator of the sorts of issues Jesus-adherents faced having been distanced from synagogue participation, worldly assimilation is far more of an issue than recent scholars have allowed.

(3) A third thing to note is that more mundane factors within the Johannine situation are helpful for noting what the Johannine Elder was addressing, rather than sketching speculative portraitures as to what imagined adversaries must have been like—such as Cerinthus and his followers or inferred Samaritan Christology (versus Brown's speculation). Lieu's and Jones's contributions help us consider such mundane plausibilities as traveling ministers creating friction by the ways they imposed upon their hosts and abused their hospitality, especially if their ventures might have been missional in their character. Less compelling is Jones's view that secessionists departed for missional reasons, despite the fact that Jesus's followers in the Gospels departed on missional ventures. The Elder clearly labels their departure as an abandonment of the community, thus questioning also their sincerity from the beginning. Jones's insight that the Elder's counsel in 2 John appears to be walking and talking like the episcopal leadership he is criticizing in 3 John, however, is important to consider. Indeed, a good deal of overlap is likely between the positional leadership

the Elder and Diotrephes seem to be exercising, and territoriality is normally most acute between members of like species (especially of the same gender), so tensions might not be suggestive of differences alone. And, the works of van der Watt, Loader, and Rensberger remind us that sometimes community tensions are factors of real social needs (caring for the hungry and the economically needy), so these factors must be appreciated, as well as larger missional concerns.

(4) The contributions of Köstenberger and Craig Koester bring into clear focus perhaps the most egregiously overlooked situational factor within the paradigms of scholars several decades ago (including Brown and Bultmann), as imperial factors played major roles in the mix within the later periods of the Johannine situation. From Koester, we are helped to face the textual facts that the words ἀντίχριστος and ἀντίχριστοι never occur in Revelation; they appear only in 1 and 2 John. And, the references are not futuristic; they imply recent and impending threats, identifying the "antichrists" as fellow believers who either left the Johannine community refusing to believe Jesus was the Messiah/Christ or were threatening to visit Johannine communities teaching doctrines supported by a nonsuffering/fleshly Jesus. Therefore, the apocalyptic speculations of Papias, Irenaeus, and Hippolytus have distorted the prophetic message of the Johannine Epistles, which is to challenge believers to authentic faithfulness in their Greco-Roman settings. With Koester, beware; we have seen the antichrist, ... and *he is us*! Likewise, Köstenberger's essay shows how, within the cosmic court case against the nations, God's love, truth, and light will finally win the day, calling believers to rest fully in the work of Christ as the Son of God, thus embracing the promise of life in his name. God wins, and such is the message of the Johannine Epistles and Apocalypse, and likewise the Johannine Gospel.

Theological and Ethical Features of the Johannine Epistles

Appreciating contextual aspects of the Johannine Epistles informs understandings of their content, and one of the greatest values of the present collection is the advances made by the six treatments of their theological and ethical thrusts.

(1) With von Wahlde, Culpepper, Köstenberger, and others, the central theological and rhetorical thrust of the Johannine Gospel continues in the Epistles—seeking to convince audiences to believe in Jesus as the Christ, the Son of God—and yet, the Epistles expand more fully on the

implications of such a faith commitment. Whereas the Gospel demonstrates the Son's agency from the Father in Jewish terms, 1 John 1:1–4 unpacks those implications in Hellenistic-friendly terms, perhaps shedding light on how the Gospel's prologue also originated in cross-cultural perspective. Interestingly, by considering the situation of the Johannine Epistles, the character and implications of the tensions within the Christology of the Johannine Gospel also become clear. As a means of convincing Jewish and gentile audiences that Jesus is indeed the Christ, the Son of God, the evangelist and the Elder are keen to show Jesus's missional connection and identification with the Father as a factor of his agency (with Jones). This accounts for high christological claims and confession in the Gospel and Epistles alike. Conversely, in emphasizing that Jesus really did suffer and die on the cross (attested by the water and the blood and the Spirit), emphases upon the suffering humanity of Jesus also are asserted (with van der Watt). Therefore, rather than reflecting disparate sources with varying christological emphases, the Johannine Gospel and Epistles reflect the tandem efforts of Johannine leaders to address differing needs within the Johannine situation, contributing to John's theologically polyvalent gospel narrative and the highly dialogical engagement design of the Epistles. In that sense, the situation-informed content of the Epistles provides a key to understanding the theology of the Johannine Gospel.

(2) Second, because faith implies faithfulness, the Johannine call to believe is also a call to abide—to remain with Jesus and his community of followers over and against the challenges of the world. With van der Watt, Loader, and Koester, those challenges thus involved ethical issues, perhaps even more than theological ones, and there was clearly a good deal of disagreement within the early Christian movement over what faithfulness to Christ required and what it did not. This would have especially been the case between believers with Jewish backgrounds versus those with gentile ones. As such, claiming to be "without sin" more likely than not (with Rensberger's pivotal essay on being *completed* in love—versus perfectionism proper) related to differences of opinion about right and wrong actions within the second and third generations of the Jesus movement. Just as Paul's earlier mission to the gentiles involved calling Jewish believers in Jesus to distinguish between matters of convictional essence and their symbolization (see Acts 15) and for gentile believers in Jesus to not abuse the liberties of grace (1 Cor 6:12), the Johannine leadership sought to advocate the covenant promise of Abraham and Moses to the nations while still calling for adherence to central features of Jewish faith

and practice. If the last word is the first word in 1 John (5:21)—little children, stay away from idols—far from representing a throw-away add-on, this admonition may indeed clarify the cluster of issues being faced within the later Johannine situation. As the imperial cult under Domitian (81–96 CE) endorsed local and regional pagan worship cults and their festivities (as long as they also referenced Caesar and added Roman festivals to their customary ones), these festivals yoked human appetites and social institutions to supporting the governing presence of empire, rewarding public loyalty and disloyalty accordingly. Therefore, with Rensberger, Loader, van der Watt, Koester, and Köstenberger, to love God and the community implies saying "no" to "the world" and its appeals—even if the way of the cross implies costly discipleship. This is likely what traveling ministers, diminishing the implications of a suffering Lord come in the flesh, sought to avoid.

(3) When viewed from this perspective, reflecting ethical debates about what is sinful and what might not be—especially between believers of Jewish and gentile origins—the appeals to sinlessness and spiritual guidance are clarified in their character and implications. With von Wahlde, the Jewishness of Spirit-led guidance is here strikingly apparent. Such a thrust thus leads into second-century Gnosticism rather than requiring a gnostic origin for its comprehension. However, if Burge is correct in his sketching the sociology of spirit-communities and their means of legitimation, it is less likely that pneumatism is the root cause of disagreement—substantiating structural approaches to ecclesial leadership over and against pneumatism. Rather, spirit-authorization seems rhetorical in its origin as well as its design. Indeed, the Johannine Elder challenges structural and episcopal leadership, but this is done in the name of apostolic memory, not against it, so Brown's inference of pneumatism as an affront to apostolic (and thus structural) leadership here receives again a needed corrective. Put otherwise, Spirit-led legitimation is just as easily claimed in advocating conservative, Jewish values on behalf of the Elder as it is would be in bolstering the liberal, assimilative teachings of the antichristic prophets, whose reluctance to embrace the way of the cross is furthered by a docetizing Christology. Again, Rensberger's emphasis on the completed and mature character of Johannine love sheds light on how that love becomes operative within community. As van der Watt has argued, loving one another in community is a direct extension of Jesus's love commands in all four of the Gospels (the commands to love God, one's neighbor, one's enemies, and even—shock!—one another). Therefore, the call to matured love becomes

a general rubric for addressing a multiplicity of issues within the Johannine situation: unity rather than defection, consideration rather than selfishness, spiritual fidelity rather than idolatry, sexual integrity rather than licentiousness, and equality of status rather than hierarchical differentiation. Thus, within a cosmopolitan setting, Jewish and gentile followers of Jesus are here seen to be struggling to understand what it means to receive grace by faith, but also to remain faithful by grace. These are the dual features of receiving and witnessing to the transformative gift of divine love.

(4) In light of these contextual issues and crises, the Johannine Elder upholds discernment-oriented leadership as the key to the way forward, involving several features. First, he grounds his teaching in historic tradition—what has been seen and heard from the beginning—he is not making this up but is furthering what eyewitnesses and others have taught and preached. Second, he calls for a faithful response to the Son's agency from the Father, whose will is also disclosed through the Holy Spirit, which is then embraced by believers and witnessed to in the world. That continuity of agency draws believers into partnership with the redemptive work of Christ as his witnesses in truth and love. Third, the Elder holds later preachers of Christ accountable to the memory of Jesus of Nazareth—come in the flesh—who suffered and died as the paradoxically glorious center of his mission. Later followers must thus commit themselves to solidarity with Jesus and his community even if hardships are implied; such is the way of the cross and the promise of the resurrection. Fourth, the Elder appeals to the love of God as the goal and measure of human endeavors and actions. Because God has first loved us, we must respond to that love in faithful gratitude; but if we claim to love God, we also ought to be willing to love one another (1 John 4:19). Echoing the Gospel (13:35), believers' love for one another is the surest sign of having received and embraced the love of God in Christ. Fifth, because truth and its discernment are the keys to effective Christian leadership, both traveling ministers and ecclesial leaders must abide in the truth, helping others to do the same, rather than resorting to societal assimilation or positional leverage. If the Spirit can indeed be trusted to lead the faithful into truth, authentic Christian leadership is a factor of authenticity and convincement rather than enticement or coercion.

Open Questions and New Directions

In addition to moving the conversation forward with a number of advances in the scholarship of the Johannine Epistles, new questions and directions are also opened in so doing. Beginning, now, with the advances made in the theological and ethical treatments of the Johannine Epistles, new questions emerge regarding understandings of the Johannine situation and the composition of the Johannine writings.

(1) Building on the advances made in understanding the meaning of completeness in love (Rensberger, van der Watt, Lieu, von Wahlde), what difference would it make for interpreting the Johannine writings if we saw their acute concerns as addressing the physical and social needs of their audiences rather than gnostic perfectionism or incorrigible pneumatism (1 John 3:17–18)? Indeed, the Elder himself can just as easily be charged with claiming that one who is in Christ cannot sin, but that does not mean that he was a gnostic or that he felt that he had attained perfection. Rather, the Jewish conviction that the Holy Spirit can and does guide the faithful (with von Wahlde) provides ample basis for his conviction, as well as his appeal to the Spirit's guidance as a means of helping his audience not to sin. Questions, therefore, that follow from such considerations involve seeking to understand what sorts of issues Jesus-adherents were dealing with in their Diaspora setting, especially regarding issues believers of Jewish and gentile origins might have debated in second and third generation Christianity. Such knowledge might also help one understand more fully what was at stake in the Elder's challenging of the assimilative teachings of the docetizing prophets, whom he labels "antichrists" in 1 John 4:1–3 and 2 John 7. That knowledge would then provide a more informed basis for understanding the original meaning of Johannine invective (with Koester) versus its distortive interpretations.

(2) A second question follows: if the sorts of issues debated by the Johannine Elder and his audiences related to calling for more Jewish-compliant approaches to aspects of faith and praxis, versus more assimilative tendencies of believers with gentile backgrounds, such a stance would challenge severely recent inferences of Johannine sectarianism. With Loader and Köstenberger, if the Elder's admonition to not love the world (including its fleshly desires and material investments) related to particular moral issues, such concerns suggest believers' extensive engagements with Greco-Roman culture and social settings rather than seeking to escape the world. Put otherwise, Johannine Christianity reflects tensions related to seeking to retain Jewish values within a cosmopolitan setting, not antiworld sectarianism such as a monastic Qumranic setting in the wilderness. Therefore, rather than seeing Johannine Christianity as an incestuous sectarian group, cut off from the world and other Chris-

tian groups, concerned only with loving one another rather than loving neighbors and enemies—as the Jesus of Nazareth taught—what if we see the Johannine leadership as continuing the love-ethic of Jesus missionally (with van der Watt and Jones) in ways that testified meaningfully to God's love in the world? Might such approaches to the Johannine writings overall (including the Gospel and Apocalypse) help us see Johannine Christianity as a central player within the larger mission to the gentiles—perhaps even within the heart of the later Pauline mission? If so, the Johannine Epistles deserve consideration for understanding the heart of the emerging Christian movement rather than its periphery.

(3) A third set of questions extends beyond the papers in the present volume, exploring implications for the history of interpretation and implications for Christian theology overall. Between the two horizons of biblical exegesis and Christian theology, a more sustained set of engagements is absolutely necessary. All too easily, theologians assume that they are in touch with state-of-the-art exegesis, expounding upon understandings decades or even centuries old, while exegetes perform their tasks with little theological sensitivity. The two disciplines are strongest if engaged dialogically, and this is especially needed regarding the interpretation of the Johannine Epistles. As one who is completing the Two Horizon Commentary on the Johannine Epistles (anticipated 2015), this is an acute concern of mine, but I am not alone. Koester, for instance, gets us back on the right track by challenging as biblically inadequate the age-old conflation of the Johannine "antichrists" with "the beasts" of Revelation and "the man of lawlessness" of 2 Thessalonians. These texts literally were *not* futuristic in their meaning, but contemporary to the first-century situation. Further, they did not relate to the same crisis or persons. Therefore, gaining a clearer understanding of the contextual and exegetical meanings of biblical invective will go some distance toward alleviating wrongheaded inferences among interpreters, as well as yielding more existentially profitable and convicting understandings for believers of later generations. Further, if the three Johannine antichristic passages referenced two distinctive threats (one a secession of community members and the other an advent of false teachers), the central issues being addressed then is clarified for later interpreters. The first antichristic threat involved the appeals of religious certainty; the second involved the ease of cultural assimilation. In both cases, faithfulness to Christ poses the existential way forward. Other issues needing to be addressed include the discerning of death-producing sins over and against venial sins; if aspects of the imperial cult were at

stake in the late first-century situation under Domitian's reign, extensive implications follow for living faithfully in contexts of imperial domination in later generations. Likewise, if the Johannine Elder was challenging the adverse effects of abrupt institutionalism as carried out by Diotrephes and his kin, such becomes a corrective to structural approaches to Christian leadership in addition to correctives to pneumatic excesses.

(4) A final set of questions then relates to the place of the Johannine corpus with relation to the other writings of the New Testament. While the present essays advance our understandings of the Johannine writings in relation to each other, what about the relations of the Johannine Gospel to other gospel narratives, and what about the relations of the Johannine Epistles to other Christian correspondence of the first-century Christian movement? While Brown stopped short of filling out a larger approach to these issues, one wonders if the early Johannine material intends to augment Mark, and likewise whether the later Johannine material appears to harmonize John's narrative with the Synoptics (with Bultmann). And, might the Johannine tradition have contributed in formative ways to Luke and Q, as well as being engaged dialectically with the early Markan and later Matthean traditions? If even some of these intertraditional features might have occupied some degree of consciousness within the Johannine tradition, might this explain the Elder's beginning his first Epistle with hearkening back to what has been seen and heard from the beginning, concerning the word of life? If such is the case, while the Johannine tradition is highly theological, it also is rife with historical consciousness, bearing implications for the historical quests for Jesus as well as the movement that developed in his memory. Likewise conspicuous are apparent contacts between the Johannine Epistles and the Pauline Epistles as well as the Petrine Epistles and the Letter to the Hebrews. As a result, the history of early Christianity cannot be fully appreciated without understanding the contexts and the content of the Johannine Epistles, as they provide an indispensable set of keys to understanding its character and complexion in the late-first-century situation.

Building on the overall theory of Brown, this collection engages his contribution by leading Johannine scholars who also lay out their overall Johannine theories in terse but robust ways. Therefore, the reader is availed a variety of lenses through which to glimpse the formation, character, and meaning of the Johannine Epistles, while also being helped to focus on their message in their own right—without the aid (or encumbrance?) of an overall-theory approach. From there, theological and ethical treatments of their content help readers appreciate what the texts might be saying, as well as what they might not be saying—in service to more adequate readings of the seven chapters of these three intriguing letters. In addition to larger paradigms facilitating closer interpretations of the text, the reverse is also true. More adequate understandings of textual issues improve our paradigms and overall theories—especially clarifying what might and might not be an actual impasse. As disputes raged in the late-first-century situation known as Johannine Christianity, they also rage among top scholars today. If the present collection points the way forward, though, here we see a number of convergences and new sets of questions emerging. As readers add their knowledge and perspectives to these contributions, the conversation continues. And, if the previous two millennia are any indication as to the disputes and questions these provocative writings evoke, the intrigue and inquiry has only just begun!

Works Cited

Akin, Daniel L. 2001. *1, 2, 3 John*. NAC 38. Nashville: Broadman & Holman.
Anderson, Bernhard W. 1999. *Contours of Old Testament Theology*. Minneapolis: Augsburg Fortress.
Anderson, Paul N. 1996. *The Christology of the Fourth Gospel: Its Unity and Disunity in the Light of John 6*. WUNT 2/78. Tübingen: Mohr Siebeck.
———. 1997. The *Sitz im Leben* of the Johannine Bread of Life Discourse and Its Evolving Context. Pages 1–59 in *Critical Readings of John 6*. Edited by R. Alan Culpepper. BIS 22. Leiden: Brill.
———. 1999. The Having-Sent-Me Father: Aspects of Irony, Agency, and Encounter in the Johannine Father-Son Relationship. *Semeia* 85:33–57.
———. 2001. John and Mark: The Bi-Optic Gospels. Pages 175–88 in *Jesus in Johannine Tradition*. Edited by Robert Fortna and Tom Thatcher. Louisville: Westminster John Knox.
———. 2002. Interfluential, Formative, and Dialectical: A Theory of John's Relation to the Synoptics. Pages 19–58 in *Für und Wider die Priorität des Johannesevangeliums*. Edited by Peter Hofrichter. TTS 9. Hildesheim: Olms.
———. 2004. The Cognitive Origins of John's Christological Unity and Disunity. Pages 127–49 in vol. 3 of *Psychology and the Bible: A New Way to Read the Scriptures*. Edited by J. Harold Ellens and Wayne Rollins. New York: Praeger. First published in *HBT* 17 (1995): 1–24.
———. 2005. Petrine Ministry and Christocracy: A Response to *Ut unum sint*. *One in Christ* 40:3–39. http://www.georgefox.edu/discernment/petrine.pdf.
———. 2006a. *The Fourth Gospel and the Quest for Jesus: Modern Foundations Reconsidered*. LNTS 321. London: T&T Clark.
———. 2006b. Review of L*ife in Abundance: Sudies of John's Gospel in Tribute to Raymond E. Brown*, by John R. Donahue. *RBL*. http://www.bookreviews.org/pdf/4874_5078.pdf.

———. 2007a. Antichristic Errors: Flawed Interpretations Regarding the Johannine Antichrists and Antichristic Crises: Proselytization Back into Jewish Religious Certainty—The Threat of Schismatic Abandonment. Pages 196–216 and 217–40 in vol. 1 of *Text and Community: Essays in Commemoration of Bruce M. Metzger*. Edited by J. Harold Ellens. Sheffield: Sheffield Phoenix Press.

———. 2007b. Aspects of Interfluentiality between John and the Synoptics: John 18–19 as a Case Study. Pages 711–28 in *The Death of Jesus in the Fourth Gospel*. Edited by Gilbert van Belle. Colloquium Biblicum Lovaniense LIV, 2005. Leuven: Leuven University Press; Leuven: Peeters.

———. 2007c. Bakhtin's Dialogism and the Corrective Rhetoric of the Johannine Misunderstanding Dialogue: Exposing Seven Crises in the Johannine Situation. Pages 133–59 in *Bakhtin and Genre Theory in Biblical Studies*. Edited by Roland Boer. SemeiaSt 63. Atlanta: Society of Biblical Literature.

———. 2007d. "*You* Have the Words of Eternal Life!" Is Peter Presented as *Returning* the Keys of the Kingdom to Jesus in John 6:68? *Neotestamentica* 41:6–41.

———. 2008a. Beyond the Shade of the Oak Tree: Recent Growth in Johannine Studies. *ExpTim* 119:365–73.

———. 2008b. From One Dialogue to Another: Johannine Polyvalence from Origins to Receptions. Pages 93–119 in *Anatomies of Narrative Criticism: The Past, Present, and Future of the Fourth Gospel as Literature*. Edited by Stephen Moore and Tom Thatcher. Resources in Biblical Studies 55. Atlanta: Society of Biblical Literature.

———. 2008c. On Guessing Points and Naming Stars: The Epistemological Origins of John's Christological Tensions. Pages 311–45 in *The Gospel of St. John and Christian Theology*. Edited by Richard Bauckham and Carl Mosser. Grand Rapids: Eerdmans.

———. 2009. Das "John, Jesus, and History" Projekt: Neue Beobachtungen zu Jesus und eine Bi-optische Hypothese. *ZNT* 23:12–26. Longer versions online in English: http://www.znt-online.de/anderson.pdf; http://www.bibleinterp.com/articles/john1357917.shtml.

———. 2010a. Acts 4:19–20: An Overlooked First-Century Clue to Johannine Authorship and Luke's Dependence upon the Johannine Tradition. *Bible and Interpretation* 2010. http://www.bibleinterp.com/opeds/acts357920.shtml.

———. 2010b. From Mainz to Marburg: A Diachronic Exchange with the Master of Diachronicity and a Bi-Optic Hypothesis. *Bible and Interpretation* 2010. http://www.bibleinterp.com/opeds/mainz357911.shtml.

———. 2011. *The Riddles of the Fourth Gospel: An Introduction to John.* Minneapolis: Fortress.

———. 2012. Discernment-Oriented Leadership in the Johannine Situation—Abiding in the Truth versus Lesser Alternatives. Pages 290–318 in *Rethinking the Ethics of John: "Implicit Ethics" in the Johannine Writings.* Edited by Jan van der Watt and Ruben Zimmermann. WUNT 291. Contexts and Norms of New Testament Ethics 3. Tübingen: Mohr Siebeck.

———. 2013a. The Community That Raymond Brown Left Behind: Reflections on the Johannine Dialectical Situation. *Bible and Interpretation* 2013. http://www.bibleinterp.com/articles/2013/09/and378030.shtml.

———. 2013b. Incidents Dispersed in the Synoptics and Cohering in John: Dodd, Brown, and Historicity." Pages 176–202 in *Engaging with C. H. Dodd on the Gospel of John: Sixty Years of Tradition and Interpretation.* Edited by Tom Thatcher and Catrin Williams. Cambridge: Cambridge University Press.

———. 2014. *From Crisis to Christ: A Contextual Introduction to the New Testament.* Nashville: Abingdon.

Anderson, Paul N., with Felix Just, S. J., and Tom Thatcher, eds. 2007. *Critical Appraisals of Critical Views.* Vol. 1 of *John, Jesus, and History.* SBLSymS 44; SBLECL 1. Atlanta: Society of Biblical Literature.

———. 2009. *Aspects of Historicity in the Fourth Gospel.* Vol. 2 of *John, Jesus, and History.* SBLSymS 44; SBLECL 2. Atlanta: Society of Biblical Literature.

Arndt, William, Frederick W. Danker, and Walter Bauer. 2000. *A Greek-English Lexicon of the New Testament and Other Early Christian Literature.* Chicago: University of Chicago Press.

Arnold, Clinton E. 1997. Satan, Devil. Pages 1077–82 in *The Dictionary of Later New Testament and Its Developments.* Edited by Ralph P. Martin and Peter H. Davids. Downers Grove, IL: InterVarsity Press.

Ashton, John. 1991. *Understanding the Fourth Gospel.* Oxford: Clarendon; New York: Oxford University Press.

———, ed. 1997. *The Interpretation of John.* 2nd ed. Edinburgh: T&T Clark.

Aune, David E. 1997–1998. *Revelation.* WBC 52a–c. Dallas: Word.

Balz, Horst. 1985. Die Johannesbriefe. Pages 156–223 in Horst Balz and Wolfgang Schrage, *Die "Katholischen" Briefe*. NTD 10. Göttingen: Vandenhoeck & Ruprecht.

Bandy, Alan S. 2007. The Prophetic Lawsuit in the Book of Revelation: An Analysis of the Lawsuit Motif in Revelation with Reference to the Use of the Old Testament. Ph.D. diss., Wake Forest.

Barrett, C. K. 1978. *The Gospel according to John*. 2nd ed. Philadelphia: Westminster.

Bauckham, Richard. 1993a. *The Climax of Prophecy: Studies on the Book of Revelation*. London: T&T Clark.

———. 1993b. *The Theology of the Book of Revelation*. New Testament Theology. Cambridge: Cambridge University Press.

———. 1997. John for Readers of Mark. Pages 147–71 in *The Gospels for All Christians*. Edited by Richard Bauckham. Grand Rapids: Eerdmans.

———, ed. 1998. *The Gospels for All Christians: Rethinking the Gospel Audiences*. London: T&T Clark.

———. 2006. *Jesus and the Eyewitnesses: The Gospels as Eyewitness Testimony*. Grand Rapids: Eerdmans.

———. 2007. *The Testimony of the Beloved Disciple: Narrative, History, and Theology in the Fourth Gospel*. Grand Rapids: Baker.

Bauer, Walter. 2000. *A Greek-English Lexicon of the New Testament and Other Early Christian Literature*. Revised and edited by F. W. Danker. 3rd ed. Chicago: University of Chicago Press.

Beale, G. K. 1999. *The Book of Revelation: A Commentary on the Greek Text*. NIGNTC. Grand Rapids: Eerdmans.

Beck, William F. 1963. *The New Testament in the Language of Today*. Saint Louis: Concordia.

Bernard, J. H. 1929. *A Critical and Exegetical Commentary on the Gospel according to St. John*. ICC. London: T&T Clark.

Beutler, Johannes. 2000. *Die Johannesbriefe*. RNT. Regensburg: Pustet.

Blank, Josef. 1981. *Das Evangelium nach Johannes 1*. Düsseldorf: Patmos.

Blumenberg, Hans. 2010. *Paradigms for a Metaphorology*. Translated by Robert Savage. Ithaca, NY: Cornell University Press.

Bogart, John. 1977. *Orthodox and Heretical Perfectionism in the Johannine Community as Evident in the First Epistle of John*. SBLDS 33. Missoula, MT: Scholars Press.

Boismard, Marie-Émile. 1990. The First Epistle of John and the Writings of Qumran. Pages 156–65 in *John and the Dead Sea Scrolls*. Edited by James H. Charlesworth. New York: Crossroad.

Borgen, Peder. 1965. *Bread from Heaven: An Exegetical Study of the Concept of Manna in the Fourth Gospel.* NovTSup 10. Leiden: Brill.
Bousset, Wilhelm. 1896. *The Antichrist Legend: A Chapter in Jewish and Christian Folklore.* London: Hutchinson.
Brooke, Alan E. 1912. *A Critical and Exegetical Commentary on the Johannine Epistles.* ICC. London: T&T Clark.
Brown, Dan. 2003. *The Da Vinci Code: A Novel.* New York: Doubleday.
Brown, Raymond E. 1965. The Qumran Scrolls and the Johannine Gospel and Epistles. Pages 138–73 in *New Testament Essays.* New York: Doubleday Image.
———. 1966, 1970. *The Gospel according to John.* AB 29, 29A. New York: Doubleday.
———. 1978. "Other Sheep Not of This Fold": The Johannine Perspective on Christian Diversity in the late First Century. *JBL* 97:5–22.
———. 1979a. *The Community of the Beloved Disciple.* New York: Paulist.
———. 1979b. The Relationship of the Fourth Gospel Shared by the Author of 1 John and by His Opponents. Pages 57–68 in *Text and Interpretation: Studies in the New Testament Presented to Matthew Black.* Edited by R. McL. Wilson and Ernest Best. Cambridge: Cambridge University Press.
———. 1982. *The Epistles of John.* AB 30. New York: Doubleday.
———. 1984. *The Churches the Apostles Left Behind.* New York: Paulist.
———. 1988. *The Gospel and Epistles of John: A Concise Commentary.* New Testament Reading Guide 13. Collegeville, MN: Liturgical Press. Originally published in 1960.
———. 1994. *An Introduction to New Testament Christology.* New York: Paulist.
Brown, Raymond E., Karl P. Donfried, Joseph A. Fitzmyer, and John Reuman, eds. 1978. *Mary in the New Testament: A Collaborative Assessment by Protestant and Roman Catholic Scholars.* New York: Paulist.
Brown, Raymond E., and John P. Meier. 1983. *Antioch and Rome: New Testament Cradles of Catholic Christianity.* New York: Paulist.
Brown, Raymond E., and Francis J. Moloney. 2003. *An Introduction to the Gospel of John.* ABRL. New York: Doubleday.
Bruce, F. F. 1970. *The Epistles of John.* New York: Revell.
Bryant, Michael. 2005. Annotated Bibliography: The Johannine Epistles, 2000–2005. *FM* 23: 83–89.
Bultmann, Rudolf. 1951; 1955. *Theology of the New Testament.* Translated by Kendrick Grobel. 2 vols. New York: Scribner.

———. 1964. ἀλήθεια κτλ. Pages 232–51 in vol. 1 of *Theological Dictionary of the New Testament*. Edited by Gerhard Kittel and Gerhard Friedrich. Translated by Geoffrey W. Bromiley. 10 vols. Grand Rapids: Eerdmans, 1964–1976.

———. 1971. *The Gospel of John: A Commentary*. Translated by G. R. Beasley-Murray, R. W. N. Hoare, and J. K. Riches. Philadelphia: Westminster. First published in German, Göttingen: Vandenhoeck & Ruprecht, 1941. Second English printing with a new foreword, Vol. 1 in the Johannine Monograph Series. Eugene: Wipf & Stock, 2014.

———. 1973. *The Johannine Epistles*. Translated by R. Philip O'Hara, Lane C. McGaughy, and Robert Funk. Hermeneia. Philadelphia: Fortress. First published in German, Vandenhoeck & Ruprecht, 1967.

Bund, Elmar. 1979. Pater Familias. Pages 545–47 in vol. 4 of *Der Kleine Pauly: Lexikon der Antike*. Edited by Konrat Ziegler and Walther Sontheimer. 5 vols. München: Deutscher Taschenbuch.

Bunkowske, Eugene W., ed. 1995. *God's Word*. Iowa Falls, Iowa: God's Word to the Nations.

Burge, Gary M. 1966. *The Letters of John*. The NIV Application Commentary. Grand Rapids: Zondervan.

———. 1987. *Anointed Community*. Grand Rapids: Eerdmans.

Caird, G. B. 1966. *A Commentary on the Revelation of St. John the Divine*. London: Black.

Calhoun, Robert L. 2010. *Scripture, Creed, Theology: Lectures on the History of Christian Doctrine in the First Centuries*. Edited by George Lindbeck. Eugene, OR: Wipf & Stock.

Callahan, Allen Dwight. 2005. *A Love Supreme: A History of the Johannine Tradition*. Minneapolis: Augsburg Fortress.

Carson, Donald A. 1987. The Purpose of the Fourth Gospel: Jn 20:31 Reconsidered. *JBL* 106: 639–51.

———. 1994. The Three Witnesses and the Eschatology of 1 John. Pages 216–32 in *To Tell the Mystery: Essays on New Testament Eschatology in Honour of Robert H. Gundry*. Edited by Thomas E. Schmidt and Moisés Silva. Sheffield: JSOT Press.

Carter, Warren. 2008. *John and Empire: Initial Explorations*. London: T&T Clark.

Cassidy, Richard J. 1992. *John's Gospel in New Perspective: Christology and the Realities of Roman Power*. Maryknoll, NY: Orbis Books.

Christ, Karl. 1984. *The Romans: An Introduction to their History and Civilisation*. London: Hogarth.

Conzelmann, Hans. 1954. Was von Anfang war. Pages 194–201 in *Neutestamentliche Studien für Rudolf Bultmann: Zu seinem siebzigsten Geburtstag am 20. August 1954*. BZNW 21. Berlin: Töpelmann.
Culy, Martin M. 2004. *I, II, III John: A Handbook of the Greek Text*. Waco, TX: Baylor University Press.
Culpepper, R. Alan. 1974. *The Johannine School: An Evaluation of the Johannine-School Hypothesis based on an Investigation of the Nature of Ancient Schools*. SBLDS 26. Missoula, MT: Scholars Press.
———. 1983. *Anatomy of the Fourth Gospel*. Philadelphia: Fortress.
———. 1995. 1-2-3 John. Pages 110–44 in *The General Letters*. Edited by Gerhard Krodel. Rev. ed. Proclamation Commentaries. Philadelphia: Fortress.
———. 1998. *The Gospel and Letters of John*. Nashville: Abingdon.
Daniell, David. 2003. *The Bible in English: Its History and Influence*. New Haven: Yale University Press.
Delling, Gerhard. 1972. τελειόω. Pages 79–84 in vol. 8 of *Theological Dictionary of the New Testament*. Edited by Gerhard Kittel and Gerhard Friedrich. Translated by Geoffrey W. Bromiley. 10 vols. Grand Rapids: Eerdmans, 1964–1976.
Deming, Will. 2004. *Paul on Marriage and Celibacy: The Hellenistic Background of 1 Corinthians 7*. 2nd ed. Grand Rapids: Eerdmans.
DeSilva, David A. 1998. Honor Discourse and the Rhetorical Strategy of the Apocalypse of John. *JSNT* 71:79–110.
Dixon, Suzanne. 1991. *The Roman Family*. London: Hopkins.
Dodd, C. H. 1937. The First Epistle of John and the Fourth Gospel. *BJRL* 21:129–56.
———. 1946. *The Johannine Epistles*. MNTC. New York: Harper & Brothers.
Donahue, John R., ed. 2005. *Life in Abundance: Studies of John's Gospel in Tribute to Raymond E. Brown*. Collegeville, MN: Liturgical Press.
Du Plessis, Paul Johannes. 1959. *TELEIOS: The Idea of Perfection in the New Testament*. Kampen: Kok.
Du Rand, Jan A. 1991. *Johannine Perspectives: Introduction to the Johannine Writings, Part I*. N.P.: Orion.
Dunn, James D. G. 1989. *Christology in the Making: A New Testament Inquiry into the Origins of the Incarnation*. Philadelphia: Westminster.
Edwards, Ruth B. 1996. *The Johannine Epistles*. Sheffield: Sheffield Academic Press.

Ellis, J. Edward. 2007. *Paul and Ancient View of Sexual Desire: Paul's Sexual Ethics in 1 Thessalonians 4, 1 Corinthians 7 and Romans 1*. LNTS 354. London: T&T Clark.
Forestell, J. Terence. 1974. *The Word of the Cross: Salvation as Revelation in the Fourth Gospel*. AnBib 57. Rome: Biblical Institute Press.
Fortna, Robert T. 1970. *The Gospel of Signs: A Reconstruction of the Narrative Source Underlying the Fourth Gospel*. SNTMS 11. Cambridge: Cambridge University Press.
Fredrickson, David. 2003. Passionless Sex in 1 Thessalonians 4:4–5. *WW* 23:23–30.
Frey, Jörg. 1993. Erwägungen zum Verhältnis der Johannesapokalypse zu den übrigen Schriften des Corpus Johanneum. Pages 326–429 in Martin Hengel, *Die Johanneische Frage: Ein Lösungsversuch*. Tübingen: Mohr Siebeck.
Freyne, Sean. 2009. Jesus and the Galilean 'Am Ha'arets: Fact, Johannine Irony, or Both? Pages 139–54 in *Aspects of Historicity in the Fourth Gospel*. Vol. 2 of *John, Jesus, and History*. Edited by Paul N. Anderson, Felix Just, and Tom Thatcher. SBLSymS 44; SBLECL 2. Atlanta: Society of Biblical Literature.
Friesen, Steven J. 1993. *Twice Neokoros: Ephesus, Asia and the Cult of the Flavian Imperial Family*. Religions in the Graeco-Roman World 116. Leiden: Brill.
Fuller, Robert C. 1995. *Naming the Antichrist: The History of an American Obsession*. New York: Oxford University Press.
Gaca, Kathy L. 2003. *The Making of Fornication: Eros, Ethics, and Political Reform in Greek Philosophy and Early Christianity*. Berkeley: University of California Press.
García Martínez, Florentino, ed. 1996. *The Dead Sea Scrolls Translated: The Qumran Texts in English*. Translated by Wildred G. E. Watson. 2nd ed. Leiden: Brill.
García Martínez, Florentino, and Eibert J. C. Tigchelaar, eds. 1997. *The Dead Sea Scrolls Study Edition*. Leiden: Brill.
Gardner-Smith, P. 1938. *Saint John and the Synoptic Gospels*. Cambridge: Cambridge University Press.
Gerhardsson, Birger. 1981. *The Ethos of the Bible*. Philadelphia: Fortress.
Gielen, Marlis. 1990. *Tradition und Theologie neutestamentlicher Haustafelethik*. Frankfurt am Main: Hain.
Gilbertson, Merrill. T. 1959. *The Way It Was in Bible Times*. London: Lutterworth.

Glare, P. G. W., ed. 1982. *Oxford Latin Dictionary*. Oxford: Clarendon.
Golden, Mark. 1990. *Children and Childhood in Classical Athens*. Baltimore: John Hopkins University Press.
Gove, Philip Babcock, ed. 2002. *Webster's Third New International Dictionary of the English Language, Unabridged*. Springfield, MA: Merriam-Webster.
Grayston, Kenneth. 1984. *The Johannine Epistles*. NCB. Grand Rapids: Eerdmans.
Griffith, Terry. 2002. *Keep Yourselves from Idols: A New Look at 1 John*. JSNTSup 233. Sheffield: Sheffield Academic Press.
Gundry, Robert M. 2002. *Jesus the Word according to John the Sectarian*. Grand Rapids: Eerdmans.
Haas, C., Marinus de Jonge, and J. L. Swellengrebel. 1972. *A Translators' Handbook on the Letters of John*. UBS Handbook Series. New York: United Bible Societies.
Haenchen, Ernst. 1960. Neuere Literatur zu den Johannesbriefen. *TRu* 26:1–43, 267–91.
Halliday, Michael A. K. 1978. *Language as Social Semiotic: The Social Interpretation of Language and Meaning*. Baltimore: University Park.
Harnack, Adolf von. 1897. *Über den dritten Johannesbrief*. TUGAL 15.3. Leipzig: Hinrichs.
Harris, J. Rendel. 1901. The Problem of the Address in the Second Epistle of John. *The Expositor* 6: 194–203.
Harris, W. Hall, III. 2003. *1, 2, 3 John: Comfort and Counsel for a Church in Crisis: An Exegetical Commentary on the Letters of John*. Dallas: Biblical Studies Press. https://bible.org/series/1-2-3-john-comfort-and-counsel-church-crisis.
Hauck, Friedrich. 1965. κοινός κτλ. Pages 789–809 in vol. 3 of *Theological Dictionary of the New Testament*. Edited by Gerhard Kittel and Gerhard Friedrich. Translated by Geoffrey W. Bromiley. 10 vols. Grand Rapids: Eerdmans, 1964–1976.
———. 1967. μένω κτλ. Pages 574–88 in vol. 4 of *Theological Dictionary of the New Testament*. Edited by Gerhard Kittel and Gerhard Friedrich. Translated by Geoffrey W. Bromiley. 10 vols. Grand Rapids: Eerdmans, 1964–1976.
Heckel, Theo K. 2004. Die Historizierung der johanneischen Theologie im ersten Johannesbrief. *NTS* 50: 425–43.
Heise, Jürgen. 1967. *Bleiben: Menein in den Johanneischen Schriften*. HUT 8. Tübingen: Mohr Siebeck.

Hengel, Martin. 1989. *The Johannine Question*. Translated by John Bowden. Philadelphia: Trinity Press International.

Hill, Charles E. 2004. *The Johannine Corpus in the Early Church*. New York: Oxford University Press.

Hirsch, Emanuel. 1936. *Studien zum vierten Evangelium*. BHT 11. Tübingen: Mohr-Siebeck.

Hoffman, Thomas A. 1978. 1 John and the Qumran Scrolls. *BTB* 8:117–25.

Houlden, James Leslie. 1973. *A Commentary on the Johannine Epistles*. HNTC. New York: Harper & Row.

———. 1973. *Ethics and the New Testament*. London: T&T Clark.

House, Paul R. 1998. *Old Testament Theology*. Downers Grove, IL: InterVarsity Press.

Howard, Wilbert F. 1947. The Common Authorship of the Johannine Gospel and Epistles. *JTS* 48:12–25.

Huebner, Hans. "μένω," Pages 407–8 in vol. 2 of *Exegetical Dictionary of the New Testament*. Edited by H. Balz and G. Schneider. ET. Grand Rapids: Eerdmans, 1990–1993.

Jauhiainen, Marko. 2005. *The Use of Zechariah in Revelation*. WUNT 199. Tübingen: Mohr Siebeck.

Jenks, Gregory C. 1991. *The Origins and Early Development of the Antichrist Myth*. BZNW 59. Berlin: de Gruyter.

Johnson, Thomas F. 1993. *1, 2, 3 John*. NIBCNT. Peabody, MA: Hendrickson.

Jones, Peter Rhea. 2009. *1, 2 and 3 John*. SHBC 29B. Macon: Smyth & Helwys.

———. 2010. A Presiding Metaphor of First John: μένειν ἐν. *PRSt* 37:179–94.

Käsemann, Ernst. 1951. Ketzer und Zeuge. *ZTK* 48: 292–311.

———. 1968. *The Testament of Jesus: A Study of the Gospel of John in Light of Chapter 17*. Translated by Gerhard Krodel. Philadelphia: Fortress.

Katz, Steven T. 1984. Issues in the Separation of Judaism and Christianity after 70 CE: A Reconsideration. *JBL* 103:43–76.

Keener, Craig S. 1993. *The IVP Bible Background Commentary: New Testament*. Downers Grove, IL: InterVarsity Press.

———. 2003. *The Gospel of John*. 2 vols. Peabody: Hendrikson.

Keil, Carl Friedrich. 1888. *Manual of Biblical Archaeology*. London: T&T Clark.

Kenney, Garrett C. 2000. *Leadership in John: An Analysis of the Situation and Strategy of the Gospel and Epistles of John*. Lanham, MD: University of America Press.

Kim, Moon-Geoung. 2003. *Zum Verhältnis des Johannesevangeliums zu den Johannesbriefen: Zur Verfasserschaft des 'johanneischen' Schriften in der Forschung.* Europäische Hochschulschriften 761. New York: Lang.

Kimelman, Reuven. 1981. Birkat Ha-Minim and the Lack of Evidence for an Anti-Christian Prayer in Late Antiquity. Pages 226–44 in *Aspects of Judaism in the Greco-Roman World.* Vol. 2 of *Jewish and Christian Self-Definition.* Edited by E. P. Sanders, Albert I. Baumgarten, and Alan Mendelson. Philadelphia: Fortress.

Klauck, Hans-Josef. 1989. Der Rückgriff auf Jesus. Pages 433–51 in *Vom Urchristentum zu Jesus: Für Joachim Gnilka.* Freiburg im Breisgau: Herder.

———. 1991a. *Der erste Johannesbriefe.* EKKNT 23.1. Zurich: Benzinger; Neukirchen-Vluyn: Neukirchener Verlag.

———. 1991b. *Die Johannesbriefe.* Erträge der Forschung 276. Darmstadt: Wissenschaftliche Buchgesellschaft.

———. 2006. *Ancient Letters and the New Testament.* Waco, TX: Baylor University Press.

Klein, Günter. 1971. "Das wahre Licht scheint schon!" Beobachtungen zur Zeit- und Geschichtserfahrung einer urchristliche Schule. *ZTK* 68: 261–326.

Klink, Edward W. 2007. *The Sheep of the Fold: The Audience and Origin of the Gospel of John.* SNTSMS 141. Cambridge: Cambridge University Press.

———. 2008. Light of the World: Cosmology and the Johannine Literature. Pages 74–89 in *Cosmology and New Testament Theology.* LNTS 355. Edited by Jonathan T. Pennington and Sean M. McDonough. London: T&T Clark.

———. 2010. *The Audience of the Gospels: The Origin and Function of the Gospels in Early Christianity.* London: T&T Clark.

Köstenberger, Andreas J. 1998. *The Missions of Jesus and the Disciples according to the Fourth Gospel: With Implications for the Fourth Gospel's Purpose and the Mission of the Contemporary Church.* Grand Rapids: Eerdmans.

———. 1999. *Encountering John: The Gospel in Historical, Literary, and Theological Perspective.* Grand Rapids: Baker Academic.

———. 2004. *John.* BECNT. Grand Rapids: Baker.

———. 2008. John. Pages 415–512 in *Commentary on the New Testament Use of the Old Testament*. Edited by G. K. Beale and D. A. Carson. Grand Rapids: Baker.

———. 2009. *A Theology of John's Gospel and Letters*. Biblical Theology of the New Testament. Grand Rapids: Zondervan.

Koester, Craig R. 2008. *The Word of Life: A Theology of John's Gospel*. Grand Rapids: Eerdmans.

———. 2014. *Revelation*. Anchor Yale Commentary 38. New Haven: Yale University Press.

Konstan, David. 1996. Friendship, Frankness and Flattery. Pages 7–19 in *Friendship, Flattery, and Frankness of Speech: Studies on Friendship in the New Testament World*. Edited by John T. Fitzgerald. Leiden: Brill.

Kretzer, Armin. 1990. πονηρός. Pages 134–35 in vol. 3 of *Exegetical Dictionary of the New Testament*. Edited by Horst Balz and Gerhard Schneider. Grand Rapids: Eerdmans.

Kruse, Colin G. 2000. *The Letters of John*. The Pillar New Testament Commentary. Leicester: Apollos; Grand Rapids: Eerdmans.

Kuhn, K. G. 1952. Die Dektenschrift und die iranische Religion. *ZTK* 49:296–316.

Kümmel, Werner G. 1966. *Introduction to the New Testament*. Translated by A. J. Masttill Jr. Nashville: Abingdon.

Kysar, Robert. 1986. *I, II, III John*. ACNT. Minneapolis: Augsburg.

———. 2005. *Voyages with John*. Waco, TX: Baylor University Press.

Lassen, Eva Maria. 1992. Family as Metaphor: Family Images at the Time of the Old Testament and Early Judaism. *SJOT* 6:247–62.

Law, Robert. 1909. *The Tests of Life: A Study of the First Epistle of St. John*. London: T&T Clark.

Lewis, Charlton T., and Charles Short. 1879. *A Latin Dictionary*. Oxford: Clarendon.

Liddell, Henry George, Robert Scott, and H. Stuart Jones. 1996. *A Greek-English Lexicon*. 9th edition with revised supplement. Oxford: Clarendon; New York: Oxford University Press.

Lieu, Judith M. 1986. *The Second and Third Epistles of John: History and Background*. SNTW. London: T&T Clark.

———. 1991. *The Theology of the Johannine Epistles*. Cambridge: Cambridge University Press.

———. 2008a. *I, II, and III John: A Commentary*. NTL. Louisville: Westminster John Knox.

———. 2008b. Us or You? Persuasion and Identity in 1 John. *JBL* 127: 805–19.
Lincoln, Andrew T. 2000. *Truth on Trial: The Lawsuit Motif in the Fourth Gospel*. Peabody, MA: Hendrickson.
———. 2004. Reading John: The Fourth Gospel under Modern and Postmodern Interrogation. Pages 127–49 in *Reading the Gospels Today*. McMaster New Testament Studies. Edited by Stanley E. Porter. Grand Rapids: Eerdmans.
Lindars, Barnabas. 1972. *The Gospel of John*. Grand Rapids: Eerdmans.
Loader, William R. G. 1989. *The Christology of the Fourth Gospel: Structure and Issues*. New York: Lang.
———. 1992. *The Johannine Epistles*. Epworth Commentaries. London: Epworth.
———. 2011a. *Philo, Josephus and the Testaments on Sexuality: Attitudes towards Sexuality in the Writings of Philo, Josephus, and the Testaments of the Twelve Patriarchs*. Grand Rapids: Eerdmans.
———. 2011b. *The Pseudepigrapha on Sexuality: Attitudes towards Sexuality in Apocalypses, Testaments, Legends, Wisdom, and Related Literature*. Grand Rapids: Eerdmans.
Lorein, Geert Wouter. 2003. *The Antichrist Theme in the Intertestamental Period*. JSPSup 44. London: T&T Clark.
Louw, Johannes A., and Eugene A. Nida. 1988. *Greek-English Lexicon*. New York: United Bible Societies.
Luz, Ulrich. 2007. *Matthew 1–7*. Hermeneia. Minneapolis: Fortress.
Mackay, Ian D. 2004. *John's Relationship with Mark; An Analysis of John 6 in the Light of Mark 6 and 8*. WUNT 2/182. Tübingen: Mohr Siebeck.
Malatesta, Edward. 1971. The Literary Structure of John 17. *Biblica* 52:190–214.
———. 1978. *Interiority and Covenant: A Study of εἶναι ἐν and μένειν ἐν in the First Letter of Saint John*. AnBib 69. Rome: Biblical Institute Press.
Malherbe, Abraham J. 1983. *Social Aspects of Early Christianity*. 2nd ed. Philadelphia: Fortress.
Malina, Bruce J., and Jerome H. Neyrey. 1991. Honor and Shame in Luke-Acts: Pivotal Values of the Mediterranean World. Pages 25–65 in *The Social World of Luke-Acts*. Edited by Jerome H. Neyrey. Peabody, MA: Hendrickson.
Malina, Bruce J., and Richard L. Rohrbaugh. 1998. *Social-Science Commentary on the Gospel of John*. Minneapolis: Augsburg Fortress.
Marcus, Joel. 2009. Birkat Ha Minim Revisited. *NTS* 55:523–51.

Marshall, I. Howard. 1978. *The Epistles of John*. NICNT. Grand Rapids: Eerdmans.

Martin, Dale B. 2006. Paul without Passion: On Paul's Rejection of Desire in Sex and Marriage. Pages 65–76 in Dale B. Martin, *Sex and the Single Savior: Gender and Sexuality in Biblical Interpretation*. Louisville: Westminster John Knox. First published 1997. Pages 201–15 in *Constructing Early Christian Families*. Edited by Halvor Moxnes. London: Routledge.

Martyn, J. Louis. 1979. *The Gospel of John in Christian History: Essays for Interpreters*. New York: Paulist.

———. 2003. *History and Theology in the Fourth Gospel*. Louisville: Westminster John Knox. First published 1968.

Marxsen, Willi. 1989. *Christliche und unchristliche Ethik im Neuen Testament*. Gütersloh: Gütersloher Verlagshaus.

Matson, Mark A. 2001. *In Dialogue with Another Gospel? The Influence of the Fourth Gospel on the Passion Narrative of the Gospel of Luke*. SBLDS 178. Missoula, MT: Scholars Press.

Maynard, Arthur H. 1984. The Role of Peter in the Fourth Gospel. *NTS* 30: 531–48.

McDonough, Sean M. Revelation: The Climax of Cosmology. Pages 178–88 in *Cosmology and New Testament Theology*. LNTS 355. Edited by Jonathan T. Pennington and Sean M. McDonough. London: T&T Clark.

McGinn, Bernard. 2000. *Antichrist: Two Thousand Years of the Human Fascination with Evil*. New York: Columbia University Press.

Meeks, Wayne A. 1972. The Man from Heaven in Johannine Sectarianism. *JBL* 91:44–72.

———. 1996. The Ethics of the Fourth Evangelist. Pages 317–26 in *Exploring the Gospel of John*. Edited by R. Alan Culpepper and C. Clifton Black. Louisville: Westminster John Knox.

———. 2003. *The First Urban Christians; The Social World of the Apostle Paul*. 2nd ed. New Haven: Yale University Press.

Menken, Maarten J. J. 2008. The Opponents in the Johannine Epistles. Pages 191–209 in *Empsychoi Logoi: Religious Innovations in Antiquity: Studies in Honour of Pieter Willem van der Horst*. Edited by Alberdina Houtman, Albert de Jong, and Magda Misset-van de Weg. AJEC 73. Leiden: Brill.

———. 2010. *1, 2 en 3 Johannes*. Kok: Kampen.

Merwe, Dirk G. van der. 2005. Understanding Sin in the Johannine Epistles. *Verbum et Ecclesia* 26:527–42.

———. 2006a. "Having Fellowship with God" according to 1 John: Dealing with the Intermediation and Environment through Which and in Which It Is Constituted. *AcTSup* 8:165–92.

———. 2006b. "A Matter of Having Fellowship": Ethics in the Johannine Epistles. Pages 535–63 in *Identity, Ethics, and Ethos in the New Testament*. Edited by Jan van der Watt. Berlin: de Gruyter.

Metzger, Bruce M. 1994. *A Textual Commentary on the Greek New Testament: A Companion Volume to the United Bible Societies' Greek New Testament*. 4th rev. ed. New York: United Bible Societies.

———. 2001. *The Bible in Translation: Ancient and English Versions*. Grand Rapids: Baker.

Miller, Ed L. 1989. *Salvation-History in the Prologue of John: The Significance of John 1:3–4*. NovTSup 60. Leiden: Brill.

Mitchell, Margaret M. 2008. John, Letters of. *NIB* 3: 370–74.

Moloney, Francis J. 1998. *The Gospel of John*. SP 4. Collegeville, MN: Liturgical Press.

Morgan, Teresa. 2007. *Popular Morality in the Early Roman Empire*. Cambridge: Cambridge University Press.

Morris, Leon. 1995. *The Gospel according to John*. Rev. ed. NIGTC. Grand Rapids: Eerdmans.

Newman, Barclay and E. Nida. 1980. *A Translators' Handbook on the Gospel of John*. New York: United Bible Societies.

Neyrey, Jerome H. 1988. *An Ideology of Revolt: John's Christology in Social-Science Perspective*. Philadelphia: Fortress.

———. 1998. *Honor and Shame in the Gospel of Matthew*. Louisville: Westminster John Knox.

Nicholson, Godfrey C. 1983. *Death as Departure*. SBLDS 63. Missoula, MT: Scholars Press.

Nicklas, Tobias. 2006. Was es heisst, "Kinder Gottes zu warden" (Joh 1,12b): Der 1. Johannesbrief für Leser des Johannesevangeliums. *BL* 79:58–61.

[North], Wendy E. Sproston. 1992. Witnesses to what was ἀπ' ἀρχῆς: I John's Contribution to Our Knowledge of Tradition in the Fourth Gospel. *JSNT* 48:43–65.

———. 2001. *The Lazarus Story within the Johannine Tradition*. JSNTSup 212. Sheffield: Sheffield Academic Press.

———. 2003. John for Readers of Mark? A Response to Richard Bauckham's Proposal. *JSNT* 25:449–68.
O'Day, Gail R. 1992. 1, 2, and 3 John. Pages 374–75 in *The Women's Commentary*. Edited by Carol A. Newsom and Sharon H. Ringe. Louisville: Westminster John Knox.
Painter, John. 1980. *John, Witness and Theologian*. 3rd ed. Kansas City: Beacon Hill.
———. 1986. The "Opponents" in 1 John. *NTS* 32:48–71.
———. 2002. *1, 2, and 3 John*. SP 18. Collegeville, MN: Liturgical Press.
Pakala, J. C. 2007. A Librarian's Comments on Commentaries: 23. 1 John, 2 John, 3 John. *Presb* 33:44–48.
Pecorara, G. 1937. De verbo "manere" apud Ioannem. *DivThom* 40:159–71.
Peerbolte, L. J. Lietaert. 1996. *The Antecedents of Antichrist: A Traditio-Historical Study of the Earliest Christian Views on Eschatological Opponents*. JSJSup 49. Leiden: Brill.
Pennington, Jonathan T. 2004. Dualism in Old Testament Cosmology: Weltbild and Weltanschauung. *SJOT* 18:260–77.
Perkins, Pheme. 2004. Preserving the Testimony in the Johannine Churches. *TBT* 42:19–23.
Polhill, John B. 1970. An Analysis of II and III John. *RevExp* 67:461–71.
Porter, Stanley E., and Tom Holmen, eds. 2010. *Handbook for the Study of the Historical Jesus*. 4 vols. Leiden: Brill.
Price, James L. 1990. Light from Qumran upon Some Aspects of Johannine Theology. Pages 9–37 in *John and the Dead Sea Scrolls*. Edited by James H. Charlesworth. New York: Crossroad.
Quast, Kevin. 1989. *Peter and the Beloved Disciple; Figures for a Community in Crisis*. JSNTSup 32. Sheffield: JSOT Press.
Rawson, Beryl. 1987. The Roman Family. Pages 1–57 in *The Family in Ancient Rome: New Perspectives*. Edited by Beryl Rawson. Ithaca, NY: Cornell University Press.
Reinhartz, Adele. 2001. *Befriending the Beloved Disciple: A Jewish Reading of the Gospel of John*. New York: Continuum.
Reis, David M. 2003. Jesus' Farewell Discourse, "Otherness," and the Construction of a Johannine Identity. *SR* 32:39–58.
Rensberger, David. 1992. Love for One Another and Love for Enemies in the Gospel of John. Pages 297–313 in *The Love of Enemy and Nonretaliation in the New Testament*. Edited by Willard M. Swartley. Louisville: Westminster John Knox.

———. 1997. *1 John, 2 John, 3 John*. ANTC. Nashville: Abingdon.
———. 2001. *The Epistles of John*. Westminster Bible Companion. Louisville: Westminster John Knox.
———. 2006. Conflict and Community in the Johannine Letters. *Int* 60:278–91.
Richter, Georg. 1968. Die Deutung des Kreuzestodes Jesu in der Leidensgeschichte des Johannesevangeliums. *BibLeb* 9:21–36.
Ricoeur, Paul. 1980. The Hermeneutics of Testimony. Pages 119–54 in *Essays on Biblical Interpretation*. Philadelphia: Fortress.
Robertson, Archibald Thomas. 1933. *General Epistles and Revelation of John*. Vol. 6. Word Pictures in the New Testament. Nashville: Broadman.
Robinson, J. A. T. 1962–1963. The Relation of the Prologue to the Gospel of St. John. *NTS* 9:120–29.
Rusam, Dietrich. 1993. *Die Gemeinschaft der Kinder Gottes: Das Motiv der Gotteskindschaft und die Gemeinden der johanneischen Briefe*. BWA(N)T. Stuttgart: Kohlhammer.
Salom, A. P. 1955. Some Aspects of the Grammatical Style of 1 John. *JBL* 74:96–102.
Schaff, Philip. 1919. *The Creeds of Christendom: The Greek and Latin Creeds with Translations*. Vol. 2. New York: Harper & Brothers.
Schmid, Hansjörg. 2002. *Gegner im 1. Johannesbrief? Zu Konstruktion und Selbstreferenz im johanneischen Sinnsystem*. BWA(N)T 159. Stuttgart: Kohlhammer.
———. 2004. How to Read the First Epistle of John Non-Polemically. *Biblica* 85:24–41.
Schmidt, Karl Ludwig. 1965. ἔθνος κτλ. Pages 364–72 in vol. 2 of *Theological Dictionary of the New Testament*. Edited by Gerhard Kittel and Gerhard Friedrich. Translated by Geoffrey W. Bromiley. 10 vols. Grand Rapids: Eerdmans, 1964–1976.
Schmithals, Walter. 1992. *Johannesevangelium und Johannesbriefe: Forschungsgeschichte und Analyse*. BZNW 64. Berlin: de Gruyter.
Schnackenburg, Rudolf. 1953. *Die Johannesbriefe*. HTKNT 13.3. Freiburg: Herder.
———. 1982. *The Moral Teaching of the New Testament*. Freiburg im Breisgau: Herder.
———. 1992. *The Johannine Epistles: Introduction and Commentary*. Translated by Reginald Fuller and Ilse Fuller. New York: Crossroad.
Schneider, Johannes. 1965. ἐξέρχομαι. Pages 678–80 in vol. 2 of *Theological Dictionary of the New Testament*. Edited by Gerhard Kittel and Ger-

hard Friedrich. Translated by Geoffrey W. Bromiley. 10 vols. Grand Rapids: Eerdmans, 1964–1976.

Schnelle, Udo. 1992. *Antidocetic Christology in the Gospel of John: An Investigation of the Place of the Fourth Gospel in the Johannine School*. Translated by Linda M. Maloney. Minneapolis: Fortress.

———. 2010. *Die Johannesbriefe*. THKNT 17. Leipzig: Evangelische Verlagsanstalt.

———. 2011. *Die Reihenfolge der Johanneischen Schriften*. NTS 57:114–44.

Scholtissek, Klaus. 2000. *In Ihm Sein und Bleiben: Die Sprache der Immanenz in den Johanneischen Schriften*. Herders Biblische Studien. Freiburg im Breisgau: Herder.

———. 2004. Die relecture des Johannesevangeliums im ersten Johannesbrief. *BK* 59:152–56.

Schrage, W. 1996. *The Ethics of the New Testament*. London: T&T Clark.

Schrenk, G. 1965. δίκαιος. Pages 182–225 in vol. 2 of *Theological Dictionary of the New Testament*. Edited by Gerhard Kittel and Gerhard Friedrich. Translated by Geoffrey W. Bromiley. 10 vols. Grand Rapids: Eerdmans, 1964–1976.

———. 1973. πατήρ. Pages 945–1014 in vol. 5 of *Theological Dictionary of the New Testament*. Edited by Gerhard Kittel and Gerhard Friedrich. Translated by Geoffrey W. Bromiley. 10 vols. Grand Rapids: Eerdmans, 1964–1976.

Schrot, Helmut G. 1979. Familia. Pages 511–12 in vol. 2 of *Der Kleine Pauly: Lexikon der Antike*. Edited by Konrat Ziegler and Walther Sontheimer. 5 vols. München: Deutscher Taschenbuch.

Schunack, Gerd. 1982. *Die Briefe des Johannes*. ZBK, NT 17. Zürich: TVZ.

Schweitzer, Albert. 1910. *The Quest of the Historical Jesus: A Critical Study of its Progress from Reimarus to Wrede*. Translated by William Montgomery. New York: Macmillan.

———. 2001. *The Quest of the Historical Jesus*. First Complete Edition. Translated by William Montgomery, J. R. Coates, Susan Cupilt, and John Bowden. Minneapolis: Fortress.

Seesemann, Heinrich. 1968. πατέω κτλ. Pages 940–45 in vol. 5 of *Theological Dictionary of the New Testament*. Edited by Gerhard Kittel and Gerhard Friedrich. Translated by Geoffrey W. Bromiley. 10 vols. Grand Rapids: Eerdmans, 1964–1976.

Segovia, Fernando F. 1982. *Love Relationships in the Johannine Tradition: Agapē/Agapan in I John and the Fourth Gospel*. SBLDS 58. Missoula, MT: Scholars Press.

———. 1991. *The Farewell of the Word: The Johannine Call to Abide*. Minneapolis: Fortress.

———. 1996. *"What is John?" Readers and Readings of the Fourth Gospel*. Edited by Fernando F. Segovia. Missoula, MT: Scholars Press.

Slater, Thomas B. 2007. 1, 2, and 3 John. Pages 496–517 in *True to Our Native Land: An African American New Testament Commentary*. Edited by Brian Blount et al. Minneapolis: Fortress.

Smalley, Stephen S. 1984. *1, 2, 3 John*. WBC 51. Waco, TX: Word.

———. 2007. *1, 2, 3 John*. Rev. ed. WBC 51. Nashville: Nelson.

Smith, D. Moody, Jr. 1965. *Composition and Order of the Fourth Gospel: Bultmann's Literary Theory*. New Haven: Yale University Press.

———. 1984. *Johannine Christianity. Essays on its Setting, Sources and Theology*. Columbia: University of South Carolina.

———. 1991. *First, Second and Third John*. IBC. Louisville: John Knox Press.

———. 1995. *The Theology of the Gospel of John*. New Testament Theology. Cambridge: Cambridge University Press.

———. 1996. What Have I Learned about the Gospel of John. Pages 217–35 in *"What Is John?": Readers and Readings of the Fourth Gospel*. Edited by Fernando F. Segovia. SBLSymS 3. Atlanta: Society of Biblical Literature.

———. 1999. *John*. Abingdon New Testament Commentaries. Nashville: Abingdon.

———. 2001. *John among the Gospels*. 2nd ed. Columbia: University of South Carolina Press.

———. 2008. John's Quest for Jesus. Pages 56–71 in *The Fourth Gospel in Four Dimensions*. Columbia: University of South Carolina Press. Originally published as pages 233–53 in *Neotestameutica et Philonica: Studies in Honor of Peder Borgen*. Brill: Leiden, 2003.

———. 2009. The Epistles of John: What's New Since Brooke's ICC in 1912? *ExpTim* 120:373–84.

Smith, Terence V. 1985. *Petrine Controversies in Early Christianity; Attitudes towards Peter in Christian Writings of the First Two Centuries*. WUNT 2/15. Tübingen: Mohr Siebeck.

Snodderley, M. E. 2008. A Socio-Rhetorical Investigation of the Johannine Understanding of "The Works of the Devil" in 1 John 3:8. Ph.D. diss., University of South Africa.

Snyder, Graydon F. 1971. John 13:16 and the Anti-Petrinism of the Johannine Tradition. *BR* 16: 5–15.

Spicq, Ceslas. 1994. *Theological Lexicon of the New Testament*. Translated by James Ernest. Peabody, MA: Hendrickson.

Stählin, G. 1964–1976. "φίλος." Pages 147–71 in vol. 9 of *Theological Dictionary of the New Testament*. Edited by Gerhard Kittel and Gerhard Friedrich. Translated by Geoffrey W. Bromiley. 10 vols. Grand Rapids: Eerdmans, 1964–1976.

Stambaugh, John, and David Balch. 1986. *The Social World of the First Christians*. London: SPCK.

Stegemann, Ekkehard. 1985. "Kindlein, hütet euch vor den Götterbildern!": Erwägungen zum Schluss des 1. Johannesbriefes. *TLZ* 41:284–94.

Stott, John R. W. 1988. *The Letters of John*. Rev. ed. TNTC. Leicester: Inter-Varsity; Grand Rapids: Eerdmans.

Stowers, 1986. *Letter Writing in Greco-Roman Antiquity*. Philadelphia: Westminster.

Strecker, Georg. 1986. Die Anfänge der johanneischen Schule. *NTS* 32:31–47.

———. 1989. *Die Johannesbriefe*. KEK 14. Göttingen: Vandenhoeck & Ruprecht.

———. 1996. *The Johannine Letters: A Commentary on 1, 2, and 3 John*. Translated by Linda M. Maloney. Hermeneia. Minneapolis: Fortress.

Streeter, Burnett Hillman. 1929. *The Primitive Church*. New York: Macmillan.

Streett, Daniel R. 2011. *They Went Out from Us: The Identity of the Opponents in First John*. BZNW 177. Berlin: de Gruyter.

Talbert, Charles H. 1992. *Reading John: A Literary and Theological Commentary on the Fourth Gospel and the Johannine Epistles*. New York: Crossroad.

———. 2010. The Fourth Gospel's Soteriology between New Birth and Resurrection. *PRSt* 37:133–46.

Taylor, Vincent. 1959. *The Gospel according to St. Mark*. New York: Macmillan.

Thatcher, Tom. 2009. *Greater than Caesar: Christology and Empire in the Fourth Gospel*. Minneapolis: Fortress.

———. 2013 Cain the Jew the Antichrist: Collective Memory and the Johannine Ethic of Loving and Hating. Pages 350–73 in *Rethinking the Ethics of John: "Implicit Ethics" in the Johannine Writings*. Edited by Jan G. van der Watt and Ruben Zimmermann. WUNT 291. Tübingen: Mohr Siebeck.

Theobald, Michael. 2002. *Herrenworte im Johannesevangelium*. Freiburg im Breisgau: Herder.

Thomas, John Christopher. 2004. *The Pentecostal Commentary on 1 John, 2 John, 3 John*. London: T&T Clark.

Thompson, Marianne Meye. 1992. *1–3 John*. IVP New Testament Commentary. Downers Grove, IL: InterVarsity Press.

———. 1993. *The Incarnate Word: Perspectives on Jesus in the Fourth Gospel*. Peabody, MA: Hendrikson.

Thompson, Michael B. 1998. The Holy Internet: Communication between Churches in the First Christian Generation. Pages 49–70 in *The Gospels for All Christians: Rethinking the Gospel Audiences*. Edited by Richard Bauckham. Grand Rapids: Eerdmans.

Thyen, Hartwig. 1971. Johannes 13 und die "kirchliche Redaktion" des vierten Evangeliums. Pages 343–56 in *Tradition und Glaube: Festgabe für K. G. Kuhn*. Göttingen: Vandenhoeck & Ruprecht.

———. 1977. Entwicklungen innerhalb der johanneischen Theologie und Kirche im Spiegel von Joh. 21 und der Lieblingsjüngertexte des Evangeliums. Pages 259–99 in *L'Évangile de Jean: Sources, rédaction, théologie*. Edited by Marinus de Jonge. BETL 44. Leuven: Leuven University Press.

Tuckett, Christopher M. 1996. *Q and the History of Early Christianity: Studies on Q*. Peabody, MA: Hendrickson.

Turner, Seth. 2004. Revelation 11:1–13: History of Interpretation. Ph.D. diss., University of Oxford.

Tyndale, William, trans. 1938. *The New Testament: A Reprint of the Edition of 1534 with the Translator's Prefaces and Notes and the Variants of the Edition of 1525*. Edited by N. Hardy Wallis. With an introduction by Isaac Foot. Cambridge: Cambridge University Press.

Vaux, Roland de. 1974. *Ancient Israel: Its Life and Institutions*. London: Darton, Longman & Todd.

Volf, Miroslav. 2005. Johannine Dualism and Contemporary Pluralism. *Modern Theology* 21:189–217.

Vogler, Werner. 1993. *Die Briefe des Johannes*. THKNT 17. Berlin: Evangelische Verlagsanstalt.

Vouga, François. 1990. *Die Johannesbriefe*. HNT 15.3. Tübingen: Mohr Siebeck.

Wahlde, Urban C. von. 1983. Review of *The Epistles of John*, by Raymond E. Brown. *BTB* 13:100.

———. 1990. *The Johannine Commandments: 1 John and the Struggle for the Johannine Tradition*. New York: Paulist, 1990.

———. 2010a. *A Commentary on the Gospel and Letters of John*. 3 vols. ECC. Grand Rapids: Eerdmans.

———. 2010b. The Johannine Literature and Gnosticism: New Light on Their Relationship? Pages 221–54 in *From Judaism to Christianity: Tradition and Transition*. Edited by Patricia Walters. NovTSup 134. Leiden: Brill.

Watson, Duane F. 1997. Antichrist. Pages 50–53 in *Dictionary of the Later New Testament and Its Developments*. Edited by Ralph P. Martin and Peter H. Davids. Downers Grove, IL: InterVarsity Press.

Watt, Jan G. van der. 1995. "Metaphorik" in Joh 15,1–8. *BZ* 38:67–80.

———. 1999. Ethics in First John: A Literary and Socioscientific Perspective. *CBQ* 61:491–511.

———. 2000. *Family of the King: Dynamics of Metaphor in the Gospel according to John*. Brill: Leiden.

———. 2006. Radical Social Redefinition and Radical Love: Ethics and Ethos in the Gospel according to John. Pages 107–33 in *Identity, Ethics, and Ethos in the New Testament*. Edited by Jan G. van der Watt. Berlin: de Gruyter.

———. 2007. *An Introduction to the Johannine Gospel and Letters*. London: T&T Clark.

———. 2009. The Good and the Truth in John. Pages 317–33 in *Studien zu Matthäus und Johannes*. Edited by Andreas Dettwiler and Uta Poplutz. Zürich: TVZ.

Weiss, Johannes. 1937. *Earliest Christianity: A History of the Period AD 30–150*. Vol. 2. Translated by Frederick Clifton Grant. New York: Harper & Row.

Wengst, Klaus. 1978. *Der erste, zweite und dritte Brief des Johannes*. ÖTK 16. Gütersloh: Gütersloher Verlagshaus Gerd Mohn; Würzburg: Echter

Westcott, Brooke Foss. 1966. *The Epistles of St John: The Greek Text with Notes and Essays*. 3rd ed. New York: Macmillan. Originally published in 1892.

Whitacre, Rodney A. 1982. *Johannine Polemic: The Role of Tradition and Theology*. SBLDS 67. Missoula, MT: Scholars Press.

Wilson, W. G. 1948. An Examination of the Linguistic Evidence Adduced against the Unity of Authorship of the First Epistle of John and the Fourth Gospel. *JTS* 40:147–56.

Wischmeyer, O. 2009. Das alte und das neue Gebot. Ein Beitrag zur Intertextualität der johanneischen Schriften. Pages 207–20 in *Studien zu Matthäus und Johannes*. Edited by Andreas Dettwiler and Uta Poplutz. Zürich: TVZ.

Witherington, Ben, III. 2006. *A Socio-Rhetorical Commentary on Titus, 1-2 Timothy, and 1-3 John*. Vol. 1 of *Letters and Homilies for Hellenized Christians*. Downers Grove, IL: InterVarsity Press.

———. 2009. *The Indelible Image: The Theological and Ethical Thought World of the New Testament*. 2 vols. Downers Grove, IL: InterVarsity Press.

Wuest, Kenneth S. 1961. *The New Testament: An Expanded Translation*. Grand Rapids: Eerdmans.

Wycliffe, John, trans. 1986. *The New Testament in English*. Rev. by John Purvey. Portland, UK: International Bible Publications.

Yarbrough, Robert W. 2008. *1–3 John*. BECNT. Grand Rapids: Baker.

Zumstein, Jean. 1996. Der Prozess der Relecture in der johanneischen Literatur. *NTS* 42:394–411.

Contributors

Paul N. Anderson is Professor of Biblical and Quaker Studies at George Fox University in Newberg, Oregon.

Gary M. Burge is Professor of New Testament at Wheaton College and Graduate School in Wheaton, Illinois.

R. Alan Culpepper is Dean and Professor of New Testament at the McAfee School of Theology at Mercer University in Atlanta, Georgia.

Peter Rhea Jones is Professor of New Testament and Preaching at the McAfee School of Theology at Mercer University in Atlanta, Georgia.

Craig R. Koester is Dean and Professor of New Testament at Luther Seminary in Saint Paul, Minnesota.

Andreas J. Köstenberger is Senior Professor of New Testament and Biblical Theology and Director of Ph.D. Studies at Southeastern Baptist Theological Seminary in Wake Forest, North Carolina.

Judith M. Lieu is Lady Margaret's Professor of Divinity at the Faculty of Divinity, University of Cambridge, England.

William R. G. Loader is Emeritus Professor at Murdoch University in Perth, Western Australia.

David Rensberger is retired Professor of New Testament at the Interdenominational Theological Center in Atlanta, Georgia.

Urban C. von Wahlde is Professor of New Testament at Loyola University in Chicago, Illinois.

Jan G. van der Watt is Professor of Exegesis of the New Testament and Source Texts of Early Christianity at the Radboud University of Nijmegen, The Netherlands.

Ancient Sources Index

Old Testament/Hebrew Bible

Genesis
- 1:1 — 173
- 1:3 — 173
- 3:6 — 229
- 4:1–16 — 208
- 18:23–26 — 214
- 39:7 — 225

Exodus
- 13:21 — 173
- 34:6–7 — 158

Numbers
- 15:39 — 225
- 35:30 — 170

Deuteronomy
- 4:26 — 173
- 17:6 — 164, 170
- 18:15–22 — 49, 66, 78
- 18:18–22 — 167, 280
- 19:15 — 164, 170
- 20:5–7 — 245
- 21:18–21 — 205

2 Samuel
- 11:2 — 225
- 22:9 — 173
- 23:4 — 173

Job
- 31:1 — 225

Psalms
- 1:6 — 214
- 51:2 — 32
- 106:14 (LXX 105:14) — 228
- 119:105 — 173

Proverbs
- 6:25 — 225
- 8:20 — 200

Ecclesiastes
- 4:8 — 224

Isaiah
- 2:5 — 200
- 6:10 — 106, 175
- 32:14–15 — 30
- 40–55 — 161
- 44:3 — 30
- 53:1 — 175
- 54:1–6 — 127
- 60:21 — 214

Jeremiah
- 9:2–3 — 203
- 24:7 — 31
- 31:33–34 — 33
- 31:34 — 31, 35, 37
- 38:34 LXX — 31, 36

Ezekiel
- 11:17–19 — 30
- 36:25–27 — 32
- 36:26–27 — 30
- 36:27 — 32

Ezekiel (cont.)		9:8	224
36:36	30	15:6	224
37:4–6	31		
37:14	31	3 Maccabees	
39:29	30	5:26	220
Daniel		4 Maccabees	
7	167	8:19	224
7:23–25	167		
12:3	214	**New Testament**	
Joel		Matthew	
2:28–29 (LXX 3:1–2)	30	5:28–30	225
		5:44	91
Deuterocanonical Books		6:23	224
		7:16	214
Judith		10:16–20	92
10:4	225	11:25–27	74
10:9	246	11:27	69, 72
16:7–9	225	16:17–19	54, 83, 91
		18:15–18	54
Wisdom of Solomon		18:15–17	92
2:6–9	230	18:16	164
5:8	224	19:12	226
17:7	224	19:19	91
		20:15	224
Sirach		22:39	91
9:5	225	23:28	214
9:8	225	26:28	164
9:9	230		
14:8	224	Mark	
23:4–6	225, 228–229	1:14	64
26:8	230	1:38	143
26:21	225	3:13–14	151
31:25–32:13	230	6	63
41:20–21	225	6:4	64
		6:7–13	167
Susanna		6:30	167
7–8	225	7:5	200
12	225	7:22	224
52–53	225	8	63
57	225	10:38–39	67
		12:25	223
2 Maccabees		12:31–33	91
6:1–9	89	13:6	190

13:11	92	1:29	162
13:32	183	1:32	169
15:7	218	1:34	181
16:9–20	76	1:36	162
		2:1	112
Luke		2:10	65
1:2	65, 74	2:11	158
1:45	246	2:22	66
6:13	167	3	55, 181
6:27–35	91	3–4	161
6:44	214	3:1–8	165
9:1–6	167	3:3	175, 181
9:10	167	3:3–8	28
10:1–20	167	3:5	175
10:1–40	167	3:6	28
10:17–20	167	3:9–12	158
10:21–22	74	3:16	174, 209, 232
10:22	69–72	3:16–17	162
10:27	91	3:18	148
11:34	224	3:19	106, 166, 153
12:11–12	92	3:19–21	147, 158, 199
18:14	214	3:20	153
21:12–15	92	3:21	153
24:11	183	3:24	64
24:24	190	3:31–36	52, 65, 87, 109
		3:32	65
John		3:34	181
1–20	101, 110	4	55, 72
1:1	158	4:10	181
1:1–4	110, 158	4:10–15	28
1:1–18	18, 52, 64, 68, 70, 87, 100, 108, 277	4:23–24	181
		4:34	14, 242, 245
1:5	162–163	4:38	174
1:7–9	158	4:42	162
1:10–11	177	4:44	64
1:10–12	162	4:53	66
1:12	148	5	55
1:12–13	165, 175	5:18	160
1:14	87, 158, 169, 174	5:19–27	87
1:14–18	109	5:19–29	160
1:15	70	5:19–30	245
1:17	158, 163	5:22	166
1:18	174	5:22–27	158
1:19–42	70	5:24	166
1:19–12:50	100	5:26–29	109

John (cont.)

Reference	Pages
5:27	166
5:28–29	112
5:29	166
5:30	158
5:32	169
5:33	169
5:36	14, 68, 70, 75, 242, 245
5:36–37	169
5:37	164, 169
5:43	148
6	55, 63–64, 66
6:27	181
6:36	112
6:40d	112
6:44c	112
6:48–58	109
6:51–58	52, 65, 87
6:51b–58	108
6:54d	112
6:60–66	115
6:68–69	92
7–8	55
7:7	106, 147, 153
7:16	147
7:17	147
7:37–38	181
7:37–39	28, 181
7:39	181
8:12	158, 199
8:24	27
8:28–29	245
8:30	206
8:34–47	158
8:38	198
8:39–44	166, 208
8:41	206
8:44	167
8:47	138
8:59	160
9	55, 172
9:1–5	245
9:4	199
9:5	158
9:22	172
9:24–31	169
9:41	27
10	55, 174
10:2	146
10:11	146, 218
10:14	146
10:15	218
10:16	146, 161, 174
10:17–18	218
10:30	158
10:33–36	160
10:37–38	245
11	55, 64–65
11:9–10	158, 199
11:49–52	161
11:51–52	174
12	55
12:20–50	161
12:23	158
12:24	198
12:28	158
12:31	158, 163
12:32	161
12:35	199
12:35–36	158
12:36	158
12:37–40	199
12:37–50	162, 175
12:40	106
12:44–50	65, 87, 109, 245
12:46	158
12:46–47	199
12:48	166
13–14	66
13–17	108
13–20	197
13:1	162, 246
13:1–20:29	100
13:19	66
13:30-31a	143
13:31–32	158
13:34	70, 87, 112
13:34–35	91, 109, 115, 168, 176, 212, 234, 253
13:35	284

ANCIENT SOURCES INDEX

13:37–38	218	19:7	160
14:6	165, 169	19:28	246
14:9–14	245	19:30	28, 246, 252
14:16	103, 112, 164	19:31–37	108
14:17	112, 164, 181	19:34	67, 112, 181
14:18	181	19:34–35	70, 87
14:23	182	19:35	67, 87
14:26	43, 92, 181	20:21	174
14:29	66	20:21–22	177
14:30	158, 163	20:22	28, 181
14:31	70, 108	20:24	67, 87
15	174	20:24–29	108
15–16	108	20:28	64, 79
15–17	52, 54, 64, 66, 68, 70, 75, 108–9, 115–16, 234, 278	20:30–31	70, 100, 158, 160, 165, 174, 177
15:1–17	109	20:30	74, 169
15:12–17	91	20:31	54, 66, 70, 174
15:16	174	21	7, 51–52, 54, 64, 66, 68, 70, 75, 101, 108–11, 114, 115–16, 277
15:18–27	169		
15:26	43, 112, 164, 181	21:1–25	100–101
15:38	218	21:14	177
16:2–13	92	21:16	146
16:11	158, 163	21:17	146
16:12	184–185	21:18–24	87
16:12–13	182	21:20–24	68
16:12–15	44	21:24	139, 169
16:13	112, 164, 181	21:24–25	70
16:33	161, 163		
17	108	Acts	
17:3	163	1:8	161
17:4	14, 245	2:17	30
17:6	148–149, 181	3	72
17:11	148–149	4	72
17:11–12	166	4:19–20	62, 65, 67, 72, 75
17:13	148–149	4:20	65
17:15	153, 167	5:28	149
17:18	174	5:40	149
17:20–24	142	5:41	149
17:23	246	8	72
17:26	148–149	11:26	148
18:1	70, 108	13:1–3	151
18:19	147	13:46–48	161
18:32	66	15	282
18:37	169	20:28	146, 164
18:38	164	20:29	146

Acts (cont.)		Philippians	
20:30	146	3:12	242
20:31	146		
21:21	200	Colossians	
28:17–31	161	1:20	164
Romans		2 Thessalonians	
1:5	148	2	11
1:14–16	161	2:1–12	167
1:17	214	2:8	51, 189
3:21–26	214	3:3	167
3:25	164		
5:1	214	1 Timothy	
5:9	164	1:20	129
7:7	228	4:14	183
8:38	245		
12:13	151	Titus	
13:13	230, 231	1:7–8	151
14:15	200		
		Hebrews	
1 Corinthians		9:12	164
1:3	128	13:1–3	234
6:10	230–231	13:2	151
6:12	282	13:12	164
7:7	226	13:23	131
7:31	225		
12:28	183	James	
14:29	183	2:1–7	234
14:32	183	2:22	243, 245
		4:16	224
2 Corinthians			
13:1	164	1 Peter	
		4:3	230–231
Galatians		4:9	151
1:1	183	4:14	149
2	132, 182	4:18	214
5:21	230–231	5:13	128
Ephesians		2 Peter	
1:7	164	1:1	129
3:5	183	2:1	183
4:11	182–183	2:14	225
5:2	200		
		1 John	
		1	105

1–4	68	2:7–11	198
1:1	228, 231	2:8	130, 168, 225–226
1:1–2	163, 190, 207	2:9–11	131, 226, 229
1:1–3	18, 36, 38, 65, 130, 136, 147	2:11	106, 200
1:1–4	67, 87, 100–101, 142, 149, 164, 168, 175, 277, 282	2:11–14	130
		2:12	148, 175
1:3	134, 142–43, 163, 166, 190, 202–3	2:12b	142
1:3b	43, 142	2:12–14	134, 231–232
1:3c	142	2:12–15	233
1:3–4	202	2:13	39
1:4	130–131, 142	2:13d	142
1:5	100, 134, 163, 173, 198	2:13–14	140, 153, 193, 211
1:5–7	198, 200	2:14c	232
1:5–10	168	2:14h	142
1:5–2:2	162	2:15–17	13, 14, 162, 169, 223, 231–33, 235
1:5–3:10	100		
1:6	142, 165, 168, 182, 200, 202–203	2:16	13, 162, 226, 229, 231
1:6–7	198, 202	2:17	169, 223
1:6–10	131	2:18	137, 162, 167, 187–88, 193, 225–26, 231–32
1:7	12, 41, 200, 203, 216		
1:7–9	136, 168	2:18–19	20, 143, 191, 232
1:7–2:2	219	2:18–20	134
1:8	168, 195	2:18–25	68, 79, 81, 88, 280
1:8–9	219	2:18–27	142, 146, 164, 233
1:8–2:2	136	2:19	9, 82, 89, 136–37, 143, 171, 175, 194
1:9	182, 213–214, 216		
1:10	165	2:20	39, 134, 183, 191
2–3	68	2:20–21	35, 142, 211
2–5	105	2:21	130, 135, 153, 168–169
2:1	90, 130, 137, 163, 175, 190, 213–15	2:21–22	175
		2:22	137, 153, 162, 167–68, 187, 189–91, 195
2:1–2	41, 134, 219		
2:1–17	80	2:22–23	20, 52, 191, 232
2:2	136, 162, 216	2:22–24	87
2:3	200	2:23	43, 145
2:3–4	40	2:24	36, 43, 134, 136, 169
2:3–6	212	2:25	207
2:4	168, 195	2:26	135, 153
2:4–6	131, 168	2:27	35, 37, 43, 142, 153, 168, 183, 191
2:5	168, 238, 240–41, 244–45, 247–48, 251, 254–70		
		2:27–28	43
2:6	142, 200, 210	2:28	135, 137, 166
2:7	36, 70, 130, 134, 136, 200	2:28–29	207
2:7–8	19, 176	2:29	150, 175, 204, 206, 210, 213–15
2:7–10	13, 199, 203	2:37	87

1 John (cont.)
3:1	40, 102, 162, 211
3:1–3	165
3:1–10	206
3:2	135, 137, 216
3:3	210, 213, 215–16
3:4–10	136, 175
3:5	211, 216, 219
3:5–6	216
3:6	38, 150, 211, 219
3:7	137, 210, 213–15
3:7–8	217
3:8	161, 165, 175, 192–93
3:8–10	165
3:9	150, 175, 203–4, 219
3:9–10	206
3:10	166, 204, 215
3:10–11	20
3:11	36, 209, 217
3:11–18	208, 217
3:11–4:21	91
3:11–5:12	100
3:12	106, 153, 162, 214–15
3:12–13	208
3:12–15	193
3:13	162, 169
3:14	209, 218, 250
3:14–15	207–9, 211
3:16	210, 215, 217–19, 250
3:16–17	217
3:16–18	253
3:17–18	285
3:17	14, 215–16, 218, 228, 231, 233–34
3:18	168
3:19	168–69
3:21	135
3:23	144, 152, 163, 190, 253
4	14, 68, 180, 237–38, 241, 244, 247, 252
4:1	135, 137, 144, 162, 167–68, 180, 192
4:1d	144
4:1–3	66, 81, 87, 90, 280, 285
4:1–6	20, 112, 146, 164, 232, 254
4:2	163, 228, 231
4:2–3	52
4:2–3a	180
4:3	42, 135, 137, 162, 167, 183, 187–88, 192–93, 232
4:4	162–63, 165, 193
4:4–5	232
4:4–6	9, 135, 159
4:5	11, 136–37, 144, 180, 193
4:6	40, 136, 162, 164, 168, 183, 192
4:7	137, 175, 204, 206–7, 211, 217, 237, 247
4:7–10	248
4:7–12	13, 209
4:7–14	190
4:7–18	253
4:7–21	193
4:8	100, 207, 217
4:9	143, 207, 209, 215
4:9–10	134, 162, 217
4:10	143
4:11	137, 210, 217, 237
4:11–18	14, 237
4:12	14, 237–38, 240–41, 245, 247–51, 254–71
4:13	181
4:13–16	237
4:13–21	166, 183
4:14	134, 136, 143, 162–163
4:14–15	175
4:14–16	149, 215
4:15	145, 163
4:16	217
4:17	162, 166, 241, 245, 250, 254–71
4:17–18	135, 237–38, 240, 250–51
4:18	238–41, 243, 254–71
4:18a	240
4:19	217, 221
4:20	168, 195
4:20–21	175
4:20–5:3	247
4:21	87, 217
5	68, 79
5:1	175, 190, 207
5:1–2	204, 206, 217

ANCIENT SOURCES INDEX

5:1–13	164	6	128, 144, 200
5:4	175	6d	144
5:4–5	159, 161–63, 165, 175, 193, 232	6e	144
5:5–6	232	7	12, 52, 66, 87, 90, 134, 137, 143–44, 146, 162–63, 167, 175, 187, 189, 190–91, 195, 232, 280, 285
5:6	41, 163, 168, 176, 190	7b	147
5:6–7	112	7bc	144
5:6–8	20, 67, 164	7–8	134
5:6–9	163, 165	7–9	144
5:6–11	163, 169, 175	7–10	254
5:7–8	164	7–11	153, 175
5:9	164	8	128, 134, 137, 145–46
5:10	43	8a	144
5:10–12	165	8b	144, 146
5:11	165, 193, 207	8–10	146
5:11–12	34, 147	9	37, 145–46
5:12	165–166, 207	9b	147
5:13	100–101, 115, 130, 136, 142, 174, 177, 207, 211	10	128, 134, 139, 145
5:14–21	100–101	10b	147
5:16	131, 207	10–11	137, 145–46
5:16–18a	38	11	106, 128, 146, 153, 203
5:16–21	80	12	128, 133–34, 141, 145–46, 150
5:18–21	169	13	128, 145
5:18	153, 175, 204, 206, 211		
5:19	153, 163, 192, 211	3 John	
5:20	163, 168, 207, 211	1	1, 150, 152
5:21	64, 89, 104, 231, 283	1a	148
		1–7	148
2 John		2	127
1	1, 144, 146	3	133, 152, 200
1c	144–145	3bc	150
1–3	127	3f	152
2	144–145	3–4	133
2bc	145	4	126–27, 137, 142, 148, 152, 200
3	144, 163, 190	5	127, 150
3a	145	5–6	126
3c	144	5–7	133
4	127–128, 134, 145–146, 200	6	133
4b	144, 146	6–8	149
4–6	134	7	166, 175
5	91, 127–128, 134, 145	7a	148
5a	144	7b	149
5d	144–145	8	137, 148, 152, 166, 175
5–6	87	8a	150

3 John (cont.)		7:1–17	170
8b	148, 150	10:1–11:13	170
9	129, 154	11	170
9a	149	11:3	170
9b	149	11:7	167, 170
9c	148	11:7–12	170
9–10	51, 133, 138	11:15	170
9–11	148	11:18	170
10	106, 133, 153, 175	12:1–15:8	170
10a	149	12:11	170
10b	149, 153	12:17	170
10c	149	13	189
10d	150	13:1–10	167
10e	150	13:1–18	170
11	127, 138, 151, 153, 175	13:8	170
11a	150	14	170
11bc	150	14:7	170
12	67, 87, 133, 138–39, 148, 150, 152	15:3	170
12–13	127	15:5	170
13	127, 141	16:2	170
13–15	127	16:5	170
14	133, 150	16:7	170
15	9, 139	16:9	170
		16:11	170
Jude		16:12–16	167, 192
1	129	17	167
4	90	17:1	170
		17:1–6	230
Revelation		17:6	170
1:1	1, 163	17:8	170
1:2	163, 170	18:3	230
1:4	1	18:8	170
1:5	163, 170	18:9	230
1:9	1, 170	18:20	170
2–3	125, 169, 175–176	19:2	170
2:9	176	19:6–9	165
2:13	170	19:9	170
2:20	183	19:10	170
2:24	176	19:11	170
3	170	19:11–21	192–193
3:7	170	19:20–21	167
3:14	170	20	171
4–20	170	20:4	170–171
6:9	170	20:7–21:4	165
6:10	170	20:10	170

20:12	170	4:17	228
20:13	170		
21:5	170	**ANCIENT JEWISH TEXTS**	
22:6	170		
22:8	1	1 Enoch	
22:11	214	8:1–2	225
22:16	170	46:4–5	230
22:18	170		
22:20	170	Apocalypse of Moses	
		19:3	227
DEAD SEA SCROLLS			
		Josephus, *Jewish Antiquities*	
1QH		2.10.7	206
8:19–20	32	4.260–64	206
14:8	32	4.289	206
		15.4	246
1QM, passim	173		
		Jubilees	
1QpHab		7:20–24	228
5:7	225	20:4	225
1QS/1Q28		Liber antiquitatum biblicarum	
1:6–7	225	43.5	225
3:18	162		
3:21	173	Philo, *De Abrahamo*	
4:9–14	173	133–135	230
4:21–22	33	135	230
4:21	32		
4:23–26	162	Philo, *De agricultura*	
5:4–5	225	37–38	230
		147–165	245
4QBer^b/4Q287		160	230, 245
8, 13	225		
		Philo, *De cherubim*	
4QInstr^e/4Q417		92	230
1 I, 27	225		
		Philo, *De vita contemplativa*	
4Q435		53–56	230
2, I, 1–2	225		
		Philo, *De decalogo*	
11QT/11Q19		28	228
59:13–14	225	120	206
		153	228
CD			
2:16	225		

Philo, *Quod Deus sit immutabilis*
    3.17–18   206
    15   230
    17–18   206

Philo, *In Flaccum*
    136   230

Philo, *De fuga et inventione*
    35   230

Philo, *Legum allegoriae*
    2.29   230
    2.33   230
    3.114   230

Philo, *Legatio ad Gaium*
    312   230

Philo, *De vita Mosis*
    1.28   230
    1.148   230
    1.150   230
    1.156   201
    2.185   230
    2.23–24   230

Philo, *De opificio mundi*
    158   229

Philo, *De posteritate Caini*
    135   228

Philo, *Quaestiones et solutiones in Genesin*
    1.12   230
    2.12   230

Philo, *De sacrificiis Abelis et Caini*
    21   225
    49   230

Philo, *De somniis*
    1.122–125   230
    1.131   245
    2.147   230

Philo, *De specialibus legibus*
    1.192   230
    1.193   230
    2.18–19   230
    2.163   230
    2.195   230
    2.236   206
    2.243   206
    3.171   225
    4.84–85   228

Philo, *De virtutibus*
    182   230
    208   230

Psalms of Solomon
    4:4–5   225
    4:9   225
    4:12   225
    9:6   32
    10:1   32

Sibylline Oracles
    1   227

Testament of Benjamin
    6:2   225

Testament of Issachar
    4:4   225

Testament of Judah
    13:2   228
    17:1   225, 228

Testament of Moses
    7:1–4   230

Testament of Reuben
    2:4   225
    3:10   225
    4:1   225
    6:1   225

ANCIENT SOURCES INDEX

CLASSICAL AND ANCIENT CHRISTIAN WORKS

1 Clement
23:5 — 246

Apuleius, *Metamorphoses*
10:29–34 — 229

Aristotle, *Ethica eudemia*
7.2, 1237b, 32f — 201
1238a, 16 — 201

Aristotle, *Ethica nicomachea*
8–9 — 201
8.5.5 — 219
8.7.1 — 219
8.7.2 — 220
8.8.5 — 220
8.11.2–3 — 204
8.12.1 — 205
8.12.3 — 205
8.12.5 — 205
8.13.1 — 220
8.13.3 — 219
8.13.8–9 — 219
8.14.2 — 220
8.14.4 — 220
9.1.1 — 220
9.11, 1159b, 31f — 201

Aristotle, *Metaphysica*
5.1021b — 244
5.1021b 15–19 — 245

Aristotle, *Politica*
2.5, 1263a, 30 — 201

Augustine, *In epistulam Johannis ad Parthos tractatus*
3.4, 8 — 12, 195

Barnabas
16:8 — 149

Cicero, *De amicitia*
14.49 — 219
16.58 — 219
20.72 — 220

Cicero, *De officus*
1.17 — 206

Cornelius Nepos, *De viris illustribus*
15.3.4 — 201

Cyprian, *De ecclesiae*
6, 149–50 — 142

Didache
11–13 — 182
11–12 — 253
11:1–6 — 147

Dio Chrysostom, *Ad Alexandrinos*
32:4 — 229

Dio Chrysostom, *De regno iv*
48.84 — 228

Dio Chrysostom, *Twelfth Discourse*
42 — 206
43 — 206

Diogenes Laertius, *Vitae philosophorum*
6.37 — 201
6.72 — 201
7.1.124 — 201

Epictetus, *Diatribai*
2.18 — 228

Euripides, *Andromache*
376f — 201

Euripides, *Orestes*
735 — 201

Eusebius, *Historia ecclesiastica*		Martial, *Epigrammata*	
3.1	67	2.43.1–16	201
3.18	67	3.36.1–3	220
3.21	67		
3.23	67	Martyrdom of Polycarp	
3.24	67	16:2	246
3.29	67		
3.31	67	Muson	
3.39	67	frg. 13	201
4.14	67		
5.1.1–5.28	125	Plato, *Leges*	
5.18	67	5, 739c	201
5.20	67		
5.24	67	Plato, *Lysis*	
		207c	201
Shepherd of Hermas, Mandates			
9:10	246	Plato, *Phaedrus*	
		279c	201
Hippolytus, *Treatise on Christ and Antichrist*	189	Plato, *Respublica*	
		4, 424a	201
Ignatius, *To the Ephesians*		5, 449c	201
2	131		
3:1	149	Pliny, *Epistulae ad Trajanum*	
7:1	147, 149	10.96–97	79, 82
12	132		
		Plutarch, *Flatterer*	
Ignatius, *To the Magnesians*		24	201
2	131		
7:1	142	Plutarch, *Moralia*	
		65AB	201
Ignatius, *To the Philadelphians*		449D	228
2	132		
8	132	Polycarp, *Philippians*	
		7:1	187
Ignatius, *To the Smyrnaeans*			
4:2	233	Tertullian, *De resurrectione carnis*	
5:2	233	38	132
6:2	233		
		Thucydides, *Historiae*	
Ignatius, *To the Trallians*		6.13	228
pref. 12	132		
Irenaeus, *Adversus haereses*			
5.25–30	189		

Name Index

Akin, Daniel L.   119, 167, 198, 212–16
Alexander   129
Anderson, Bernhard W.   169
Anderson, Paul N.   1–2, 4, 6, 7, 47, 48, 55, 57–59, 62–63, 71–72, 77, 86, 93, 99, 109, 113, 119, 179, 253, 275
Antiochus Epiphanes   89
Antoninus Pius   206
Arian   206
Aristotle   201, 204, 219, 220, 244, 245
Arnold, Clinton E.   166
Ashton, John   56, 57, 64, 158
Augustine   12, 195
Aune, David E.   169
Balch, David   205
Balz, Horst   224
Bandy, Alan   170
Barre, Michael L.   47
Barrett, C. K.   55, 277–278
Bauckham, Richard   6, 59, 64, 123, 149, 154, 163, 169, 170, 174
Bauer, Walter   243
Beale, G. K.   169
Beck, William   14, 241, 269
Bengel, Johann Albrecht   148
Beutler, Johannes   21, 23, 119
Black, Matthew   179
Blank, Josef   197
Blumenberg, Hans   198
Bogart, John   118
Boismard, Marie-Émile   173
Bonaparte, Napoleon   194
Bonsirven, Joseph   148
Borgen, Peder   278
Bousset, Wilhelm   188
Bromiley, Geoffrey W.   244
Brooke, Alan   19, 98, 101–3, 105, 113, 117, 147, 176
Brown, Raymond E.   2, 4–6, 10, 12–13, 17, 19–20, 22–27, 30–31, 34, 36–37, 41, 43–45, 47–63, 67, 69, 71–72, 76, 78–79, 81, 86–87, 93, 97–100, 102, 104, 107–8, 110, 113–14, 116, 118, 123, 141–43, 147–49, 153, 158, 172–73, 179–80, 182, 184, 187, 190–92, 197–203, 207–14, 216–19, 223–26, 229, 232, 251, 277–81, 283, 287
Bruce, F. F.   143, 147
Bultmann, Rudolf   5, 17, 26, 27, 52–57, 63, 67, 78, 95, 97–98, 117, 130, 143, 147, 152, 158, 160, 172–73, 187, 197, 211–12, 278, 281, 287
Bund, Elmar   205
Bunkowske, Eugene W.   241
Burge, Gary   4, 12, 179, 279, 283
Caesar   79, 80, 82, 89, 283
Caird, G. B.   169
Callahan, Allen Dwight   98, 105
Carson, Donald   164, 173, 174
Carter, Warren   79
Cassidy, Richard   79
Clement of Rome   52, 145, 151
Cerinthus   50, 51, 53, 184, 280
Charondas   227
Christ, Karl   206
Cicero   206, 219, 220
Conzelmann, Hans   98, 102, 117
Cornelius Nepos   201
Culpepper, R. Alan   1–4, 7, 23, 55, 57, 60, 86, 95, 118, 164, 178, 275–77, 281

Culy, Martin M.	251	Griffith, Terry	105, 119, 164, 214
Daniell, David	238	Gundry, Robert M.	80
Danker, Frederick W.	243	Haas, C.	105, 117, 199, 207, 211–15, 218
Delling, Gerhard	243–45		
Deming, Will	227	Haenchen, Ernst	97, 149
DeSilva, David A.	170	Halliday, Michael A.K.	172
Dio Chrysostum	206, 228, 229	Hamartalos, George	67
Diogenes Laertus	201	Harris, J. Rendel	126
Dionysius	89	Hauck, Friedrich	145, 201, 202
Diotrephes	10, 51, 53–54, 61, 65, 69–70, 75, 82–83, 85, 91–92, 105, 121–22, 124, 129, 133, 138–39, 147–53, 156, 279, 281, 287	Heckel, Theo	99, 110, 113, 119
		Heise, Jürgen	145
		Hengel, Martin	99, 109, 113, 118, 154
		Heracleon	51, 85
Dixon, Suzanne	206	Hippolytus	11, 189, 281
Dodd, C. H.	3, 96, 98, 117, 229, 247	Hirsch, Emanuel	109, 113, 117, 126
Domitian	61, 64, 67, 75, 79–82, 84, 89, 279, 283, 287	Hoffman, Thomas A.	173
		Houlden, James Leslie	117, 145, 148, 197
Donahue, John R.	47		
Du Plessis, Paul Johannes	252	House, Paul R.	158
Du Rand, Jan A.	117–18	Howard, Wilbert F.	95, 96, 143, 214, 224, 251
Edwards, Ruth B.	119, 127–28, 224		
Ellis, J. Edward	227	Huebner, Hans	145
Epictetus	206, 228	Hymenius	129
Epicurus	228	Ignatius	8, 20–21, 50–52, 58, 60, 79, 81–82, 90–91, 125, 127, 131, 133, 142, 146–47, 149, 151, 184, 233, 276
Euripides	201		
Eusebius	67, 125		
Forestell, J. Terence	26	Innocent IV	194
Fortna, Robert	95	Irenaeus	11, 67, 189, 281
Frederick II	194	Jauhiainen, Marko	170
Friedrich, Gerhard	93	Jenks, Gregory C.	188
Friesen, Steven J.	80	Johnson, Thomas	80, 99, 118, 142, 146, 199, 213, 215, 218
Fuller, Robert C.	194		
Gaca, Kathy L.	227	Jones, Peter Rhea	9, 10, 99, 105, 119, 141–42, 145, 229, 231–32, 244, 279–80, 282, 286
Gaius	1, 8, 10, 69, 70, 124, 126, 127, 129, 133, 137–39, 148, 149, 150–53		
Gerhardsson, Birger	197	Jonge, Marinus de	105, 214
Gielen, Marlis	205, 206	Josephus	206, 246
Gilbertson, Merrill T.	205, 206	Justin	71
Glare, P. G. W.	242	Käsemann, Ernst	92, 152
Golden, Mark	206	Kasper, Walter (Cardinal)	48
Goodspeed, Edgar J.	240, 268	Katz, Steven T.	6, 58, 59
Gove, Philip Babcock	242	Keener, Craig S.	206, 219–20
Grayston, Kenneth	22, 87, 99, 104, 107, 108, 118, 176	Keil, Carl Friedrich	205
		Kimelman, Rueven	6, 58–59
Gregory the Great	195	Klauck, Hans-Josef	21–22, 99, 111,

NAME INDEX

118, 124, 126–27, 191–92, 197–200, 202–4, 208, 211–15, 223–26, 229–30, 233, 251
Klein, Günter 102, 117
Klink, Edward 58, 157–58, 161, 168, 174
Koester, Craig 11, 187, 189, 190, 194, 281–83, 285–86
Konstan, David 219
Köstenberger, Andreas 10, 119, 157–58, 162, 171, 174–76, 278–79, 281, 283, 285
Kretzer, Armin 153
Kruse, Colin 99, 109, 119, 145, 154, 165–66, 175, 199
Kuhn, K. G. 29, 30
Kümmel, Werner G. 151, 153
Kysar, Robert 118, 147, 251
Lassen, Eva Maria 205, 228
Law, Robert 146
Lewis, Charlton T. 242
Liddell, Henry George 211, 244
Lieu, Judith 4, 8–10, 22–23, 31–32, 37–38, 83, 95, 99, 102, 105–6, 116, 118–19, 123, 126–27, 129, 132, 134–35, 139, 141, 143, 146–48, 152, 190, 194, 200, 210, 214, 223–24, 226, 228–29, 231, 234, 250–51, 253, 278–80, 285
Lincoln, Andrew 160–61, 164–65
Lindars, Barnabas 64, 66
Loader, William 13–14, 108, 118, 147, 223, 228, 230–31, 233, 279, 280–83, 285
Lorein, Geert Wouter 167
Louw, Johannes 212, 214, 216
Luz, Ulrich 188
Mackay, Ian D. 64
Malatesta, Edward 145, 201
Malherbe, Abraham J. 154
Malina, Bruce J. 158, 172–73, 205–6
Marcion 85
Marshall, I. Howard 95, 99, 107, 118, 143, 207, 212, 214–15, 224, 228, 251
Martial 201, 220
Martin, Dale 227
Martinez, Garcia 32, 34

Martyn, J. Louis 10, 56–60, 64, 76, 123, 172, 176, 279
Marxsen, Willi 203, 209
McDonough, Sean M. 169
McGinn, Bernard 187–88, 194–95
Meeks, Wayne 5, 10, 27, 80, 88, 158, 172–73
Meier, John P. 47
Menken, Maarten 197, 199, 202–4, 233
Menoud, Philippe 97
Merwe, Dirk G. van der 197, 201
Metzger, Bruce M. 142, 211, 238
Miller, Ed L. 103
Mitchell, Margaret M. 119
Moffatt, James 14, 240, 267
Moloney, Francis 6, 54, 55
Montanus 51, 85, 184
Morgan, Teresa 198
Morris, Leon 161
Musonius Rufus 201, 227
Newman, Barclay 214
Neyrey, Jerome H. 148, 158, 205–6
Nicholson, Godfrey 26
Nicklas, Tobias 102–3, 119
Nida, Eugene A. 212, 214, 216
Ocellus 227
Ockham 52, 67
O'Day, Gail R. 118
Painter, John 23, 99–101, 113–14, 119, 144–47, 153, 188, 197, 199, 201, 208, 211–12, 214, 216, 218–19, 224–25, 229, 232, 251
Papias 67, 72, 281
Pecorara, G. 145
Peerbolte, L. J. Lietaert 188
Pennington, Jonathan T. 173–74
Peterson, Eugene 240
Petronius 230
Philip of Sidetes 67
Phillips, J. B. 240, 269
Philo 201, 206, 225–226, 228–30, 245
Plato 201, 227, 230
Pliny 79, 80, 82, 146
Plutarch 210, 228
Polhill, John B. 147

Polycarp 67, 125, 127, 131, 146, 187
Polycrates 67
Pope Benedict XVI 48
Pope Gregory IX 194
Pope John Paul II 48
Price, James L. 173
Quispel, Gilles 148
Rawson, Beryl 205–6
Reinhartz, Adele 6, 58–59
Reis, David M. 103, 119
Rensberger, David 14–15, 108–9, 119, 167, 187, 199–200, 237, 247, 253, 280–83, 285
Ricoeur, Paul 164–65
Richter, Georg 99, 109, 113, 117
Robertson, Archibald Thomas 147
Robinson, J. A. T. 103
Rohrbaugh, Richard L. 158, 172–73
Rusam, Dietrich 103, 118
Salom, A. P. 96
Schmid, Hansjörg 137, 164, 165
Schmidt, Karl Ludwig 149
Schmidt, Thomas E. 149
Schmithals, Walter 99, 118
Schnackenburg, Rudolf 17, 20, 23, 95, 97, 99, 107, 117–18, 145, 147, 149, 152, 173, 197, 209, 224–26, 228, 251, 253
Schnelle, Udo 21, 98, 104, 118, 129, 197, 223–24, 228
Scholtissek, Klaus 145
Schrage, Wolfgang 197
Schrenk, G. 206
Schrot, Helmut G. 205–6
Schunack, Gerd 118
Scott, Robert 211, 244
Seesemann, Heinrich 152
Segovia, Fernando 99, 109–10, 113, 118
Seneca 227
Short, Charles 242
Siewert, Frances 241
Slater, Thomas B. 119
Smalley, Stephen 19–20, 118, 152, 192, 197–201, 203–4, 208, 211–18, 224–25, 228–29, 251

Smith, D. Moody, Jr. 19, 22–23, 26–27, 59, 95, 99, 111, 118, 251
Snodderley, M. E. 197
Spicq, Ceslas 152
Sproston, Wendy E. 105, 118–19, 123
Stählin, G. 201
Stambaugh, John 205
Stegemann, Ekkehard 98, 118
Stott, John R. W. 118, 231
Stowers, Stanley K. 145
Strecker, Georg 20–21, 98–99, 101, 104–6, 118, 145, 154, 188, 190–91, 213, 226, 228, 232
Streeter, Burnett Hillman 153
Streett, Daniel R. 164, 169, 173, 175, 178
Swellengrebel, J. L. 105, 214
Talbert, Charles H. 98, 99, 118, 145
Taylor, Kenneth 240
Taylor, Vincent 143
Tertullian 132
Thatcher, Tom 194
Theobald, Michael 197
Thomas, John Christopher 118
Thompson, Marianne Meye 251
Thompson, Michael B. 151, 165–66, 175
Thucydides 228
Thyen, Hartwig 109, 113, 115
Tigchelaar, J. C. 32, 34
Trajan 67, 70, 79–80, 82
Tuckett, Christopher M. 151
Turner, Seth 170
Tyndale, William 14, 238–39, 246, 255
Valentinus 85
Vaux, Roland de 205
Vogler, Werner 224–25
Volf, Miroslav 158
Vouga, François 118, 225
Wahlde, Urban C. von 4, 5, 17, 19, 27, 37, 65, 87, 95, 99, 111, 113–15, 118–19, 179, 252, 275–81, 283, 285
Watson, Duane F. 154, 167
Watt, Jan van der 12, 197, 202–4, 207, 209, 279, 281–83, 285–86
Weiss, Bernhard 148
Weiss, Johannes 146

NAME INDEX

Wengst, Klaus 224
Westcott, Brooke F. 142, 228, 251
Weymouth, Richard Francis 240
Whitacre, Rodney A. 118
Wilson, W. G. 96
Wischmeyer, Oda 197
Witherington III, Ben 224
Wuest, Kenneth 241, 268
Wycliffe, John 14, 238, 243, 246, 254
Yarbrough, Robert W. 163–69, 173, 175–77
Zumstein, Jean 101, 119

www.ingramcontent.com/pod-product-compliance
Lightning Source LLC
Chambersburg PA
CBHW020639300426
44112CB00007B/169